# Mainstreaming Unpaid Work

# Mainstreaming Unpaid Work
## Time-use Data in Developing Policies

*Edited by*
INDIRA HIRWAY

OXFORD
UNIVERSITY PRESS

# OXFORD
## UNIVERSITY PRESS

Oxford University Press is a department of the University of Oxford.
It furthers the University's objective of excellence in research, scholarship,
and education by publishing worldwide. Oxford is a registered trademark of
Oxford University Press in the UK and in certain other countries.

Published in India by
Oxford University Press
YMCA Library Building, 1 Jai Singh Road, New Delhi 110001, India

© Oxford University Press 2017

ISBN-13: 978-0-19-946825-6
ISBN-10: 0-19-946825-7

Typeset in Bembo Std 10.5/13
by Tranistics Data Technologies, New Delhi 110044
Printed in India by Replika Press Pvt. Ltd

# Contents

**PART ONE**   Producing Quality Time–use Statistics: Issues
Related to Methodology and Harmonization of Concepts
and Methods

# Tables, Figures, and Box

## TABLES

## FIGURES

## BOX

प्रो. टी. सी. ए. अनन्त
**PROF. T.C.A. ANANT**

भारत के मुख्य सांख्यिकीविद्
**Chief Statistician of India**

सत्यमेव जयते
Government of India

राष्ट्रीय सांख्यिकीय आयोग
**National Statistical Commission**
भारत सरकार / **Government of India**
सरदार पटेल भवन, संसद मार्ग, नई दिल्ली-110001
Sardar Patel Bhavan, Sansad Marg,
New Delhi-110001
फोन /Tel.: 23742150  फैक्स / Fax: 23742067
E-mail : tca.anant@nic.in

# Foreword

This volume, with its collection of papers on measuring and producing time-use statistics, is a welcome contribution to our state of knowledge. The importance of this area of statistics cannot be understated especially now in the context of the decisions of the 19th International Conference of Labour Statisticians (ICLS) held in October 2013.

The 19th ICLS provided a more complete conceptual framework for statistics of work, employment, and labour underutilization. This conceptual framework emphasized the importance of all forms of work both paid and unpaid with a view to measuring well-being better.

The chapters in the current volume will be useful for labour economists and statisticians seeking to develop frameworks to analyse and implement the conceptual framework of the 19th ICLS. I congratulate the authors for this timely production.

*T.C.A. Anant.*

(T.C.A. Anant)
Chief Statistician of India

October 2016
New Delhi

# Preface

At the outset, I would like to congratulate the Centre for Development Alternatives for this publication, and express my gratitude to them for partnering with UN Women in this regard. I am particularly grateful to Dr Indira Hirway for her leadership and contribution to the global discourse on women's unpaid work, particularly in the context of the Global South and in developing economies. At UN Women, we feel that the time is ripe now to take sound research and methodological learnings to the next level, in order to create a more enabling environment for women's work, paid and unpaid.

Last year, in September 2015, world leaders committed to a common agenda for global development for the next decade and a half. This vision, called the Sustainable Development Agenda 2030, comprising 17 development goals, is both transformative and ambitious. This agenda has a stand-alone goal on gender equality and women's empowerment (GEWE), thanks to the importance given to the issue by member states, and also due to UN Women's advocacy in partnership with women's movements across the world. Moreover, it is now clear to world leaders and to development partners that the other goals cannot be achieved without embedding GEWE in every goal. This is an important gain, moving forward.

A discussion on women's unpaid work was first initiated at the Commission on the Status of Women (CSW) in the early 1970s, where the issue was addressed in terms of the double burden of household responsibilities on women workers in the labour market. Demand for equity between men and women in household responsibilities consequently emerged as an agenda point at the Mexico Conference in

1975. Thereafter, the discourse expanded to include the roles of not just men within the family but also the state and community in sharing women's unpaid work, especially in a globalizing context where women were often called upon to subsidize state investments in health, water, agriculture, food security, and fuel through their unpaid labour. This was the contribution of feminist economists and women's organizations from the Global South. In 1980, the UN World Conference on Women, Copenhagen, identified the provision of safe water, sanitation, and energy as state responsibilities to counter burdens of unpaid work on women. The Beijing Platform for Action in 1995 later highlighted the significance of capturing unpaid work through systems of national accounts.

The Convention on the Elimination of All Forms of Discrimination against Women (CEDAW) and the International Covenant on Economic, Social, and Cultural Rights (ICESCR), to which a vast majority of countries are signatory, enshrine the role of the State to address unpaid work when the distribution of such work creates or perpetuates gender inequality or proves an obstacle to full and equal human rights enjoyment. The Report on Unpaid Care Work by the UN Special Rapporteur on Extreme Poverty and Human Rights and the global consensus on the Social Protection Floor (SPF), 2012, show important links between macroeconomics and unpaid care work. Many years, perhaps decades, of advocacy and research around unpaid work has contributed to the inclusion of unpaid care work as a target in Goal 5 on GEWE in the Sustainable Development Agenda to 'recognize and value unpaid care and domestic work through the provision of public services, infrastructure, and social protection policies and the promotion of shared responsibility within the household and the family as nationally appropriate'.

Gender equality advocates and feminists globally have constantly raised the need to recognize women's unpaid work. Women bear a disproportionate burden of unpaid work, including care that prevents them from participating in other activities. They are responsible for much of the production of goods and services that poor households consume, yet this is often not reflected in economic measurements. Moreover, evidence shows that women and girls have to forego their basic rights to education, healthcare, decent work, and leisure time in order to balance all these activities.

Feminist economists argue that unpaid work entails a systemic transfer of hidden subsidies to the rest of the economy that go unrecognized, imposing a time-tax on women throughout their life cycle. They argue that this gets exacerbated within a framework of macroeconomic policies that promotes structural adjustment programmes (SAP), including trade liberalization and privatization of basic rights and essential services. The relationship between unpaid work and macroeconomic policies, especially fiscal policies that involve cutting down expenditure on social sectors such as health, childcare, nutrition, sanitation, and so on, is well-known. These hidden subsidies that women are forced to bear signal the existence of power relations between men and women. Also, they connect the 'private' worlds of households and families with the 'public' spheres of markets and the state in exploitative ways.

In India, women are employed in large numbers in informal jobs in the manufacturing sector, construction, and agricultural activities (National Sample Survey [NSS] 2009–10). Their work in these sectors is characterized by informality, invisibility, vulnerability, and drudgery. Even when they are remunerated, the conditions of work and wages remain grossly exploitative and in contravention of international and national labour standards. The marginalization of these women is further exacerbated due to their socio-economic position in society.

However, entering the labour market does not mean women abandon their unpaid care work. Instead, the expectation is that they will continue with the multitasking. Therefore, the understanding of women's unpaid work in developing economies requires analysis not just of the duration, but also the distribution, of time between paid/unpaid work and the allocation of unpaid time among a range of activities as well as the presence or absence of enabling conditions. As already mentioned, the burden of unpaid work is further exacerbated by the lack of adequate public provisioning in critical sectors such as health, water and sanitation, food security, and livelihoods. Researchers have argued that while earlier governments took up a substantial part of the costs for provision of such services, now it is mostly left to private markets: for poor women, this often results in increasing their burden of paid and unpaid work, and also substantially increasing the volume and drudgery of unpaid work.

Ninety-three per cent of the workforce in India is in informal employment, with a majority being women. Where only 22 per cent of the labour force comprises women workers and where nearly 80 per cent of all women workers are associated with the farm economy with little or no social recognition and limited access to social protection, a discussion on unpaid work and its consequences for women workers' identity and their rights at work becomes important.[1] While this is the case in many parts of the Global South, it is especially relevant in the Indian context because women's labour force participation has seen a declining trend between 1993 and 2011, with data pointing to the fact that 21 million women have exited the workforce, and a large majority has moved into the realm of 'domestic responsibilities'. These trends further necessitate more robust research on the issue of unpaid work, towards building a legal policy and programmatic framework that can effectively contribute towards create an enabling environment for women's work, both paid and unpaid, and specifically ensure the recognition, reduction, and redistribution of women's unpaid work.

It is in this broad context that UN Women's interventions have been focused. Over the last couple of decades, UN Women (and United Nations Development Fund for Women [UNIFM] prior to that) has supported research and advocacy on women's unpaid work, and supported national governments in developing robust methodologies for capturing data on women's work (including through time-use surveys [TUS]). In 2015, UN Women published the Progress of the World's Women (POWW) report that once again used empirical analysis and normative bases to argue that on one hand, unpaid care and domestic work, which aggravates women's socio-economic disadvantage in labour markets, must be urgently addressed, and on the other, decent work opportunities and paid work that is dignified, secure, and sufficiently remunerative must be

---

[1] Women in India spend nearly 10 times more time on unpaid care work than men, and, on average, a woman spends between 30 minutes to 5 hours each day in provisioning water for the household. Given that the results of the NSS indicated a strong correlation between adequate sanitation infrastructure and high female labour force participation rates (particularly in households where there is a working tap), the effect of unpaid work on upward mobility should not be understated.

made available to women. The 2015 POWW report also emphasized
the need to invest in women's rights organizations to transform
economies towards achieving women's rights.

In India, UN Women has been playing a catalytic role since 2013
in the formation and strengthening of the first-ever national alliance
called the Collective on Women's Unpaid Work, which now comprises
202 individuals, organizations, and networks, which work collectively
towards the recognition, reduction, and redistribution of women's
unpaid work through campaigns, training, research, and advocacy, in the
realm of care, labour rights, and universal social protection. Following
the first-ever national workshop supported by UN Women in April
2015, a roadmap for action was developed, which included recommendations for influencing and informing from a gender perspective,
sectoral policies and budgets, public provisioning for 'care', and data
systems on women's work as well as supporting the organizing efforts
of rights holders.

At the workshop of the Collective on Women's Unpaid Work, it was
also discussed that despite normative frameworks being in place for
women's right to work, rights at work, and equality and non-discrimination, the translation of these frameworks into existing legislation,
policy, and programmes has remained restricted to conceptualizing
the rights of workers in remunerative employment, such as in the
Factories Act, 1948; the Minimum Wages Act, 1948; the Mahatma
Gandhi National Rural Employment Guarantee Act, 2005; and the
Unorganised Workers Social Security Act, 2008. This limits the very
understanding of 'work' to that which is done for an income and of
a 'worker' to one who provides services in return of remuneration,
thereby restricting workers' rights (in the absence of universal social
protection) to those in paid employment only.[2] Consequently, the cur-

[2] Statistical accounts systems and time-use studies suggest that worldwide,
and across developed and developing economies, the daily time of a woman
spent in undertaking unpaid work is far higher when compared to men's
participation in unpaid work. Women daily dedicate an average of six hours
in Mexico and Italy, five hours in India, and over four hours in the US and
France to unpaid work. Men spend an hour and a half in Mexico and Italy, less
than an hour in India, and over two hours in the US and France (Antonopoulos 2009) in participating in unpaid work.

rent discourse on workers' rights excludes a vast majority of individuals in unpaid or non-remunerative work.

The roadmap for action developed by the Collective on Women's Unpaid Work re-emphasizes the need to document and inform policy and programme on the links between the paid–unpaid, productive–reproductive, and public–private, and to break the binaries therein. Taking forward the roadmap, UN Women has recently commissioned an action research to map the continuum of work (paid and unpaid) undertaken by women working in the unorganized sector, with special focus on construction workers and agricultural workers (including subsistence farmers). The action research will also involve evidence generation, capacity-building, and advocacy in select sectors impacting women's unpaid work, such as 'care', water, and energy, and will draw upon the rich literature on time use being presented in this book, and elsewhere.

**Rebecca Reichmann Tavares**
Representative, UN Women Multi-country Office
for India, Bhutan, Maldives, and Sri Lanka

# Abbreviations and Acronyms

| | |
|---|---|
| ACGSD | African Centre for Gender and Social Development |
| ACS | African Centre of Statistics |
| AGDI | African Gender and Development Index |
| BBS | Bangladesh Bureau of Statistics |
| BIA | Benefit Incidence Analysis |
| CAUTAL | Classification of Time-use Activities for Latin America and the Caribbean |
| CSO | Central Statistical Organisation/Office |
| CTUR | Centre for Time Use Research |
| ECD | Early Childhood Development |
| ECLAC | United Nations Economic Commission for Latin America and the Caribbean |
| EGM | Extraordinary General Meeting |
| EIM | Enterprise Information Management |
| EMICoV | l'Enquête Modulaire Intégrée sur les Conditions de Vie des Ménages |
| EPWP | Expanded Public Works Programme |
| ESCAP | United Nations Economic and Social Commission for Asia and the Pacific |
| Eurostat | Statistical Office of the European Communities |
| FAO | Food and Agriculture Organization of the United Nations |
| GIZ | Deutsche Gesellschaft für Internationale Zusammenarbeit |
| GLSS | Ghana Living Standards Survey |
| GRB | Gender Responsive Budgeting |
| HBHC | Home-based Healthcare |

| HCBC | Home- and Community-based Care |
|------|-------------------------------|
| HETUS | Harmonized European Time-use Survey |
| IATUR | International Association for Time Use Research |
| ICATUS | International Classification of Activities for Time-Use Statistics |
| IDRC | International Development Research Centre |
| IFPRI | International Food Policy Research Institute |
| ILO | International Labour Organization |
| INSTRAW | United Nations International Research and Training Institute for the Advancement of Women |
| LFS | Labour Force Survey |
| LSMS | Living Standards Measurement Study |
| MDG | Millennium Development Goal |
| MPCE | Monthly Per Capita Expenditure |
| NBS | National Bureau of Statistics |
| NLF | Not in the Labour Force |
| NMW | Non-market Work |
| NPISH | Non-profit Institutions Serving Households |
| NSO | National Statistical Office |
| NSSO | National Sample Survey Organisation/Office |
| OECD | Organisation for Economic Co-operation and Development |
| PAYEM | Payroll Employment |
| PHS | Periodic Household Survey |
| PRA | Participatory Rural Appraisal |
| SAM | Social Accounting Matrix |
| SIDA | Swedish International Development Cooperation Agency |
| SNA | System of National Accounts |
| TUS | Time-use Surveys |
| UNDP | United Nations Development Programme |
| UNECA | United Nations Economic Commission for Africa |
| UNECE | United Nations Economic Commission for Europe |
| UNFPA | United Nations Population Fund |
| UNSD | United Nations Statistics Division |
| USAID | United States Agency for International Development |
| WPR | Workforce Participation Rate |

# Introduction

## Indira Hirway

This book primarily argues that (a) there is an urgent need to measure unpaid work using sound concepts and methods to produce quality time-use data, as it is an important component of the economy; (b) there is a need to include this work in analysing critical concerns of an economy, which include gender inequality, poverty, unemployment, human development, etc., and to incorporate this work in major policy designing and monitoring; and (c) there is a need to integrate unpaid work in national policies, so as to optimize the use of total labour force in an economy to maximize development, to promote well-being of its people, and to ensure quality professional care to those who need it.

Unpaid work is essentially work that does not receive direct remuneration. It includes unpaid work that falls within the production boundary of the UN System of National Accounts (SNA)[1] as well as unpaid work that falls within the general production boundary but outside the production boundary (non-SNA).[2] The former unpaid

---

[1] SNA is the internationally agreed standard set of recommendations on how to compile measures of economic activity in accordance with strict accounting conventions based on economic principles (ISWGNA [2008]). This document defines the 'production boundary', which determines the goods and services that need to be included in national income accounts. This boundary is also known as the boundary of SNA.

[2] Non-SNA work is defined as all work carried out outside the production boundary that can be delegated to others.

work, which is a part of the national accounts and is expected to be covered under national income accounts, includes three types of work: (a) first, unpaid family work in family enterprises; (b) subsistence production of goods by households and free collection of products (such as water, fuel-wood, fish, and fruit) for own consumption; and (c) collection of free goods for use for production purposes (such as fodder, wood, and craft material). Unpaid non-SNA work, on which 35–50 per cent of total work time is spent by economies (Antonopoulos 2009; Hirway 2011), includes daily activities for household upkeep (cooking, washing, cleaning, shopping for own household, etc.), care work (of children, the old, the sick, the differently abled, and others who require care), and unpaid voluntary services. Unpaid SNA work, which is covered under national income accounts, is expected to be visible in national statistical systems,[3] while unpaid non-SNA work, which is outside the national income accounts, is usually invisible. This book deals with both categories of unpaid work.

The book is divided into two parts: Part One, 'Producing Quality Time-use Statistics: Issues Related to Methodology and Harmonization of Concepts and Methods', focuses on producing quality time-use statistics, as this is the first step in moving towards integrating unpaid work in policymaking. Part Two, 'Analytical Tools for Addressing Critical Concerns', presents the chapters that have developed different analytical tools to use time-use statistics in conjunction with other statistics to address critical socio-economic concerns of economies.

## PRODUCING QUALITY TIME–USE STATISTICS

The main survey technique available to us today for collecting data on unpaid activities is time-use surveys (TUS). Though this technique has recently spread in the developing and emerging countries of Asia, Africa, and Latin America, there are problems pertaining to producing quality time-use statistics.

Time-use statistics provide detailed and comprehensive information on how individuals spend their time on a daily or weekly basis and on different activities, that is, activities that fall within the purview of

---

[3] National income estimates frequently do not follow the production boundary due to methodological problems or due to the lack of required data.

national income accounts, non–SNA activities that fall outside these accounts but within the general production boundary, and personal services that are non-delegable activities. Time-use statistics are, thus, quantitative summaries of how individuals allocate their time over a specified time period (typically over 24 hours of a day or over the seven days of a week) on different activities and how much time they spend on each of these activities. Time-use statistics have three major components: (a) information on major socio-economic characteristics of households and individuals (for whom data is collected) through a background schedule or through the main schedule in case TUS is a module in a major survey; (b) time spent by individuals on SNA and non–SNA activities and personal services collected through a time diary or by direct questions to respondents; and (c) context variables that collect information on the basis of the context of different activities carried out by respondents.[4] This comprehensive data set opens up immense possibilities for understanding the total economy consisting of paid and unpaid work as well as human life in general.

For developing and emerging countries today, time-use statistics have become an important data set to understand and address development-related concerns, including the multiple dimensions of gender-based inequalities and the socio-economic life of people: it gives visibility to all forms of work (remunerated and non-remunerated) and personal activities; provides full visibility to the care economy by estimating paid and, particularly, unpaid care work; helps improve estimates of the workforce and understands its characteristics better, along with throwing light on informal work that may be scattered and/or sporadic in nature; aids the measure of socio-economic changes by describing the variations in levels/types of paid and unpaid work and how such work is shared among different socio-economic groups and over time; throws light on the nature of poverty and human well-being; explains the dynamics of intra-household sharing and gender inequality; provides valuation of unpaid non–SNA work and estimates

---

[4] The context variables in time-use statistics usually refer to the location of the activity (where), the presence of other people there (with whom), the beneficiary, person, or institution of the activity (for whom the activity was carried out), the motivation of the activity (for example, whether the activity was paid or unpaid), etc.

of total well-being; and, finally, provides a total picture of the economy consisting of paid and unpaid work and thereby presents input for macroeconomic policymaking and monitoring. The last has emerged as an important use recently, as it is realized that paid and unpaid work are closely interlinked and macroeconomic policies need to be formulated and monitored keeping in mind their impact on unpaid work. In short, time-use statistics can be a critical tool in designing policies for inclusive growth.

## STATUS OF TUS

Out of the total 193 member countries of the UN (that is, independent sovereign countries in the world), 125–30 countries (65–7 per cent) have conducted at least one small or big TUS so far (2011–12). This is a positive development, as it reflects the wide reach of its technique. However, only 35–40 per cent of countries have conducted at least one national TUS.

As regards the countries located in the Global North (that is, the USA, Canada, parts of Europe, parts of East Asia, and Australia), TUS was introduced sometime during the second half of the twentieth century, or even earlier in some countries. Most of these countries have mainstreamed TUS in their respective national statistical systems, though about 10 countries, such as Greece, Luxembourg, New Zealand, South Korea, Ireland, Lithuania, Estonia, and Czech Republic, have not.

Of the countries in the Global South (that is, countries located in Africa, Latin America, and developing Asia, including the Middle East), the situation is quite different. Of the 54 countries in the African union, around 30 countries, or 57 per cent, have conducted at least one TUS. Of the 44 countries from the members of the UN Economic Commission for Latin America and the Caribbean (ECLAC), more than 50 per cent of countries have conducted at least one TUS. From the 53 members of the United Nations Economic and Social Commission for Asia and the Pacific (ESCAP), about 30 countries, or 56 per cent, have conducted at least one TUS (2013).

The first four chapters discuss the status of TUS in the different regions within the Global South. Chapter 1 discusses the status in Asia, Chapters 2 and 3 discuss the status in Latin America, while Chapter 4 focuses on Africa. There are two chapters dealing with Latin America because there is a huge debate going on in the region on use of stylized questions versus 24-hour time for collecting time-use data. These chapters show that TUS began as small surveys in all the three continents, each covering a small sample and short questionnaire. Many of them were like anthropological surveys. Such surveys were conducted in Nepal (1976–7), India (1976–7), Cameroon (1976), Kenya (1970s), Peru (1966), Gambia (1952), etc. The more systematic surveys, however, started in the 1990s and particularly after the Beijing Conference in 1995.

Over the years, TUS have spread very well in all the three continents, with Latin America leading because many countries in this region adopted a relatively easy approach of collecting data using stylized questions in national or large household surveys. These surveys are cheaper, simpler, and relatively easy to conduct, as there is no time diary used, no context variables, or no data collection on simultaneous activities. On the other hand, Africa, which started with the TUS module in the Living Standard Measurement Survey (LSMS) (the World Bank), shifted to 24-hour time-diary-based surveys. Somehow, for historical reasons, Asian countries in most cases used 24-hour diary-based surveys. India was one of the first countries from the developing and emerging countries in Asia to conduct this survey using the 24-hour time diary.

## Asia-Pacific Countries

Chapter 1, 'Assessment of Concepts and Methods used in Selected Countries in ESCAP Region', reviews the TUS in the 31 selected countries of the Asia-Pacific region (developed countries are excluded) to see how far these countries have been able to produce sound time-use data and how far the data is useful in designing national policies. Seven countries (Afghanistan, Brunei Darussalam, Maldives, Marshall Islands, Myanmar, Palau, and Singapore) have not conducted a single TUS so far, while 24 developing and emerging countries have conducted at least one small or big TUS. Of these, nine countries have conducted only small-scale surveys, eight have conducted national modular surveys, and six countries have conducted a national/large TUS using 24-hour time diaries.

Small-scale surveys, including anthropological surveys, are useful, as they provide valuable insight into the time use of people. However, they cannot be considered representative of their respective countries, and, therefore, cannot be used for national-level policymaking. The review presented in the first four chapters of the volume focuses on national surveys and assesses the objectives in depth, sampling design, background questionnaires, data collection methods used, classification systems of activities, context variables, etc. On the positive side, the review observes rapidly growing awareness about the need to collect time-use data for various reasons, and despite the limitations, concrete data has emerged in a large number of countries on the time use of people that not only gives visibility to their non-SNA activities and personal activities, but also throws useful and additional light on the SNA activities. Clearly, a new understanding has emerged on the contribution of women to national economies and the nature and extent of gender inequalities prevailing in these economies. In spite of these positive developments, it needs to be recognized that these surveys suffer from several weaknesses in designing sampling, background questionnaire, data collection methods, classification, context variables, etc., with the result that the data produced is not up to the mark. The main constraints faced by countries can be listed as poor appreciation of the utility of time-use statistics by their respective national statistical offices (NSOs) and policymakers, poor expertise with their statistical offices to collect and analyse the data, and frequent lack of adequate funds to conduct these expensive surveys.

These constraints have led several countries in the region to go for modular TUS, which are easier to conduct, are much less expensive, and convenient to mainstream. Several global agencies and donor agencies have sponsored and financed such modular surveys. However, the author believes that it is better to prepare these countries for 24-hour diary-based surveys by providing capacity-building to them. After all, mainstreaming modular TUS in the national statistical systems is not a sound decision.

The next steps suggested by the author include standardization of concepts and methods of data collection to improve the quality of the data; promote cross-country comparability of data; capacity-building of data producers, data users (on how to analyse the raw data with analytical tools), and other government departments; and promotion and mainstreaming of TUS in national statistical systems in the region.

## Latin American Countries

Valeria Esquivel, in Chapter 2 'Time-use Surveys in Latin America', observes that the decade of 2005–15 has witnessed rapid expansion of TUS in Latin America. During this decade, the Dominican Republic (2007), Honduras (2011), Peru (2010), Panama (2011), El Salvador (2010), Venezuela (2011–12), and Colombia (2012–13) completed their first nation-wide TUS. Uruguay (2013), Ecuador (2012–13), Guatemala (2011), and Mexico (2009) conducted their third round. Brazil (2010) and Bolivia (2010) conducted 'pilot' surveys, the former big enough to cover five states. There have also been new city-wide TUS, like those in Gran Santiago, Chile (2008); Rosario, Argentina (2010); and Gran San José, Costa Rica (2011). The latest TUS follows the methodological paths set at the end of the 1990s and the beginning of the 2000s by Mexico (2002), Ecuador (2005), Uruguay (Montevideo 2003), Nicaragua (1998), Guatemala (2000), and Argentina (Buenos Aires 2005). Different countries have, however, used different methods of data collection, namely short tasks lists, stylized diaries, the exhaustive activity lists, and the 24-hour recall activity diaries.

The chapter discusses the different methodological approaches used in the Latin American countries in the context of the ongoing regional debate in the continent. Overall, the use of 24-hour time diary is limited in Latin America as compared to other regions. Though some observers have a highly positive view of the use of different methods, the author does not quite agree, as she believes that TUS based on the 24-hour time diary gives sound and reliable data. On a more positive note, one can state that Latin America has experienced a strong learning-by-doing process in time-use data-collection methods, which have gained complexity, and wider local consensuses (including law mandates) have supported bigger, year-long standalone TUS.

There are at least four methodological trade-offs that arise when choosing a particular approach to time-use data collection: (a) compromises over time-use data quality; (b) respondents' burden versus fieldwork burden; (c) surveying households versus surveying individuals; and (d) appropriately considering (or not) simultaneous activities. The quality of time-use data collected depends primarily on the survey instrument chosen (activity diaries are the least biased time-use data collection instrument) and the respondents' burden (which is minimized through the use of activity diaries). The 24-hour self-reported time diaries are better than 24-hour recall diaries filled in by enumerators. However, stylized diaries also filled in by enumerators are problematic. Fieldwork has to be carefully calibrated in order to correctly select methodology of data collection. Also, inclusion of simultaneous activities in questionnaire design helps in collecting comprehensive information on time-use activities.

Over this period, the debates around TUS methods in Latin America have been defined by the stark opposition to the idealized standalone, Eurostat-type self-administered activity diary, which is known to be the best way of collecting time-use data. It is regarded by some as infeasible in the Latin American context, because a part of the population is not literate, and is therefore not in a position to fill in self-reported time diaries. The other methods are cheaper and better suited to illiterate populations. It seems that the use of methodology depends significantly on the institutions involved. When respectable academic institutes such as NSOs, research institutes, and universities are involved, they select the 24-hour time-diary approach, and self-reported or interview-based recall system. On the other hand, donors tend to economize costs and, being spread in a large number of countries, they recommend stylized methods.

For TUS to support gender-aware public policy in Latin America, we need a thorough and open dialogue on time-use data methods, and on the difficult trade-offs involved in choosing among existing options, making the process of TUS design explicit, and the compromises made (Esquivel and Folbre 2008).[5] We need to elaborate much more, and give more sophistication to policy-impact analyses. This means, among other things, that TUS methods have to be designed with policy-impact analysis in mind. We need to have good background data in order to analyse the access and need for health and education services. We also need a theoretical framework to develop the complex relationship between time and income poverty. It is not

---

[5] In the section 'Methodological Challenges: The (Role) for the National Statistical Offices', Marco Navarro (2012: 23) restricts her recommendations to those that apply to exhaustive activity lists only ('restrict activity length', 'add questions on…', 'beware of interview length'), but stated in a general way, as if they applied to *all* existing time-use surveys.

enough to state that 'unpaid care work is impoverishing for those who perform it' (Marco Navarro 2012: 5).[6] In other words, we need to frame advocacy for 'time-use data collection not as a precursor to the construction of household-sector satellite accounts, but as an irreplaceable source of information for the design of polices that support the reduction and redistribution of unpaid care work within a framework that recognizes both caregivers' contributions to well-being and the costs of care-giving—that is, within an economic justice framework' (Esquivel 2011: 230).

Sonia Montaño, in Chapter 4 'Measurement of Total Working Time with a Gender Perspective: Development of Time-use Surveys in Latin America', has a slightly different view on TUS in Latin America. The author observes that with the exception of Brazil, which was a pioneer in TUS in this region until the 1990s, no other government in the region took any action. There was, however, a spur in TUS in Latin America, particularly after the Beijing Conference, where participants were inspired by the results of an Italian time-use survey that were widely distributed in the conference. The tenth session of the Regional Conference on Women in Latin America and the Caribbean (2007), which recognized gender parity as 'one of the key driving forces of democracy', also inspired the ECLAC member states to request the Commission 'to promote gender equality that will help strengthen national gender mechanisms'.

Independent TUS is now considered the most appropriate source of information to construct indicators that show the uneven distribution of time between men and women. However, due to institutional considerations and scarce resources available, many countries have opted for a module on time use as part of regular household surveys. While this is considered a more minimalist approach which does not allow for the same level of analysis, it has permitted more countries to reach the principal objective of measuring women's unpaid work. In practice, therefore, TUS in the region are frequently incomplete, as they have not incorporated all of the activities that define and cover unpaid work,

[6] The Levy Economics Institute Measure of Time and Income Poverty (LIMTIP) is a valuable step towards this direction. LIMTIP measures were calculated for Mexico, Chile, and Argentina. See Antonopoulos et al. (2012, 2013).

and the amount of time people spend doing various activities such as household activities, childcare, volunteering, and personal work.

This problem is further compounded by the difficulty in applying ad hoc methods for obtaining the data and deciding what strategies to use at various stages of the research while maintaining the requirement to keep interview times short, to maximize response rates and keep the costs within a tight budget. Producers of information on time use are confronted with big challenges. Under tremendous pressure, they lack a sufficient conceptual understanding of the issue and face a rigorous methodological challenge. They have a very limited budget and little understanding of how to incorporate a gender perspective in collecting information; they also lack models or prototypes to follow that are similar in circumstances to the reality of their country. This problem is faced by most of the statistical systems in the region, where there are too many variables to fit into an equation, making it difficult to reach a common solution.

In the end, some recommendations are made to spread TUS in the context of Latin America: (a) when institutional and financial restrictions do not allow for an independent survey, a well-constructed module within multipurpose household surveys can be an important source of information as the present analysis shows; (b) TUS should be conducted by NSOs and not by women's ministries; (c) efforts to measure time use need to be integrated into official statistics and have a standard periodicity to allow comparison over time; and (d) political commitment is required on behalf of national and international institutions, backed by the experience, knowledge, and support of academia and non-governmental organizations.

## African Countries

In the case of Africa, one observes a spur in national TUS (before this, several small-scale TUS were conducted by researchers) after the Beijing Conference in 1995. Chapter 3 by Jacques Charmes, 'Time-use Surveys in Africa: Problems and Prospects', reviews the national TUS carried out in Africa since the end of the 1990s in terms of methodological characteristics (sample size, survey instruments, etc.) as well as in terms of findings (gender gaps in time devoted to productive activities [SNA production as measured by GDP], to extended

SNA production [care work], or to activities, such as water and wood fetching). Regarding problems and prospects, issues in harmonization and in the better measurement of women's economic participation are identified, but the chapter mainly stresses that, with some rare exceptions, most of the time-use findings on the continent have been useful for academic research, but far less for the design of policies aiming at reducing the gender gaps and the empowerment of women.

Historically speaking, the first national TUS was conducted in Morocco in 1997–8 (it excluded men's time use), followed by Benin, then by Madagascar, Mali, and later by many other countries. At present, about 23 African countries have conducted modular or stand-alone TUS.

The major concerns related to African TUS discussed by the author are: (a) most African TUS have been conducted without much concern about their use by policymakers (except for South Africa) and this lack of use has definitely got to change for the next generation of surveys, though the African Gender Development Index (AGDI) is a good beginning; (b) quality concern should focus on higher response rates at an individual level and on seasonal variations; (c) concern of improvement of labour-force statistics through time-use statistics should become a priority, especially in countries where female activity rates remain low; (d) harmonization issues continue to arise despite efforts made towards generalization of international classifications; and (e) simultaneous activities are not given the importance they should have; their capture and analysis remain secondary.

One major area of concern, which is related to comparisons between time-use data and labour-force data, raises some difficulties in terms of concepts, periods, and classifications (Charmes 2011): in particular, the International Classification of Activities for Time Use Surveys (ICATUS), which has been used by most countries in Africa, does not allow a reclassification of the unemployed and the inactive who have actually worked during the period of the survey, unless the questionnaires provide for the capture of the detailed industry, occupation, and status in employment. There is a need to redesign the classification.

The decade of the 2010s will probably be a decade of intense data collection on time use in Africa, thanks to the intense efforts of the United Nations Economic Commission for Africa (UNECA). Also, the African Centre for Gender and Social Development (ACGSD) and the African Centre of Statistics (ACS) have supported TUS and the elaboration of satellite accounts of household production, gender budgets, and gender-aware modelling. It can be taken for granted that African TUS will lead to national time accounts and detailed satellite accounts of household production as well as gender-aware modelling. Policymakers should then be more sensitive to the challenges towards gender equality and empowerment of women and more open to designing policy measures towards these aims.

## SOME CRITICAL COMMON OBSERVATIONS

There are several common weaknesses in the methodologies of TUS conducted in all the three continents, according to the four chapters discussed in the preceeding paragraphs. These are:

1.  The type of TUS that can provide reliable data is a stand-alone survey that uses the 24-hour time diary. In other words, one should avoid using modular TUS based on stylized questions. In the short run, countries may be tempted to use modular TUS, but in the long run, these methods should be avoided.
2.  Classification of time-use activities is an important issue. The ICATUS (1997), which is one of the most commonly used classifications, is not good enough, particularly for SNA activities. Even the United Nations Statistics Division (UNSD) has now rejected it. Some countries have a modified version of this classification, and some others have used the classification employed in European Union (EU) countries. At present, UNSD is working on finalizing the classification, and it will be useful to wait for it at least for future TUS.
3.  The reference period is usually inadequate in most TUS. It could be of one day, one month, one season, or a few months. The proportion of countries that have used the one-year reference period is less than 30 per cent. Most surveys, therefore, do not provide information on seasonal variations in the time use of people.
4.  The same is true about reference population. The geographical coverage of the surveys is frequently one city, a few villages, only rural areas or only urban areas, or only some regions of a country. Even in case of India and China, which are both large countries

having a large coverage area, their surveys do not cover their complete geographic areas. There are also wide variations regarding the sample size, number of persons selected from a household, the minimum or maximum age of household members, or the number of days per person selected for the survey. There is a need to standardize these concepts for reliable data and for cross-country comparison of the data.

5.  Another weak point of many surveys is that they have not been able to tap the full potential of the different survey instruments, such as background questionnaire, context variables, and simultaneous activities. Either the relevant data is not collected or is not adequately analysed. There is considerable scope for improvement in these areas.

6.  The use of the data in formulating national policies in most countries is very limited. As Charmes has pointed out in Chapter 4, while researchers have used the data in many cases, the policymakers have usually ignored the data. The likely reasons for this seem to be: (a) the data is not of good quality; (b) NSOs do not have the funds to analyse the data because donors do not give funds for analysis; (c) NSOs do not have the expertise to use the data; or (d) the official policymakers do not appreciate the utility of the data. It is observed by all experts that there is a need to work on all these fronts.

## USING TIME–USE DATA IN POLICY DESIGNING

Part Two presents chapters that apply time-use data along with other data for addressing and analysing critical concerns of these economies. These studies have been undertaken by experts from a variety of countries. The issues taken up by the chapters are varied. Chapters 5 and 6 are related to employment and unemployment, Chapters 7 and 8 are about time poverty, while Chapters 9, 10, and 11 analyse public policies and programmes that incorporate time-use statistics.

### Employment and Unemployment

Indira Hirway, in Chapter 5 'Challenges to Measuring (SNA) Workforce/Labour Force in Global South', presents the new challenges that have emerged in getting correct measurement of workforce and labour force. She argues that labour force surveys (LFS) do not appear to be adequate to estimate 'workforce' and 'labour force' and to understand their characteristics in most economies today. This is because of the changing labour market structures in most economies on the one hand and the recent groundbreaking resolution on statistics on work of the International Labour Organization (ILO) on the other. There is, therefore, a need to look for additional sources of data on work and labour force. This chapter examines, conceptually as well as empirically, how these developments have made it difficult for LFS to correctly estimate and comprehensively understand the work and labour force in an economy and how far these difficulties can be addressed by TUS.

The chapter argues that these challenges can be addressed by TUS, as they provide comprehensive information on all human activities without bias. TUS can, therefore, capture underemployment (intensity of work), multiple jobs performed by persons, and the scattered nature and flexibility of work. It can also collect better the sporadic, unstable, scattered, and precarious types of work. At the end, the chapter presents an empirical study of India to show how time-use data can address the new concerns effectively.

Chapter 6 by Maria Sagrario Floro and Hitomi Komatsu, 'Time Use and Job Search among the Unemployed and Underemployed', is about the search for jobs by the unemployed and underemployed. The authors argue that the use of time-use data to explore the issue of job search has received little attention in economic analysis. Using data from the 2000–1 South African national TUS produced by Statistics South Africa, the authors demonstrate the usefulness of time-use data in policy discourses, such as those pertaining to the problem of unemployment. The chapter aims to examine: (a) the time-use patterns and incidence of job search among the 10,465 adult respondents, women and men aged between 16 and 64 years, as a means of assessing their ability to improve their labour market situation and (b) the determinants that likely influence the unemployed person's ability to look for jobs. These include gender-based constraints as well as household- and community-level factors that may affect the search for a wage employment or the development of a new enterprise activity. Controlling for economic, social, and demographic factors, which include race, household life cycle, education, household composition, as well as area characteristics, for example, access to basic social services, the authors examine the link between the incidence and time spent in job search and gender role indicators by means of probit and tobit regression analyses. The chapter also shows that unemployed and underemployed men have a significantly higher incidence and intensity of job search as compared to women.

The findings of the study suggest that an examination of time allocation is crucial for a comprehensive assessment of the gender inequalities in the labour market, including differences in rates of unemployment and underemployment.

## Time Poverty

Ajit Zachariah, in Chapter 7 'The Measurement of Time and Income Poverty', presents the major existing approaches to time and income poverty within a unified framework. As will be obvious, this purpose has compromised certain subtle aspects of the various approaches. However, the framework captures the essential aspects of the different contributions. Subsequently, the author proposes a modification to the standard time-income poverty measure to account for intra-household disparities. The author starts with a discussion on a two-dimensional measure of poverty, time, and income dimensions, followed by a discussion on potential time deficit or surplus with no income deficit, and potential income with no time deficit. Based on these concepts, intra-household disparities are discussed, followed by policy implications for addressing poverty separately for households which are either time poor and income non-poor, income poor and time poor, or time non-poor and income poor. The chapter underscores the benefits of separating income and time poverty and the different combinations of the both.

Omar Ismael Abdourahman, in Chapter 8 'Time Poverty: A Contributor to Women's Poverty? Analysis of the Time-use Data in Africa', observes that inequality is a major challenge to development and an obstacle to achieving the millennium development goals (MDGs). It takes several forms, including income inequality; inequality in access to and control over property and resources; inequality in access to civil and political rights; and unequal access to social, cultural, and economic rights. Additionally, the form of inequality that has received much less attention but has adverse implications for accessing economic rights is that relating to time. The allocation of time between women and men in the household and in the economy is a major gender issue in the evolving discourse on time poverty. In the first part of the chapter, the author shows how allocation of time by women leads to time poverty among women, and how it impacts adversely on achievement of the MDGs. Using TUS methodologies and tools, the author shows how sex-disaggregated time-use data help in empirical analysis. The chapter argues that such analysis will help policymakers to incorporate time-poverty analysis as one of the components of the overall poverty-reduction strategies and the assessment and monitoring of MDGs. In the end, the author observes that the impact of macroeconomic policies on paid and, particularly, unpaid work (using TUS) helps in analysing the relationship between macroeconomic policies and time poverty of women.

## Unpaid Work and National Policies and Programmes

Chapters 9, 10, and 11 deal with different well-known policy initiatives taken in several countries. These include (a) employment guarantee schemes; (b) gender budgeting; and (c) neo-liberal policies or opening of economies.

Rania Antonopoulos and Kijong Kim, in Chapter 9 'Public Job-Guarantee Programmes: The Economic Benefits of Investing in Social Care—Case Studies of South Africa and the United States', discuss employment programmes in South Africa and the USA. It demonstrates the strong pro-poor impact that social provisioning of care has on employment creation and poverty reduction. Though not all job-guarantee programmes (such as Mahatma Gandhi National Rural Employment Guarantee Scheme [MGNREGS] in India) include care-related work, the countries where this is included show several positive results. The chapter shows that mobilizing underutilized domestic labour and targeting it to bridge gaps in community-based services yields substantial pro-poor income growth. In fact, such social care provision in the programmes contributes to gender equality, as women (especially from low-income households) constitute a major portion of the workforce in the care sector. The chapter presents ex ante policy simulation results from South Africa and the USA using social-accounting-matrix-based (or SAM-based) multiplier analysis and propensity-ranking-based micro-simulation. Both methods provide evidence of the pro-poor impact despite different levels of economic development.

Chapter 10 by Lekha Chakraborty, 'Integrating Time Use in Gender Budgeting', discusses the relevance of time-use data in gender budgeting and shows, in the context of India, how an addition of this dimension adds to enriching the policy of gender budgeting. Chakraborty argues that the gender budgeting policies often rest on a highly restricted assumption that 'all public expenditure cannot be gender partitioned'. This is especially with reference to the mainstream expenditure, such as public infrastructure, which is assumed to be non-rival in nature and, therefore, applying the gender lens to this expenditure is not feasible. The author refutes this argument by using time-budget statistics. The time-budget data reveals that this argument is often flawed, as there is intrinsic gender dimension to the non-rival expenditure.

The results shown in the chapter suggest that the time allocation in the economic activities carried out in the unpaid care sector involves more girls and women and, therefore, infrastructure investment with gender-sensitive water and energy policies can really benefit women. Another important contribution of the chapter is that without looking at time-use data, any exercise of gender budgeting will remain partial and inadequate.

Indira Hirway, in Chapter 11 'Trade Liberalization and Unpaid Work: Integrating Unpaid Work into Macroeconomic Policies', discusses the impact of trade liberalization policy on paid and unpaid work of men and women, and the macroeconomic processes emerging from this. The main objective of this chapter is to understand the impact of a major macroeconomic policy, which is trade liberalization, on the pattern of employment in the market economy and on the allocation of time on SNA and non-SNA activities by labour, particularly by women workers. While the impact on SNA has been studied well in the literature, the impact on non-SNA, which has important implications for designing and monitoring of macroeconomic policies, has not been given adequate attention. This chapter argues that examining the macroeconomic policies on a broader framework makes the policies more relevant and valid for an economy.

The chapter opens with a conceptual framework and presents the impact of liberalization in the textile and garment industry on the pattern of the use of labour in the industry. It shows that trade liberalization pressurizes producers in the industry to restructure production for flexibility and restructure labour for flexibility and cost reduction. This tends to promote home-based work of men and, particularly, of women. Women manage this work, which is at the lowest rung of the labour market, along with their unpaid work. With the use of the time-use data of the members of the selected households engaged in home-based work, the chapter shows that the impact of this work on paid and unpaid work of women and children tends to result in significant macroeconomic losses in several ways. It shows that there is a need to address these losses by appropriate policy interventions. Home-based work that tends to increase under trade liberalization in several industries needs a fresh look at the policy level.

## NEED TO GO BEYOND MEASURING UNPAID WORK

Part One of the volume shows that despite the progress of countries in the Global South towards expansion of TUS, they have a long way to go to produce quality time-use statistics using sound concepts and methods as well as to mainstream TUS in their respective national statistical systems.

Measurement of unpaid work is just the first phase. There is a need to go beyond measurement and to use the data in addressing critical socio-economic concerns of countries. The studies in the second part show that inclusion of unpaid work or time-use data in analysing socio-economic concerns provides additional insight, which can be useful in designing suitable interventions. In fact, absence of this data in examining and addressing these concerns can lead to partial, biased, and even wrong solutions. In other words, time-use data needs to be used along with other data to get a complete and correct diagnosis of problems. Similarly, macroeconomic policies impact paid and unpaid work differently. Unless both the impacts are included, it is difficult to get a comprehensive view of macroeconomic policies. It therefore, becomes essential, to incorporate unpaid work or time-use data in monitoring macroeconomic policies. These policies could be related to labour and employment; trade, taxation, and fiscal policies; and gender equality and women's economic empowerment, among others.

Unpaid work is not fixed or static. It has a dynamic relationship with paid work. The empirical studies in Part Two of the volume show that the nature and size of unpaid work depends on household-level factors (size and composition of a household; its income and socio-cultural characteristics; and the age, sex, literacy, education, etc. of its members) as well as on macroeconomic factors (level of development of the economy,[7] status of the economy on business cycle,[8] etc.). Understanding the dynamic relationship between paid and unpaid work is an important question for studying any economy.

Finally, unpaid work or its relationship with paid work is not merely a gender issue, but it is also a macroeconomic issue. This is because without understanding this relationship, it is difficult to understand the microeconomic and macroeconomic concerns and policies.

## REFERENCES

Antonopoulos, Rania. 2009. 'The Unpaid Care Work–Paid Work Connection', Working Paper No. 86, Policy Integration and Statistics Department. Geneva: International Labour Office.

———. 2013. 'The Value Added of the Levy Institute Measure of Time and Income Poverty (LIMTIP)', Working Paper No. 600, Levy Economics Institute of Bard College, New York.

Antonopoulos, Rania, Thomas Masterson, and Ajit Zacharias. 2012. 'Why Time Deficit Matters', Policy Brief No. 126, Levy Economics Institute of Bard College, New York.

Charmes, J. 2005. 'A Review of Empirical Evidence on Time Use in Africa from UN- Sponsored Surveys', in *Gender, Time Use and Poverty in Sub-Saharan Africa*, Washington, DC: International Bank for Reconstruction and Development.

[7] For example, in relatively poor economies, a large number of services are performed at home (such as taking care of the sick, old, and differently abled), while in rich economies, many of the services are accessed through the market.

[8] For example, during a slump period when employment and incomes are falling, households tend to raise their unpaid work as a coping strategy by bringing in some paid activities within the household. Conversely, during a boom, when employment and incomes are rising, households tend to reduce their unpaid work by taking this work to the market, as they can now afford to buy services. This anti-cyclical behaviour of unpaid work is a good indicator of the macroeconomic interactions of both categories of work.

Elson, Diane. 2008., 'The Three R's of Unpaid Work: Recognition, Reduction and Redistribution', Paper presented at the Expert Group Meeting on Unpaid Work, Economic Development and Human Well-Being, UNDP, New York, November 2008.

Esquivel, Valeria. 2008. 'A "Macro" View on Equal Sharing of Responsibilities between Women and Men' (EGM/ESOR/2008/EP.8), Expert Group Meeting on 'The Equal Sharing of Responsibilities between Women and Men, including Caregiving in the Context of HIV/AIDS', 53rd Meeting of the Commission for the Status of Women (CSW), United Nations Division for the Advancement of Women (DAW), New York.

Esquivel, Valeria. 2011. 'Care in Households and Communities', background paper on conceptual issues, Oxfam GB, October.

Esquivel, Valeria, Nancy Folbre, and Indira Hirway. 2008. 'Explorations: Time Use Studies in The Global South', _Feminist Economics_, June–September 2008.

Hirway, Indira. 2011. _Restructuring of Production and Labour under Globalization: A Study of the Textile and Garment Industry in India_, ILO Decent Work Team for South Asia programme. Geneva: International Labour Organization (ILO).

Inter-secretariat Working Group on National Accounts (ISWGNA). 2008. System of National Accounts. New York: United Nations.

Marco Navarro, Flavia. 2012. 'La utilización de las encuestas de uso del tiempo en las políticas públicas', Serie Mujer y Desarrollo No. 119 (LC/L.3557), Santiago, CEPAL.

# PART ONE

Producing Quality Time-Use Statistics:
Issues Related to Methodology and
Harmonization of Concepts and Methods

# 1 Assessment of Concepts and Methods Used in Selected Countries in ESCAP Region

## Indira Hirway*

Time-use surveys (TUS) provide comprehensive and detailed information on how individuals spend their time, on a daily or weekly basis, on different activities. These activities include activities that fall within the production boundary of the UN System of National Accounts (SNA),[1] non-SNA activities that fall outside the production boundary but within the general production boundary,[2] and personal activities that are non-delegable activities.[3] Time-use statistics are, thus, quantitative summaries of time allocation by men and women

* The author is thankful to Atanu Chatterjee, Research Associate at Centre for Development Alternatives, for his research support. She is also thankful to Dr Sukti Dasgupta, Senior Economist and Member of the Regional Economic and Social Analysis Research Team, ILO (Bangkok) for giving the permission to use the material from an earlier assignment with the ILO, 'Review of time use surveys in selected countries in Asia Pacific'.

[1] These activities constitute those that are included in national income accounts.

[2] Non-SNA activities are not included in national accounts, but are covered under the General Production Boundary. They include all delegable production of services not covered under the national income accounts.

[3] Personal services are non-delegable services, that is, the services that cannot be delegated to others. For example, sleeping, watching TV, etc.

on different activities. The TUS expand the conventional statistical paradigm and provide data on multiple dimensions of human life not otherwise obtainable from conventional data sources. This survey technique, thus, opens up immense opportunities for understanding critical concerns of an economy and society.

This chapter reviews TUS in 35 countries selected from the Asia-Pacific region, especially the members of the United Nations Economic and Social Commission for Asia and the Pacific (ESCAP)[4] to see how far these countries have been able to produce sound time-use data and how far the data is useful in designing national policies in the areas discussed earlier. The chapter essentially studies the strengths and weaknesses of the concepts, methods, and classifications used by these countries in conducting TUS, and explores the need for their standardization and harmonization. The chapter also attempts to examine why some countries have not yet conducted a national TUS, and why the countries that have conducted a national TUS not mainstreamed the survey in their respective national statistical systems. What are their constraints and problems, and what support do they need for mainstreaming TUS?

## OVERALL STATUS OF TUS IN THE SELECTED COUNTRIES

This review is based on desk research on the available material on TUS in the selected 35 countries. This includes the websites of the national statistical offices (NSOs) of the selected countries, the websites of other global agencies that store time-use data (such as United Nations Statistics Division [UNSD] and Centre for Time Use Research [CTUR]), as well as of the global organizations that have sponsored TUS (such as the World Bank [Living Standards Measurement Study (LSMS)], Food and Agriculture Organization of the United Nations [FAO] [studies under 'Righting the Wrong'], United Nations Development Programme [UNDP], and UN Women, etc.). Apart from this literature, the chapter uses a large number of research reviews (Budlender 2000; Hirway 2010; UNDP 2008, 2010) and other research papers.[5] We also had

---

[4] ESCAP is the regional development arm of the UN for the Asia-Pacific region. Made up of 53 member states and 9 associate members, it is the largest UN body serving the Asia-Pacific region with over 600 staff.

[5] As listed in the References at the end of the chapter.

an opportunity to discuss some time-use studies with NSOs of some countries at a recent conference and workshop. The list of references shows that we could lay hands on a large number of sources. However, we could not get much information on some countries like Sri Lanka, Myanmar, Vietnam, etc.

The Asia-Pacific countries under this review are highly heterogeneous as regards their status on TUS. On the one extreme, there are four developed countries—Australia, Japan, South Korea (Republic of Korea or RoK), and New Zealand—where TUS has been mainstreamed in their respective national statistical systems (Table 1.1). These countries conduct regular TUS at an interval of 3–10 years and analyse the data for different uses. On the other extreme, there are seven countries—Afghanistan, Brunei Darussalam, Maldives, Marshall Islands, Myanmar, Palau, and Singapore—which have not conducted a single TUS so far. Between these two extremes are 24 developing and emerging countries (77.4 per cent of the 31) which have conducted at least one TUS (small or big), but several of them have not yet mainstreamed the surveys. These countries are at different levels of conducting or mainstreaming TUS (Table 1A.1).

**TABLE 1.1** Status of TUS in the Selected Countries

| Status | Countries |
| --- | --- |
| Developed Countries where TUS is Mainstreamed | Australia, Japan, South Korea (RoK), New Zealand |
| No TUS Conducted | Afghanistan, Brunei Darussalam, Maldives Marshall Islands, Myanmar, Palau, Singapore |
| Small TUS Only | Indonesia, Fiji, Kiribati, Papua New Guinea, Samoa, Solomon Islands, Sri Lanka, Tuvalu, Vanuatu |
| Official Pilot TUS Only | Philippines |
| Only Rural/Urban TUS | Iran (only urban TUS) |
| National Modular TUS | Cambodia, Lao PDR, Nepal, Timor Leste, Malaysia, Vietnam, Cook Islands |
| National/Large TUS Using Time Diary | Bangladesh, China, India, Mongolia, Pakistan, Thailand |

*Source*: Author's compilation from the respective TUS data and from various organizations.

Of the 24 developing and emerging countries, nine have conducted only small-scale surveys, covering a small numbers of households in a few villages or an urban centre. The NSOs in seven countries (Fiji, Kiribati, Malaysia, Papua Guinea, Samoa, Solomon Island, Sri Lanka, and Vanuatu) have not yet taken any initiative to conduct a pilot or a large/national TUS. Of the other two—Philippines and Iran—the NSO in Philippines has conducted a pilot TUS in 2000 and Iran has conducted two TUS covering only urban areas. However, both the countries have not conducted any national TUS so far.

As Table 1.1 shows, only 14 countries out of the 24 have conducted a national TUS so far. Of these, eight countries have conducted national modular surveys attached to LSMS, Labour Force Surveys (LFS), or income/expenditure surveys, etc. Of these, only three—Lao People's Democratic Republic (Lao PDR), Timor Leste, and Vietnam—have conducted 3–4 TUS, and seem to have mainstreamed them. There are only six (out of the 24) developing and emerging countries in the region that have conducted national/large TUS using 24-hour time diaries, and of these India, China, and Bangladesh have conducted only pilot surveys. But we have included them in the category of national surveys, because they are large surveys covering large parts of the countries. It is interesting to add that of these six countries, only Thailand and Mongolia have conducted more than one survey (that is, four surveys). In other words, only two countries have mainstreamed these surveys in their respective national statistical systems.

## TUS IN DEVELOPING AND EMERGING COUNTRIES

As this chapter focuses on developing and emerging countries in the Asia-Pacific region, there is no in-depth discussion on the TUS in the four developed countries. There is no discussion on the countries which have not conducted any TUS, because we have no information on the reason why they have not conducted a survey (Table 1.1). As shown in Table 1.1, the 24 developing and emerging countries that have conducted TUS can be divided into two categories, namely those that have conducted only small-scale TUS, and those that have conducted national TUS. The countries with national TUS are again of two types: countries that conducted a TUS as a module of a large national survey, and countries which conducted independent national TUS that use 24-hour time diaries for data collection.

## Countries with Only Small-scale TUS

It will be useful to understand the nature of these surveys and see why the concerned countries have not conducted any national survey and whether they want to conduct one.

Many of these are small island countries, located in and around the Pacific—Fiji, Kiribati, Samoa, Solomon Islands, Papua New Guinea, Vanuatu, Indonesia, and Sri Lanka. The small countries like Palau, Marshall Islands, Maldives, Brunei Darussalam, Singapore, and Myanmar have not conducted any TUS so far, while Cook Islands is the only island country to have conducted a national modular TUS. Leaving out the more prosperous Singapore and Brunei Darussalam, some of the other island countries have low literacy and their people have a poor sense of time. In addition, the NSOs of the Philippines, Indonesia, Tuvalu, and Iran have conducted only a pilot survey or a small survey.

Time-use researchers in these countries, including anthropologists, have conducted TUS with a variety of objectives. They are primarily interested in understanding and measuring wide inequalities in the burden of work borne by men and women, and the consequent fewer opportunities in life for women. Some of them also want to make women's work visible, mainly in informal work, subsistence work, household upkeep, and care work, including care provided to chronic patients like those suffering from HIV. FAO conducted small TUS under its programme entitled 'Righting the Wrongs'[6] that aimed at giving visibility to women's work in agriculture and allied activities and to promote their role in decision-making and overall empowerment.

The tourism department in Fiji conducted a TUS in 2003 to assess the burden of work on women and to see how women can be involved in the growth of tourism in the region, while a small survey was conducted in Vanuatu using participatory rural appraisal (PRA) methods to create awareness about unequal sharing of work by men and women

---

[6] This project was undertaken by FAO in a large number of developing countries where agriculture is predominant.

and to prepare a daily gender calendar to highlight wide gender gaps. Kiribati conducted a small TUS to get 'a snapshot of the day' and to see whether and how women can help in forestry and nursery promotion in the region. A TUS in Fiji and one in Tuvalu were conducted in 2003 to understand lifestyle and culture as well as well-being of people. Another survey was conducted in Tuvalu later to estimate the impact of climate change on the livelihoods of people. Benjamin White (1983) conducted the first small-scale surveys in Indonesia in 1972–3 and 1977–8 to estimate gender inequalities in the time spent on paid and unpaid work. Though the reference period was one year, the sample was very small, consisting of only 80–100 households.

One can discern a variety of methods used in these surveys. Participant observation is common among anthropologic surveys, where the researcher observes the time use while living with the subjects. Some researchers used community-based surveys conducted through PRAs, including focus group discussions. Apart from these, the other methods used are: (a) non-participant observation method (under which time use of the subjects is observed from a distance); (b) random observation method; (c) PRA methods, including focus group discussions or community methods (community meets to discuss and comes to a conclusion on sharing of work by men and women); (d) stylized activity list under which respondents are asked about the time they generally spend on the listed activities—sometimes they include specific reference period, such as one week or one day; and (e) 24-hour time diary—usually with time slots of 1–3 hours. FAO's TUS wanted to test eight methods of data collection, namely rapid appraisal by checklist, interview questionnaire, participant observation, non-participant observation, group feedback analysis, group discussion using checklist, 24-hour self-reported time diary, and 24-hour recall. They gathered that the best methods are men observing men and women observing women.

Apart from these, the Philippines conducted a pilot TUS in 2000 covering one rural and one urban area, after researchers conducted small-scale surveys in 1975, 1976, and 1977. Given the fact that the women's movement is very strong in the Philippines and that input-based satellite accounts are prepared for 2000, it is indeed surprising that the country has not yet conducted a single national TUS. However, somehow this has not happened. Statistics Indonesia conducted a pilot TUS in a rural area (100 villages) in 1998–9, and twice in urban areas—in

2004 (five municipalities) and in 2005 (four urban centres). A 24-hour time diary was filled by the respondents above the age of 15 years from the selected households. As literacy is low in Indonesia, only literates were asked to fill in the diary and time slot was kept for 1–3 hours in the diary.

The NSO in Iran (Statistical Centre, Government of Iran) conducted two small TUS in selected urban centres in 2008 and 2009. The 2009 survey was spread over two periods: December 2008–March 2009 and June–September 2009. These pilot surveys have small coverage, because it is believed that rural respondents will not be able to fill in time diaries. Though these surveys have followed the established methods—background questionnaire, 24-hour self-reported time diaries with 15-minute time slots, and 15 activity groups—the urban surveys are conducted only for the literate population. The NSO of Tuvalu conducted a pilot TUS in 2003 as a part of its 'social and well-being surveys' under the 'Participatory Monitoring and Evaluation Project'. The objective was to measure the impact of the Island Development Trust on the quality of life of the subjects. Along with the household and individual characteristics, the time-use data was collected from the selected household members (between the ages of 18 and 82 years) for the week previous to the survey.

There is no doubt that small-scale surveys, including anthropological surveys, are useful, as they provide valuable insight into the dynamics of gender inequalities of different types at the ground level, are useful in addressing local socio-economic and cultural issues, and create awareness among communities as well as in policy advocacy. However, given the variety of concepts and methods used, their results are not comparable with each other. Also, they cannot be considered representative of their respective countries, and, therefore, cannot be used for national-level policymaking. Our review showed that many of these countries want to conduct national TUS using more sophisticated methods.

However, these countries face certain constraints in undertaking national TUS. To start with, the low level of literacy in many of these countries has made it difficult for them to use self-reporting 24-hour time diaries. Second, the limited use of timepieces/clocks (in some countries, this is observed mainly in remote and backward areas) does not allow detailed reporting of the time use. For example, the NSO in

Indonesia has observed that the problems that they face in conducting TUS are: (a) rural people have no concern with time; (b) many of the respondents are not interested responding to time diaries even when they are being interviewed; and (c) the diaries, therefore, are half-filled. This happens even when the time slots are of 1–3 hours. Duncan Ironmonger has also observed that in several island countries, time does not make much sense to people (UNDP 2005).

Some experts have also observed that the main reasons why developing countries hesitate to conduct national TUS are: (a) statistical offices and policymakers in many countries do not appreciate enough the utility of time-use data in addressing major socio-economic concerns at the national level; (b) they do not have the required capacity to collect, analyse, and use the data; (c) the funds required to conduct these surveys are not available; (d) the data collected frequently has serious limitations with respect to its quality; and (e) there is a lack of standardized and harmonized concepts and methods, including activity classification, at the global level for conducting TUS (Budlender 2002; Corner 2003; Hirway 2003; UNDP 2004).

## Countries with National TUS

Most of the 14 countries, which conducted a national-level TUS, started with small-scale surveys conducted by private researchers including anthropologists during the 1970s, 1980s, and the 1990s, covering small number of villages, households and/or one or two urban centres. As mentioned in the earlier discussion, these surveys used a variety of methods and activity classifications and investigated specific issues, sectors, or regions. Some of the countries conducted the surveys around the following timelines: Bangladesh 1974 onwards, India 1976 onwards, Indonesia 1972 onwards, Nepal 1977 onwards, Thailand 1990–1 onwards, Mongolia 2000 onwards, and Malaysia 1972–3 onwards. Though most of these countries also faced the constraints mentioned above, they have somehow been able to conduct national TUS.

All the 24 countries faced several constraints while maintaining 24-hour time diaries, as discussed earlier. These countries, therefore, depend on alternative ways such as (a) linking the time use to major common events (such as, office time, school time, timings of TV/radio programmes) to help respondents to recall time use; (b) using bigger time slots (that is, 30-minute to 1-hour time slots) to fill in or discard time diaries; and (c) asking questions to respondents to report the time spent on a given list of activities (that is, stylized questions). Also, being predominantly agricultural, these countries need seasonal data on the time use to reflect seasonal variations. This being expensive, many countries have done single day/period TUS and failed to provide seasonal variations in the time use of people.

In addition, the countries (including the NSOs and policymakers) also faced constraints like lack of adequate funds, lack of expertise, and poor appreciation of the utility of time-use data. However, their own experiences with small TUS as well as global literature and outside consultants made them realize the importance of conducting national surveys. The *Human Development Report*, 1995; the global women's conference in Beijing in 1995 and its declaration entitled 'Platform For Action'; and the SNA 1993 have been a major source of motivation for these countries to conduct national TUS.[7] Financial as well as technical support from global organizations and donor agencies helped the countries undertake these time-consuming and expensive surveys. As donor agencies frequently tried (and try) to minimize costs, maybe to cover a large number of countries under these surveys, many developing countries faced difficult trade-offs, and ended up with making several 'pragmatic' compromises in sample size and coverage, survey design, data collection methods, etc. This pragmatic approach is reflected in reduced sample size, smaller time samples (and avoiding collection of data by seasons), simpler methods of data collection, shorter list of time-use activities, etc. Our study will throw light on these compromises and shortcuts.

The relevant question, however, is whether, despite the compromises, the data is of good quality, is usable, and whether it is actually used. Our framework of assessment basically includes the following areas: type of the TUS, concepts and methods, objectives of the surveys, background questionnaire, sampling methods and reference period, data collection methods, classification of used and context variables, response rates, publication of the report, and the overall quality of the

---

[7] A number of countries began conducting TUS in the developing world as a result of these events.

survey data. The following sections deal with these points in the context of the developing and emerging countries of the region.

It is important to note at the outset that when these countries started their official pilot surveys or large/national TUS, they needed standard methodologies and classifications to meet their specific needs and constraints. These were not available, firstly because the methods and classifications, designed for developed countries, did not suit them fully, and secondly because UNSD, the global agency in charge of TUS, has not yet fully completed its task of developing methods and classifications.[8] Many of the countries that have conducted national/large TUS have, therefore, modified the available methods and classifications adapting from the sources, including UNSD Guidebook, UNSD's classification, and Harmonized Guidelines of Eurostat.

## TYPES OF NATIONAL TUS

There are two types of national TUS: independent standalone TUS and non-independent or modular TUS, that is, surveys conducted as a part (module) of a major national survey, such as LSMS, LFS, National Income and Expenditure Survey (NIES), etc. Independent TUS collect comprehensive information on the time use of the reference population without missing out any details. It has three components: (a) a background schedule that collects background information of the responding household and the respondent; (b) the time–use schedule/diary that collects data on the time use of the reference 24 hours; and (c) context variables, which provide information on the context of the time–use activities. Time–use surveys started out as independent surveys, largely because they collected information that was not collected through other surveys.

The national modular TUS have been mainly sponsored by international organizations. For example, the World Bank sponsored such surveys as a part LSMS in Vietnam, Nepal, and Timor Leste; the UNDP promoted such surveys in Malaysia (with LFS), Cambodia

---

[8] The custodian of TUS is UNSD at the global level. Given the complex task of combining interests of the Global North and Global South, it is not easy to harmonize methods and classification. The task, therefore, is a 'work in progress'.

(socio-economic survey), Cook Islands (Household Income and Expenditure Survey [HIES]) and Lao PDR (expenditure and consumption survey); and the ILO supported a modular TUS with LFS in Nepal in 1998–9.

## Living Standards Measurement Study and Modular TUS

The LSMS was established by the World Bank in 1980 to explore ways of improving the type and quality of household data collected by developing countries. The goal of LSMS is to foster the use of household data as basis for policymaking in these countries. So far, the World Bank has conducted LSMS in about 40 developing countries. Since time-use data is a critical part of understanding the living standards of people, LSMS frequently uses a module that collects time-use data of men and women in the selected households. Time-use data measures the burden of paid and unpaid work of men and women and their leisure time, provides accurate measures of employment and unemployment in developing countries, and helps movement of work from market to non-market domain and vice versa (Acharya 2000).

The details of the activity list used in a country depend on the specific needs of the country. The NSO in Vietnam has conducted five LSMS (1992, 1997, 2002, 2004, and 2010) in collaboration with the World Bank. These surveys collected time-use data of selected household members (older than 15 years) using stylized questions. However, not many details are accessible about these surveys.[9] Nepal also collected time-use data as a module of its LSMS in 1982, 1996, 2003, and 2010. It is not clear whether the module on TUS was there in all these surveys, but the available literature shows that this module was definitely there in the LSMS of 1982 and 2010. The activity list is developed by Nepal as per its requirements. The Nepal LSMS has seven major groups and other detailed activities. Timor Leste conducted LSMS in 2001 and 2007 and the time-use survey module was in both these national surveys (TLSLS or Timor Leste Survey of Living Standards). The last LSMS was launched in 2007, but it concluded in

---

[9] One major problem faced by us in this chapter was to access information on time-use studies from several countries. Despite trying all possible sources of information on TUS, we could not get information on a few countries.

2008 due to internal conflicts. The survey collected very limited data on the time use of the respondents.

If LSMS collects time-use data for only a single day, the information will be limited to that specific day only. As LSMS needs general/average patterns of time use, stylized questions are asked about the general pattern of time use of men and women. The matrix developed for data collection, therefore, is the list of activities on the x-axis and the details of the time spent on the activities, wages paid, mode of payment, distance from home, etc., on the y-axis.

## Other Global Organizations and Modular TUS

UNDP's approach to TUS basically aims at giving visibility to women's unpaid work, to gender inequalities in the time spent by men and women on paid and unpaid work, and to collect information on how people spend their leisure time. UNDP has frequently used funds from the Swedish International Development Cooperation Agency (SIDA) to promote modular TUS. The idea is to reduce the cost of conducting a TUS so that it can spread to many more countries. Cook Islands conducted a TUS in 1998 as a module of its national HIES, which was conducted by its NSO under the UNDP Poverty Strategies Initiative Trust Fund. The national survey, which provides major indicators of economic health of the nation and well-being of its people, covered 15 per cent of its households. The reference period of the time-use module was one week, and the respondents (over the age of 15 years) were asked to give details on the time use during the past week. The activity list included 10 groups—domestic work, childcare, church and religious activities, education, personal care, social entertainment, community work, sports and hobbies, cultural activities, and free-time activities. This survey did not collect data on simultaneous activities and did not use ant context variables.

Though Malaysia started with a small TUS under FAO, in 2014, the Ministry of Women, with the financial and technical support of UNDP, conducted a national TUS to assess women's burden of work and to recommend ways of raising their workforce participation rate in the labour market in order to raise economic growth (Ministry of Women and UNDP 2014). The study was undertaken as a module of the national LFS. It covered women between 20–60 years and was conducted from August to September 2014. There were 2,640 respondents who reported how much time they spent on listed activities during the past 24 hours.[10] Lao PDR conducted its first national expenditure and consumption survey in 1992. The survey has been conducted every five years. It included a module to collect information on time use of men and women in the household. Nepal also started with small-scale TUS in the 1970s, 1980s, and 1990s (1992 and 1993–4), and started national modular TUS (by the NSO) in 1996 with LSMS. In 1998–9, the NSO conducted it as a module to the national LFS (helped by ILO). It continued with an annual modular survey with LFS in 2003 and 2009–10. The data on the time use was collected using stylized questions.

Cambodia conducted its first TUS in 2004 as a module of the national Cambodia socio-economic survey. The period of the survey was from November 2003 to January 2005. It is the only country whose modular TUS used 24-hour self-reported time diaries and collected information on simultaneous activities (primary and secondary) and used context variables (location, transportation mode, and with whom/persons present). The activity list included six major groups and other details. The survey, however, faced several limitations that will be discussed later.

## National Independent Surveys

As discussed earlier, six countries—India, China, Pakistan, Bangladesh, Mongolia, and Thailand—have conducted TUS using 24-hour time diaries. Of these, India, Bangladesh, and China have conducted large surveys with a representative sample, which are, therefore, considered here as national surveys. These countries have expressed their intention to conduct national TUS in the near future).

The National Bureau of Statistics (NBS) of China conducted a pilot TUS in two regions (Zhejiang and Yunnan) in 2005. The respondents

---

[10] The background schedule of the main survey included questions related to the socio-economic profile of individuals, work status, work–life balance, barriers and facilities to their participation in the labour market, barriers and facilities to career progression, reasons for leaving employment, and care and attitudes towards work. It was also accompanied by focus group discussions with women.

reported two 24-hour self-reported time diaries that collected data on different activities that were divided into seven broad groups. In May 2008, the NBS conducted its first large TUS covering 10 provincial cities and rural areas. The survey collected information on simultaneous activities and used context variables also.

After two small TUS in the 1970s by researchers, the Government of Bangladesh conducted national LFS in 1984–5 and 1990–1 using a small-size time-use module. However, the Bangladesh Bureau of Statistics (BBS) of the Ministry of Planning did not consider the data good enough for publication. The Dhaka University with the support of International Development Research Centre (IDRC) conducted a small TUS (1,000 households) using anthropological (observation) methods to collect data on distribution of expenditure within household members. In 2012, however, the BBS conducted a pilot survey using 24-hour time diary and United Nations Trial International Classification of Activities for Time Use Statistics (ICATUS) 1997. The time diary was filled in by interviewers. The Time Use Survey 2012 Report was published by the BBS.

In Pakistan, the first TUS was conducted as a small survey in 1986–9, which was funded by United States Agency for International Development (USAID). The survey was also supported by the International Food Policy Research Institute (IFPRI), the Government of Pakistan, and various researchers. The study covered 800 households from 44 villages with the objective of assisting food-related policies, food security, and food management. FAO conducted a small TUS in Pakistan in 1990–1 to try out eight methods of collecting time-use data.[11] At last in 2007, the Federal Bureau of Statistics of the Government of Pakistan conducted a national, independent, and standalone TUS. This survey covered 97 per cent of the total population and collected data throughout the year to assess seasonal changes in the time use of people.

India has a long history of having small-scale TUS conducted by scholars (1976–7, 1980, 1987, 1990, and 1990–1). In 1990–1, FAO conducted a small TUS under its programme 'Righting the Wrongs'. In 1996, the Directorate of Statistics of the state government of Tamil

---

[11] These methods are rapid appraisal by checklist, diary method, interview questionnaire, participant observation, non-participant observation, 24-hour recall, group discussion, and group feedback analysis.

Nadu also conducted a small-scale survey. At last in 1998–9, under the Central Statistical Organization (CSO), Ministry of Statistics and Programme Implementation, Government of India, the first national pilot TUS was conducted, covering six major states that represented the entire country (Hirway 2015). The survey was conducted in all the four seasons of the year and covered 18,648 households (CSO 2000).

Thailand and Mongolia are the only two countries among the emerging and developing countries in the region that have mainstreamed TUS as independent and standalone surveys. Thailand's first TUS was conducted in 1990–1 under the 'Righting the Wrongs' programme, which is aimed at giving visibility to women's work in agriculture and to promote their role as decision makers. In 2000–1, however, the NSO of Thailand conducted the first national independent standalone TUS. This survey was repeated every 3–4 years—in 2004, 2009, and 2014–15. There has been continuous improvement in the content and coverage of these surveys over the years: (a) the 2001 and 2004 surveys were conducted in August, the 2009 survey covered three months (June–August), while 2015 has covered one whole year (July 2014–June 2015); (b) the sample size has increased over the surveys; (c) the classification has become more detailed—the last survey has a five-digit classification; (d) the time slot was reduced to 5 minutes in the time diary; and (e) the age limit (10+ years) was reduced to 6+ years in the 2014–15 survey. One person was selected from each household and she filled in one time diary. Systematic reports are published by the NSO of the Government of Thailand.

In the case of Mongolia, the first TUS, a pilot TUS, an independent TUS, was conducted in 2000. This survey, supported by UNDP, used a 24-hour self-reported time diary. In 2004, a statistical law was passed according to which a national TUS should be conducted after every four years. The survey was, therefore, conducted in 2007 and 2011 (the 2015 survey was being conducted when the chapter was written). Mongolia also improved over the years with the expansion of the reference period and people. The survey was conducted throughout the year, in March, June, September, and December. Regular reports are published with preliminary (tables) analysis in the local language.

The third type of TUS, namely small-scale surveys, could be in the form of anthropological surveys or small surveys conducted by private researchers, or systematic TUS that are specific to a sector, area, or an issue. The former throws useful light on the dynamics of specific issues at the ground level, and have limited use at the national-level database. The latter surveys aim at understanding time use on specific issues, sectors, or areas for specific policymaking.

## Concerns Relating to Modular TUS

It will be relevant here to discuss the ongoing debate on modular versus independent TUS. As discussed earlier, a modular TUS is a non-independent survey, which is a part (module) of a major survey. It is frequently argued that there are several advantages of a modular TUS: (a) it is less expensive when compared to an independent survey, as information is collected in the form of replies to a list of questions and not through a 24-hour time diary; (b) it is easy to conduct, as it needs less effort in data collection and analysis; and (c) it is easy to institutionalize, as it is usually conducted with a regular national survey. Compared to this, an independent survey has relatively high start-up costs and, therefore, it is not easy to institutionalize. Since it is conducted every 4–7 years, its survey operations are irregular, and that makes it difficult to accumulate and absorb the knowledge and experience to achieve efficient and reliable survey results. They also limit the opportunity to develop independent technical and field staff well trained in time-use methods. Many countries, therefore, favour modular TUS.

On the other hand, it is argued that a modular survey has a limited scope for data collection. A time-use module of a large survey cannot be a very large module that can collect comprehensive data, as it is a part of a major national survey. Also, such a module tends to collect information that is related to the main survey, as its scope is restricted by the main survey. The collected information may not be adequate to understand the time use of men and women in a comprehensive manner. For example, a time-use module in an LFS may not provide the data needed to compile satellite accounts of unpaid work, or a time-use module in an income and expenditure survey (IES) may not provide the data needed to estimate and understand informal and subsistence economy.

Again, most modular TUS collect data by asking stylized questions. Investigators present a list of activities and ask respondents to report how much time they spent on each of those activities during the reference day (the previous day) or the reference week. This is usually a short list of the activities of specific interest, as it would be difficult to manage a long, exhaustive list and check that the total time adds up to 24 hours. Respondents usually do not reply keeping in mind the total time. In practice, therefore, one observes a short or a slightly long list, but not an exhaustive list consisting of all activities. Some post-survey reviews have observed (Charmes and Hirway 2006) in Madagascar and Malawi that the listed activities missed out several relevant activities, as the list is predetermined, and is not always exhaustive. Also, this method does not give information on the total time use, for 24 hours.

Questions have also been raised in the literature about the quality of the data collected through stylized questions. The UN Guidebook, for example, has observed that stylized questions tend to produce results with a high degree of error (UNSD 2005). This is because respondents tend to under-report the time spent on the activities that are less important or desirable and over-report the time on the activities of more importance or desirability. Also, respondents may find it difficult to report the time spent on intermittent or scattered activities. Bonke (2002) compared the performance of both these methods (time diaries based on one-day recall and stylized questions) at the field level. He observed that there are clear errors emerging from the stylized questions. The studies have shown that the error comes not only from the problems of recall, but also from social desirability of the activities. Respondents tend to over-report the activities of their interest and under-report the activities in which they have low interest. The error varies across different socio-economic groups also. Bonke (2002) also found that the gap in the results of both the methods is larger in the case of women than in the case of men.

In addition, there are several other problems of stylized methodology. First, stylized questions do not provide the time of the day when the activity was performed. Second, one cannot collect time-use data on simultaneous activities accurately under this approach, as respondents find it difficult to provide this data, because they are not able to identify these activities and the time spent on these correctly. Third, it is also not easy to use context variables efficiently under this method. Respondents also find it difficult to respond to context variables, such as for whom, with whom, for each of the episodes while responding to stylized questions. And finally, recall can be a serious problem with stylized questions when the reference period is more than one day. A one-week reference period in the TUS of Nepal and Papua New Guinea is seen as a serious problem. It seems to have affected the quality of time-use data to very rough approximation of the time use.

If time diaries are used in a modular survey, it becomes difficult for investigators and respondents to respond suddenly to a totally new method of data collection; the quality of the data at the end of the main survey is, thus, likely to be less than satisfactory. It is, therefore, recommended to organize a staggered and independent TUS after the main survey is conducted if one is interested in collecting related time-use data (for example, India has decided to do so).

In short, it is recommended by UNSD (the custodian of TUS globally) that for good quality national time-use data, NSOs should use independent standalone TUS that use time diaries—filled in by any reliable method.

## OBJECTIVES OF NATIONAL TUS

Table 1A.2 presents information on the objectives of the TUS in the selected 35 countries. There are clear differences in the objectives of conducting TUS in developed and developing countries. In the selected developed countries (Australia, Japan, RoK, and New Zealand), where it is assumed that conventional LFS are able to provide reliable estimates of their workforce and labour force,[12] time-use data is seen to be useful in estimating non-SNA work, valuing unpaid work in satellite accounts, and in understanding a number of socio-economic issues, such as gender inequalities, transportation, balancing family and work, loneliness of the old, and social capital.

One major objective of TUS in all four developed countries is to collect information on how people spend their time on different activities. All four state this in so many words. The other objectives, which seem to be important, particularly in the 1990s and 2000 onwards,

---

[12] This assumption is not fully acceptable, as the informal sector is emerging in these economies also. Again, the details of different work-time arrangements and what people do at the workplace is not revealed by the conventional surveys in these countries.

are related to gender inequalities—'to analyse gender inequalities', 'to estimate time spent by men and women on care', including childcare, and compiling satellite accounts of unpaid work in monetary terms to estimate women's contribution to the economy (Centre for Time Use Research, various years). In the case of RoK and Japan also, the TUS were conducted by the broadcasting companies (NHK in Japan and KBS in South Korea). These companies were mainly interested in collecting data on how people spend leisure time and in knowing the socio-cultural lives of people. On the contrary, the NSOs shifted the focus of TUS on estimating gender inequalities and measuring contribution of unpaid work to national well-being from the late 1990s onwards. Another set of objectives of these countries was related to social concerns, such as to estimate work–life balance, to understand how men and women spend their leisure time, lifestyle of people, as well as some socio-economic concerns related to ageing (how old people spend their time), health, childcare, environment-related issues, traffic and transportation policy, etc. Clearly, objectives related to poverty, the informal sector, or employment are almost absent from their list of objectives.

A common objective of the national TUS in the developing and emerging countries is to improve estimates of paid work or SNA work, particularly in informal and subsistence work. This has been put differently by different countries. Cambodia, Malaysia, Lao PDR, and Mongolia have put this as 'to get information on participation and time spent on agriculture and allied activities, handicraft, and collection of water and fuel wood' or 'to get information on how individuals in rural areas spend their time'. India, Pakistan, Nepal, Thailand, Mongolia, and Bangladesh have put it as 'getting improved estimates of workforce, or getting detailed information on paid and unpaid work of men and women, or to get reliable estimates on labour input in an economy (the last is applicable to Lao PDR). China has put it as 'to measure women's unremunerated work'. Vietnam has put it as 'to get reliable data on living standards of people'. The objective indicates the belief of these countries that LFS does not provide complete data on the labour/work force and the time spent by them on different paid and unpaid SNA activities, particularly those relating to informal sector units, unpaid work in family business, subsistence work, and collection of free goods.

Another major objective, again of most of the developing and emerging countries, is to estimate gender inequalities in paid and unpaid work. This was expressed by most countries as 'to get detailed information on how men and women spend their time on unpaid work'. Most countries aimed at estimating gender inequalities in the time spent by men and women on paid and unpaid work. Bangladesh put it as 'to estimate all forms of work by men and women', while Cambodia, India, Lao PDR, Bangladesh, Mongolia, Thailand, etc., have expressed as 'to estimate inequalities in paid and unpaid work'. Several countries have also put compiling satellite accounts of unpaid work as their objective (China, India, Pakistan, Thailand, and Philippines).

In both the objectives, the focus is on getting (improved) estimates of paid and unpaid work of women (and men) and on estimating gender inequalities prevailing in paid and unpaid work.

The other objectives are varied. China has stated 'to measure quality of life of people' as one of its objectives. Malaysia wants to test eight methods of collection of time-use data to see which method gives the most accurate data on women's agrarian labour.[13] Mongolia wants to study household patterns and change, while Thailand wants to understand people's participation in cultural and custom-related activities and to produce internationally comparable data (Table 1A.2). The small surveys also have expressed their objectives to give visibility to women's paid and unpaid work, to understand and measure wide inequalities in the burden of work borne by men and women, and to estimate how men and women spend their leisure time.

In short, the focus on getting improved estimates of all forms of work, of national workforce and labour force; a measurement of gender inequalities; and a valuation of unpaid work are very much in line with the major needs of these countries. There is also realization that the conventional LFS are not adequate to capture adequately the size and characteristics of informal and subsistence work prevailing in these countries.

---

[13] FAO's TUS wanted to test eight methods of data collection, namely rapid appraisal by checklist, interview questionnaire, participant observation, non-participant observation, group feedback analysis, group discussion using checklist, 24-hour self-reported time diary, and 24-hour recall. They observed that the best methods are men observing men and women observing women.

## BACKGROUND QUESTIONNAIRE

There are two types of background schedules used in national TUS: in the case of modular TUS, the main survey can be treated as the background schedule, while in the case of independent standalone surveys, a background questionnaire is designed specifically keeping in mind the objectives of the survey. In the former case, the background schedule is determined by the main objectives of the main survey (such as LFS, IES, LSMS, or any other household survey), which may not accommodate the specific objectives of the objectives of the TUS. For example, a time-use module in an LFS will have different background data from that in an IES. The subject of the main survey, thus, is likely to restrict the analysis of time-use data. An LFS may not help in compiling household satellite accounts or estimate the care economy; an IES may not provide the required data on estimating informal and subsistence employment. The selection of the main survey to latch on a TUS module needs to be done carefully. Also, to design another elaborate background for the time-use module will be impractical. In general, modular surveys are weak in designing background information for facilitating analysis of the time-use data. This puts a restriction on the use of the data.

In the case of independent standalone TUS, there is a good scope for collecting the required data on households and individuals. All developed countries have a long tradition of collecting background information on selected households and selected members from these households. Household information includes major household characteristics, such as, place of residence (province and city/village and rural/urban), size and composition of the household, race and social groups, total income and expenditure, main source of income, and housing conditions. The individual questionnaire includes an individual's characteristics, such as, age, sex, marital status, occupation, education, health status (if sick), and details of employment (industry and occupation status) if any, and incomes earned. Whether the background questionnaires of the selected national TUS are adequate to meet the objectives of the surveys, or not, is an important consideration.

The background schedule of a TUS is designed keeping in mind the objectives of the survey. It is an important component of a TUS, as the time-use data is usually analysed with reference to the information collected in the background schedule. This schedule, therefore, is expected to collect all the data required to analyse the time-use data in the context of the objectives of the survey. For example, if an objective of the survey is to value the unpaid non-SNA work in the economy, it is necessary that the background questionnaire collects data on equipment and assets of the household; their ownership by sex, technologies used in cooking, cleaning, washing, etc.; prevailing wages in the locality; the presence of children, elderly, disabled, and others, in the household; market prices of the goods produced at home; among other such factors. If the objective is to understand the care economy, it will be necessary to collect information on the need for care of the households, that is, size of the household, presence of children in the household (in the age groups of 0–6 years and 7–18 years), presence of disabled persons and the elderly that need care, how the care is shared within household members, and how the care is organized between the household, government organizations, the market, and voluntary agencies).

The background questionnaires of the TUS in Bangladesh, China, India, Mongolia, Pakistan, and Thailand have collected rich information on household and individual characteristics. The Chinese TUS has collected these individual characteristics: age, sex, marital status, occupation, education, income earned, and distance between home and the workplace. The official report of the Chinese TUS, which has presented main tables based on the data, has used these variables. One problem with the Chinese TUS is that the report does not use all the data collected on households and individuals. The Chinese survey also has general questions about the nature of the day (too busy, normal, etc.). The TUS in Mongolia also has included more or less the same details in the background schedules. In the case of employment, however, they have used details such as occupation, employment status, unemployment, and part-time employment.

In the case of Thailand's TUS, the background questionnaires have collected the usual information on selected households. In the case of individuals, the data includes relationship with the household's head, age and sex, marital status, religion, employment status, occupation, and the industry in which the person is working. The TUS in India included an elaborate background questionnaire. The household questionnaire included questions on head of the household, size and composition of the household, social group (religion and caste), average monthly consumption expenditure and per capita monthly consumption expenditure, household assets, land owned and operated, housing, main industry (code) and main occupation (code) of the household, and whether there is any disabled person in the household. The individual questionnaire included questions on age, sex, marital status, education, relation with the household head, usual activity status (principle and subsidiary), industry and enterprise status, and participation in decision-making. The survey also asked general questions on the type of the day (normal or abnormal, week day or weekend), and the nature of the questionnaire (easy, difficult, etc.).

Pakistan has used an elaborate background questionnaire comprising five to six pages. The information on the selected households includes head of the household, the respondent's name and sex, household income by sources, and the main source of income; consumption, savings, investment; housing conditions (earthquake-affected, kutcha, pucca, etc.); sources of energy for cooking, lighting, and heating; use of firewood and distance to the sources; source of water supply and distance to the source; access to transportation facility (distance); access to major government services (distance); number of children in the household (0–7 years and 8–18 years); who does the household work, and so on. The individual questionnaire is also elaborate and it collects information on age, sex, education, marital status, children in the household, and a number of questions on employment. These questions include whether the person has worked at least one hour in the last week, whether he has work/job in general, employment status (whether the person is unemployed, looking for work, or is available for work), income earned, designation, and details of the enterprise where he/she is working, such as nature of the establishment; whether it files accounts, employs regular workers; and the number of workers employed. Interestingly, the questionnaire also includes questions like: (a) whether the person uses a watch or has a clock; (b) whether the day of the interview was normal or not; and (c) how the person is feeling about his/her time use—is he/she too busy?

The Bangladesh TUS also has an elaborate background questionnaire. The household information collected includes details of head of the household, source of energy for light and for cooking, source of water supply, participation in selected household occupations (livestock, poultry, dairy, horticulture, small and cottage industry, and pisciculture), occupational assets owned, and primary and other sources of income. The individual questionnaire included questions on economic activities of individuals—whether the person worked for at least one hour during the past seven days, if he/she has a employed, was he/she looking for employment, the nature of the enterprise where he/she is working—industry code, employment status, designation, ownership of the enterprise, whether full-time/part time work, etc.

There appear to be variations across countries in the way they have designed background questionnaires. On the one hand, there are China and Mongolia, which have collected the details that are usually collected in any household surveys, while on the other hand, there is Pakistan, which has designed an elaborate background questionnaire. It seems to us that none of the background questionnaires is adequate to provide information to meet the objectives of the surveys laid down by them, for the following possible reasons:

1. None of the background schedules helps in understanding the care economy in their respective countries because: (a) none has collected household level data on the need for care in the household (presence of the disabled, chronically sick people, old needing care and children by age group)[14] and (b) how it is organized at the household level, that is, who provides care: household women, other household members, elder child, government support, the market, or NGO groups. The result is that it is different to understand the total care needed at the household and macro levels and how it is shared at the household level and at the macro level by different agencies.

2. Similarly, household upkeep needs data on the technology used for cooking (fuel and stove used), washing, cleaning, shopping,[15] etc. This information helps in assessing the drudgery component of

---

[14] The nature of childcare depends on the age of children. The ages of children are, therefore, necessary.

[15] As the time needed depends on the technology used, this information helps in identifying drudgery of household work.

this work. Also, information on how this work is shared within the household, and between household members and hired workers will help in assessing sharing of burden of this work. While Pakistan has collected some of the data (not all), other countries have missed it.

3. For valuation of unpaid work, the background questionnaires need to collect data on value of assets along with its ownership by sex. Though data on assets is collected by a few countries, the asset ownership is missing from all questionnaires.

4. Collection of data on employment—occupation, industry, employment status, number of jobs done, wages earned, whether the person has worked for at least one hour in the past seven days or whether he has looked for work or is available for work—is important data. However, there is no provision to get this information from the additional work that is captured through the details of the time use of respondents. Also, in the case of multiple jobs, there is no way to link this information with the time use of the respondent.

To conclude, there is need to give more attention to the designing of the background questionnaires. The usual details in households and individuals are far from adequate. It appears that there is a poor appreciation of the potential uses of this schedule in enriching time-use data.

## SAMPLING UNDER TUS

Sampling under TUS includes sampling of households and household members as well as sampling of time—number of days per selected household members and the period of the year for which the TUS is undertaken, that is, the reference period.

### Sampling of Households and Members under Independent TUS

The basic issues for sampling for a TUS are the standard ones as faced by any household-based survey except that the sample size of national TUS is usually smaller than the other national surveys, which are more time-consuming and more expensive than regular surveys. Sometimes

NSOs/researchers reduce the sample size to an unacceptable level. This tends to raise sampling errors on the one hand and limits the possibility for disaggregated analysis on the other. Both these factors tend to reduce the utility of the data. The size of a sample for TUS is, therefore, an important issue.

There are certain factors that must be taken care of while selecting the number of households for a TUS. Firstly, it is important that the household sample is drawn systematically using multi-stage stratified random sampling techniques. The random element is more important than the size of the sample per se. One can also use a geographical cluster approach to reduce sampling errors as well as sample size. It is important, however, to draw a sufficiently large sample to have more than enough numbers to analyse the small cells. The issue of sample size is also tied to the issue of minimizing field costs. As mentioned above, the cluster design approach, which geographically concentrates fieldwork, saves on travel and administration costs. The population can be broken down into geographical units and a multi-stage method is used to randomly select some units.

The sample size of a TUS can be raised with least cost by: (a) increasing the number of persons in the survey and (b) increasing the number of days of each person selected for the survey. Selecting more than one day per person is definitely another way of raising the sample size. An important sample design decision is whether to include all household members belonging to the sampled (reference population of) households or not. Several countries have selected one member (Thailand) or two members (Pakistan) of the household randomly.

There are important advantages of selecting all eligible members (above a minimum age) in the sample: (a) it helps in estimating the distribution of tasks across household—the larger the household, the more options for variation in the performance of different tasks across members; (b) it provides better detail of the power and task dynamics within a household; and (c) it helps in unpacking the intra-household dynamics by assessing how those dynamics work.

An additional reason for selecting multiple persons per household is cost efficiency. Most population surveys are based on household samples. It is generally less expensive to collect the survey data from a sample of persons clustered in a smaller number of households than to spread the sample over a larger number of households. From the perspective of cost efficiency, the most efficient design is the one that minimizes the sampling errors of the survey estimates for a given budget. Determining an efficient design, therefore, requires an evaluation of the effects on sampling error of clustering the sample of persons within households. This evaluation involves both the effect of weighting for unequal selection probabilities and the effect of cluster homogeneity.

A further factor, however, to be considered in determining the numbers of persons to be selected from sampled households is that of household response burden. If time-use data is collected for several persons in selected households, the burden of interviewing all of them may be perceived as excessive on the household, even though it is distributed among the sampled persons. This perception may then lead to unacceptable levels of non-response. Household response burden is particularly high with large households and when all persons are selected per household. Methods should be devised to reduce this burden on individuals, such as interviewing each household independently.

When we look at the selected countries, one common point that emerges in all national TUS is that sampling has been done using multi-stage stratified random sampling, that is, samples of households have been selected systematically. The size of the sample, however, varies from country to country depending on the size of the country, population of the country, the coverage of the survey and the sampling techniques used. The Chinese surveyed 16,661 households (for selected provinces), Pakistan surveyed 196,000 households, the last Thai survey has 27,000 households, and Indian pilot TUS has 18,600 households (six states). All these surveys have used variations of multi-stage stratified random sampling methods.

The minimum age for the sample varies from 5 years in Nepal, Timor Leste, and Cambodia, to 15 years in China, Cook Islands, Indonesia, and Malaysia. India has kept it at 6 years, while Lao PDR, Pakistan, and Thailand have used 10 years. Mongolia has kept it 12 years. There are countries where there is a maximum age limit too. China has selected 74 years as the maximum age for respondents and Malaysia has selected 64 years. The countries interested in studying problems of children's time use, including child labour, have reduced the minimum age. Though time diaries are to be reported by the respondent herself, in the case of children, a parent or any elderly household members is allowed to help.[16] The uneven coverage of minimum and maximum ages is likely to create some problems in cross-country comparability of time-use data.

## TIME SAMPLING UNDER INDEPENDENT TUS

Sampling of time for which the data is collected needs to be representative of the total time of the sampled households. Two decisions are important here for selecting a representative time sample. How many diary days should be sampled per household member? What should be the reference period of the survey, that is, for how many months the data on time use of people should be collected?

The simplest design collects time-use data for a single day for each sampled person. This design avoids problems of collecting data for several days and places the least burden on the selected persons. Considering the fact that time use on weekdays and weekends is usually different, it will be useful to select two days per person. UN Guidebook, UN Economic Commission for Europe (UNECE) Guidelines, and EU Guidelines on TUS recommend selection of two diary days for each person: one weekday and the other a weekly variant day (could be Sunday or any other variant day), as it is argued that selection of these two days represents time use of persons fairly satisfactorily.

Most countries follow this pattern. It is important to maintain randomness in the selection. It can be argued that selection of four days per person enables two weekdays, one Saturday, and one Sunday to be chosen (where this weekly pattern is the norm). It will also cut down the costs. From these four days, a synthetic week estimate can be constructed. Survey designers should consider the minimum number of representations of a particular day of the week and select the sample to produce tolerable standard errors given specific analytical objectives (Bittman 2000).

Again, ideally a TUS should represent a full 12-month period. Failing that, a purposive selection of a 'representative' set of, say, two, three, or four individual months may be used, or if resource constraints so dictate, the data collection may be confined to a single 'typical' time

---

[16] For example, several countries have allowed even adults to refer to each other while responding to time-use diary.

period. Whatever the chosen period, within that period, the day or days for which each respondent reports time use should be pre-specified and chosen by a random selection procedure.

In the selected countries, China and Thailand have collected time-use data for one person and Pakistan for two persons. The rest of the countries have selected all eligible persons (above a certain age) for collecting time-use data. Countries also differ in the number of days selected to collect time-use data. China, Cambodia, and Bangladesh have collected time-use data for one diary day per person, while India,[17] Pakistan, Mongolia, and Thailand have selected two diary days per person. The two days usually include one weekday and the other weekly variant day. Mongolia has grouped the days of a week into three groups and selected days in a manner that each day gets an equal probability of getting selected. Several modular TUS have selected more than one day—usually the past seven days. Nepal has collected time-use data for the previous day, seven days, and one month.

## Sampling in Multipurpose or Modular Surveys

Sampling for two combined household surveys—one the main household survey and the other the TUS—raises several issues. One major issue is whether it is possible to create an efficient dual-purpose sampling design in which the objectives of the time dimension are properly represented. As this sampling is usually done keeping in mind the objectives of the large survey, it will help if the time-use module has matching objectives.

Apart from TUS, very few household surveys require that data be collected for specific days. Thus, the need to represent the time dimension appropriately in a design that combines a TUS with another survey type requires a modification in the data collection procedures so that it represents the criteria that would be used by the other survey if it were a standalone survey. Since the modification will almost certainly impose restrictions on the timing of interviews, it may lead to a lower

[17] In the case of India, instructions were given to find out whether the day selected was an abnormal day, and if the interviewers were asked to select another day, a normal day.

response rate for the combined survey than would be achieved if the other survey was conducted alone. This factor also needs to be taken into account when a combined survey is being considered. A TUS will most readily fit together with another survey that also involves spreading data collection over time. The other survey may itself require a similar representation of the time dimension as, for example, is often the case with a nutrition or family budget survey. The main concern here is that of response burden. The response burden in such surveys is often substantial so that, when combined with the high burden of a TUS, the overall burden may become excessive.

The main complexity of sample design in TUS is encountered when incorporating the time dimension in the design. Most household surveys collect data that relates to a specific point or period of time (cross-sectional data) or that is assumed to change little over the period of time of data collection. In TUS, however, the estimates of interest are not for the activities that people engage in during a particular day or week, but for a longer period of time, typically a year. Since people's activities can substantially vary in terms of the day of the week and the season of the year, the TUS needs to ensure that the sample design provides a suitable representation of the time period for which estimates are required.

Should a modular TUS cover all days of the year or all four seasons of the year? One basic option is to conduct the survey on a periodic or continuous basis over the entire year and to spread the total sample of households over each survey period. The ideal design, with data collected over a 12-month period, gives representation to the time dimension throughout the period. In many countries, a fieldwork plan can be developed to satisfy this requirement, for instance, spreading the interviews evenly over the 12 months, both at national and subnational levels. However, is such a design is not possible, the aim should be to approximate the ideal to the extent possible.

In practice, however the number of time periods selected is generally small, say, from two to four, and is chosen by purposive selection: data collection may cover a few separate months, chosen carefully to be 'representative' accounting for seasonality and spread over the year. Within the chosen months, the sample can then be spread across weeks and across days of the week. An alternative is to take a sample of time periods, such as weeks or months, and concentrate the data collection in those periods. The more periods that can be covered, the better. The key here is to choose a set of such time periods that are representative of the full 12 months on an average.

Whether the sample is spread across a full year or concentrated in certain periods, it is important to select days by probability methods, to avoid selection bias. Interviewers or respondents might choose days that are convenient for them—for instance, days when the respondent is at home. Such choices may lead to distorted estimates of time use. Probability sampling of days theoretically guarantees time-use estimates that are free of selection bias, but only if the data is collected for the specified sample days. Every effort should, therefore, be made to respect specified days.

Constraints posed by limited resources, or the use of a multi-purpose survey, may restrict a TUS to a single period of one or two months. Interpreting the resulting estimates as typical of time-use patterns over a year is not possible. Another option would be simply to conduct a single-period survey and acknowledge the analytical limitations of such an approach.

## METHODS FOR DATA COLLECTION

Getting correct and detailed response from respondents is an important part of data collection. The selected developed countries usually employ 24-hour self-reported time diaries, with a 10-minute time slot, for collecting information on how people spend their time. Many of the developing and emerging countries need to work out their strategy for data collection carefully, since literacy levels could be low and in certain remote backward areas people may not use timepieces or watches to be able to report their exact time use, which could make accurate data collection a difficult task.

As seen in the case of small-scale TUS earlier, several methods of time-use data collection have been used. In national surveys, however, the choice of the methods declines because one has to deal with a larger sample size. The PRA-based or community-based methods will not be feasible here.

As seen earlier, there are three categories of methods available in large TUS: (a) the observation method; (b) the 24-hour time diary-based method; and (c) stylized questions.

## Observation-based Methods

Under this approach, a person is appointed to observe and record the time use of a person accurately. There are two types of approaches here. Under the participant observation method, a researcher, usually an anthropologist, observes and records time use and also tries to understand it by participating in the life of the respondents. Under the non-participant observation, the observer simply observes and records time use of respondents. There is no direct involvement of the person being observed. The observation method has been regarded by practitioners as very successful for local community empowerment and change. The main advantage of the observation method is that the person whose activities are recorded does not have to be able to read and write, or have a western concept of time.

There are several problems with this method: (a) continuous observation tends to make respondents conscious and leads them to behave differently and (b) if an investigator has to observe the entire household, he/she may find it difficult do so, but if an investigator has to observe only one person, then there will be a need for a full-time investigator for each respondent, which may be a costlier alternative. In a large survey, this method will not be practical. However, the researcher can train local volunteers supervised by educated volunteers (Mulik and Werner 2002) or use a literate younger member of the household to assist in the observation (Waring 2006).

One alternative version of this method is to do random observations, for example, the observer can come back every hour to see what the respondent is doing. This method allows one researcher to monitor more than one person in a day. However, it gives an incomplete picture of activities and is not considered reliable (Sillitoe 2006). Observation-based methods are, thus, the least used methods at present.

## Stylized Questions Method

The stylized questions are asked mainly in modular TUS. Under this approach, respondents report their time use by answering questions as per a set of listed activities. These questions are about the time they spend on each of the listed activities during the reference day (usually the previous day), the reference week, or even a month (as in the case of Nepal). There can be a short list of the activities of specific interest or a long list covering all activities. It would be difficult to manage a long, exhaustive list and to check that the total time adds up to 24 hours, because the respondents usually do not reply keeping in mind the total time. Also, when simultaneous activities are included, it becomes almost impossible to keep the total time to 24 hours. In practice, therefore, one observes a short or a slightly long list, but not an exhaustive list consisting of all activities. In all the modular surveys, the list varies between 9 and 90.

We have already examined the limitations of this method of time-use data collection earlier. It needs mention here that since this is a less expensive and easy method, it is used by many developing and emerging countries. The UN International Research and Training Institute for the Advancement of Women (INSTRAW) has rated this method as having low validity, reliability, and flexibility (INSTRAW 1995: 89). There are several versions of this method of data collection which are discussed in the following sections. These versions do not deal with simultaneous activity at all. Use of context variables is also avoided in these methods. Also, as discussed earlier, there are problems with the accuracy and reliability of the data.

ACTIVITY LOG

Under this version, the person whose activities are being studied is asked to write down on the questionnaire each time he/she does a particular activity. For example, during the next three days, each time the respondent prepares any food, or gets or prepares a drink, he/she is required to provide the following information: time started, time ended, and purpose (morning meal, midday meal, etc.). This method assumes that the person is literate, and that they have a watch or clock. It also assumes that the person is motivated enough to remember and write down each time they do the activity. It requires a lot from the respondent and, therefore, has a high dropout rate.

STYLIZED ACTIVITY LIST

This method would usually be part of another questionnaire, or constitute a questionnaire on its own. It involves questions such as the following, with a block in which the person can write the number of hours and minutes for each activity: 'What does your actual day look like?'

'How many hours per day do you usually spend on the following activities?'[18] Ideally, the question should be asked separately for weekdays and weekends, because the activities and the time spent on those activities are likely to be different. As with the stylized questions, there is no way of checking for answers, unless you are sure that the list covers every possible activity. Another problem with this method is that as the list grows longer to include all possibilities, the fatigue level of the respondents and collectors grows. Such a list may prompt recall, but it is hard to get the balance right for every situation. It is rated the same as the activity log—low reliability, validity, and flexibility (INSTRAW 1995).

### TIME ACTIVITY MATRIX

This method is similar to the stylized method, in that it has an activity list. However, it adds a list of time periods. The INSTRAW example has the activities listed along the top (y-axis), while the x-axis collects data on the time spent on the activities (INSTRAW 1995). The periods could be 10 minutes for a very detailed sub-division, or one hour for a much cruder division. The person recording the activities marks off in each row which activity was being carried out. There must be at least one activity for every time period. This method helps the respondent to remember what they were doing. By insisting on at least one activity for each time period, it produces a comprehensive record. It does not avoid the conceptual problem, whereby the respondent must be able to classify each of their activities according to the activity categories provided. It assumes that the person is able to remember all the activities undertaken and assign them to the categories. Both, a good memory and good calculation skills are needed.

## 24-hour Time Diaries

Under this approach, a 24-hour time diary is designed for each respondent and they are expected to fill in fairly detailed information on how

---

[18] For example, housework and related errands, childcare, occupation (includes travel to work and secondary work), training/education, handiwork/repairs in the home and car, garden work, television/video, hobbies, and other free-time activities.

they spent their time during the past 24 hours. In countries where the respondents are literate, the diaries are self-reported, and the information is provided in 10-minute (or 5-minute) time slots. However, when literacy level is inadequate, face-to-face interviews are organized and the interviewer fills in a 24-hour time diary for the respondent.

A self-reported time diary is filled in different ways: in some cases it is filled in on the next day, in some cases at the end of the day (evening) or it is filled continuously throughout the day as activities are performed, or at frequent intervals during the day. The last method is considered better than the others. Among the countries that conducted independent standalone TUS, Thailand and China[19] have used self-reported diaries, while Mongolia and Pakistan have used such a diary for its literate population and have conducted face-to-face interviews for the illiterates or those with low literacy levels. It is interesting to note that Indonesia canvassed time diaries only from literate persons.

Under the one-day recall-based time diary (face-to-face interview), interviewers ask how respondents spent their time the previous day and record all their activities comprehensively in chronological order. This method avoids many of the problems of the stylized questions. However, the role of the interviewers is very critical here, as they have to get the right response from respondents. Designing of a survey manual, intensive training of interviewers, and strong follow-ups are very critical (Hirway 2003). The interviewer has to establish a good rapport with respondents and get their replies without asking any leading question. He has to collect the right data without any biases. Interviewers frequently have to get the timings of the activities when the respondents do not wear watches or use clocks.

One important limitation of the face-to-face recall diary is that it needs a larger time slot—half an hour to one-hour slots. India, Bangladesh, Pakistan, and Mongolia (when doing face-to-face interviews) used half an hour as the time slot, while, as seen earlier, Indonesia used time slots of two to three hours. Larger time slots imply a smaller number of episode[20] reporting (usually three episodes are reported)

---

[19] In the case of Thailand, literacy level is very high—near 100 per cent, while in the case of China, a pictorial diary was also used when the respondents were not literate.

[20] An episode is an activity carried out during a particular time slot.

and fewer details of the time use. The time-use data, therefore, tends to be approximation rather than accurate estimates. In the case of Pakistan, three activities are reported in each half hour and the time recorded for each activity is 10 minutes.[21] Also, under collection of time-use data by recording the time use chronologically through a face-to-face interview, recalling could be a problem, as the respondent may not be able to remember the exact time spent on different activities.

It is desirable that a time diary is filled in only by the respondents themselves (to get reliable information), and if it is filled in by an interviewer, nobody else should be present to help the respondents (except in the case of children above a fixed age). It is observed that this rule is frequently not observed. For example, the Pakistan TUS (2007) points out that time diaries were filled in with 'mutual help'.

In the case of modular surveys, we observed that the seven countries that conducted them used activity lists ranging from 9 to 90 activities, while of the nine countries that used the 24-hour time diary, three countries—Thailand, China, and Mongolia—used self-reported time diaries. Pakistan used self-reported time diaries for urban people, while one-day recall diary for the rest of the respondents. The others used only one-day recall diaries filled by interviewers. The time slot for self-reported diaries was 10 minutes, while for the others it was 30 minutes.

## SIMULTANEOUS ACTIVITIES

Context variables and simultaneous activities are critical components of a time diary, as they provide additional information about the activities undertaken. Information on simultaneous activities is particularly important, as the poor as well as women have been observed to perform more than one activity at a time. Data on simultaneous activities helps in improved estimates of both paid and unpaid work as it adds and does not miss out the time spent on work that is a part of simultaneous activities.

---

[21] In the case of the TUS (2007) in Pakistan, the time slot was 30 minutes. The time spent on an activity was derived by dividing 30 minutes by the number of activities conducted during that time. This was too simplistic an approach to collect data.

Simultaneous activities are likely to generate time stress when both (or all) the activities performed simultaneously involve (hard) work. For example, if a woman cooks and at the same time attends to livestock, it could be strenuous. Such work can be useful in estimating time poverty. On the other hand, if a man watches TV and has his lunch along with it, it could be relaxing. It is, therefore, necessary to analyse and address simultaneous activities keeping in mind the nature of the activities. This data also helps in designing interventions for reducing time stress of the poor, particularly poor women.

However, it is not easy to collect such data, as people do not provide this information easily. Respondents do not always report their simultaneous activities on their own, although there is a column in the diary. One has to make special efforts in face-to-face interviews (the interviewer may need to ask each question specifically, and, if necessary, repeat the questions) as well as in self-reported time diaries (specific instructions on reporting simultaneous activities need to be provided and then checked while collecting time diaries). It also not easy to analyse the data since it needs good analytical tools.

Usually, the activities performed simultaneously are divided into primary and secondary activities and the total time spent on simultaneous activities is divided between the two activities as per the weight allotted to each activity (the total time has to be 24 hours). When countries find this difficult, they divide the total time spent on simultaneous activities into two equal parts and allot one part to each of the activities, which is not accurate. A slightly complex approach could be of developing time grids for simultaneous activities and or let the total time go beyond 24 hours. This area, however, has not received much attention in developing countries.

Our review of national TUS shows that modular surveys (even with a time diary) do not collect data on simultaneous activities. When stylized questions are asked, respondents find it difficult to report this data, and when time diaries are used, the results are not likely to be accurate or useful, as the number of activities would be very limited. We, therefore, find that no country with modular surveys has collected data on simultaneous activities. In the case of independent surveys, except for Malaysia, all countries (Bangladesh, China, India, Mongolia, Pakistan, and Thailand) have collected data on simultaneous activities. However, China and Bangladesh have not analysed this data, while

India and Pakistan have divided the time into two equal parts without bothering and classifying activities into primary and secondary activities. It is only Thailand and Mongolia that have divided the time as per their primary and secondary status (see Table 1A.4).

In short, 'simultaneous activities' is another weak point of the surveys conducted in these developing and emerging countries. Most of the countries have missed the advantages of collecting data on these activities.

## TIME-USE ACTIVITY CLASSIFICATIONS

Classification of time-use activities is an important component of TUS, as it organizes the information on the time use in a systematic manner. Along with context variables, it provides rich information on how people use their time on different activities, with reference to the objectives of TUS.

One can list certain norms for a good time-use activity classification:

1.  The classification should be comprehensive and inclusive of all activities performed by men and women.
2.  It should be hierarchical, reflecting the different levels of activities in different digits (for example, the first digit represents the major group, the second digit represents the subgroup, and so on).
3.  It should be compatible with other relevant classifications (in this case, with established time-use classifications to maintain comparability of data.
4.  It should be simple, easy to understand and clear.
5.  Very importantly, it should be compatible with the objectives of the survey, such as, valuation of unpaid work and compilation of satellite accounts of household work, estimation of informal and subsistence work or estimate all categories of work (ICLS 2013), and so on.

### Available Time-use Classifications

Since time-use studies were first developed in industrialized countries, there is a well-developed set of classifications of time-use activities designed in the context of the needs of these countries. One widely popular classification divides time-use activities into four broad categories: contracted time, necessary time, committed time, and free time.[22] These four broad categories are then sub-divided into: (a) personal care activities; (b) employment-related activities; (c) education activities, (d) domestic activities; (e) childcare activities; (f) purchasing goods and services; (g) voluntary work and care activities; (h) social and community interaction; and (i) recreation and leisure. These broad groups are again divided into sub-groups and into activities. The classifications developed by Australia, Canada, Eurostat (the statistical body of the EU) as well as several European countries, and the US have many similarities, and the data is comparable across countries. The harmonized time-use project of the Eurostat has developed a time-use classification that is intended to serve as a standard for the region. Most industrialized countries seem to be using this classification, with minor changes, except Japan.[23]

## ICATUS and Its Versions

The UNSD, as the custodian of TUS, is expected to develop globally accepted concepts and methods of conducting TUS and also a global classification of time-use activities that meets the needs of countries located in the Global North as well as in the Global South. Looking to the specific needs of developing countries, UNSD had set up an Extraordinary General Meeting (EGM) in 1997 in order to develop a

[22] In 1978, Dagfinn developed a classification, which was widely used by several countries from the 1970s to 1990s. According to this framework, time spent by human beings is basically of four types, namely, necessary time (time spent on necessary activities for survival), contracted time (time that human beings spend on to fulfil the contracts that they have made), committed time (time committed to fulfil social responsibilities), and free time (the residual time left after performing contracted, committed, and necessary time).

[23] Harmonized European Time-Use Surveys (HETUS 2008), http://ec.europa.eu/eurostat/ramon/nomenclatures/index.cfm?TargetUrl=LST_NOM_DTL&StrNom=TIMEUSE_08&StrLanguageCode=EN&IntPcKey=&StrLayoutCode=HIERARCHIC New Zealand, http://www.stats.govt.nz/surveys_and_methods/methods/classifications-and-standards/classification-related-stats-standards/activity-time-use-survey.aspx Republic of Korea, http://ffb.uni-lueneburg.de/iatur2009/downloads/paper_presentation/Friday/H5/Choi___New%20approaches%20of%20the%202009%20Korean%20Time%20Use%20Survey%20(Paper).pdf

global time-use activity classification.[24] The expert group developed a trial ICATUS in 1997. It had 10 major groups, followed by two-digit sub-groups and then three-digit activity lists.

The EGMs of 2000 and 2012 resulted in two new classifications. However, none of these has been found to be fully satisfactory. The work on finalization of ICATUS is still going on, and was expected to be over by the end of 2016.

As regards the 24 countries of the region, we observed that under modular surveys, the classification is developed largely by the countries themselves. This primarily included: (a) agriculture and allied activities—animal husbandry, dairy, poultry, fishery, etc.; (b) collection of free goods, particularly fuel wood, water, fodder, and other raw material for economic activities, including craft as well as making cow dung, etc.; (c) paid work in manufacturing and construction; (d) non-market production of goods; (e) domestic work; (f) care-related work; and (g) leisure and personal activities. Cambodia has a list of 22 activities, while Lao PDR developed a list of 22 activities that include a detailed list of SNA activities (wage/salary earner, own business owner, tending rice, tending animals, fetching water, fetching firewood, hunting, fishing, construction, weaving, dewing, etc.) as well as care and household work, leisure, education, and personal activities. In all, there are 12 SNA, four non-SNA, and six personal activities.

Cook Islands also has a focus on non-market SNA activities. The activity classification in Cook Islands (1998) has 14 categories of work of which four are SNA (along with a long list of non-market SNA activities), two non-SNA (15 activities), and eight personal activities. Nepal had a rather large list of non-market activities focused on unpaid SNA activities—milling and food processing, handicraft, construction, fetching water, collecting firewood, animal care, poultry-related work, etc. The unpaid non-SNA work is divided into cooking, cleaning and washing, shopping, repairing, childcare, other care-related activities, volunteer work, community services, etc. In all, there are 114 questions have been asked to each household/respondent. Questions are also posed on reasons for not working, hours of work, location, and other details. We could not get much information on the classification used in Timor Leste and Vietnam, which have the time-use module in the LSMS.

---

[24] The author has been involved with all EGMs on the time-use classification.

In the case of independent national TUS, the most popular method is ICATUS 1997. This is perhaps because for many years this was the only classification that was developed by UNSD for developing and emerging countries. Bangladesh (2012) used the ICATUS developed in 2000 (onwards) and divided time-use activities into 15 major categories: there were four major groups for SNA activities, three groups for domestic and voluntary services and care, and seven groups for personal activities. India, China, Mongolia, Thailand, and Pakistan used modified versions of ICATUS 1997. China developed nine major groups that included four SNA groups, two non-SNA groups, and three personal activities. It is important to note that it called the first group 'formal' employment.[25] China also used occupation groups for SNA activities. The National Bureau of China has developed its own time-use activity classification (2008). It has three major activity groups: SNA productive activities, non-SNA productive activities, and leisure activities (which include study and training, meals, watching television, sleeping and other personal activities, and other free-time activities).[26]

----

[25] Clearly this group could not reflect the formal sector. In fact, it is accepted by EGM 2012 that TUS cannot collect data on formal and informal work—given the complex and varied definitions of 'informal sector' and 'informal employment'.

[26] Time-use activity classification in China (2008)

| SNA activities | Non-SNA activities | Leisure activities |
| --- | --- | --- |
| Workers | Domestic work | Watching television |
| Clerks | Food preparation | Listening to radio |
| Farmers | Cleaning up | Reading |
| Rural immigrant workers | Washing clothes | Surfing Internet |
| Rural immigrant salesmen | Shopping | Physical exercise |
| Drivers and conductors | Pet raising | Playing card or chess |
| Workers in the service sector | Repairing and maintenance | Visiting museum or park |
| Officials | Management and arrangement | Social life |
| Staff of ESCH | Caring for family members | Relative travel |
| Individual businesses | Unpaid help to others | |
| Owners of private enterprises | Community work and voluntary activities | |
| Unemployed | Relative travel | |
| Retirees | | |
| Students | | |
| Domestic workers | | |
| Others | | |

Thailand has used two sets of classifications, the ICATUS 1997 and the classification used by Eurostat. In other words, the main groups of the Thailand classifications are: (a) necessary time, committed time, and contracted time along with the major groups of the classification used in developed countries and (b) the nine groups of the ICATUS 1997. Mongolia used the ICATUS 1997 as well as an economic activity classification of 21 activities that was developed by Mongolian NSO. The Pakistan TUS (2007) used the 10 major groups of the ICATUS 1997. It has 122 three-digit activities. In fact, it is necessary to note that each of these countries has divided activities into two-digit and three-digit. Though the two-digit classification is as per the ICATUS, there are cross country variations in the three-digit activities.

India observed that one major problem with the ICATUS 1997 was relating to the first three groups. The first group was expected to capture the 'formal work' (in establishments), while the second and third groups were expected to capture 'informal work' in the primary and non-primary sectors, respectively. However, the term 'establishment' is vague and does not really reflect formality—a unit can be: (a) an informal unit; (b) can employ informal workers even with a fixed structure (establishment); or (c) a formal unit without a fixed structure. The first three groups, therefore, could not describe formality or informality of activities. The Indian survey, therefore, changed the SNA groups to: (a) primary production activities; (b) secondary production activities (industry and construction); and (c) tertiary economic activities (trade, business, and services).

## CONTEXT VARIABLES

Unlike mainstream statistics, time-use statistics provide comprehensive information on all human activities, which are not restricted to any one sector or one type of activities. In order to understand and analyse these activities meaningfully, it is important to see these activities in their proper context, so that they can be classified properly. For example, cooking could be either an unpaid domestic service, a free voluntary service if done for the community, or could be an employment if done in a restaurant by chefs. Context variables are, thus, a unique feature of TUS that provide physical, social, economic, or temporal features of the environment in which the activity takes place. Context variables are put in time diaries against each activity to collect additional information on these.

Context variables give meaning to activities and provide additional dimension to activities—they help in reducing the list of activities, in classification of activities, and in recall of time associated with the activity, thereby reducing under-reporting of time and activities. They provide useful information on physical, social, cultural, and economic contexts of activities.

## Types of Context Variables

Context variables can be broadly divided into the following types:

1.  Location-based context variables: 'where'
2.  Persons present: 'with whom' and 'in the presence of whom'
3.  Beneficiary of activity: 'for whom'
4.  Motivation of activities: 'paid or unpaid'
5.  Instrument used and mode of travel (means of transportation)

Most developed countries use almost similar context variables: 'where', 'with whom', 'for whom', and mode of transportation.

## 'Where'

The variable 'where' can provide information on whether the activity is performed in own house, someone else's house, public area, etc. Australia has divided location into two parts: Physical location (own house, someone else's house, public area, workplace, leisure place, educational institute, etc.), and spatial location (indoor, outdoor, in transit, waiting, etc.). Pakistan (2007) has used two context variables, namely, location 1 and location 2. Location 1 has six codes: at home, at somebody's home, field, farm or other agriculture workplace, educational establishment, public area, travelling, waiting, or others. Location 2 has nine codes: inside, outside, travelling by foot, taxi, train, bicycle, any other public transport, or 'other means of transport'.

## 'With whom' or 'In the presence of whom'

This context variable can provide information on whether a person was alone, with spouse, with friends, family members, children, colleagues, etc. Australia has used codes like spouse, family member, friends, neighbours, colleagues, crowd, no one, etc. Japan has used four variables: alone, with family members, with colleagues or classmates, and others.

## 'For whom'

This context variable provides information on the motive of an activity. For example, if the activity was performed for own children, family members, friends, community, etc. This helps in understanding the social behaviour of respondents, and identification of voluntary work. This variable can also provide information on whether the activity is for self-consumption, consumption by one's household, or for sale. Australia has used codes like: for own family, for outside the family, for community, for friends, relatives, etc.

## Context Variables for Mode of Transport

People travel by multiple modes of transport for multiple reasons. Factors, such as how one travels and how much time is taken in travelling, are important input for transportation and infrastructure planning. People walk the required distances by foot or they use different types of private and public vehicles.

Different guidebooks and guidelines have recommended three context variables—where, with whom, and for whom. In addition, the mode of transport is also a recommended variable. As seen above, UNSD (2012) Expert Group proposed three context variables, such as 'for whom', 'paid/unpaid', and 'location' for the consideration of the experts.

## Context Variables for Specific Uses

The use of context variables has expanded to several new areas recently, and it is now used for different new areas of policymaking, as discussed further.

## CONTEXT VARIABLES FOR WORK AND EMPLOYMENT

For the most accurate description of activities related to employment and other forms of work, contextual information is very important. This information needs to relate to: (a) the motivation or ultimate purpose of the activity (whether for pay, profit, or family gain as in employment); (b) the organization of the working time (whether it is overtime or not); (c) the details of work place (for which institutions/ organizations the activity is carried out); and (d) the location of the work activity (whether the activity is done at home, at work, during the commute, etc.) for the main and secondary jobs. Contextual information may also relate to characteristics that are part of the status of employment (paid work, home-based work, self-employment, unpaid work, etc.) and are useful to distinguish between the different forms of work such as household services or voluntary services.

To ensure that activities are captured, if these carried out as part of employment or of other forms of work, it is important that all time intervals can be coded to both the type of activity done and to the variables that will describe the context in which the activity was undertaken. These context variables may refer to: (a) for whom the activity is carried out (institutional units, households, enterprises that either market or non-market oriented, etc.) and (b) to the ultimate purpose of the work activity (to generate an income, for own final use, to acquire skills, to serve/benefit others, including own community, to seek work, etc.).

Clear instructions need to be given to respondents indicating that such information should be included and how to record it in their report of activities. Specifying contextual information regarding the time spent in employment, which uses between one-fourth and one-third of a majority of the adult population's time (and of many children in some countries), while adds to the complexity of the recording, but it also improves the use of the resulting statistics significantly. This relates to the fact that many of the activities described may be done in the context of employment or of other forms of work, and yet be the same type as those done in other contexts, such as leisure and personal activities. Activities producing goods, services, travelling, reading and writing, waiting on-call, preparing food, caring for the elderly, household management, etc., may belong to different work categories.

Even sleeping and eating may also be work activities in some jobs. This overlap will require that the classification system, to which these activities are coded, serves to eliminate duplications between activity descriptions, using relevant contextual information. Some of the examples are:

1. Understanding whether the activity is for self-consumption, for sale, or for barter, can help in distinguishing in subsistence production, unpaid domestic services, and SNA work.
2. The variable 'for whom' can also provide information on whether the activity is performed for own household/own use, for other households—unpaid, for voluntary or community organization, for sale or market, etc.
3. The other codes could be with respect to institutions/organizations for whom the work is done—for government, quasi government, for corporate units, for the private sector, or for household units.
4. The variable 'paid' or 'unpaid' can also help in identifying whether an activity is 'paid' or 'unpaid'. The details of unpaid services can also be collected using proper codes.
5. The variable 'where' can help in estimating home-based work, work of street vendors, and work in workplaces.

## CONTEXT VARIABLES FOR SOCIAL POLICY

Context variables can also provide information on the social life of people as well as input for social policy designing.

1. 'With whom' helps in estimating time spent with spouse/family, which, in turn, can help in assessing the person's marital life, work–life balance, or social life. Time spent alone can reveal loneliness of people, particularly old, sick, etc.
2. Assessment of time spent with children or those who need care in the family can help in assessing passive care requirements.
3. Time spent on other organizations/members can reflect net time spent on work, and this may be useful in estimating social capital formation.

## Context Variables for Environmental-related Policies

Time spent in the presence of 'whom' (persons present), or the surroundings can provide useful input in environment policies.

1. Time spent in a polluted environment can be used to estimate the adverse impact of pollution on human health with the help of dose-response coefficients. A study in India has estimated the impact of use of fuel wood with traditional technology on women's health using the time spent by women in cooking with this technology and dose–response coefficients of impact on carbon monoxide on human health.
2. Time spent with people with ineffectual diseases will reflect the impact on health of people, again with the help of dose–response coefficient.
3. Time spent can be related to energy use and carbon footprints, using the data on how often electricity is consumed by people or how long the electric connection is on in the households.
4. Finally, time spent in a healthy, open environment or sunlight may reflect consumption of Vitamin D.

### CONTEXT VARIABLES AND TRANSPORTATION PLANNING

Time spent on travelling and the mode of travel throws useful information on the commuting pattern of the population.

1. Time spent on travelling by different modes, on waiting, in traffic jams, etc., provide useful input about the transport-related problems of any population. This can be used in planning for public transport—its routes, frequency, etc.
2. Information on the mode of transport may also reveal requirements for speedy and cheap transportation (for example, if people are walking long distances on foot).
3. If long hours are spent in accessing basic services—in reaching basic infrastructural facilities, in waiting, or in meeting the service providers—will help in understanding the population's access to basic services and infrastructure. This data can be used in planning for infrastructure and policymaking for efficient basic services.

## Subjective Context Variables

Context variables can also be divided into subjective and objective variables. Objective variables refer to the variables discussed above, while subjective variables refer to personal feelings and perception of people towards activities:

- Did you feel stressed while performing this activity? How much? (codes)
- Did you feel time-stressed/exhausted while doing the activity? (codes)
- How happy you are doing each activity? How much did you enjoy the activity?

Robinson and Michelson (2010), and Harvey (2014), have used these context variables to estimate time stress or happiness of the population. These variables are also used in computing time poverty and happiness indices.

## Context Variables in the Selected Countries

Modular TUS do not usually employ any context variables, as it is not easy to get a good response to stylized questions asked. Cambodia, which has used a time diary under its modular TUS, has used the common context variables, but the quality of the responses may be doubtful. In the case of Nepal, questions have been asked for each activity about the location of the activity (where), whether any pay was received (paid or unpaid), and whether they did any other activity with the first activity. In addition, general questions were asked to respondents about the wages received, reasons for not working, and terms of work.

In the case of independent TUS, however, context variables help in estimating the time spent on activities accurately. Bangladesh (2012) has used two context variables, namely, 'where' and 'with whom'. The former has several codes for the first variable (at home, in a car, train, bus, etc.), while the latter context variable has three codes (alone, with a household member, and other known person). Pakistan (2007) has used two context variables, namely, location 1 and location 2. Location 1 has six codes: at home, at somebody's

home, field, farm or other agriculture workplace, educational establishment, public area, travelling, waiting, or others. Location 2 has
nine codes: inside, outside, travelling by foot, taxi, train, bicycle, any
other public transport, or other means of transport. Pakistan has also
used subjective context variables. China (2008) has used two contexts: 'with whom' and 'mode of transport'. India (1998–9) also has
used two contexts: paid/unpaid and inside/outside home. Mongolia
has used four context variables: 'where', 'with whom', 'paid/unpaid',
and 'mode of transportation'.

Which context variables should be used for a TUS essentially
depends on the specific objectives of the survey. For example, if an
important objective is to estimate and understand work and employment, the context variables should collect data on as well as the codes
could be decided carefully. As discussed above, additional contexts or
codes can also be designed to get more information on the nature
and characteristics of work. However, the selected countries have not
gone beyond the common patterns of context variables to tap the full
potential of context variables to enrich time-use information. This is a
missed opportunity to add rich information to the time-use data.

### Response Rate in a TUS

The data on the response rates is available only for some countries
(Table 1A.3). This is partly because the response rates are not calculated and partly because these rates are not reported in the documents/
papers/material that were available to us. In the case of developed
countries, the response rate was between 60–70 per cent in Australia,
75–80 per cent in Japan, 72 per cent in New Zealand, and 98 per cent
in RoK. In the case of RoK, substitution was allowed with the result
that the response rate is high. Out of the 13 developing and emerging
countries that conducted national TUS, nine have not reported the
response rate. Of the rest, Mongolia had 80–3 per cent, Cook Islands
has 98 per cent, while India and Pakistan had 99 per cent as their
response rate.

It appears that developed countries have a relatively low response
rate. One main reason for the high response in developing countries
appears to be the use of face-to-face interviews. Interviewers are
usually allowed to substitute one person for another when the first

person was not available. In the case of self-reported time diaries, however, people tend to avoid recording or record half-heartedly their time use. In fact, low and declining response rate is one of the concerns of TUS in developed countries. It seems that the interview method has at least one clear advantage over the self-reported diary method.

## QUALITY OF TIME-USE STATISTICS

There are serious quality problems with the TUS collected through 24-hour time diaries, particularly where face-to-face interviews are used in filling in time diaries. As seen earlier, modular TUS, with all their advantages, are not really equipped to produce quality data. As has been discussed, these surveys have several methodological limitations that do not all production of data with high quality.

The TUS using 24-hour time diaries has also shown many weaknesses. First, almost none of these diary-based TUS have designed a background questionnaire well enough to address the required objectives. Consequently, the data is not good enough to provide reliable estimates of WF/LF along with the industry, occupation, and employment status-based classification. Most of the background questionnaires do not have enough data for studying the care economy or for valuing unpaid work in satellite accounts.

Second, although systematic sampling techniques have been used in drawing samples for TUS, the selection of household members and the diary days per person are not always selected well. Also, there are problems with the time sample (reference period), as not all surveys have collected data for seasonal variations in time use. Use of 24-hour time diaries despite low literacy levels and poor use of timepieces is definitely a positive development. This has helped in the expansion of TUS in developing countries. However, countries have not implemented this approach very well because: (a) this interviewer-centric data collection method calls for a detailed instruction manual, intensive training of investigators, and strong follow-ups—which are frequently not there; (b) earlier visits to the respondent households to build rapport have been cut short frequently; and (c) long duration of time slots along with dividing the total time by the three activities to get activity time have not been sound methods.

Most countries have failed to tap the potential of simultaneous activities and context variables. The data on simultaneous activities is either not collected or not used in many cases. Those countries who use the data have divided the time by the number of activities rather than estimating primary and secondary activities. Context variables also have huge potential in enriching time-use data; somehow countries, which have largely followed developed countries, do not seem to be aware of this. Again, as discussed in the details, the classification of activities, mostly adapted from the available classification systems, are not adequate to meet the major objectives laid down by the countries. The SNA classification is particularly a major limitation. The absence of a harmonized classification, of course, is a major reason for this.

★★★

Our review shows that on the positive side, there are quite a few achievements made by these countries. First, one finds rapidly growing awareness about the need to collect time-use data to estimate paid and unpaid work of men and women in the economy, to measure and address gender inequalities prevailing in the society, and to value the unpaid non-SNA work in money terms. Time-use surveys, which began as small-scale surveys in several countries in the 1970s and 1980s, are now increasingly graduating into large and national surveys. Second, though the specific objectives of conducting TUS differ across the countries to an extent, the broad objectives are not drastically different. Third, despite the constraints arising from the specific problems faced by these countries while conducting TUS (such as poor literacy levels, limited use of timepieces in some remote areas, lack of funds, etc.), the countries have been able to conduct TUS. These countries have used a kind of learning-by-doing approach in conducting TUS. Last, despite the indifferent quality of time-use data, concrete data has emerged in a large number of countries on the time use of people that not only gives visibility to their non-SNA activities and personal activities but also throws useful and additional light on the SNA activities. Clearly, a new understanding has emerged on the contribution of women to national economies and the nature and extent of gender inequalities prevailing in these economies.

Even with these positive developments, it needs to be recognized that these countries have a long way to go to reach the goal of main-streaming TUS in their respective national statistical systems. If we exclude the four developed countries, of the remaining 31 countries, seven have not conducted any TUS so far, and 11 have conducted only small-scale TUS, mainly by private researchers, or official small pilot surveys. The Pacific Islands region lags behind the most, where except for Cook Islands (modular TUS) no country has conducted a national TUS. Only 13 countries have conducted national TUS, and only 6 of them have conducted independent national surveys by using 24-hour time diaries. And finally, there are only two countries (6.5 per cent) that have mainstreamed independent 24-hour diary-based TUS.

The main constraints faced by countries that have not conducted TUS, national or otherwise, have: (a) poor appreciation of the utility of time-use statistics in designing sound national policy to address their critical socio-economic concerns; (b) poor expertise with their statistical offices to collect and analyse the data; and (c) lack of adequate funds to collect these expensive surveys. The other set of constraints relates to the low level of literacy and poor use of timeprices, particularly in remote rural areas. It is believed that these constraints will not allow people to fill in 24-hour time diaries.

These constraints have led many countries in the region to go for modular TUS, which is easier to conduct, is much less expensive, and convenient to mainstream. Several global agencies and donor agencies have sponsored and financed these modular surveys, perhaps because they believe that these countries are not yet ready to employ 24-hour self-reported time diaries, and that some time-use data is better than no time-use data, or maybe these agencies are interested in covering a large number of countries with their limited funds. However, we believe that it is better to prepare these countries, by providing capacity-building in using 24-hour time diaries, to conduct independent diary-based TUS. After all, main-streaming modular TUS in national statistical systems is not a sound decision.

In short, there are serious questions about the methodological rigour and quality of time-use data produced in the region.

## Inferences for the Future

### STANDARDIZATION AND HARMONIZATION

In order, to ensure sound quality of time-use statistics, it is important to standardize the different components of conducting the survey as well harmonize these concepts at the regional level (at least to start with) for facilitating cross-country comparability of the data. Some broad details of the framework and formats of TUS at the global level may help in developing details at the regional and national levels.

### CAPACITY-BUILDING OF STAKEHOLDERS

Capacity-building of data producers and data users (within the government as well as researchers) will not only help data producers produce (improved) time-use data, but it will also encourage users to use the data. Capacity-building, therefore, should be for officers from NSOs and other government departments (such as women-related ministries, labour ministry, agriculture and industry ministries, ministry of social policy and human development), and for researchers and activists.

### MAINSTREAMING OF TIME-USE SURVEYS

There are strong reasons to mainstream TUS in national statistical paradigms in all countries in the ESCAP region. This mainstreaming implies that: (a) TUS is conducted regularly and periodically (5–7 years) to provide meaningful time-series data; (b) these surveys use sound concepts and methodologies and produce quality data; and (c) the data is used in a range of policymaking exercises so as to tap its potential uses.

## APPENDIX 1A

**TABLE 1A.1** TUS in Selected 35 Countries: Preliminary Information

| S.No. | Name of the Country | Years | Type of Survey | Coverage | Name of the Organization Conducting the Survey |
|---|---|---|---|---|---|
| 1. | Afghanistan | | | —No TUS conducted so far— | |
| 2. | Australia | 1974 | Independent survey (Diary) | Small survey: Leisure – An Inappropriate Concept for Women | YWCA Australia |
| | | 1974 | Independent survey | Australians' Use of Time, (Albury- Wodonga and Melbourne) | Cities Commission funded and oversaw the design in collaboration with The Australian National University |
| | | 1987, 1992, 1997, 2006 | Independent pilot survey | National survey | Australian Bureau of Statistics |
| | | 1996–2009 | Time Use Modular survey | Australian national Longitudinal Study on Women's Health (Women's Health Australia) | The Research Centre for Gender, Health and Ageing, the University of Newcastle |
| | | 2004–10 | Independent survey: Growing Up in Australia: The Longitudinal Study of Australian Children (National) | Small, limited coverage | Australian Institute of Family Studies in partnership with the Australian Government Department of Families, Housing, Community Services and Indigenous Affairs |

| | | | | | |
|---|---|---|---|---|---|
| | | 2005–6 | Independent survey: Time-use Survey of New Mothers | Large but not a national survey Independent | Dr. Julie Smith, National Centre for Epidemiology and Population Health, Australian National University, with funding from the Australian Research Council grant |
| | | 2007 wave: June 2007 to June 2008, 2009–10 | Independent survey: The Victorian Integrated Survey of Travel and Activity (VISTA) (2007, 2009) | Transportation sector only | Urban Transport Institute and I-View Pty Ltd on behalf of the Victorian Department of Transport |
| 3. | Bangladesh | 1974, 1976 | Independent survey: Time Use Among Employees in Bangladesh (Small) | Small coverage | Private Researcher |
| | | 1984–5, 1990–1 | Small modular survey – module of a labour force survey | Small coverage | National Statistical Agency |
| | | 2005 | Small independent survey | Only some villages | Dhaka University |
| | | 2012 | Pilot independent TUS | Large but not a national survey | National Statistical Agency |
| 4. | Brunei Darussalam | ————————No TUS conducted so far———————— | | | |
| 5. | Cambodia | 2003–4 | National modular survey | National coverage (with Socio-economic survey) | National Statistical Office |

*(Cont'd)*

**TABLE 1A.1**  (*Cont'd*)

| S. No. | Name of the Country | Years | Type of Survey | Coverage | Name of the Organization Conducting the Survey |
|---|---|---|---|---|---|
| 6. | China | 2005 | Independent Pilot Time-use Survey | Small coverage | National Bureau of Statistics |
| | | 2008 | Independent survey | Large but not a national survey | National Bureau of Statistics |
| 7. | Cook Islands | 1998 | National Modular use survey with HH income and expenditure survey | National survey | NSO and UNDP (funded) survey under UNDP Poverty Strategies Initiative Trust Fund |
| 8. | Fiji | 1987 | Independent survey | Small survey | Private Researchers |
| 9. | India | 1976–7, 1980 | Time-use Survey – independent survey without a 24-hour time diary | Small survey | ISST (Research Institute) |
| | | 1980 | Small Surveys – without a time diary | Small surveys | Private Researchers |
| | | 1990–1 | Modular survey: Use of Time by Women and Men | Small rural sample | Food and Agriculture Organization of the United Nations |
| | | 1990 | Small independent survey without a 24-hour time disry | Small survey: Time Allocation of Children in Agricultural Households | Private Researchers |
| | | 1996 | Independent survey | Small survey covered only one state of India | Directorate of Economics and Statistics |

| | | | | | |
|---|---|---|---|---|---|
| | | 1998–9 | Independent Time-use Survey | Large but not a national survey | Central Statistical Organization (CSO) |
| | | 1975–2006 | Small surveys Anthropological survey | Small villages level studies | The International Crops Research Institute for the Semi-Arid Tropics (ICRISAT) conducted the study |
| 10. | Indonesia | 1972–3 | Independent Small Survey: Measuring Time Allocation | Small coverage | Private Researcher |
| | | 1975–6 | Small Independent survey | Patterns of Household Labour Allocation in a Javanese Village | Private |
| | | 1976 | Small anthropological survey | Covered one village Patterns of Household Labour Allocation in a Javanese Village | Private |
| | | 1977–8 | Small anthropological survey | Small coverage – a few villages Studying Rural Women in West Java | Private |
| | | 1998–9 | Small pilot independent survey | Small survey covered a few villages | BPS, Statistics Indonesia |
| | | 2005 | Pilot time-use survey (360 HH) | Small survey | BPS, Statistics Indonesia |
| 11. | Iran | 2008, 2009 | Independent survey | Only urban areas covered | Statistical Centre of Iran |

*(Cont'd)*

**TABLE 1A.1** (*Cont'd*)

| S. No. | Name of the Country | Years | Type of Survey | Coverage | Name of the Organization Conducting the Survey |
|---|---|---|---|---|---|
| 12 | Japan | 1993–2004 1976, 1981, 1986, 1991, 1996, 2001, 2006, 2011 | National independent survey | National survey: Time Use and Leisure Activities in Japan | Statistics Bureau |
| | | 1960–1, 1965, 1970, 1975, 1980, 1985, 1990, 1995, 2000 | National independent survey | National surveys: How Do People Spend Their Time Survey | NHK |
| 13. | Maldives | | | No TUS conducted so far | |
| 14. | Marshall Islands | | | No TUS conducted so far | |
| 15. | Kiribati | 2001–2 | Small independent survey | Small survey: Time-use Survey of the Gilbert Island Group, Republic of Kiribati | Private Researcher |
| 16. | Korea, South (RoK) | 1981, 1983, 1985, 1990, 1995, 2000, 2005 | National independent survey | National survey | Korean Broadcasting System (KBS) |

| | | | | | |
|---|---|---|---|---|---|
| | | 1999, 2004, 2009, 2014 2005 | National independent survey Small independent survey Time-use Patterns of Korean Farm Couples | National survey Small Independent survey – Time Use Patterns of Korean Farm Couples | Korean Statistical Institute (KOSTAT) Private Researcher |
| 17. | Lao (PDR) | 1997–8, 2002–3, 2008 | National modular survey – module in national Lao Expenditure And Consumption Survey | National survey – with Expenditure and Consumption Survey. | National Statistical Office |
| 18. | Malaysia | 1990–1, 2003 | Small independent survey | Small rural sample | FAO / UN-Malaysia's Ministry of Women, Family & Community Development with NSO |
| 19. | Mongolia | 2000 2007, 2011 | Pilot independent Time-use Survey National independent surveys | Pilot survey National surveys | National Statistical Office National Statistical Office |
| 20. | Myanmar | | ——————No TUS conducted so far—————— | | |
| 21. | Nepal | 1977 1980s 1992/1993–4 | Small surveys Small modular surveys—with LSMS surveys Small surveys: | Small coverage Small surveys Small coverage | Women's Department and other government departments and scholars Private Researcher Women's Department and other government departments and scholars |

*(Cont'd)*

**TABLE 1A.1** (Cont'd)

| S. No. | Name of the Country | Years | Type of Survey | Coverage | Name of the Organization Conducting the Survey |
|---|---|---|---|---|---|
| | | 1998–9 | National modular survey – module of Labour Force Survey | National survey | National Statistical Office |
| | | 1996, 2003, 2010 | Small modular surveys – a module of LSMS surveys | Small surveys | The Central Bureau of Statistics |
| 22. | New Zealand | 1990 | National Pilot independent Time-use Survey | Pilot survey | Ministry of Women's Affairs, Statistics New Zealand |
| | | 1998–9, 2009–10 | National independent TUS | National surveys | Ministry of Women's Affairs, Statistics New Zealand |
| 23. | Pakistan | 1986–9 | Small modular surveys – modules of Rural HH Surveys | Small surveys | IFPRI and USAID Mission for Pakistan |
| | | 1990–1 | Small surveys: Use of Time by Women and Men | Small Surveys | FAO/ UN |
| | | 2007 | National independent survey | National survey | Pakistan Bureau of Statistics |
| 24. | Palau | ———————— No TUS conducted so far ———————— | | | |
| 25. | Papua New Guinea | 1962 | Small survey | Small survey – Kapauku Papuan Economy | Private Researchers |
| | | 1977 | Pilot small survey | Small Pilot survey | Private Researchers |

| | | | | | |
|---|---|---|---|---|---|
| | | 1998 | Small anthropological surveys: Environmentally Sound Agricultural Development in Rural Societies: A Comparative View from Papua New Guinea and South China | Small surveys: Environmentally Sound Agricultural Development in Rural Societies: A Comparative View from Papua New Guinea and South China | Private Researcher |
| 26. | Philippines | 1975, 1976, 1977 | Small survey: A Synopsis of Several Laguna Household Studies | Small survey – Nutrition, Work and Demographic Behavior in Rural Philippine Households: | Private Researcher |
| | | 2000 | Pilot independent TUS | Pilot survey – one rural and one urban area | National Statistical Office |
| 27. | Samoa | 1991 | Small anthropological survey | Small survey in two villages | Private Researcher |
| 28. | Singapore | | —No TUS conducted so far— | | |
| 29. | Solomon Island | 1985 | Small anthropological survey | Small survey | Private Researcher |
| 30. | Sri Lanka | 2001 | Small independent survey | Small survey | Research Scholar |
| 31. | Thailand | 1990–1 | Small independent survey: Use of Time by Women and Men | Small survey Use of Time by Women and Men | Food and Agriculture Organization of the United Nations |
| | | 2000–1, 2004, 2009, 2015 | National independent Time Use Surveys | National surveys | National Statistical Office |

*(Cont'd)*

**TABLE 1A.1** (*Cont'd*)

| S. No. | Name of the Country | Years | Type of Survey | Coverage | Name of the Organization Conducting the Survey |
|---|---|---|---|---|---|
| 32. | Timor Leste | 2001 and 2007 | National modular surveys – a module in LSMS survey | Small module in LSMS surveys | World Bank |
| 33. | Tuvalu | 2003 | National modular survey – a module in Social and Economic Wellbeing Survey | National survey with socio-economic well being | Prepared for the Government of Tuvalu, Funded under ADB |
|  |  | 2013 | Modular survey Under climate change adaptation project – How Men And Women Spend Their Time | National survey | UNDP and Government of Tuvalu |
| 34. | Vanuatu | 1983–4 | Small modular survey module in Agricultural Census | Small survey | The Government of Vanuatu |
|  |  | 1995 | Small anthropological survey | Small coverage | Private Researcher |
|  |  | 1999 | Small independent survey | Small surveys – a few villages | Jenny Whyte, the Foundation of the Peoples of the South Pacific International |
| 35. | Vietnam | 1992, 1997, 2002, 2004 | National modular surveys – a module in LSMS survey | National survey | In collaboration with the World Bank |

*Source:* Author's compilation from the respective TUS data and from various organizations.

**TABLE 1A.2** Objectives of the TUS of the Selected 35 Countries

| S. No. | Name of the Country | Years | Objectives |
|---|---|---|---|
| 1. | Australia | 1974 | • To collect detailed information on the daily activity patterns of people in Australia. |
| | | 1974 | • To access leisure opportunities for women in Melbourne, particularly those who were not employed or worked fewer than 20 hours per week. |
| | | 1987 | • To collect detailed information on the daily activity patterns of people in Australia. |
| | | 2005–6 | • To collect information on daily activities of mothers with infants. |
| | | 2004–10 | • To investigate the contribution of children's social, economic, and cultural environment, along with their adjustment and well-being. A major aim is to identify policy opportunities for improving support for children and their families and for early intervention and prevention strategies. |
| | | 1992, 1997, 2006 | • To collect detailed information on the daily activity patterns of people in Australia.<br>• To examine how people allocate time to activities, such as paid and unpaid work and to analyse such issues as gender equality, care giving, and balancing of family and paid work responsibilities.<br>• The balance between paid work, unpaid work, and leisure is important for a person's well-being and economic welfare. |
| | | 1996–2009 | • To examine the needs, views, lifestyles, currents health and other factors affecting the long-term health of individual women in Australia. |

*(Cont'd)*

**TABLE 1A.2**   *(Cont'd)*

| S. No. | Name of the Country | Years | Objectives |
|---|---|---|---|
| | | 2007 series: June 2007–June 2008, 2009, 2010 | • To understand the travel patterns and inform transport and land-use planning decisions being made by the government.<br>• To understand the travel pattern of residents living in Australia. |
| 2. | Bangladesh | 1974 | • To understand the time-use pattern of government employees, agricultural workers, tribal community, employees in the manufacturing sector. |
| | | 1976 | • To understand the economic activities pattern of children in a village in Bangladesh. |
| | | 1984–5 and 1990–1 | • To estimate informal and subsistence work of men and women. To understand gender inequalities in the time spent on paid and unpaid work. |
| | | 2005 | • To understand and estimate all forms of work done by men and women. To understand gender inequalities in sharing of different categories of work. |
| | | 2012 | • To provide estimates of the amount of time spent in various activities of the population aged 15 years and above;<br> ▪ average hours worked by employment status;<br> ▪ average hours spent in doing household activities;<br> ▪ average hours spent in leisure activity;<br> ▪ average hours spent by SNA, non-SNA and non-productive work; and<br> ▪ paid and unpaid work. |
| 3. | Cambodia | 2003–4 | • To collect information on how men and women in the country spend their time on different activities—market production, non-market production as well as house work, study, personal care, etc. |

|   |   |   |   |
|---|---|---|---|
|   |   |   | • To collect detailed information on non-market production in agriculture and allied activities, production within household (handicraft, fetching water and fuel wood, etc.). |
| 4. | China | 2005 | • To estimate the different kinds of activities performed by men and women. |
|   |   | 2008 | • To measure quality of life in time-use aspects. |
|   |   |   | • To improve methodology on women's contribution to national income and social development. |
|   |   |   | • To develop new measurement on women's unremunerated work. |
|   |   |   | • To enlarge social statistics to meet increasing demand from governments, NGOs, and other parts of civil society. |
| 5. | Cook Islands | 1998 | • To estimate distribution of income and expenditure. |
|   |   |   | • To value subsistence activities and other unpaid work. |
|   |   |   | • To estimate workforce participation rates of men and women. |
|   |   |   | • To design government income support policy. |
| 6. | Fiji | 1987 | • To understand how individuals in rural Fiji spend their time. |
| 7. | India | 1976–7 | • To measure female work participation in India. |
|   |   |   | • To try to identify the variable determinants of female labour supply. |
|   |   |   | • To re-group productive and non-productive activities and define gainful activity on the basis of evidence. |
|   |   | 1990 | • To understand the pattern of time allocation of children in agricultural sector of rural India. |
|   |   | 1990–1 | • To understand the role of women in agricultural development by collecting information on their time use. |

(*Cont'd*)

**TABLE 1A.2**   (*Cont'd*)

| S. No. | Name of the Country | Years | Objectives |
|---|---|---|---|
| | | 1996 | • This pilot study was conducted in Tamil Nadu which sought to measure:<br>  ▪ non-market economic activity; and<br>  ▪ how households distribute labour by looking at the use of time of people aged six and above in households. |
| | | 1998 | • To collect and analyse time-use patterns of men and women to understand the time spent on marketed and non-marketed economic activities.<br>• To generate more reliable estimate of workforce.<br>• To estimate and value unpaid work.<br>• To develop a conceptual framework and a suitable methodology for designing and conducting time-use studies in India. |
| 8. | Indonesia | 1972–3 | • To collect information on how men, women, and children spend their time in rural Indonesia.<br>• To get a view of the relative influences of husbands and wives in the decision-making of households.<br>• To understand the changes in the mode of labour recruitment and payments to look at the incomes. |
| | | 1975–6 | • To understand the pattern of household labour allocation in rural Indonesia. |
| | | 1998–9 | • To find the time allocation of activities conducted by each household member.<br>• To find the time allocation of household members, representing children within the ages of 0–11 months, 1–5 years, 6–21 years; women aged 15–49 years; and head of the household.<br>• To see the contribution of parents and youth in the domestic works, particularly in caring for children. |

|     |          |                                                                            |                                                                                                                                                                                                                                                                              |
| --- | -------- | -------------------------------------------------------------------------- | --- |
|     |          | 2004, 2005                                                                 | • To find the time allocation of activities conducted by each household member.<br>• To estimate the contribution of parents and youth in domestic works, particularly in caring for children. |
| 9.  | Iran     | 2008, 2009                                                                 | • To identify types of activity that people engaged in and amount of time spent by people on various activities.<br>• To review changes in people's lifestyle in successive sessions of the year to determine the main unpaid domestic and other activities of urban married housewives. |
| 10. | Japan    | 1960–1, 1965,<br>1970, 1975,<br>1980, 1985,<br>1990, 1995,<br>2000, 2005   | • To investigate how much time Japanese people spend on various daily activities. |
|     |          | 1976, 1981,<br>1986, 1991,<br>1996, 2001,<br>2006, 2011                    | • To obtain comprehensive data on daily patterns of time allocation and on leisure activities. The eighth survey was conducted in 2011.<br>• To provide statistics on the economic aspect of living.<br>• To improve the interpretation and the understanding of various social and economic phenomena.<br>• To assist the formulation of policy aimed at promoting better work–life balance, maintaining a vital ageing society, improving the childcare environment, facilitating gender equality, etc., taking the current social background (for example, ageing society with fewer children, and diversification of lifestyles) into account. |
|     |          | 1993–2004                                                                  | • To identify, explain, and forecast social changes in Japan at the individual and household level. |
| 11. | Kiribati | 2001–2                                                                     | • To identify the daily activities of Kiribati women to uncover the amount of unpaid work women perform in the community. |

(*Cont'd*)

**TABLE 1A.2**    *(Cont'd)*

| S. No. | Name of the Country | Years | Objectives |
|---|---|---|---|
| 12. | South Korea (RoK) | 1981, 1983, 1985, 1990, 1995, 2000, 2005 (Korean Broadcasting Service) | • To collect information on the total amount of time people spend in a day for various activities, such as sleep, meals, leisure, work, and the like.<br>• To understand the changes in Korean people's leisure time patterns during the last two decades in an effort to analyse the relationship between social development and changes in people's concepts and attitudes towards leisure. |
| | | 2005 | • To examine the time-use patterns of Korean farm couples with a focus on gender equity. |
| | | 1999, 2004, 2009, 2014 | • To provide basic data required for understanding people's lifestyle and quality of life by measuring how people spend their 24 hours.<br>• To understand time spent on unpaid housework in order to analyse the economic value of housework.<br>• To provide basic data required for integrating satellite account of households in the national account system.<br>• To provide basic data for establishing various policies related to labour, welfare, culture, and traffic, and for academic research. |
| 13. | Lao (People's Democratic Republic) | 1998 | • To measure productivity in farming, mainly rice cultivation.<br>• To measure labour input work in small-scale businesses and the informal sector. |
| | | 2002–3 and 2008 | • To estimate production in household agricultural activities and business activities. A 'light' time diary is used to capture time use for members of the household that are 10 years and above.<br>• This enables measurement of labour input in hours in the Lao economy. |

| | | |
|---|---|---|
| 14. Malaysia | 1990–1 | • To understand the role of women in agricultural development. |
| | | • To test eight methods of time-use data collection to access which methods yield the most accurate data on women's agrarian labour. |
| | 2003 | • To determine what unpaid work people do and how much they do of it. |
| 15. Mongolia | 2000 | • To collect data on employment and the informal sector to come up with a realistic assessment of employment. |
| | | • To collect data on gender inequality and women's paid and unpaid work. |
| | | • To determine what unpaid work men and women do and how much they share. |
| | 2007 | • To collect data on employment and the informal sector to come up with a realistic assessment of employment. |
| | | • To collect data on gender inequality and women's paid and unpaid work. |
| | | • To determine what unpaid work men and women do and how much they share. |
| | 2011 | • To determine time spent in unpaid and paid work by women and men. |
| | | • To determine Mongolian household patterns and its change. |
| | | • To obtain data essential to monitoring progress in the National Programme of Gender Equality. |
| 16. Nepal | 1977 | • To measure all form of work done by women. |
| | | • To measure children's work as well as voluntary work. |
| | 1980, 1992–3 | • To understand female economic participation in the largely subsistence economy of rural Nepal. |
| | | • To investigate the relationship between these variables and the extent of women's input into the household decision-making process. |

*(Cont'd)*

**TABLE 1A.2**   (*Cont'd*)

| S. No. | Name of the Country | Years | Objectives |
|---|---|---|---|
| | | 1998–9 | • To improve the estimation of national workforce and labour force to collect the information on all forms of work performed by men and women |
| | | 2010, 1996, 2003 | • To collect information of people's living standards in Nepal. |
| 17. | New Zealand | 1990 | • To integrate time-use information with its role of informing the government of the impact on women of policy developments. |
| | | | • To collect empirical information on women's involvement in the domestic and voluntary sectors. |
| | | | • To promote the recognition and valuing of women's unpaid work. |
| | | 1998–9 | • To measure the amount of time people aged 12 years and over spend on the main categories and sub-categories of activity. |
| | | | • To determine whether significant differences in time use exist between different population groups. |
| | | | • To determine the proportionate allocation of time to various activities. |
| | | | • To provide information on the context in which people undertake various activities and whether other activities are taking place simultaneously. |
| | | | • To provide data to improve significantly the estimates of the contribution of GDP to the domestic services of households industry and the employment component of the contribution to GDP, in the sector of non-profit institutions serving households, within the national accounts. |

|  |  |  | • To provide time-use data for New Zealand, which is internationally comparable at a broad level of the activity classification, focusing on four basic categories—contracted time, committed time, necessary time, and free time. |
|---|---|---|---|

|  |  | 2009–10 | • To understand and analyse:<br>▪ how people divide their time between paid work, unpaid work, family, and leisure;<br>▪ how people schedule their paid work and where do they do it;<br>▪ how socially connected people are with their family, friends, from inside and outside their household;<br>▪ how much unpaid work contributes to the New Zealand economy;<br>♦ how people spend their leisure time; and<br>♦ who cares for whom, for how much time, and where. |
| 18. | Pakistan | 1986–9 | • To assist with collecting data to shape food-related policies in the rural areas of Pakistan.<br>• To give insight into labour, income, and consumption dynamics. |
|  |  | 1990–1 | • To test eight methods of time-use data collection to assess which method yields the most accurate data on women's agrarian labour.<br>• To understand work performed by men and women in agricultural and related activities. |
|  |  | 2007 | • To account for the 24-hour time of the full spectrum of activities carried out by people.<br>• To profile the quantum and distribution of paid and unpaid work to infer policies and programmes for gender equality.<br>• To draw inferences for designing employment policy and welfare programmes. |

(*Cont'd*)

**TABLE 1A.2**   *(Cont'd)*

| S. No. | Name of the Country | Years | Objectives |
|---|---|---|---|
| | | | • To estimate production within the production boundary and the general production boundary. |
| | | | • To generate more reliable estimates of the national workforce. |
| 19. | Papua New Guinea | 1962 | • To collect information on time spent by agricultural workers on different agricultural activities. |
| | | 1977 | • To document differences and inequalities in the daily activities of men and women. |
| 20. | Philippines | 1975, 1976, 1977 | N.A. |
| | | 2000 | • To collect information on how individuals allocate their time on daily activities. |
| | | | • To measure and evaluate unpaid housework. |
| 21. | Samoa | 1991 | • To access the role of time in daily activities with a focus on female time use |
| 22. | Solomon Islands | 1985 | N.A. |
| 23. | Sri Lanka | 2001 | • To collect information on men and women's paid and unpaid work. |
| 24. | Thailand | 1990–1 | • To understand the participation of people in cultural and custom-related activities. |
| | | 2000–1, 2004, 2009, 2015 | • To get comprehensive knowledge on how people above the age of 10 years spend their time on different paid and unpaid work. |
| | | | • To understand gender differences in paid and unpaid work. |
| | | | • To provide data to markedly improve the estimates of labour contribution to the GDP. |
| | | | • To provide internationally comparable time-use data for the country. |
| 25. | Timor Leste | 2001, 2007 | • Time spent on free goods collection and on household chores by individuals. |

| | | | |
|---|---|---|---|
| 26. | Tuvalu | 2003 | • The aim of the Participatory Monitoring and Evaluation (PME) project was to measure the effects of the Island Development Trust and particularly the Falekaupule Trust Fund on the quality of life in the islands over a six-year period. |
| | | | • Household questionnaires were used to identify, for example, water and electricity access, development priorities, and the number of people living in the dwelling. |
| | | | • Respondents were asked about the amount and type of unpaid work that was undertaken by various household members during the previous week. |
| | | | • Although not designed to be a time-use survey, it does give some indication of time use by gender. |
| | | 2013 | • To address some of the adverse effects of climate change. |
| | | | • To gather evidence on how men and women use their time during a typical day in various locations of Tuvalu. |
| 27. | Vanuatu | 1984 | • To develop a beer agricultural system. |
| | | | • To test eight different questionnaires to access the time-use activities of residents and local farmers. |
| | | 1995 | • To outline of how to do a Daily Gender Calendar at a village meeting and then give the results found. Men and women describe their day from waking until sleeping and form a consensus of an average day. |
| | | 1999 | • The aim was for a daily time-use record for seven days for each person more than 10 years old. Activities were put into 12 categories, including family and household care. |
| 28. | Vietnam | 1992, 1997, 2002, 2004 | • To collect data on time use of people to understand the living standards of people. |

*Source:* Author's compilation from the respective TUS data and from various organizations.

*Note:* We could get this information from only 28 countries out of 35 countries.

**TABLE 1A.3** Details of Methodology of the TUS

| S. No. | Name of the Country | Years | Sample Size | Surveyed Population | Reference Period | Method of Data Collection | Response Rate | Background Questionnaire | Time Slot |
|---|---|---|---|---|---|---|---|---|---|
| 1. | Afghanistan | | | | — No TUS conducted — | | | | |
| 2. | Australia | 1974 | 1,491 dairies | Aged 18–69; one random person from the HH | March–September 1974; one single day | Self-reported 24-hour time diary | 67% in Albury–Wodonga, 58% in Melbourne | Household and individual questions | 24-hour time dairy with 10-minute |
| | | 1974 | 834 women | Women with children aged 16–46 years | 24 June–5 July 1974;last week | Self-reported 24-hour time diary | 87.3% of eligible households responded | Yes | 10 minutes |
| | | 1987 | 681 fully responding HHs | All HH members aged 15 years and above | 23 May to 4 June 1987; single day | Self-reported 24-hour time diary | 74.2% | Yes | 48-hours time dairy with 15-minute interval |
| | | 1992 | 4,367 HHs | All HH members aged 15 years and above | Between February and December 1992; Four collection periods | Self-reported 24-hour time diary | 69% | Yes | 48-hour time dairy with 5-minute time slot |

| | | | | | | | |
|---|---|---|---|---|---|---|---|
| 1997 | 7,246 individuals in 3,684 HHs | All HH members aged 15 years and above | Four collection periods: 27 January to 8 February; 21 April to 3 May; 23 June to 5 July; 27 October to 8 November 1997 | Self-reported 24-hour time diary | 72% | Yes | The questions of time use like time spent doing various activities on account of the respondent's health, hours worked, time spent in waiting room of health-care providers, satisfaction with time with doctors is included with other individuals and health related questions | 48-hour time dairy with 5-minute time slot |
| 1996–2009 | 106,000 women | Three age groups: 18–23, 45–50, 70–75, randomly selected women from national health system database | 1996 to 2009; Recent week | Self-reported 24-hour time diary | Not relevant | | The questions of time use like time spent doing various activities on account of the respondent's health, hours worked, time spent in waiting room of health-care providers, satisfaction with time with doctors is included with other individuals and health related questions | Activities which were performed for 20 minutes or more were counted |

(Cont'd)

**TABLE 1A.3**   (*Cont'd*)

| S. No. | Name of the Country | Years | Sample Size | Surveyed Population | Reference Period | Method of Data Collection | Response Rate | Background Questionnaire | Time Slot |
|---|---|---|---|---|---|---|---|---|---|
| | | 2004–10 | 49,938 Children | HHs with children aged 0–7 years | Four times a year every two years | Self-reported time diary; two diaries—one for the week day and one for the weekend | 68% | Yes | 15-minute time slot |
| | | 2005–6 | 188 mothers participated, completing 327 weeks, resulting in around 2,223 diary days | Mothers of children aged 3, 6, or 9 months | April 2005–April 2006 (Last week) | Self-reported time diary | Not relevant | Yes | 10 minutes |

| | | | | | | |
|---|---|---|---|---|---|---|
| 2006 | 3,870 HHs | All HH members aged 15 years and above | Four sessions: 20 February–4 March 2006; 24 April–6 May 2006; 26 June–8 July 2006; 23 October–4 November 2006 (Two consecutive days: one week day and one weekend) | Self-completed time dairy: one week day and one weekend | 72.7% | Yes | 48-hour time dairy with 5-minute time slot |
| 2007–10 | 4,932,422 respondents | Representative sample of the residents living in Victoria | 2007 wave: June 2007–June 2008; 2009 wave: July 2009–July 2010 | Travel diary of 24-hours time period | – | Yes | 5 minutes |
| 2009–10 | 17,000 HHs | One day diary of all trips made by members on their randomly selected day | April 2009–March 2010 (randomly selected dairy day) | Travel diary of 24-hour time period | – | Yes | 5 minutes |

(Cont'd)

**TABLE 1A.3**  (*Cont'd*)

| S. No. | Name of the Country | Years | Sample Size | Surveyed Population | Reference Period | Method of Data Collection | Response Rate | Background Questionnaire | Time Slot |
|---|---|---|---|---|---|---|---|---|---|
| 3. | Bangladesh | 1974 | 700 HHs(100 HHs from each of the 7 unions) | Professional public service workersone sampled HH | One year | Face-to-face interview (recall method) | N.A. | Not mentioned | – |
| | | 1976 | 120 parents and children | Universe of parents: one set of either a currently married couple (or a once-married but now single) with at least one living child aged 5 or above | Whole year(single day) | One-day self-reported diary | Not relevant | Not mentioned | Not mentioned |

| 1984–5 and 1990–1 | Small sample | All HH members aged 6 years and above | Yesterday—single period | Face-to-face interview: Stylized questionnaire | N.A. | N.A. | N.A. |
| 2005 | Small; 1000 HHs; (R + U) | All HH members aged 6 years and above | Yesterday—single period | Face-to-face interview: Stylized questionnaire | N.A. | Yes | N.A. |
| 2012 | Pilot; 3,780 HHs (U: 1,400 HHs, R: 2,380 HHs) | All HH members aged 15 years and above | One year:one week day and one weekend | Self-reported time diary for the interviewed households and face-to-face interview for uneducated respondents | N.A. | Yes | 24-hour time diary with 30-minute slots |

*(Cont'd)*

**TABLE 1A.3** *(Cont'd)*

| S. No. | Name of the Country | Years | Sample Size | Surveyed Population | Reference Period | Method of Data Collection | Response Rate | Background Questionnaire | Time Slot |
|---|---|---|---|---|---|---|---|---|---|
| 4. | Brunei Darussalam | | | | ——— No TUS conducted ——— | | | | |
| 5. | Cambodia | 2003–4 | National: 2,000 HHs | All HH members aged 5 years and above | November 2003–January 2005: A random day of the month | One-day self-reported dairy | N.A. | Modular with CSES | 24-hour diary with 30-minute time slotEach half hour is classified according to the activity taking most time during that half hour. |

| | Country | Year | Sample | Population | Reference period | Method | | | Interval |
|---|---|---|---|---|---|---|---|---|---|
| 6. | China | 2005 | Pilot (U + R) 4,290 HHs, 9,400 respondents | All HH members aged 15–74 years | One day—single period | Self-reported 24-hour time diaries (illiterates were helped) | N.A, | Yes | 10-minute interval |
| | | 2008 | National37,142 respondents (16,661 HH) | All HH members aged 15–74 years | One dayMay 2008–Single period;Two diaries–one week day and one weekend | Self-reported 24-hour time diaries (illiterates were helped) | N.A. | Yes | 10-minute interval |
| 7. | Cook Island | 1998 | 15% of the total population | 15 years and above | One week | Stylized questions | 98% | | N.A. |
| 8. | Fiji | 1987 | Small sample: 600 individuals | Farming household | Autumn 1987—on a week day | Face-to-Face interview (recall) | N.A. | Not mentioned | N.A. |

*(Cont'd)*

TABLE 1A.3   (*Cont'd*)

| S. No. | Name of the Country | Years | Sample Size | Surveyed Population | Reference Period | Method of Data Collection | Response Rate | Background Questionnaire | Time Slot |
|---|---|---|---|---|---|---|---|---|---|
| 9. | India | 1976–7 | Rural India: 6 villages were sampled—3 from dry millet region of Rajasthan and 2 from wet paddy cultivation in West Bengal127 households—52 in Rajasthan and 75 in West Bengal15% sample households in each sampled villages | Every HH member aged 5 and above | September 1976–December 1977; Pilot phase for two month from July–August 1976; Main phase from December 1976 to December 1977; Households were visited once in two months | 45% data was collected through recall method and the rest through the observation method (15 hours from 6.00–21.00 hours) | Households which refused were replaced by a similar household in each village, so the total desired sample size was achieved | Yes | 30-minute interval |
| | | 1990 | Small:451 children | Children aged 5–17 years in rural India | Single day: Yesterday | Self-reported dairy | N.A. | N.A. | N.A. |

| | | | | | | | | |
|---|---|---|---|---|---|---|---|---|
| | 1990–1 | – | Men and women | 6 days in a week | Eight methods of data collection | N.A. | N.A. | N.A. |
| | 1996 | Pilot study in rural and semi-urban areas in Tamil Nadu: 241 people from 64 HHs | All HH members aged 6 years and above | August–September 1996 (every other day in a week) | Recall interview direct observation | Refusing households were replaced | Yes | 30 minutes |
| | 1998–9 | Pilot8, 620 HHs | All HH members aged 6 years and above | 2 day in a week with three types of days in a week—normal, abnormal, 'weekly-variant' | Face-to-face interview One-day recall time diary | 99% | Yes | All activities recorded within one-hour interval |
| 10. Indonesia | 1972–3, repeated in 1977–8 | 64 adults in 44 sample HHs | All HH members aged Aged 15 years and above | November 1972–October 1973 (six days in one year) | Face-to-face interview (over 24-hour recall method) | Not relevant | Not mentioned | Not mentioned |

(*Cont'd*)

**TABLE 1A.3** (*Cont'd*)

| S. No. | Name of the Country | Years | Sample Size | Surveyed Population | Reference Period | Method of Data Collection | Response Rate | Background Questionnaire | Time Slot |
|--------|--------|--------|--------|--------|--------|--------|--------|--------|--------|
| | | 1975–6, repeated in 1976 | Rural; 518 HHs | All HH members aged 6 years and above | Two monthly interview periods during 1975–6's wet season rice cycle; November–December 1975 peak demand; February–March 1976, which was part of the slack period before harvest | Interview method | Not relevant | Yes | N.A. |
| | | 1998–9 | Pilot; 1,200 HHS (rural) | One HH member aged 0–21 years; women age 15–49 years; and head of the HH | Two times in 1998 (August and December), and two times in 1999 (May and October): 1 randomly selected dayOne day—single period | Time diaries—recall | Not relevant | Yes | N.A. |

| | | | | | | | |
|---|---|---|---|---|---|---|---|
| | 2004 | Pilot; 1,024 people (urban) | One literate person aged 15 years and above | 2004 (A week divided into 3 days—2 days on week days and one day on weekend) | One-day 24-hour time diary and stylized questionnaire | 90% | Yes | 2-hour time slot |
| | 2005 | Pilot; 360 HHs | One person aged 10 years and above from sampled HHs | 2005 | Self-reported 24-hour time diary method | 90% | Yes | 3 different time instruments—one-hour time interval, four-hour time slot, 15-minute time slot |
| 11. Iran | 2008 | Urban 12,000 HH | All HH members aged 15 years and above | Autumn (21 September 2008 to 21 November 2008 | 24-hour self-completion method | 90% | Yes (most likely) | 15-minute time slot |
| | 2009 | Urban 12,000 HHs | Population aged 15 years and above | Summer and winter (22 December 2008 to 20 March 2009) | 24-hours self-completion method | N.A. | Yes | 15-minute time slot |

(*Cont'd*)

*Mainstreaming Unpaid Work*

**TABLE 1A.3** (*Cont'd*)

| S. No. | Name of the Country | Years | Sample Size | Surveyed Population | Reference Period | Method of Data Collection | Response Rate | Background Questionnaire | Time Slot |
|--------|---------------------|-------|-------------|---------------------|------------------|---------------------------|---------------|--------------------------|-----------|
| 12. | Japan | 1960–1 | 170,000 persons | All HH members aged 10 years and above | Yesterday—single day | Self-completed 24-hour time diary | N.A. | Yes | 24 hours in 15-minute interval |
| | | 1965 | National: 900 HHs | All HH members aged 10 years and above | 1–28 October 1965 Yesterday—single Day | Self-completed 24-hour time diary | N.A. | Yes | 24 hours in 15-minute interval |
| | | 1970 | 37,974 HHs | All HH members aged 10 years and above | 3–25 October 1970 (two weekdays, two Saturdays, two Sundays) | Self-completed 24-hour time diary | Weekdays: 84.1%; Saturdays: 82.4%; Sundays: 82.0% | Yes | 24 hours in 15-minute interval |
| | | 1975 | 12,000 HHs | All HH members aged 10 years and above | 14–26 October 1975 (two weekdays, two Saturdays, two Sundays) | Self-completed 24-hour time diary | Weekdays: 83.3%; Saturdays: 80.7%; Sundays: 80.6% | N.A. | 24 hours in 15-minute interval |

| 1976 | National | All HH members aged 10 years and above | One year (Oct. 1976) two consecutive days | Self-completed 24-hour time diary | All non-respondents were replaced | Yes | 24 hours in 15-minute interval |
| 1980 | 67,680 | All HH members aged 10 years and above | 14–26 October 1980 (two weekdays, two Saturdays, two Sundays) | Self-completed 24-hour time diary | N.A. | Yes | 24 hours in 15-minute interval |
| 1981 | 209,000 individuals in 83,000 HHs | All HH members aged 10 years and above | Two consecutive days | Self-completed 24-hour time diary | N.A. | Demographic questionnaires | 24 hours in 15-minute interval |
| 1985 | 14,400 | All HH members aged 10 years and above | 15–27 October 1985 (two week days, two Saturdays, two Sundays) | Self-completed 24-hour time diary | Weekdays: 80.5%; Saturdays: 79.0%; Sundays: 78.6% | N.A. | 24 hours in 15-minute interval |
| 1986 | 95,000 HHs | All HH members aged 10 years and above | One day in October 1986 Two consecutive days | Self-completed 24-hour time diary | N.A. | N.A. | 24 hours in 15 minutes interval |

*(Cont'd)*

**TABLE 1A.3** *(Cont'd)*

| S. No. | Name of the Country | Years | Sample Size | Surveyed Population | Reference Period | Method of Data Collection | Response Rate | Background Questionnaire | Time Slot |
|---|---|---|---|---|---|---|---|---|---|
| | | 1990 | Sample of 90,240 people, 67,898 people completed effective diaries (112,800 weekday diaries; 33,840 Saturday diaries; 33,840 Sunday diaries) | All HH members aged 10 years and above | 15–28 October 1990 | Self-completed 24-hour time diary | 75.2% in total (weekdays 74.8%; Saturdays 74.3%; Sundays 74.4%) | Yes | 24 hours in 15-minute interval |
| | | 1991 | 99,000 HHs | All HH members aged 10 years and above | One day in October 1991 | Self-completed 24-hour time diary | Overall: 63.8%; 63.8% on weekdays, 62.6% on Saturdays, 64.8% on Sundays | Yes | 24 hours in 15-minute interval |

| Year | Sample | Population | Diary days | Method | Response rate | Replacement | Interval |
|---|---|---|---|---|---|---|---|
| 1995 | – | All HH members aged 10 years and above | Two randomly selected days in October 1995 | Self-completed 24-hour time diary | 75% | Yes | 24 hours in 15-minute interval |
| 1996 | 99,000 households | All HH members aged 10 years and above | Two consecutive diary days | Self-completed 24-hour time diary | N.A. | N.A. | 24 hours in 15-minute interval |
| 2000 | Sample of 45,120 people; at least 32,984 completed | All HH members aged 10 years and above | 12–22 October 2000; two randomly selected days | Self-completed 24-hour time diary | 73.1% of people approached completed at least 1 diary | N.A. | 24 hours in 15-minute interval |
| 2001 | Approximately 10,000 people in 4,000 HHs | All HH members aged 10 years and above | October 2001; two consecutive days | Self-completed 24-hour time diary | All non-respondents were replaced | N.A. | 24 hours in 15-minute interval |
| 2005 | 12,600 people | All HH members aged 10 years and above | 11–24 October 2005; two consecutive days | Self-completed 24-hour time diary | Of 12,600 people contacted, 7,718 (61.3%) completed a valid diary for at least one of the two days | Yes | 24 hours in 15-minute interval |

(Cont'd)

**TABLE 1A.3** (*Cont'd*)

| S. No. | Name of the Country | Years | Sample Size | Surveyed Population | Reference Period | Method of Data Collection | Response Rate | Background Questionnaire | Time Slot |
|---|---|---|---|---|---|---|---|---|---|
| | | 2006 | Around 200,000 people in around 80,000 HHs | All HH members aged 10 years and above | 14–22 October 2006; Two consecutive days | Self-completed 24-hour time diary | N.A. | Yes | 24 hours in 15-minute interval |
| | | 2011 | Around 200,000 people in around 83,000 HHs | All HH members aged 10 years and above | 15–23 October 2011; Two consecutive days | Self-completed 24-hour time diary | N.A. | Yes | 24 hours in 15-minute interval |
| 13. | Kiribati | 2001–2 | 226 surveys in 11 islands Not representative of the HHs | People aged 18 years and above One man and one woman from the households | November 2001– March 2002 | Diary in 48-hour period Non-participant observation | N.A. | N.A. | 48-hour time slot divided into 15-minute time interval |
| 14. | Korea, South (RoK) | 1981, 1983, 1985, 1990, 2000, 2005 | 3,500 respondents | All HH members aged 10 years and above | Three days in a week (Friday, Saturday, and Sunday) through the year | 24-hour self-reported diary | N.A. | Household and individuals' background details | 15 minutes |

| 1999 | National 46,109 diarists in 17,000 sample households | All HH members aged 10 years and above | September 1999 (two selected diary days: one week day and one weekend) | Self-completion 24-hour dairy | 94.70% | Household and individuals' background details | 10 minutes |
|---|---|---|---|---|---|---|---|
| 2004 | 64,000 diaries from 32,000 persons in 12,750 households | All HH members aged 10 years and above | September 2004; Two selected diary days | 24-hour self-completion | 98.10% | Household and individuals' background details | 10 minutes |
| 2005 | Small 324 couples (rural) | Farm couples | 17 June 2005–30 June 2005; 28 November 2005–10 December 2005 Two diary days | Self-completion 24-hour diary | This survey collected a quota sample, and replaced non-respondents | Socio-demographic details | 10 minutes |
| 2009 | 40,526 diaries | Aged 10+ years: all HH members | March and September 2009 Two diary days—one week day and one weekend | Self-reported time diary | N.A. | Same | 10 minutes |

*(Cont'd)*

**TABLE 1A.3**  (*Cont'd*)

| S. No. | Name of the Country | Years | Sample Size | Surveyed Population | Reference Period | Method of Data Collection | Response Rate | Background Questionnaire | Time Slot |
|---|---|---|---|---|---|---|---|---|---|
| | | 2014 | The survey aims to collect 63,600 diaries from 31,800 persons in 12,720 HHs | | Either April and August 2014 or July, September, November 2014 | Self-reported 24-hour time diary | N.A. | Household and individual questionnaire | 10 minutes |
| 15. | Lao PDR | 1997–8 | National: 8,882 persons | One HH member aged 10 years and above | One year | One-day recall interview | N.A. | Modular with consumption and expenditure survey | 24 hours with one-hour time interval |
| | | 2002–3 | National: 8,100 | All HH members aged 10 years and above | One year | One-day recall interview | N.A. | Modular with consumption and expenditure survey | 24 hours with one-hour time interval |
| | | 2008 | National: 8,100 | All HH members aged 10 years and above | One year | One-day recall interview | N.A. | Modular with consumption and expenditure survey | 24 hours with one-hour time interval |

| | | Year | Sample | Population | Reference period | Method of data collection | | | Diary |
|---|---|---|---|---|---|---|---|---|---|
| 16. | Malaysia | 1990–1 | Small sample; Rural | Men and women | Agricultural season of the year | Eight methods of data collection | N.A. | N.A. | N.A. |
| | | 2003 | National; 32,000 respondents | Aged 15–64 years | Single time period | Stylized questionnaire | None | N.A. | N.A. |
| 17. | Maldives | | | | — No TUS conducted — | | | | |
| 18. | Marshall Islands | | | | — No TUS conducted — | | | | |
| 19. | Mongolia | 2000 | Pilot; 2,753 individuals in 1,086 households | Three HH members aged 12 years and above | 8 April–1 May 2000, Single time period | Self-reported 24-hour time diary and face-to-face one-day recall | 82.1% in total, 83.5% for men and 80.4% for women | Yes | 24-hour diary with 10-minute slot |
| | | 2007 | National; 3,200 HHs (R + U) | All HH members aged 12 years and above | Four quarters—one Year | Self-reported 24-hour time diary and face-to-face one-day recall | N.A. | Yes | 24-hour diary with 10-minute slot |

*(Cont'd)*

**TABLE 1A.3** (Cont'd)

| S. No. | Name of the Country | Years | Sample Size | Surveyed Population | Reference Period | Method of Data Collection | Response Rate | Background Questionnaire | Time Slot |
|---|---|---|---|---|---|---|---|---|---|
| | | 2011 | National; 4,000 HHs | All HH members aged 12 years and above | Four quarters—full year | Self-reported 24-hour time diary and face-to-face one-day recall | N.A. | Yes | 24-hour diary with 10-minute slot |
| 20. | Myanmar | | | | ——— No TUS conducted ——— | | | | |
| 21. | Nepal | 1977 | 251 children | Aged 6–19 years in the households | 7–10 months, once a month | Observation method | Not a probability Sample | N.A. | N.A. |
| | | 1980s | 192 HHs, approximately 1,200 individuals, including 252 children | Men, women and children aged 10–14 years; Two HH members | Six months; Two randomly selected hours in a day | Observation method | Not a probability Sample | N.A. | N.A. |

| | Year | Sample | Members | Reference period | Method | | | |
|---|---|---|---|---|---|---|---|---|
| | 1992/1993–4 | 3 small surveys: 192 HHs, 24 HHs, and 420 HHs | All HH members aged 6 years and above | Carried out in different seasons | Observation methods—random observations from morning to evening | Not a probability Sample | N.A. | N.A. |
| | 1998–9 | National | All HH members aged 5 years and above | Last week—one year | Face-to-face interview—stylized questions | N.A. | N.A. | N.A. |
| | 2010–11 | 7,200 HH | All HH members aged 5 years and above | One year—past seven days | Face-to-face interview—stylized questions | N.A. | Modular with LSMS | N.A. |
| 22. New Zealand | 1990 | Pilot: 627 HHs | Two HH members aged 12 years and above | Last week | Self-reported time diary (two diary days) interview | 45% | Yes | 48-hour diary with 5-minute interval |

*(Cont'd)*

**TABLE 1A.3** (*Cont'd*)

| S. No. | Name of the Country | Years | Sample Size | Surveyed Population | Reference Period | Method of Data Collection | Response Rate | Background Questionnaire | Time Slot |
|---|---|---|---|---|---|---|---|---|---|
| | | 1998—9 | National: 8,532 individuals | Two HH members aged 10 years and above | 4 July 1998 – 7 July 1999 (last week) | Self-reported time diary | 72% | Yes | 48-hour diary with 5-minute interval |
| | | 2009–10 | National: 9,159 individuals, 8,543 HHs | Two HH members aged 12 years and above | 1 September 2009–31 August 2010 (last weeks) | Self-reported time diary | 72% | Yes | 48-hour diary with 5-minute interval |
| 23. | Pakistan | 1986–9 | 800 HHs: Rural household labour | All HH members aged 6 years and above | July 1986 and September 1989 (12 rounds) previous week | Interview methods (one-day recall dairy) | N.A. | Yes | N.A. |
| | | 1990–1 | Small; Women agricultural labour | | One day—single period | 8 methods | N.A. | N.A. | N.A. |
| | | 2007 | National: 19,380 individuals | Two HH members aged 10 years and above | January 2007–December 2007 (four quarters) | Time diary of 24 hours | 98.9% | Yes | 24-hour time diary with 30-minute interval |

|  | Country | Year | Sample | Members | Reference period | No TUS conducted | | |  |
|---|---|---|---|---|---|---|---|---|---|
| 24. | Palau | 1962 | Small; Agricultural workers | N.A. | N.A. | Not relevant | Not relevant | N.A. | N.A. |
| 25. | Papua New Guinea | 1974 Repeated in 1977 | Small; 25 people | N.A. | 72 days | 24-hour recall method | Not relevant | N.A. | N.A. |
|  |  | 1998 | Read the article | N.A. | N.A. | N.A. | N.A. | N.A. | N.A. |
|  |  |  |  |  |  |  | 80%, and 36.30% in 1977 | N.A. | N.A. |
| 26. | Philippines | 1975, followed up in 1976 and 1977 | 576 HHs Rural community 99 HHs in 1976 and 245 HHs in 1977 | All HH members and children aged 3–17 years | 1975 Previous seven days | One-day recall method | | | |
|  |  | 2000 | Pilot (1 rural, 1 urban area) | Three HH members aged 10 years and above | 3-day period | Self-reported 24-hour time diary and face-to-face interview and one-day recall interview | 98% | yes | N.A. |

*(Cont'd)*

**TABLE 1A.3** (Cont'd)

| S. No. | Name of the Country | Years | Sample Size | Surveyed Population | Reference Period | Method of Data Collection | Response Rate | Background Questionnaire | Time Slot |
|---|---|---|---|---|---|---|---|---|---|
| 27. | Samoa | 1991 | Small; two Samoa villages | N.A. | Both dry and wet season (every home was visited over two one-week periods) | One-day recall method | Not relevant | N.A. | N.A. |
| 28. | Singapore | | | | — No TUS conducted — | | | | |
| 29. | Solomon Island | 1985 | Small | N.A. | N.A. | N.A. | Not relevant | N.A. | N.A. |
| 30. | Sri Lanka | 2001 | Small | N.A. | N.A. | N.A. | N.A. | N.A. | N.A. |
| 31. | Thailand | 1990–1 | Small | N.A. | One day-single period | 8 method | not relevant | N.A. | N.A. |
| | | 2000–1 | National 27,000 HHs | 10 years +: 1 per HH | One day (August 2001) | Self-reported 24-hour time diary | Not relevant | Household and individual questions | 10 minutes |
| | | 2004 | N.A. | 10 years +: 1 per HH | One day (August 2001) | Self-reported time diary | Not mentioned | Household and individual questions | 10 minutes |

| No. & Country | Year | Sample | Age / Respondent | Reference period | Method | | Survey design | Duration |
|---|---|---|---|---|---|---|---|---|
| | 2009 | National: 7,956 HHs | 10 years +: 1 per HH | 3 months | Self-reported time diary | Not mentioned | Household and individual questions | 10 minutes |
| | 2014 | National; 83,881 HHs | 10 years +: 1 per HH | Round the year | Self-reported 24-hour time diary | Not mentioned | HH and individual questions | 10 minutes |
| 32. Timor Leste | 2001, 2007 | National: 1,800 HHs | All HH members aged 5 years and above | Whole year Last seven days | Stylized questions | Not mentioned | Modular with LSMS in the Employment section—individual time use | N.A. |
| 33. Tuvalu | 2003 | Small, with socio-economic well-being survey | N.A. | N.A. | N.A. | Not mentioned | Modular with socio-economic well-being survey | N.A. |
| | 2013 | Small | All HH members aged 18–81 years | Single day | 24-hour recall | Not mentioned | Yes | Households details |
| 34. Vanuatu | 1983-84 | Small; 600 agricultural HHs | N.A. | N.A. | Eight methods tested | Not mentioned | N.A. | N.A. |

(Cont'd)

**TABLE 1A.3**  *(Cont'd)*

| S. No. | Name of the Country | Years | Sample Size | Surveyed Population | Reference Period | Method of Data Collection | Response Rate | Background Questionnaire | Time Slot |
|---|---|---|---|---|---|---|---|---|---|
| | | 1995 | Small | N.A. | One day—single | PRA method | Not mentioned | N.A. | N.A. |
| | | 1999 | 5 sample HHs | All HH members aged 10 years and above | Last seven days | Time dairy—recording | Not mentioned | N.A. | N.A. |
| 35. | Vietnam | 1992, 1997, 2002, 2004 | National | All HH members aged 10 years and above | All the year | Modular stylized questions | Not mentioned | Modular with LSMS: employment section | N.A. |

*Source:* Author's compilation from the respective TUS data and from various organizations.

*Note:* For small surveys (not pilot surveys), the response rate is not relevant, as these are small surveys and usually all information is collected. For large surveys we have put N.A. – not available when the rates are not calculated or not available.

**TABLE 1A.4**  Context Variables, Simultaneous Activities, and Classification of Time-use Activities

| S. No | Name of the Country | Years | Context Variables | Simultaneous Activities | Activity Classification |
|---|---|---|---|---|---|
| 1. | Australia | 1974 | Mode of transport, distance, technology used, locations | Not collected | Own classification |
| | | 1974 | Unpaid | Not collected | Own classification |
| | | 1987 | None | Not collected | Own classification |
| | | 1992, 1997, 2006 | With whom, where, mode of transport | Collected | Own classification (Major activities have been classified into 4 categories: necessary time, contracted time, committed time, free time). In 2006, 9 broad categories were introduced |
| | | 1996–2009 | With whom, where, mode of transport | Not collected | Own classification |
| | | 2004–10 | None | Not collected | Own classification |
| | | 2005–6 | | Not collected | Own classification |
| | | 2007 wave: June 2007 to June 2008, 2009, 2010 | Location | Not collected | Own classification |

*(Cont'd)*

**TABLE 1A.4** (*Cont'd*)

| S. No | Name of the Country | Years | Context Variables | Simultaneous Activities | Activity Classification |
|---|---|---|---|---|---|
| 2. | Bangladesh | 1974, 1984–5, 1990–1, 2005 | None | Not collected | Small list of activities:<br>• Men were asked to account for 11 categories of activities,<br>• Women were asked to account for 10 categories of activities |
| | | 2012 | Where, with whom | Collected | 15 activities—Own classification (For comparison with ICATUS developed by the UN |
| 3. | Cambodia | 2003–4 | None | Not collected | Own classification—22 list of activities |
| 4. | China | 2005 | With whom, mode of transport | Collected | Own classification |
| | | 2008 | With whom, mode of transport | Collected | Own classification |
| 5. | Cook Islands | 1998 | None | Yes | Own classification—14 main groups |
| 6. | Fiji | 1987 | None | Not collected | Own classification |
| 7. | India | 1976–7, 1990–1, 1990, 1996 | None | Not collected | Own classification |
| | | 1998–9 | Paid/unpaid, where | Collected | Indian classification—9 broad categories |
| 8. | Indonesia | 1972–3, 1975–6, 1998–9 and 2005 | None | No | Own classification |
| | | | Where, with whom | Collected | Own classification |

| | | | | | |
|---|---|---|---|---|---|
| 9. | Iran | 2008 (Autumn) | None | No | 15 broad categories of activities in accordance with the ICATUS |
| | | 2009 | None | No | 15 broad categories of activities in accordance with the ICATUS |
| 10. | Japan | 1960–1, 1965, 1970, 1975, 1980, 1985, 1990, 1995, 2000, 2005 | | Collected | Own classification—28 activities |
| | | 1993–2004 | With whom and where | Not collected | Own |
| | | 1976, 1981, 1986, 1991, 1996, 2001, 2006, 2011 | | Collected | 19 categories of daily activities were set, and grouped into the three broad categories: Leisure, personal, and households. In 2001, one more category was added: Time spent on Internet |
| 11. | Kiribati | 2001–2 | | No | Own classification—11 short list of activities |
| 12. | Korea, South (RoK) | 1981, 1983, 1985, 1990,1995 and 2000, 2005, 2010 | Where, with whom, paid/ unpaid, mode of transport | Not collected | Own classification—11 categories of activities After 2000, a new category 'New Media' use was added to the existing category |
| | | 2005 | Where, with whom, paid/ unpaid, mode of transport | Not collected | Own classification |
| | | 1999, 2004, 2009, 2014 | Where, with whom, paid/unpaid, mode of transport | Collected | Classification adopted from EUROSTAT and the UNSD. There are 9 main groups of activities. In 2009, they added 3-digit activity codes |

(*Cont'd*)

**TABLE 1A.4** (*Cont'd*)

| S. No | Name of the Country | Years | Context Variables | Simultaneous Activities | Activity Classification |
|---|---|---|---|---|---|
| 13. | Lao PDR | 1997–8 | None | Not collected | Own classification—21 activities |
|  |  | 2002–3 | None | Not collected | Own classification—22 activities |
|  |  | 2008 | None | Not collected | Own classification—22 activities |
| 14. | Malaysia | 1990–1, 2003 | None | Not collected | Own classification |
| 15. | Mongolia | 2000, 2007, 2011 | Where, with whom, paid/unpaid, mode of transport | Collected | UN trial classification (ICATUS)—1997 |
| 16. | Nepal | 1977, 1980, 1992–3 | None | Collected | Own classification |
|  |  | 1998–9 | None | Not collected | Own list of activities |
|  |  | 2010 | None | Not collected | Own list of activities |
| 17. | New Zealand | 1990 | Where, with whom, paid/unpaid work | Collected | Own classification |
|  |  | 1998–9, 2009-10 | Where, with whom, paid/unpaid work | Collected | Own classification—11 broad categories |
| 18. | Pakistan | 1986–9, 1990–1 | | Not collected | Own classification |
|  |  | 2007 | Locations 1&2 | Collected | UN trial classification |

| | | | | | |
|---|---|---|---|---|---|
| 19. | Papua New Guinea | 1962 | | No | Own |
| 20. | Philippines | 1977 | None | No | Own |
| | | 1975, 1976, 1977 | | No | Own |
| | | 2000 | Information not available | Collected | UN trial classification |
| 21. | Samoa | 1991 | | No | Own |
| 22. | Solomon Islands | 1985 | | No | Own |
| 23. | Sri Lanka | 2001 | | No data collected | N.A. |
| 24. | Thailand | 1990–1 | | No | Own |
| | | 2000–1 | Where, with whom, for whom and paid/unpaid | No data collected | UN trial classification 1997 and Dagfinn's concept of type of time use |
| | | 2004, 2009, 2015 | Where, with whom, for whom and paid/unpaid | Collected | UN trial classification 2000 (15 categories) |
| 25 | Timor Lester | 2001, 2007 | None | Not collected | Own classification |
| 26. | Tuvalu | 2003 | None | No | Own classification with 16 broad categories |
| | | 2013 | | No | Own classification with 16 broad categories |
| 27. | Vanuatu | 1983–4, 1995, 1999 | None | No | Own classification |
| 28. | Vietnam | 1992, 1997, 2002, 2004 | None | Nos | Own list of activities |

*Source:* Author's compilation from the respective TUS data and from various organizations.

## REFERENCES

Acharya, Mina. 2000. 'Time Budget Studies For Measurement of Human Welfare', presentation for Workshop of Integrating Paid and Unpaid Work into National Policies, Seoul, 28–30, submitted to United Nations Development Programme (UNDP), New York.

Bittman, Michael. 2000. 'Methodological Issues in Conducting Time Use Survey at the Global Level and Emerging Lessons', in *Mainstreaming Time Use Surveys in National Statistical System in India*. New Delhi: Ministry of Women and Child Development, Government of India.

Bonke, J. 2002. 'Paid Work and Unpaid Work: Diary Information Versus Questionnaire Information', paper presented at the Conference of the International Association for Time Use Research, Lisbon, 16–18 October.

Budlender, Debbie. 2000. 'Major Issues in Developing the South African Time Use classification', Expert Group Meeting on Methods for Conducting Time-Use Surveys, New York, 23–27 October.

Budlender, Debbie and Ann Lisbet Brathaug. 2002. 'Calculating the Value of Unpaid Labour: A Discussion Document' Working Paper 2002/1, Statistics South Africa, Pretoria.

Central Statistical Organization (CSO). 2000. *Report of the Time Use Survey*. New Delhi: Ministry of Statistics and Programme Implementation, Government of India.

Charmes, Jacques and Indira Hirway. 2006. 'Estimating and Understanding the Informal Employment through Time Use Studies', paper presented at Expert Group on Informal Sector Statistics (Delhi Group), 11–12 May.

Corner, Lorraine. 2003. 'Use of Time Use Data for Policy Advocacy and Analysis', in *Applications of Time Use Statistics*, pp. 57–66. New Delhi: Central Statistical Organization, Government of India.

Harvey, Andrew S. 2014. 'Activity and Contextual Codes – Implications for Time-Use Coding Schemes, Activity and Contextual Codes Implications for Time Use Coding Schemes', electronic *International Journal of Time Use Research*, 8(1): 66–80.

Hirway, Indira. 2003. 'Indian Experience of Time Use Survey', in *Applications of Time Use Statistics*, pp. 3–24. New Delhi: Central Statistical Organization, Government of India.

———. 2010. 'Time Use Surveys in Developing Countries: An Assessment', in Rania Antonopoulos and Indira Hirway (eds), *Unpaid Work and the Economy: Gender, Time Use and Poverty in Developing Countries*. London: Palgrave Macmillan.

———. 2015. 'Unpaid Work and the Economy: Linkages and Implications', *Indian Journal of Labour Economics*, 58(1): 1–22.

International Council of Labour Statistics (ICLS). 2013. 'Resolution on Statistics on Work, Employment and Labour Underutilization', 19th International Council of Labour Statistics, ILO, Geneva.

International Research and Training Centre for the Advancement of Women (INSTRAW). 1995. 'Time Use Surveys in Developing Countries', INSTRAW, Santo Domingo, Dominican Republic, mimeo.

Ministry of Women and Child Development and UNDP. 2014. *Report of the International Seminar on Mainstreaming Time Use Survey in National Statistical Systems.* New Delhi: Government of India and UNDP.

Mulik, James and Laura Werner. 2002. 'Time Use Survey of the Gilbert Island Group, Republic of Kiribati', CTUR, Oxford University.

Robinson, John and William Michelson. 2010. 'Sleep as a victim of the "time crunch" – A multinational analysis', electronic edition, *International Journal of Time Use Research*, 7(1): 32–41.

Sillitoe, Paul. 2006. 'What Labour Engenders: Women and Men, Time and Work in the New Guinea Highlands', *The Asia Pacific Journal of Anthropology*, 7(2): 119–51.

United Nations. 2005. 'Guide to Producing Statistics on Time Use: Measuring Paid and Unpaid Work', Economic and Social Affairs, United Nations Publications, New York.

United Nations Statistics Division (UNSD). 1999. 'Towards International Guidelines in Time Use Surveys: Objectives and Methods of National Time Use Surveys in Developing Countries', paper presented at the International Seminar on Time Use Studies, United Nations Economic and Social Commission for Asia and the Pacific, Ahmedabad, 7–10 December.

———. 2012. Minutes of the Expert Group Meeting on Time Use Activity Classification, organized by UNSD, New York.

United Nations Development Programme (UNDP). 2004. 'Project Document on Gender Equality in the Asia-Pacific Region', UNDP, New York.

———. 2005. *Guide to Producing Statistics on Time Use: Measuring Paid and Unpaid Work*, Series F, No. 93. New York: Department of Economics and Social Affairs, United Nations.

———. 2008. *Report of the EGM on Equal Sharing of Responsibilities between Women and Men including Care-giving in the Context of HIV/AIDS.* Geneva: UNDP.

———. 2010. *Human Development Report.* New York: HDR Office, UNDP.

Waring, Marilyn. 2006. *If Women Counted: The New Feminist Economics*, Kennedy School of Administration. Massachusetts: Harvard University Press.

White, Benjamin. 1983. 'Measuring Time Allocation, Decision-Making and Agrarian Changes Affecting Rural Women: Example from Recent Research in Indonesia', paper prepared for methodology workshop, Jakarta, 1982.

# 2 Time-use Surveys in Latin America: 2005–15

## Valeria Esquivel*

The decade of 2005–15 has witnessed the expansion of time-use surveys (TUS) in Latin America at an unprecedented rate. During this decade, Dominican Republic (2007), Honduras (2011), Peru (2010), Panama (2011), El Salvador (2010), Venezuela (2011–12), and Colombia (2012–13) completed their first nation-wide TUS. Uruguay (2013), Ecuador (2012–13), Guatemala (2011), and Mexico (2009) conducted a third round. Brazil (2010) and Bolivia (2010) conducted 'pilot' surveys, the former being big enough to cover five states. New city-wide TUS have also been conducted in Gran Santiago, Chile (2008); Rosario, Argentina (2010); and Great San José, Costa Rica (2011).

The latest surveys follow the methodological paths set at the beginning of the 2000s by Mexico (2002); Ecuador (2005); Montevideo, Uruguay (2003); Guatemala (2000); and Buenos Aires, Argentina (2005). These methodological paths are quite distinct. There have been at least four forms of questionnaires: (a) the short tasks lists: Colombia (2006–11), Bolivia (2001), Montevideo, Uruguay (2003, 2007, and

* The views expressed in this chapter are those of the author and do not represent the position of the ILO or the United Nations. The article this chapter is based on a version that was written when the author was Associate Professor of Economics at Universidad Nacional de General Sarmiento and Researcher at CONICET (Argentina).

2013), Ecuador (2004), and Honduras (2009); (b) the stylized diaries:
Nicaragua (1998), Guatemala (2000, 2006, and 2011), Costa Rica
(2004), and El Salvador (2004, 2010); (c) the exhaustive activity lists:
Mexico (2002, 2006, and 2009), Ecuador (2005, 2007, and 2012–13),
Peru (2010), Great San José, Costa Rica (2011), Panama (2011), and
Colombia (2012–13); and (d) the 24-hour recall-based activity diaries: Buenos Aires, Argentina (2005); Rosario, Argentina (2010); Gran
Santiago, Chile (2008); Brazil (2010); Bolivia (2010); and Venezuela
(2011–12). All these questionnaire types are explained in detail later in
this chapter. Diversity in methods is also evident in coverage (national/
urban/city or group of cities), reference period (yesterday/previ-
ous week), sample unit (household/individual), reference population
(respondent's minimum and maximum age), and the inclusion and
recording of simultaneous activities (see Appendix 2A).

This chapter is an updated version of a previous review (Esquivel
2008). It addresses the different methodological paths discussed earlier and goes beyond the methods to lay emphasis on the state of the
regional debate, and the institutional and political frameworks that
supported data collection of time use. Some observers have a highly
positive view of these developments (López and Scuro 2012). In the
present author's view, however, the picture is rather mixed: the following
discussion shows that the advancement of TUS in the Latin American
region has been very heterogeneous, that this reflects lack of agreement
on best suited methodological approaches. On a more positive note,
Latin America has experienced a strong learning-by-doing process in
time-use data collection methods, which have gained complexity and
wider local consensuses (including law mandates) that support a bigger,
year-long, and standalone TUS (Aguirre and Ferrari 2014).

## DIFFERENT APPROACHES TO TIME-USE DATA COLLECTION IN LATIN AMERICA

### Short Tasks Lists

Short tasks lists, which are survey instruments based on stylized questions that target specific tasks, aim to obtain data on the time spent
performing these tasks (UNSD 2005: 57). What differentiates this
approach from others is not so much the length of the list—which,
in some cases, can be fairly long—but the fact that the lists are never
exhaustive. When focusing on unpaid care work, these lists exclude

personal care (particularly sleeping time) and leisure, and, therefore, never equate to 24 hours a day. Examples of this approach include Uruguay (2003 [Montevideo] and 2007) and Honduras (2009).[1] Reference periods are either 'yesterday', 'last working day', 'last week', or an 'average week day/weekend day' during the last week.

In the case of Honduras (2009), the list included three questions on tasks, that is, (a) cooking, cleaning, food shopping, laundering, and ironing; (b) taking care of children and/or frail adults; (c) voluntary work; and two on activity types, that is; (d) education; and (e) self-care (excluding sleep time) performed 'yesterday'. For each task or activity type, there was an 'hours and minutes' slot to fill in (Leiva 2010).

Following in its design the first Uruguayan TUS (that is, Montevideo 2003) (see Aguirre and Batthyány 2005), the 2007 national TUS sought to identify the total workload (paid and unpaid) by certain demographic characteristics and to calculate how household time was distributed across members. The survey listed 32 tasks and six leisure activities. Its main type of respondent was the household member who considered herself/himself the main person in charge of' unpaid care work (Instituto Nacional de Estadística [INE] and Universidad de la República 2008). In other words, the task survey was not self-referred, which could give biased results if 'the main person in charge of' unpaid care work was not a full-time homemaker/housewife, as he/she might not have exact information on other household members' uses of time—particularly those that refer to activities in spaces other than the household or leisure time.[2] In all other Latin American short tasks list surveys, respondents were all household members above a certain age (see Appendix 2A).

Though the least expensive of all time-use data collection methods, this approach is prone to reporting errors. In an analysis of five of the Latin American cases—Nicaragua (1998), Guatemala (2000), Bolivia (2001), Mexico (2002), and Ecuador (2004)—Milosavljevic (2006) shows that the longer the tasks list, the longer the time women report as devoting to unpaid work. Thus, as the prompting questions become

[1] Other countries also conducted short tasks surveys, but reverted to more complex methodologies afterwards. These are Mexico (1996), Ecuador (2003–11), and Colombia (2006–11) (see Appendix 2A and Comunidad Andina 2012; Esquivel 2008; Freire Delgado 2011; Marco Navarro 2012).

[2] See also INE (2014) for details on the 2013 Uruguayan TUS.

more detailed, respondents produce more accurate accounts, because their recall improves. This, in turn, means that time-use estimations are affected by both the length and detail of the tasks list. Among the many reasons for this are that list items are necessarily broad, making respondents 'add up' all activities comprised under a general heading and inevitably miss some. Problems of activity wording—what the respondent understands by 'housework' or 'childcare', for example— also affect survey responses. In addition, as this approach does not capture simultaneous activities, short tasks lists show a tendency to underreport activities that are frequently performed simultaneously, such as total unpaid care work, when compared to activity diaries.

Additionally, it should be noted that short tasks lists that are too concise do not allow for a detailed analysis of particular activities, a sensitive issue when time-use data feeds modelling exercises or well-being indicators.

## Stylized Diaries

The stylized diary approach was followed by Nicaragua (1998), Guatemala (2000, 2006, and 2011), Costa Rica (2004), and El Salvador (2004 and 2010). In solving the difficult trade-off between respecting the 24-hour cap and keeping the interview short, this approach resorts to a short but comprehensive list of activities (which, in many cases, corresponds to the one-digit International Classification of Activities for Time-Use Surveys [ICATUS]).[3] For example, in the case of Guatemala (2011), the third round of the time-use module reverted to its initial (2000) form of 24 questions because the shortened version of 2006 got lost in detail and comparability (Monzón 2012).

In stylized diaries, respondents provide information on the time spent on these broad activities during 'yesterday', that is, the day before the survey. An exception was the 2004 survey of El Salvador, where the opening question of the diary was, 'How much time do you devote to the following activities in a given day?', without specifying a particular day. This can potentially be problematic, as some activities (for example, productive work and social events) most frequently take

---

[3] These are not 'light diaries': there is no information on the chronology of activities (see the discussion on activity diaries in the following section).

place on different weekdays. This is the reason the 2010 round of the Salvadorian TUS—which expanded the list to 47 activities—changed this question for a 'normal' day (Dirección General de Estadística y Censos [DIGESTYC] 2012; Meléndez 2011).

Some countries using this approach to TUS still encountered methodological challenges. While in the Nicaraguan TUS (1998), a specific check was included in order to verify that all activities added up to 24 hours, serious problems arose in the analysis of the 2004 Costa Rican time-use data, since the time did not always add up to 24 hours. If the reported hours exceed 24, it can be inferred that some activities were simultaneously performed, but nothing can be inferred if the time adds up to less than 24 hours. In anticipation of this problem, the Costa Rican questionnaire differentiates between time devoted exclusively to care—which is one of the 15 activity types asked for—and time devoted to care 'at the same time', which is asked separately. However, these two questions did not always work well: sometimes, respondents declared total time devoted to care without really considering whether it was 'exclusive' and became confused when prompted to differentiate the two. In other cases, where chronic patients were present in the household, answers to time devoted to care in combination with other activities were 24 hours, indicating of being constantly on call (Sandoval 2005). In the case of Guatemala, the TUS also included a final question asking the respondent to identify which activities were performed simultaneously because any one activity can be performed at the same time as many others, in different episodes along a given day (Miranda 2011).

It is observed that the inclusion of simultaneous activities within this approach is still problematic, particularly because emphasis is given to 'exclusive' time while prompting the respondent to indicate the time spent on each activity type. Indeed, this approach only works well if respondents are forced to think of activities not performed at the same time as others.

## Exhaustive Activity Lists

Dissatisfaction with built-in list aggregation and the difficulties of unpacking this information have prompted an effort to refine task data collection with the use of an 'exhaustive' activity list. This was applied by Mexico (2002 and 2009), Ecuador (2005, 2007, and 2010), Peru (2010), Costa Rica (2011), and Panama (2011).[4] These lists are similar to stylized diaries in being comprehensive (they include time devoted to personal care, paid work, leisure time, education, etc.), and also resemble short tasks lists in the way they emphasize capturing unpaid care work. Like some short tasks lists, the reference period is the previous week. The cap of 24 hours per day/168 hours per week is neither respected nor checked, and there is no explicit provision for capturing simultaneous activities.

A distinct feature of this approach is the extent of the activity list. For example, Mexico (2002) included 86 activities, Ecuador (2005) 110, Panama (2011) 107, and Peru (2010) 207 (Comunidad Andina 2012; INEC 2013). This allowed for the inclusion of very detailed activities (for example, 'preparation of home-made medicines') that would not be included in stylized approaches. The wide reference period (last Monday to Friday, and last weekend) also allowed for capturing less frequent/extraordinary activities (for example, 'attending funerals').

But the advantage of this approach also represents a weakness. There cannot be an activity list that is completely exhaustive—problems of wording and omitted activities still arise, as is evident from the inclusion of the 'other activities' residual category. Differing activity frequencies might lead to respondents reporting 'averages' and not actual time use. For example, 'washing the dishes' takes place many times a day, so respondents have to add up the time to answer according to the reference period, while 'attending a party' takes place on very specific days and contexts. Respondent fatigue (and concomitant list-ordering biases) can also arise because each questionnaire is extensive and because it is applied to every family member (above a certain age). Successive TUS (Mexico 2009 and Ecuador 2007) sought to avoid some of these problems by re-designing the questionnaire's passes, in order to pose some of the questions to persons/households that had already ascertained

---

[4] Armas, Contreras, and Vásconez (2009); Consejo Nacional de las Mujeres, Presidencia de la República (CONAMU) (2006); Instituto Nacional de Estadística y Censo (INEC) (2013); Instituto Nacional de Estadística, Geografía e Informática (INEGI) (2005, 2010); Instituto Nacional de Estadística e Informática (INEI) (2011); Instituto Nacional de las Mujeres (INAMU) et al. (2012); Pedrero (2012); Pérez Avellaneda (2011); Sandoval (2012).

they could have devoted time to these activities (that is, only asking whether time was devoted to care for a frail household member if there was one in the household).[5]

Variations of this approach can be found in Colombia (2012–13), where the list is exhaustive and similar to that used in Mexico and Ecuador (93 activities, some of them grouped and preceded by a 'yes/no' question, plus room for additional activities), but the reference period is 'yesterday', as researchers felt that recall was much more accurate if it referred to the day before the interview (Departamento Administrativo Nacional de Estadística [DANE] 2013). Given this reference period, one could argue that the Colombian TUS is, indeed, a (quite long) 'stylized diary'. However, as it is the case with other exhaustive activity lists, the 24-hour cap does not hold.

Both the Mexican (2009) and the Colombian (2012–13) surveys have attempted to cater to simultaneous activities, requesting the respondents to identify pairs of simultaneous activities (five in Mexico, four in Colombia), and the frequency (in case of Mexico) or the actual time (in case of Colombia) devoted to them. Moreover, in the case of Colombia, passive care ('being on call') was one of the listed activities, and for this activity alone the respondent is asked to indicate what she/he was doing during the same time. This information could eventually help in adjusting time-use data, particularly when the total hours collected per interview are less than 24 per day/168 per week.

## Activity Diaries

Activity diaries are 24-hour schedules, divided in fixed time slots (10, 15, or 30 minutes long) with room for one, two, or three activities in each of them.[6] In contrast to short tasks lists and exhaustive activity lists, activity diaries follow what could be termed a 'bottom-up approach' to time-use data collection. Instead of starting from aggregate types of activities and eventually disaggregating them further (a top-down

---

[5] Mexico (2009) also slightly shortened the number of activities to 76 (see Appendix 2A).

[6] There are other diaries that use open time slots, like the 1998 Mexican TUS. Results from that survey have not been published, precluding its analysis.

approach), diaries invert this principle by collecting detailed information on time use. The data is subsequently post-coded and eventually aggregated according to the survey's activity classification. Following the initial attempts of Cuba (2001) and Buenos Aires, Argentina (2005) (Esquivel 2010; Oficina Nacional de Estadística [ONE] 2002), many of the most recent TUS have been activity diaries: Gran Santiago, Chile (2008); Rosario, Argentina (2010); Brazil (2010); Bolivia (2011); and Venezuela (2011–12). Regrettably, both Brazil and Bolivia view their attempts as 'pilot' surveys, and, as a consequence, have not published their results yet.

With the exception of Cuba (2001) (ONE 2002), all other surveys based on activity diaries in Latin America have collected data through an interview.[7] In the 24-hour recall activity diary, respondents use their own words to report on what they did 'yesterday' while the interviewer fills in the diary. This type of diary emphasizes minimizing the respondents' recall efforts. In doing so, the burden moves from respondents' extensive reports on their activities over a long period in the exhaustive activity list approach, to sampling design and fieldwork. If correctly designed, 'less frequent activities' will come up less frequently in the activity diaries of the sampled days, provided they are representative of the reference population on all different weekdays.

In the cases of the two Argentinian surveys—Buenos Aires (2005)[8] and Rosario (2010)—fieldworkers working with this type of diary were responsible for activity coding, which was post-edited, so data quality ultimately depended on fieldworkers' ability to transform respondents' answers into diary activities with appropriate coding. Thus the number of codes had to be manageable (10-digit 1997 trial ICATUS), most

[7] In the case of Venezuela, a pilot survey showed that leaving the diary behind to aid recall, and filling it in through an interview the following day, apparently scared people who had previously accepted answering background questions, making non-response rates unacceptably high. In the case of Brazil, the paper diary was left behind, with an indication of the reference day, but in many cases ended up being completed by fieldworkers (Gama 2010).

[8] The Buenos Aires TUS drew heavily on the 2000 South African TUS, though it introduced several changes in interviewers guiding questions, activity classification, context variables, probing questions, and the way in which simultaneous activities were recorded (Budlender 2007).

of them quite aggregate (two-digit). Time slots were of 30 minutes long, from 4 a.m. to 4 a.m., allowing for up to three consecutive and/ or simultaneous activities. The Buenos Aires and Rosario surveys also included probing questions that asked for frequently underreported simultaneous activities (for example, passive care) or checked whether an activity was done for pay (for example, taking care of a neighbour's child for pay) (Esquivel 2010; Ganem, Giustiniani, and Peinado 2012).

By contrast, the Brazilian and Venezuelan TUS were collected with the aid of personal digital assistants that had built-in dictionaries and automatically coded the activities, a feature that enormously reduced fieldworkers' burden.[9] In the case of Venezuela, respondents, who reported time spent in housework, care work, or voluntary work, were prompted to give more detail on these activities with a built-in questionnaire, which had 'where', 'for whom', and 'with whom' questions. Time slots were 10 minutes long (Llavaneras Blanco 2011). In the case of Brazil, time slots were 15 minutes long, and the questions 'where' and 'with whom' were included for all main activities.

All activity diaries collected in the region were self-referred. In the cases of Buenos Aires and Brazil, one randomly selected household member answered about her/his previous day.[10] In all other cases, all members of the household equal or older than a predefined age (such as 10, 12, or 15 years) answered the questionnaire.

Time-use data collected from diaries features a chronology of events that can be analysed (not only total time devoted to a certain activity type, but also when that activity takes place). Daily rhythms can be analysed to inform a number of policy issues as a result. In the case of Venezuela, for example, one of the TUS objectives was the analysis of transportation times and paid work schedules (INE and Banco Central de Venezuela [BCV] 2011). In the case of Buenos Aires, it was found that working parents adjusted their daily timetables differently to make them compatible with care provision once schools are closed for the day (Esquivel 2012).

---

[9] Statistical offices had already used PDAs for other household surveys, or population censuses.

[10] A distinctive feature of the 2005 Buenos Aires TUS is that all household members' socio-demographic and labour market data is available from the core Annual Household Survey it was attached to (Esquivel 2010).

Time-use data collected from diaries better captures simultaneous activities by asking, 'what else were you doing?', at any given time. Diaries may or may not include hierarchical simultaneity: they can pre-establish a 'main' activity and a 'secondary' activity (as in the Venezuelan and Brazilian surveys) or simply capture them without attaching any intrinsic ranking to the responses (as in the Buenos Aires and Rosario surveys).

## A Comparison of TUS Methods used in Latin America

This cursory review of TUS methods used in Latin America indicates that there are at least four methodological trade-offs that arise when a particular approach is chosen for time-use data collection: (a) compromises over time-use data quality; (b) respondents' burden versus fieldwork burden; (c) surveying households versus surveying individuals; and (d) appropriate consideration, or not, of simultaneous activities.

First, the quality of time-use data collected depends on the survey instruments chosen. The international view that activity diaries are the least biased time-use data collection instrument is also confirmed by Latin American scholars. In a comparison between exhaustive activity lists and activity diaries for the case of Mexico, Parker and Gandini (2011) found strong differences in time-use estimations. The authors found that activities with pre-established time schedules—paid work and education—got higher estimated times in exhaustive activity lists than in activity diaries, possibly because the former do not capture interruptions that are evident in activity diaries. They also found that estimated times of unpaid care work are higher in exhaustive activity lists, and they attribute this to the biases brought about by repeatedly probing by using long lists of care-related activities, and possibly prejudice and social norms. On the contrary, authors found that highly 'individualized' activities (socialization, sleeping time, media use) get higher estimated times in activity diaries.

Second, if the respondents' burden is to be minimized through the use of activity diaries (24-hour recall diaries or even stylized diaries, which are both filled in by enumerators) as opposed to exhaustive activity lists, fieldwork has to be carefully calibrated. This is done in order to correctly select households, individuals, and days to collect information on, something that might not always be guaranteed or even be possible depending on the core survey characteristics to which the time-use module is attached. Indeed, restrictions imposed by the core survey are among the main reasons for not choosing activity diaries (Pedrero 2005). On the contrary, if the exhaustive activity list approach is followed, extreme caution should be applied to the length and ordering of the list to minimize respondent dropout.

Third, while household surveying makes it possible to analyse intra-household time-use distribution and, therefore, calculate average distributive measures, it may also raise non-response rates (defined on household bases) when one or some of household members refuse, are absent, or cannot be contacted to conduct the survey. Yet, household 'total unpaid workload' and intra-household unpaid work shares need be estimated in order to calculate individual time-poverty rates (Antonopoulos, Zacharias, and Masterson 2012). On the contrary, picking only a limited number of randomly selected members of the household—depending on average household size—can shorten the total interview time and widen the number of surveyed households when the ultimate unit of analysis is the surveyed individual, but at the cost of making intra-household analyses harder.

A fourth trade-off arises with the inclusion of simultaneous activities in questionnaire design. Making respondents' answers comply with the cap of 24 hours per day/168 hours per week by artificially avoiding capturing of simultaneous activities, allowing for these limits to be surpassed and, therefore, implicitly allowing for simultaneous activities to take place (in aggregate terms), or allowing for predefined 'simultaneous tasks' are not satisfactory ways of dealing with simultaneity. As previously mentioned, problems arise when the total hours surveyed is less than the limit, and ad hoc (and highly disputable) adjustments might be required.

Activity diaries (either 24-hour recall or self-administered ones) are the only approaches to consistently monitor simultaneous activities. An interesting question to address is whether simultaneous activities should be ranked and how time is to be accrued to each one of the activities performed at the same time. One solution is to divide or average time while analysing the chronology of activities or daily rhythms to comply with the 24-hour cap and give the full time to each of the activities when aggregating them (irrespective of when they were performed), as it was the case in the Buenos Aires and Rosario surveys (Esquivel 2010; Ganem, Giustiniani, and Peinado 2012).[11]

## LATIN AMERICAN DEBATES ON TUS METHODS: THEN AND NOW

### Modules versus Standalone Surveys

Over the decade of 2005–15, the debates around TUS methods in Latin America have been defined by the stark opposition between two distinct approaches to time use data collection. On the one hand is the idealized standalone, Eurostat-type self-administered activity diary, as the best way of collecting time-use data—yet regarded as infeasible in the Latin American context and ultimately a misuse of scarce social resources by practitioners and UN regional agencies alike. On the other hand are the modules of ongoing household surveys in the form of short tasks lists. regarded as *the* feasible way of collecting time-use data because they are cheaper than standalone surveys and better suited to largely illiterate populations.[12]

However, the Latin American experience proves that whether the TUS is standalone or a module to an existing household survey, it is relatively independent of the chosen TUS data collection method. More importantly, activity diaries need not be left behind self-administered diaries, but can in fact be (and have been) adapted to suit regional needs.

The relative independence between the time-use data collection methods and whether the surveys are modules or standalone endeavours has worked both ways. During 1995–2004, almost all the Latin American TUS were modules in ongoing household surveys: a modular approach to TUS (as opposed to standalone surveys) had given way

---

[11] In a different treatment of hierarchical (main/secondary) activities, the *Guide to Producing Statistics on Time Use: Measuring Paid and Unpaid Work* (or the *Guide*) (UNSD 2005: 143) defines simultaneous activities as main and secondary performed in parallel. However, parallel activities need not be prioritized (Waring 2006: 6).

[12] See, for example, Milosavljevic and Tacla (2007); Durán (2007) cited in Marco Navarro (2012: 16); and Sonia Montaño (Chapter 4 of this volume).

to all the data collection methods summarized above (see Appendix 2A). On the other hand, during 2010–15, the exhaustive activity lists of Mexico (2009), Ecuador (2010), and Colombia (2012–13) have been standalone surveys, as were the 24-hour recall activity diaries collected in Brazil (2010) and Venezuela (2011–12). In all five cases, cost considerations were not the primary driver for choosing one or the other method of time-use data collection—all these surveys were costly.

Other considerations, like available statistical infrastructure (including skilled fieldworkers and technological devices), knowledge of available options, and, more often than not, donor preferences and pressures, seemed to have been much more prominent in shaping choices (see the section, 'Institutional Frameworks' further in the chapter). Regrettably, neither the abovementioned methodological trade-offs, nor the specific, policy-driven TUS objectives beyond the aggregate measurement of women's and men's unpaid care work seem to have been as central as they should have in informing and shaping countries' methodological choices.[13]

## Path Dependency and the Hard Road to Harmonization

Latin America seems to have taken a time-use data collection path that diverges from those taken by other developing and developed regions of the globe. While the *Guide* (UNSD 2005) almost restricts time-use data collection to activity diaries, dismissing other methodological approaches, the region has seen the emergence of an array of methodological approaches to time-use data collection. These have resulted from a mix of well-intended attempts at local adaptation, the expansion of regional path-breaking experiences (particularly that of Mexico, which 'exported' exhaustive activity lists to Ecuador, Peru, Costa Rica, Panama, and Colombia), and the influence of successful stories elsewhere (the Uruguayan TUS is modelled after a Spanish design [García Sainz 2005], and the Buenos Aires TUS takes after the South

---

[13] Indeed, TUS objectives have not guided methodological choices. In most cases, the stated main objective of TUS is 'measuring total workloads (paid and unpaid)' (Comunidad Andina 2012), a very aggregate measure that could be calculated—albeit with differing data quality—from very simple short tasks lists.

African TUS [Esquivel 2010]). However, there is also a strong belief held by the Division of Gender Affairs at ECLAC[14] and the institutions that convene the regional expert meetings on 'Time Use Surveys and Unpaid Work'[15] that activity diaries cannot be collected, and, therefore, should not be recommended in the region. Indeed, if one follows the meetings' programmes, one gets the idea that activity diaries have not been collected in the region at all—no presenters from Brazil, Venezuela, Bolivia, or Argentina are not invited.[16]

A pattern that emerges after more than a decade of time-use data collection in the region is one of a strong methodological path dependency: countries that started with one of the above-mentioned data-collection methods persist with them, try to learn from past experience, and tweak and fine-tune whatever is in need of improvement. This is not surprising: abandoning any of these paths is too costly, as it means losing inter-temporal comparability.

In this regional context, the multiplicity and path dependency in methods can jeopardize regional harmonization, given that it means finding the least common denominator (Rydenstam 2011). Work on a regional classification of activities, the 'Latin American Classification of Time-Use Activities' (CAUTAL for its Spanish name, *Clasificación de Actividades de Uso del Tiempo para América Latina y el Caribe*) has been seen as the way towards regional harmonization (Gómez Luna 2010). This is perhaps true, given that Bolivia's (2011) 24-hour recall activity diary and Ecuador's (2010) exhaustive activity list have both used or adapted

---

[14] See, for example, Marco Navarro (2012); Milosavljevic and Tacla (2007); Montaño (Chapter 4 of this volume).

[15] Reunión de Expertos y Expertas en Encuestas de Uso del Tiempo y Trabajo no Remunerado. Conveners of the meeting, which takes place in Mexico City, are ECLAC, UN Women, The Americas Statistical Conference (Conferencia de Estadistica de las Américas, or CEA), the local Instituto Nacional de Estadística y Geografía (INEGI), which is the Mexican National Statistical Office, and the National Institute for Women (Instituto Nacional de las Mujeres). See López and Scuro (2012) for an interpretation of the role of these expert meetings in advancing time-use data collection in the region.

[16] As an example, the programme of the 2014 meeting can be found at http://cedoc.inmujeres.gob.mx/documentos_download/Uso_Tiempo_2014.pdf, last accessed in September 2015.

CAUTAL (Comunidad Andina 2012).[17] Interestingly, CAUTAL is not useful if short tasks lists are adopted—a signal that Latin America has finally left short tasks lists behind.

## Institutional Frameworks

All major TUS in Latin America have emerged from broad consensuses, sometimes painstakingly achieved. The 2010 Brazil TUS was collected by the Instituto Brasileiro de Geografia e Estatística (IBGE), the National Statistical Office of Brazil, with the support of the Technical Committee for the Study of Gender and Time Use, coordinated by the Secretariat of Policies for Women (SPM) and with Instituto de Pesquisa Econômica Aplicada (IPEA), IBGE, the International Labour Organization (ILO) and the Organization of United Nations Gender Equality and the Empowerment of Women (UN Women) as members (Gama 2010). The 2011–12 Venezuelan TUS was collected by INE with the funding and technical support of the Venezuelan Central Bank, which oversees the building of national accounts (Llavaneras Blanco 2011). In the cases of Costa Rica and Uruguay, the broad consensuses included one or more faculties/universities, aside from national statistical offices and women's machineries (Marco Navarro 2012). In some cases, the fact that there was a strong legal mandate binding statistical offices was instrumental in providing the political will and the budget for time-use data collection, like in the cases of Colombia, where a national law (Ley 1413 de Economía del Cuidado, 2010) mandated regular collection of time-use data to monitor the care economy (López 2011), and Buenos Aires, where a city-level law mandated regular time-use data collection to inform gender-aware policies (Esquivel 2010).

Donors have had a strong role in defining countries' methodological choices as well, as the case of Bolivia exemplifies: Bolivia was offered funding to support its TUS both from SIDA, the Swedish International Cooperation Agency, and from AECID, the Spanish International Cooperation Agency through ECLAC. The SIDA funding was tied to the activity diary data collection method, while AECID funds were

---

[17] However, the ultimate goal of CAUTAL is not being used both by activity diaries and by exhaustive activity lists, although it suits the latter (Gómez Luna 2010).

tied to a tasks/activity list (Tapia 2010). Although having two donors vying for the recipient country is not usual, it was clear that the funds offered were not 'method-free'.[18] In fact, there is a strong correlation between AECID-funded initiatives, the concurrence of Spanish experts, and the use of time-use data collection methods other than the activity diary. On the contrary, no international resources corseted the Venezuelan, Brazilian, and Argentinean initiatives.

## THE ROAD AHEAD: TIME-USE DATA TO INFORM GENDER-AWARE AGENDAS IN LATIN AMERICA

Where it exists, time-use data has not been applied to inform gender-aware policies as broadly as was expected before collecting it. This has been a source of concern in the region and elsewhere (Esquivel 2011). The present author concurs with Marco Navarro (2012: 10) on the importance of the fact that time-use data informs policy agendas at the meso level: employment, social security, and health policies are immediate examples. However, while Marco Navarro emphasizes lack of knowledge as one of the drivers of the lack of impact of time-use surveys on public policy—and, therefore, suggests more emphasis in dissemination strategies—I have argued that data quality problems, particularly those stemming from excessive aggregation in results, might hinder an analytical use of time-use data particularly in policies that have the highest potential to be informed by such use (Esquivel 2011). In other words, there is not much scope of truly influencing employment, health, social security, and anti-poverty policies if our TUS analyses are lean, showing mainly aggregate profiles. This is also emphasized by Aguirre and Ferrari (2014), when they assert the need for more refined statistical

---

[18] A similar point was made by Sonia Montaño (2011), head of Gender Affairs Division, ECLAC, at the time, in her presentation at the International Workshop on Harmonization of Time Use Surveys at the Global Level with Special Reference to Developing Countries. She argued that a major driver for methodological choices is the source of funding: if SIDA were to fund time-use data collection in the region, then diaries would be recommended. If AECID funds time-use data collection, it will go for short tasks lists or exhaustive activity lists at most. AECID has a long-standing cooperation agreement with ECLAC http://www.cepal.org/aecid/ last accessed in September 2015.

treatment of time-use data—something that can only happen when data is sufficiently detailed and of good quality.

For TUS to inform gender-aware public policy in Latin America, a thorough and open dialogue is needed on time-use data methods as well as on the difficult trade-offs involved in choosing from existing options, making explicit the process of TUS design, and the compromises to be made (Esquivel and Folbre 2008).[19] Policy-impact analyses need to be elaborated further and mode more sophisticated. This means, among other things, that TUS methods have to be designed with policy impact analysis in mind. Thus, adequate background data is required in order to perform analyses on the access to and needs for health and education services. Moreover, a theoretical framework is needed to develop the complex relationship between time and income poverty—it is not enough to state that 'unpaid care work is impoverishing for those who perform it' (Marco Navarro 2012: 5).[20] In other words, advocacy ought to be framed for 'time-use data collection not as a precursor to the construction of household-sector satellite accounts, but as an irreplaceable source of information for the design of polices that support the reduction and redistribution of unpaid care work within a framework that recognizes both caregivers' contributions to well-being and the costs of care giving—that is, within an economic justice framework' (Esquivel 2011: 230).

[19] In the section 'Methodological Challenges: The (Role) for the National Statistical Offices', Marco Navarro (2012: 23) restricts her recommendations to those that apply to exhaustive activity lists only ('restrict activity length', 'add questions on ...', 'beware of interview length'), but stated in a general way, as if they applied to all existing TUS.

[20] The Levy Economics Institute Measure of Time and Income Poverty (LIMTIP) is a valuable step towards this direction. LIMTIP measures were calculated for Mexico, Chile, and Argentina. See Antonopoulos, Zacharias, and Masterson (2012 2013).

# APPENDIX 2A

**TABLE 2A**  TUS in Latin America

| Country | Survey Title | Type of Survey and Coverage | Survey Instrument | Reference Period | Surveyed Population | Mode of data collection |
|---------|--------------|------------------------------|-------------------|------------------|---------------------|--------------------------|
| Argentina | Buenos Aires Time-use Survey 2005 | Module of the Buenos Aires annual household survey 2005; Buenos Aires City | Activity diary; 30-minute intervals with up to three activities in each one; non-hierarchical simultaneous activities. Adapted the 1997 trial ICATUS | Yesterday (4 a.m. to 4 a.m. today) | A randomly selected household member, between 15 years and 75 years of age | Face-to-face interview, self-referred, one-dairy day |
| | Rosario Time-use and Voluntary Work Survey 2010 | Standalone survey; Rosario City | Same as Buenos Aires. Further adapted the 1997 trial ICATUS to differentiate voluntary work | Yesterday (4 a.m. to 4 a.m. today) | All household members 15 years or older | Face-to-face interview, self-referred, one-dairy day |
| Bolivia | Continuous Household Survey 2001, Housework and Unpaid Work Module | Module of labour force survey; national | Short tasks list (7 housework/care tasks) | Last week (weekdays/ weekends) | All household members 7 years or older | Face-to-face interview (sometimes to key informant) |
| | Bolivia Pilot Time-use Household Survey 2010–11 | Standalone survey; national | Activity diary; 10-minute intervals with up to 2 simultaneous activities. CAUBOL, adapted CAUTAL | Predefined days | All household members 7 years or older | Face-to-face interview, self-referred, two predefined diary days |

*(Cont'd)*

**TABLE 2A**  (*Cont'd*)

| Country | Survey Title | Type of Survey and Coverage | Survey Instrument | Reference Period | Surveyed Population | Mode of data collection |
|---|---|---|---|---|---|---|
| Brazil | Brazilian Time-use Survey 2010 | Standalone survey; 5 states | Activity diary; 10-minutes interval with up to 2 simultaneous activities | Yesterday | A randomly selected household member 10 years or older | Face-to-face interview, self-referred |
| Chile | Gran Santiago Time-use Survey 2008 | Standalone survey | Activity diary; 10-minutes interval with up to 2 simultaneous activities | Yesterday | All household members 12 years or older | Face-to-face interview, self-referred |
| Colombia | 'Other Activities' Module 2007–11 | Module of the Great Integrated Household Survey (GEIH) | Short tasks list (10 tasks) | Last week | All household members 10 years or older | Face-to-face interview |
|  | National Time-use Survey 2012–13 | Standalone survey | Exhaustive activity list (93 activities) | Yesterday | All household members 10 years or older | Face-to-face interview, self-referred |
| Costa Rica | Continuous Household Survey 2004; Time-use Module | Module of labour force survey; national | Stylized diary (15 predefined activities); attempt to differentiate between childcare performed simultaneously | Yesterday except for Mondays' interviews, which referred to Saturdays and Sundays | All household members 12 years or older | Face-to-face interview (sometimes to key informant) |

| | | | | | |
|---|---|---|---|---|---|
| | Time-use Survey: Metropolitan Area (San José) 2011 (First) | Standalone survey; Great San José | Exhaustive activity list (104 activities) | Last week (weekdays/weekends) | All household members 12 years or older | Face-to-face interview, self-referred |
| Cuba | Cuban Time-use Survey 2001 | Standalone survey; 5 municipalities | Activity diary; 10-minute intervals; simultaneous activities as main and secondary. Adapted the 1997 trial ICATUS | Predefined days | All household members 15 years or older | Self-administered; two pre-defined diary days |
| Dominican Republic | Time-use Survey 1995 | Standalone; national | Activity diary; 15-minute intervals; simultaneous activities as main and secondary; 'for whom' | Yesterday (5 a.m. to 5 a.m. today) | All household members 10 years or older | Interview with adult women, plus participant observation; one-day diary |
| Ecuador | Labour Force Survey since 2003–4; Unpaid Housework Module | Permanent module of labour force survey; national | Yes/no question on housework, plus short tasks list (5 tasks) | Last week | All household members 5 years or older | Face-to-face interview (sometimes to key informant, particularly in the case of children) |

*(Cont'd)*

**TABLE 2A** (*Cont'd*)

| Country | Survey Title | Type of Survey and Coverage | Survey Instrument | Reference Period | Surveyed Population | Mode of data collection |
|---|---|---|---|---|---|---|
| | Time-use Survey 2005 | Module of labour force survey; Quito city plus 2 provinces, including rural areas | Exhaustive activity list (99 activities plus 11 tasks asked in case there are household members who are mentally or physically in need of continuous care) | Last week (weekdays/weekends) | All household members 12 years or older | Face-to-face interview, self-referred |
| | Time-use Survey 2007 | Module of labour force survey; national | Exhaustive activity list (124 activities) | Last week (weekdays/weekends) | All household members 12 years or older | Face-to-face interview, self-referred |
| | Time-use Module 2010 | Module of employment household survey; national | Reduced exhaustive activity list (34 questions) | Last week | All household members 12 years or older | Face-to-face interview |
| | Time-use Module 2012 | Module of employment household surveys; national | Reduced exhaustive activity list (34 questions) | Last week | All household members 12 years or older | Face-to-face interview |
| | Time-use Survey 2012–13 | Standalone survey; national | Exhaustive activity list, CAUTAL | Last week (weekdays/weekends) | All household members 12 years or older | Face-to-face interview, self-referred |

| El Salvador | Natural Environment and Time-use Survey 2004 | Module of a standalone specific survey; national | Stylized diary (6 productive work activities plus 24 predefined activities) | 'In a given day' | All household members 10 years or older | Face-to-face interview (sometimes to key informant) |
|---|---|---|---|---|---|---|
| | Time-use Survey 2010 | Module of household survey; national | Stylized diary (47 activities, in 13 groups) | 'In a given day' (provided that day is not a holiday) | All household members 10 years or older | Face-to-face interview |
| Guatemala | National Living Conditions Survey 2000; Time-use Module | Module of living conditions survey; national | Stylized diary (23 predefined activities); up to 3 simultaneous activities grouped in up to 4 groups | Yesterday | All household members 7 years or older | Face-to-face interview (in the case of children younger than 12 years, key informant) |
| | National Living Conditions Survey 2006; Time-use Module | Module of living conditions survey; national | Stylized diary (17 predefined activities) | Yesterday | All household members 7 years or older | Face-to-face interview (in the case of children younger than 12 years, key informant) |

*(Cont'd)*

TABLE 2A   (Cont'd)

| Country | Survey Title | Type of Survey and Coverage | Survey Instrument | Reference Period | Surveyed Population | Mode of data collection |
|---|---|---|---|---|---|---|
| | National Living Conditions Survey 2011; Time-use Module | Module of living conditions survey; national | Stylized diary (23 predefined activities, as in 2000); simultaneous activities as groups (as in 2000) | Yesterday | All household members 7 years or older | Face-to-face interview (in the case of children younger than 12 years, key informant) |
| Honduras | National Multi-purpose Household Survey 2009 | Module of a household survey; national | Short tasks list (3 housework/care tasks, plus 2 questions on education and self-care, excluding sleeping time) | Yesterday | All household members 10 years or older | Face-to-face interview, self-referred |
| Mexico | Labour, Time-use, and Contributions to Household Expenditures Survey 1996 | Module of an income and expenditure survey; national | Short tasks list (34 activities) | Last week | All household members 8 years or older | Face-to-face recall interview, self-referred |
| | Time-use Survey 1998 (results were never published) | Module of an income and expenditure survey; national | Activity diary, open time slots | Yesterday | All household members 8 years or older | Face-to-face recall interview, self-referred |

| | | | | | |
|---|---|---|---|---|---|
| Time-use Survey 2002 | Module of an income and expenditure survey; national | Exhaustive activity list (87 activities) | Last week (weekdays/weekends) | All household members 12 years or older | Face-to-face recall interview, self-referred |
| Time-use Survey 2009 | Standalone survey; national | Exhaustive activity list (76 activities); frequency of simultaneous activities, plus up to 5 combinations | Last week (weekdays/weekends) | All household members 12 years or older | Face-to-face recall interview, self-referred |
| Nicaragua  Valuing Nicaraguan Women's Work, 1995–6 | Standalone survey; national, rural/urban designed and collected by Fundación Internacional para el Desafío Económico Global (FIDEG), an independent research centre | Short tasks list (9 housework/care tasks, plus questions on household production for paid and auto-consumption work) | 'A typical day' | N.A. | N.A. |

*(Cont'd)*

**TABLE 2A** (*Cont'd*)

| Country | Survey Title | Type of Survey and Coverage | Survey Instrument | Reference Period | Surveyed Population | Mode of data collection |
|---|---|---|---|---|---|---|
|  | Living Conditions Survey 1998; Time-use Module | Module of living conditions survey; 50% of core survey coverage (national) | Stylized diary (22 predefined activities), plus 2 questions on simultaneous activities (childcare, other) | Yesterday | All household members 6 years or older | Face-to-face interview (sometimes to key informant) |
| Panama | Time-use Survey 2011 | Standalone survey; national (except province of Daren) | Exhaustive activity list (107 activities) | Last week (weekdays/ weekends) | All household members 15 years or older | Face-to-face interview; self-referred |
| Peru | Time-use Survey 2010 | Standalone survey; national | Exhaustive activity list (207 activities) | Last week (weekdays/ weekends) | All household members 12 years or older | Face-to-face interview, self-referred |
| Uruguay | Montevideo Time-use Survey 2003 | Standalone survey; Montevideo City and suburban areas | Short tasks list (housework/care tasks), plus information on household paid domestic work | Last week | Household | Face-to-face interview to he/she who is 'mainly responsible' for unpaid domestic work |

| | | | | | | |
|---|---|---|---|---|---|---|
| | Time-use Survey 2007 | Module of the continuous household survey; national | Short tasks list (32 tasks and 6 leisure activities) | Last working day; last weekend | Household | Face-to-face interview to he/she who is 'mainly responsible' for unpaid domestic work |
| | Time-use Survey 2013 | Module of the continuous household survey; national | Short tasks list (36 activities) | Yesterday | All household members 14 years or older | Face-to-face interview to he/she who is 'mainly responsible' for unpaid domestic work |
| Venezuela | Time-use Survey 2011–2 (First) | Standalone; national | Activity diary; 10-minute intervals with up to 2 simultaneous activities; on-the-spot questions on housework and care work | Yesterday | All household members 12 years or older | Face-to-face interview, self-referred |

*Source*: Author's compilation from the respective TUS data.

## REFERENCES

Aguirre, Rosario and Karina Batthyány. 2005. *Uso del tiempo y trabajo no remunerado: Encuesta en Montevideo y área metropolitana 2003*. Montevideo: UNIFEM/Universidad de la República.

Aguirre, Rosario and Fernanda Ferrari. 2014. *Las encuestas sobre uso del tiempo y trabajo no remunerado en América Latina y el Caribe. Caminos recorridos y desafíos hacia el futuro*. Serie Asuntos de Género 122, Santiago de Chile: CEPAL.

Antonopoulos, Rania, Ajit Zacharias, and Thomas Masterson. 2012. *Why Time Deficits Matter: Implications for the Measurement of Poverty*. Annandale-on-Hudson: Levy Economics Institute and United Nations Development Programme (UNDP).

———. 2013. *The Interlocking of Time and Income Deficits: Revisiting poverty measurement, informing policy responses*, part of the *Undoing Knots, Innovating for Change* series. Panama: United Nations Development Programme (UNDP)'s Regional Centre for Latin America and the Caribbean, Gender Practice Area.

Armas, Amparo, Jackeline Contreras, and Alison Vásconez. 2009. *La economía del cuidado, el trabajo no remunerado y remunerado en Ecuador*, Bogotá: Comisión de Transición hacia el Consejo de las Mujeres y la Igualdad de Género, Instituto Nacional de Estadística y Censos (INEC), AECID, and UNIFEM.

Budlender, D. 2007. 'A Critical Review of Selected Time Use Surveys', Gender and Development Programme Paper 2, United Nations Research Institute for Social Development, Geneva.

Comunidad Andina. 2012. 'Informe. II Reunión de expertos gubernamentales en encuestas del uso del tiempo de la Comunidad Andina, 11–13 de abril de 2012', Lima: Secretaría General de la Comunidad Andina.

Consejo Nacional de las Mujeres, Presidencia de la República (CONAMU). 2006. 'Encuesta de uso del tiempo en Ecuador 2005', Serie Información Estratégica II, Quito.

Departamento Administrativo Nacional de Estadística (DANE). 2013. 'Encuesta nacional de uso del tiempo (ENUT)'. Available at http://www.dane.gov.co/index.php/estadisticas-sociales/encuesta-nacional-del-uso-del-tiempo-enut, last accessed in September 2015.

Dirección General de Estadística y Censos (DIGESTYC). 2012. 'Medición del uso del tiempo en El Salvador.' San Salvador: Agosto.

Durán, M. Ángeles. 2007. 'El desafío de una innovación necesaria: el trabajo no remunerado en las economías actuales' in Rosario Aguirre (coord.) *Encuestas de uso del tiempo y trabajo no remunerado. Reunión técnica subregional*. Montevideo: UNIFEM/ PNUD/Universidad de la República.

Esquivel, Valeria. 2008. 'Time-Use Surveys in Latin America' in Valeria Esquivel, Debbie Budlender, Nancy Folbre, and Indira Hirway, 'Explorations: Time-Use Surveys in the South', *Feminist Economics*, 14(3): 107–52.

———. 2010. 'Lessons from the Buenos Aires Time Use Survey: A Methodological Assessment', in Rania Antonopoulos and Indira Hirway (eds), *Unpaid Work and the Economy: Gender, Time Use and Poverty*, pp. 181–214. New York: Palgrave-Macmillan.

———. 2011. 'Sixteen Years after Beijing: What Are the New Policy Agendas for Time-Use Data Collection?', *Feminist Economics*, 17(4): 215–38.

———. 2012. 'El cuidado infantil en las familias. Un análisis en base a la Encuesta de Uso del Tiempo de la Ciudad de Buenos Aires', in Valeria Esquivel, Elizabeth Jelin, and Eleonor Faur (eds). *Las lógicas del cuidado infantil: entre las familias, el estado y el mercado*, pp. 73–105. Buenos Aires: UNFPA/UNICEF/IDES.

Esquivel, Valeria, and Nancy Folbre. 2008. 'Introduction' in Valeria Esquivel, Debbie Budlender, Nancy Folbre, and Indira Hirway, 'Explorations: Time-Use Surveys in the South', *Feminist Economics*, 14(3): July.

Freire Delgado, Eduardo Efraín. 2011. 'Medición de trabajo no remunerado', in *Magazínib de la Gestión Estadística*, Edición Especial. Bogotá: Departamento Administrativo Nacional de Estadística (DANE).

Gama, Lara. 2010. 'A pesquisa piloto de Uso do Tempo do IBGE 2009/2010', presented at *II Seminário Internacional sobre Pesquisas de Uso do Tempo*, hosted by Instituto Brasileiro de Geografia e Estatística (IBGE), 9–10 September, Rio de Janeiro.

Ganem, Javier, Patricia Giustiniani, and Guillermo Peinado. 2012. *Los usos del tiempo en la ciudad de Rosario. Análisis económico y social*, Rosario: Editorial Foja Cero.

García Sainz, Cristina. 2005. 'Aspectos conceptuales y metodológicos de las encuestas de uso del tiempo en España', in Rosario Aguirre, Cristina García Sainz, and Cristina Carrasco (eds), *El tiempo, los tiempos, una vara de desigualdad*, pp. 35–49. Serie Mujer y Desarrollo No. 65. Santiago: Women and Development Unit, CEPAL.

Gómez Luna, Eugenia. 2010. *Directrices y referentes conceptuales para armonizar las encuestas sobre uso del tiempo en América Latina y el Caribe. Documento para discusión*, CEPAL, Grupo de Estadísticas de Género. Mexico City: Instituto Nacional de las Mujeres/INEGI/UNIFEM/CEPAL.

Instituto Nacional de Estadística (INE). 2014. 'República Oriental del Uruguay - Encuesta de Uso del Tiempo y Trabajo No Remunerado, Marzo 2013, Segunda Encuesta Nacional', Montevideo, Uruguay: INE. http://www3.ine.gub.uy/anda4/index.php/catalog/673/datafile/F2 (accessed September 2015)

Instituto Nacional de Estadística (INE) and Banco Central de Venezuela (BCV). 2011. 'I Encuesta de Uso del Tiempo', press presentation, Caracas, Venezuela.

Instituto Nacional de Estadística (INE) and Universidad de la República. 2008. *Uso del tiempo y trabajo no remunerado en el Uruguay. Módulo de la Encuesta Continua de Hogares Septiembre 2007,* Montevideo, Uruguay: INE/INMUJERES/UNIFEM/Universidad de la República/Facultad de Ciencias Sociales/Departamento de Sociología.

Instituto Nacional de Estadística, Geografía e Informática (INEGI). 2005. *Encuesta nacional sobre uso del tiempo 2002: Tabulados básicos definitivos,* Aguascalientes, México: INEGI.

———. 2010. *Informe técnico de la operación de la Encuesta Nacional sobre el Uso del Tiempo 2009, 2° Premio Regional a la Innovación Estadística,* Aguascalientes, México: INEGI.

Instituto Nacional de Estadística e Informática (INEI). 2011. *Encuesta nacional de uso del tiempo 2010, Principales resultados,* Lima, Perú: INEI and Ministerio de la Mujer y Desarrollo Social.

Instituto Nacional de Estadística y Censo (INEC). 2013. 'Informe sobre la planificación y ejecución de la Encuesta de uso del tiempo', Panama City, Panama: INEC.

Instituto Nacional de las Mujeres; (INAMU) Universidad Nacional, Instituto de Estudios Sociales en Población; Instituto Nacional de Estadística y Censos. 2012. *Encuesta de uso del tiempo en la Gran Área Metropolitana 2011: una mirada cuantitativa del trabajo invisible de las mujeres,* Colección Estadísticas de la desigualdad por género No. 5, San José: Instituto Nacional de las Mujeres; Universidad Nacional, Instituto de Estudios en Población; Instituto Nacional de Estadística y Censos.

International Research and Training Institute for the Advancement of Women (INSTRAW) and Oficina Nacional de Estadística (ONE). 1995. 'Time Use Pilot Survey for the Measurement and Evaluation of Work: Paid and Unpaid: Guidelines for Interviewers', Santo Domingo: Dominican Republic.

Leiva, Martha. 2010. 'Módulo Uso del Tiempo-EPHPM. Mayo 2009, Honduras', presented at *8° Reunión Internacional Estadísticas sobre Uso del Tiempo y Políticas Públicas,* hosted by UNIFEM/CEPAL, 30 June to 2 July, Mexico City.

Llavaneras Blanco, Masaya. 2011. 'Aproximación conceptual a la Cuenta Satélite de Hogares de Venezuela. La economía del cuidado y el trabajo no remunerado como puntos de partida', Caracas: Banco Central de Venezuela (BCV).

López, Cecilia. 2011. 'La mujer latinoamericana, su nivel de autonomía y la economía del cuidado', in *Magazín ib de la Gestión Estadística,* Edición

Especial, Bogotá: Departamento Administrativo Nacional de Estadística (DANE).

López, María de la Paz and Lucía Scuro. 2012. 'Una década de reuniones internacionales de expertas y expertos en encuestas de uso del tiempo y trabajo no remunerado', presentation for *10° Reunión Internacional de Expertas y Expertos en Encuestas de Uso del Tiempo y Trabajo no emunerado,* hosted by ONU MUJERES/CEPAL, 11–12 October, Mexico City.

Marco Navarro. Flavia. 2012. *La utilización de las encuestas de uso del tiempo en las políticas públicas,* Serie Mujer y Desarrollo No. 119 (LC/L.3557), Santiago: CEPAL.

Meléndez, Evelyn. 2011. 'Módulo del Uso del Tiempo en El Salvador 2010', presentation at *9° Reunión Internacional 'Políticas Públicas, Uso del tiempo y Economía del Cuidado: La importancia de las estadísticas nacionales',* hosted by UNIFEM/CEPAL, 29–30 August, Mexico City.

Milosavljevic, Vivian. 2006. 'Análisis de la aplicación de módulos de uso del tiempo en América Latina', presentation at *Taller Internacional sobre Cuentas Satélites de los Hogares: Género y salud—Midiendo la contribución del trabajo no remunerado de la mujer en la salud y el desarrollo,* hosted by the Pan-American Health Organization (PAHO) and CEPAL, 5–6 June, Santiago, Chile.

Milosavljevic, Vivian and Odette Tacla. 2007. 'Incorporando un módulo de uso del tiempo a las encuestas de hogares: restricciones y potencialidades', Serie Mujer y Desarrollo 83, Unidad Mujer y Desarrollo, CEPAL, Santiago.

Miranda, Brenda. 2011. 'Medición del Uso del Tiempo a través de la Encuesta Nacional de Condiciones de Vida (ENCOVI)', presentation at *9° Reunión Internacional 'Políticas Públicas, Uso del tiempo y Economía del Cuidado: La importancia de las estadísticas nacionales',* hosted by UNIFEM/CEPAL, 29–30 August, Mexico City.

Montaño, Sonia. 2011. 'Measurement of Total Working Time with a Gender Perspective: Development of Time-use Surveys in Latin America', presentation at the International Workshop 'Towards Harmonization of Time Use Surveys at the Global Level with Special Reference to Developing Countries', hosted by the Centre for Development Alternatives (CFDA), April, New Delhi.

Monzón, Orlando. 2012. 'La medición del trabajo no remunerado en Guatemala', presentation at *XIII Encuentro Internacional de Estadísticas de Género,* hosted by INEGI, 8–10 October, Aguascalientes.

Oficina Nacional de Estadísticas (ONE). 2002. 'Encuesta sobre el Uso del Tiempo, La Habana', Cuba: Oficina Nacional de Estadísticas.

Parker, Susana W. and Luciana Gandini. 2011. 'Cuantificación de sesgos en la contabilización del uso del tiempo a partir de metodologías de diarios y cuestionarios', Cuadernos de Trabajo No. 30, Mexico DF: Instituto Nacional de las Mujeres.

Pedrero, Mercedes. 2003. *La encuesta de uso del tiempo y sus potencialidades para conocer las inequidades de género.* Mexico City: Instituto Nacional de las Mujeres.

———. 2005. *Trabajo doméstico no remunerado en México:una estimación de su valor económico a través de la encuesta nacional sobre uso del tiempo 2002.* Mexico City: Instituto Nacional de las Mujeres.

———. 2012. 'Encuestas sobre uso del tiempo en la región de América Latina. Una mirada comparativa', presentation at *10° Reunión Internacional de Expertas y Expertos en Encuestas de Uso del Tiempo y Trabajo no emunerado,* hosted by ONU MUJERES/ CEPAL, 11–12 October, Mexico City.

Pérez Avellaneda, Alba. 2011. 'Logros y retos pendientes de la implementación de las encuestas de Uso del Tiempo en la Región para su articulación con las políticas públicas: Ecuador', presentation at *Seminario internacional. Políticas de tiempo, tiempo de las políticas (International Meeting. Policies on Time, Time for Policymaking),* hosted by CEPAL, 28–30 November, Santiago.

Rydenstam, Klas. 2011. 'Multi-country Time Use Statistics: Lessons for Developing Countries', presentation at the International Workshop 'Towards Harmonization of Time Use Surveys at the Global Level with Special Reference to Developing Countries', hosted by the Centre for Development Alternatives (CFDA), April, New Delhi.

Sandoval, Irma. 2005. 'Módulo uso del tiempo EHPM 2004 Costa Rica,' presentation at the international meeting 'Las Encuestas de Uso del Tiempo: Su diseño y aplicación', hosted by CEPAL, Santiago, 21–23 November, Chile.

———. 2012. 'Encuesta del Uso del Tiempo. Gran Área Metropolitana, Costa Rica 2011,' San José: Universidad Nacional de Costa Rica.

Tapia, Carmen. 2010. 'Producción de información estadística sobre el trabajo no remunerado del hogar y su valoración en las cuentas públicas', presentation at *II Seminário Internacional sobre Pesquisas de Uso do Tempo,* hosted by IBGE, 9–10 September, Rio de Janeiro.

United Nations Statistics Division (UNSD). 2005. *Guide to Producing Statistics on Time Use: Measuring Paid and Unpaid Work.* New York: Department of Economic and Social Affairs, United Nations.

Waring, Marilyn. 2006. 'Remarks for the International Workshop on Household Satellite Accounts', paper presented at *Taller Internacional sobre Cuentas Satélites de los Hogares: Género y salud—Midiendo la contribución del trabajo no remunerado de la mujer en la salud y el desarrollo,* Santiago, 5–6 June, Chile.

# 3 Time-use Surveys in Africa: Problems and Prospects

Jacques Charmes

Concerns for time use in Africa are not new, but they were limited to monographic studies and time devoted to agricultural tasks, for instance. By the end of the 1990s and as a result of the 1995 Beijing Conference, real concerns had emerged. A number of time-use surveys (TUS) have been carried out since 1998 at national level throughout the continent. One must also notice that the surveys of the World Bank programme of the Living Standard Measurement Study (LSMS) and the assimilated so-called 'integrated' surveys have systematically included a short set of stylized questions or a short module in their already long, multipurpose questionnaire.

The following section enumerates and describes the national experiences of the region, while the subsequent section assesses some of the problems that can be identified on the methodological side or the users' side.

## TIME-USE DATA COLLECTION IN AFRICA: PROGRESS IN THE LAST 15 YEARS

Ignoring the studies/surveys at the local level that focus primarily on agricultural works or energetic consumption, the first set of TUS ever conducted in Africa have been the LSMS-type surveys of the World Bank, which, as early as the mid-1980s, devoted a short module to the question. In some countries (such as in Ghana with the Ghana Living Standards Survey [or the GLSS] or in Guinea with the integrated survey of households), a few questions were asked about the number of persons and the number of hours dedicated to activities such as fetching of water and wood, and housekeeping activities. It is true and was recognized that water and wood fetching were quite time-consuming tasks, especially for women, and it needs to be reminded here that these activities were included in the GDP calculations even before the fourth revision of the System of National Accounts (SNA) in 1993.

Such data collection, through short modules of already long multipurpose questionnaires, has continued in the successive rounds of these surveys, and many more countries have recently introduced this set of questions in their multipurpose questionnaires, some with even more details (for instance, the Nigerian Living Standard Survey collects time data on 15 activities and the Zambian Labour Force Survey (LFS) on 22 activities). Twelve countries have been collecting such data and some of them for more than two decades (see Table 3.2, given later in the chapter). Such data would certainly deserve a systematic analysis and also, in the case of Ghana, a comparison with the results of the ad hoc TUS.

Although comparisons are difficult because of the heterogeneity of the classifications used, Ky (2013) has prepared a table for seven countries from which it appears that the time spent by women, as compared to men, in fetching water is 4.6 times more in case of Guinea; 1.4 to 1.7 times more in three countries (Malawi, Ghana, and Liberia); and as much time in two countries (Nigeria and Rwanda). In some countries, men spend more time than women in cooking (Rwanda) and in caring of children (Liberia, although for a very small time slot). In two countries, total female unpaid work exceeds male unpaid work (in typical female household chores) by only 1.2 times (Nigeria, Malawi, and Uganda). These results so dramatically diverge from the findings of specific TUS that one can legitimately question their reliability.

However, it is only at the end of the 1990s that time-use data collection—encouraged by the Beijing Platform of Action in 1995—really started on a broad scale with a national survey in Morocco in 1997–8. Unfortunately, this first attempt, although funded by the United

Nations Population Fund (UNFPA), was not gender-appropriate, as it was restricted to women's time budgets, ignoring men's. Approximately at the same time, Nigeria conducted a pilot survey, the results of which have not been published.

The second experience was carried out in Benin in 1998, where a detailed diary (with 63 activities classified as SNA and non-SNA) was attached to the survey of household activities in urban areas and to the survey of living conditions in rural areas, in order to prepare the 1998 national human development report on gender. For the first time, it was demonstrated that women's work (including extended SNA activities) exceeded men's by more than 40 per cent. The same type of survey was carried out in Madagascar in 2001 (with a diary attached to the LSMS-type Periodic Household Survey (PHS) on a sub-sample of the PHS) and in Mali in 2008 (specific survey). In these three surveys, all household members aged between 6 and 65 years were interviewed (in Mali, however, it was decided to limit the number of household members to be interviewed to six).

South Africa followed in 2000 with a national standalone survey and a detailed questionnaire accompanying the diary. Only two adults (15 years and older) were randomly selected in the sampled households. The Mauritian survey (2003) and the Tanzanian survey (2006) were of the same type, but they were attached to the multipurpose continuous household survey for the former and to the integrated LFS for the latter (Charmes 2005).

Tunisia carried out a TUS in 2005–6 (attached to the household budget-consumption survey), which could have been potentially interesting for the understanding of the 'feminization of poverty', if only this feature had been used for the analysis. Still, the Tunisian survey can be considered as a standalone survey, given that a detailed list of household members with their demographic, educational, economic and health characteristics, and other questions on volunteer work, for instance, were attached to the diary. Tunisia's Ministry for Women's Affairs published the results only in 2011.

Ghana (with the support of the United Nations Economic Commission for Africa [UNECA]) conducted its own standalone survey in 2009, the results of which were released in November 2011. Djibouti conducted its TUS in 2012, also with the support of UNECA.

Morocco and Algeria followed with their national standalone surveys in 2012 with the support of United Nations Entity for Gender Equality and the Empowerment of Women (or simply, UN Women).

Finally, three countries (South Africa, Tanzania, and Benin) conducted another TUS in 2010, 2012, and 2015 respectively, and one more country, Cameroon, carried out its first TUS in 2015.[1] Till date, 13 African countries have carried out a TUS (not including the pilot surveys in two countries). Among the TUS conducted, seven were standalone, and six were complete modules of regular household surveys.

Table 3.1 lists—by chronological order—these two types of surveys (specific/standalone surveys and complete modules of household surveys) with their main characteristics. Table 3.2 lists the 12 African countries that have included short modules on time use in selected activities in their multipurpose household surveys.

The minimal sample size (compared to the total population) is observed in Mali (0.016 per cent), Tanzania (0.026 per cent), and South Africa (0.032 per cent), and the maximum sample size in Mauritius (1.6 per cent), and Benin (2 per cent). Sampling is generally a two-stage procedure: (a) a random selection of enumerations areas (with urban/rural and/or agro-ecological zones stratification) and (b) a random selection of households (with a probability proportional to the number of households) within each selected area. Then, in the selected households, all members above a certain age are interviewed, or only two members, one female and one male, randomly selected.

The minimum age is 5 years in one country (Tanzania), 6 years in four countries (Benin, Madagascar, Mali, and Morocco), 10 years in six countries (South Africa, Mauritius, Ghana, Djibouti, Algeria, and Ethiopia) and 15 years in one country (Tunisia). The question arises of how a diary can be filled in for young boys and girls aged between 6 and 10 years without the presence and help of the mother or the person who takes care of them. Only three countries used a maximum age limit (65 years), which can be explained by the fact they were using the same methodology.

---

[1] A complete review of time-use surveys across the world was recently completed by Charmes (2015).

**TABLE 3.1** TUS and Time-use Modules in Household Surveys in Africa in Chronological Order (1998–2013)

| Country | Year(s) | Type of Survey | Sample | Survey Instruments | Mode of Data Collection | Observations |
|---|---|---|---|---|---|---|
| *Morocco* | 1997–8 | Ad hoc | 2,776 women; age 15–70 years; one per HH | Open diary | Face-to-face recall interview. One diary day | Only women interviewed |
| Benin | 1998, repeated in 2015 | TUS diary occasionally attached to a regular survey (EMICoV in 2015) | 1,787 HHs and 5,834 respondents in rural;, 1,419 HHs and 6,770 respondents in urban; age 6–65 years; 15,560 individuals in 2015 | Diary with a pre-listing of 63 activities classified as SNA and non-SNA, 15-minute time slots | Face-to-face recall interview. One diary day | Sponsored by UNDP in 1998, by GIZ in 2015 |
| *Nigeria* | 1998 | Pilot survey | 243 respondents; age 10+ years | Open diary with chronological recording of activities, starting and ending times recorded as well total number of minutes | Self-reporting and face-to-face recall interview. One diary day | Unpublished results |
| South Africa | 2000, repeated in 2010 | Standalone TUS | 8,564 HHs; 14,553 respondents; 2 individuals randomly selected in each HH; age 10+ years | Open diary, 30-minute time slot with 3 activities maximum, ICATUS classification | Face-to-face recall interview. One diary day, 3 rounds (February, June, October) | |

*(Cont'd)*

**TABLE 3.1** *(Cont'd)*

| Country | Year(s) | Type of Survey | Sample | Survey Instruments | Mode of Data Collection | Observations |
|---|---|---|---|---|---|---|
| Madagascar | 2001 | TUS, sub-sample of the permanent household survey | 2,663 HHs; 7,743 respondents; age 6–65 years | Diary with a pre-listing of 77 activities classified as SNA and non-SNA, 15-minute time slots | Face-to-face recall interview. One diary day | Sponsored by UNDP |
| Mauritius | 2003 | TUS, module occasionally attached to a continuous multipurpose survey | 6,480 HHs, 19,907 respondents, age 10+ years | ICATUS classification, 30-minute time slots | Face-to-face recall interview. One diary day, 4 quarters | |
| Tunisia | 2005–6 | TUS diary, sub-sample of the budget-consumption survey | Rotating sample, 4,261 sampled HHs, 11,594 individuals, age 15+ years | Open diary, 15-minute time slots, adapted European time-use classification | One diary for one weekend day and one for a normal week day | |
| Tanzania | 2006, Repeated in 2014 | TUS, module of the Integrated LFS (sub-sample) | 3,193 HHs, 10,553 respondents, age 5+ years | Open diary, ICATUS classification | Face-to-face recall interview. One diary day, 7 consecutive days, 4 quarters | |

| | | | | | | |
|---|---|---|---|---|---|---|
| Mali | 2008 | Standalone TUS | 680 HHs, 2,249 respondents (2 individuals per age group: 6–14, 15–49, 50–65 years) | Diary with a pre-listing of 63 activities classified as SNA and non-SNA, 15-minute time slots | Face-to-face recall interview. One diary day | |
| Ghana | 2009 | Standalone TUS | 4,800 HHs, 9,203 individuals, age 10+ years | Open diary, ICATUS classification, one-hour slot with up to 5 activities | Face-to-face recall interview. One diary day | Sponsored by UNECA Ghana Statistical Service |
| Djibouti | 2012 | TUS, module attached to the third Household Survey (EDAM III-EDETEM) | 6,250 HHs, age 10+ years | Open diary, ICATUS classification, one-hour slot with up to 5 activities | Face-to-face recall interview. One diary day | Sponsored by UNECA Not published |
| Morocco | 2011–12 | Standalone survey | Rotating sample on the entire year, 9,200 HH, with 1 male and 1 female adult randomly selected within each sampled HH and 1 child aged 6–14 years selected in 1 out of 3 selected HHs | Adapted European time-use classification, starting and end time for each activity | Self-reporting for the literate. Face-to-face-recall interview. One diary day | Sponsored by UN Women |

(Cont'd)

**TABLE 3.1** (*Cont'd*)

| Country | Year(s) | Type of Survey | Sample | Survey Instruments | Mode of Data Collection | Observations |
|---|---|---|---|---|---|---|
| Algeria | 2012 | Standalone survey | 9,015 HHs, 22,138 individuals, age 10+ years | Adapted European time-use classification, 15-minute time slot | Face-to-face recall interview. One diary day | Sponsored by UN Women |
| Ethiopia | 2013 | Standalone survey | 20,280 HHs, age 10+ years | Open diary, ICATUS classification, one–hour slot with up to 5 activities | Face-to-face recall interview. One diary day | Sponsored by UNDP |
| Cameroon | 2015 | TUS, module attached to the fourth Household Survey (ECAM) | 5,077 HHs, 12,568 individuals | Open diary, ICATUS classification | Face-to-face recall interview | |

*Source:* Respective TUS data.

*Notes:* (a) For the countries whose names are italicized, the given results cannot be used (see the 'observation' column in each case).

(b) ECAM: Enquête Camerounaise auprès des Ménages (Cameroonian Survey of Households); EDAM III EDETEM: Enquête Djiboutienne auprès des Ménages III Enquête Djiboutienne sur l'Emploi du Temps (Djiboutian Survey of Households/ Djiboutina Survey on Time Use); EMICoV: Enquête Modulaire Intégrée sur les Conditions de Vie des ménages (Modular Integrated Survey on Living Conditions of the Households); GIZ: Deutsche Gesellschaft für Internationale Zusammenarbeit (GIZ) GmbH.

**TABLE 3.2** Short Time-use Modules in Household Surveys in Africa in Chronological Order (1991-2013)

| Country | Years | Type of Survey | Sample | Survey Instruments | Mode of Data Collection |
|---|---|---|---|---|---|
| Lesotho | 2002–3 | Module of Household Budget Survey | 8,182 adults, age 15+ years | Time recorded for 12 activities | 24-hour diary with 15-minute time slots |
| Comoros | 2003 | Module of EIM | Age 7+ years | Time recorded for 8 activities | Face-to-face recall interview, last 7 days |
| Guinea | 2003 | Module of EIBEP | Age 6+ years | Time recorded for 9 activities | Face-to-face recall interview, last 7 days |
| Sierra Leone | 2003–4 | Module of SLIHS | | | |
| Malawi | 2004, 2010–11 | Module of the second Integrated Household Survey | Age 5+ years | Time recorded for water, wood, and other household chores | Face-to-face recall interview, last 7 days |
| Nigeria | 2003–4 | Module of NLSS | Age 5+ years | Time recorded for 14 activities | Face-to-face recall interview, last 7 days |
| Rwanda | 2005, 2010 | Module of EICV 2 and 3 | Age 6+ years | Time recorded for 6 activities | Face-to-face recall interview, last 7 days |
| Zambia | 2005 | Module of the LFS | 7,886 HHs, age 5+ years | Time recorded for 22 activities—SNA/non-SNA | Face-to-face interview, one diary day |
| Uganda | 2005–6 2009–10 | Module of the UNHS | 7,400 HHs: age 14–64 years | Time recorded for 4 activities (water, wood, cooking, and care) | Face-to-face recall interview, last 7 days |

*(Cont'd)*

**TABLE 3.2** (Cont'd)

| Country | Years | Type of Survey | Sample | Survey Instruments | Mode of Data Collection |
|---|---|---|---|---|---|
| Ghana | 1991–2 1998–9 2005–6 | Module of the third, fourth and fifth rounds of the GLSS | 8,687 HHs: age 7+ years among the 37, 128 members | Ad hoc classification with 8 activities. Time spent recorded | Face-to-face recall interview, last 7 days |
| Cameroon | 2007 | Module of the third Household Survey (ECAM 3) | 10,397 HHs, 1 HH out of 2, or 5,695 HHs, 21,733 individuals, age 5+ years | Time recorded for 8 activities | Face-to-face recall interview, last 7 days |
| Liberia | 2010 | Module of the LFS | 6,233 HHs: age 5+ years | Time recorded for 6 non-market activities and 7 HH activities | Face-to-face recall interview, last 7 days |

*Source:* Respective TUS data.

*Notes:* ECAM: Enquête Camerounaise auprès des Ménages (Cameroonian Survey of Households); EIBEP: Enquête Intégrée de Base pour l'évaluation de la Pauvreté (Integrated Baseline Survey for Poverty Assessment); EICV: Enquête Intégrée sur les Conditions de Vie des ménages (Integrated Household Living Conditions Survey); EIM: Enquête Intégrale auprès des Ménages (Integrated Survey of Households); NLSS: Nigerian Labour Force Survey; SLISH: Sierra Leone Integrated Household Survey; UNHS: Uganda National Household Survey.

In the first surveys (Benin, Madagascar, and Mali), the diary is broken down according to a list of 60–80 activities, simplifying the United Nations trial International Classification of Activities for Time Use Statistics (ICATUS) and in 15-minute time slots over the 24 hours of the previous day. Most of the other surveys used an open diary of a half-hour slot and, more recently, a one-hour slot, with the possibility of identifying five different activities, which is the method now recommended. Questionnaires take care of simultaneous activities, but the survey reports devote little room to them. The ICATUS is commonly used, except in North Africa where the Harmonised European Time Use Survey (HETUS) was preferred and adapted, which raises some comparability issues. One country (Morocco) did not fix a time slot in order to capture even the shortest activities, such as praying. All surveys used the face-to-face recall interviews, except Morocco and Tunisia which used self-reporting for the literate interviewees.

Most African surveys renounced to capture seasonal variations except five: South Africa (2000) organized data collection in three rounds (February, June, and October); Mauritius (2003) and Tanzania (2005) organized data collection in four quarters, and Tunisia (2005–6); and Morocco (2011–12) designed rotating samples (the sample is broken down in 12 monthly samples distributed across the country). As to the variations within the week, only one survey (Tanzania) collected data for seven consecutive days and one (Tunisia) collected data for one ordinary day and for one weekend day. All other surveys have ensured that all days of the week are equally represented.

Finally, one can note that three surveys have been funded by the United Nations Development Programme (UNDP), three have been sponsored or technically supported by UNECA, and two funded and technically supported by UN Women.

Tables 3.3 and 3.4 summarize the main findings of standalone and complete modules in household surveys, in terms of female (and male) work burden (SNA and non-SNA) illustrating the gender distribution of time in several sub-Saharan African countries (Charmes 2009, updated with data of Tanzania, Mali, Tunisia, Ghana, Algeria, and South Africa, 2010).

In the 11 countries presented in Table 3.3 and Figure 3.1, it is only in Benin (in 1998) that women are participating in economic activities (that is, within the production boundaries defined by the SNA for the

**TABLE 3.3**   Time Devoted to Economic Activity and to Work, by Gender in Nine African Countries (hours and minutes per day)

| Country | Women/Men | SNA Production | Extended SNA Production: Domestic and Care Activities | Total Work | % SNA in Total Work |
|---|---|---|---|---|---|
| Benin | Women | 4h 37m | 3h 15m | 7h 52m | 58.7 |
| (1998) | Men | 4h 26m | 1h 4m | 5h 30m | 80.6 |
| | Women/Men | 104% | 308% | 143% | 72.8 |
| South | Women | 1h 55m | 3h 48m | 5h 43m | 33.5 |
| Africa | Men | 3h 10m | 1h 15m | 4h 25m | 71.7 |
| (2000) | Women/Men | 61% | 304% | 129% | 47.0 |
| Madagascar | Women | 3h 42m | 3h 35m | 7h 17m | 50.8 |
| (2001) | Men | 5h 40m | 44m | 6h 24m | 88.5 |
| | Women/Men | 65% | 489% | 114% | 57.4 |
| Mauritius | Women | 1h 56m | 4h 37m | 6h 33m | 29.5 |
| (2003) | Men | 4h 56m | 1h 13m | 6h 9m | 80.2 |
| | Women/Men | 39% | 379% | 106% | 36.8 |
| Tunisia | Women | 1h 32m | 5h 22m | 6h 54m | 22.2 |
| (2005-06) | Men | 4h 17m | 43m | 5h | 85.7 |
| | Women/Men | 36% | 749% | 138% | 25.9 |
| Tanzania | Women | 3h 25m | 3h 33m | 6h 58m | 49.0 |
| (2007) | Men | 4h 36m | 1h 12m | 5h 48m | 79 .3 |
| | Women/Men | 74% | 296% | 120% | 61.8 |
| Mali | Women | 3h 45m | 4h 2m | 7h 47m | 48.2 |
| (2008) | Men | 5h 10m | 14m | 5h 24m | 95.8 |
| | Women/Men | 73% | 1795% | 144% | 50.3 |
| Ghana | Women | 4h 6m | 3h 29m | 7h 35m | 54.1 |
| (2009) | Men | 5h 9m | 1h 9m | 6h 18m | 81.7 |
| | Women/Men | 80% | 303% | 120% | 66.7 |
| South | Women | 2h 10m | 3h 49m | 5h 59m | 36.2 |
| Africa | Men | 3h 34m | 1h 37m | 5h 11m | 68.8 |
| (2010) | Women/Men | 61% | 236% | 115% | 52.6 |
| Algeria | Women | 30m | 5h 24m | 5h 54m | 8.4 |
| (2012) | Men | 3h 30m | 48m | 4h 18m | 81.4 |
| | Women/Men | 14% | 675% | 137% | 10.3 |
| Ethiopia | Women | 3h 20m | 4h 51m | 8h 11m | 40.7 |
| (2013) | Men | 5h 1m | 2h 5m | 7h 6m | 70.7 |
| | Women/Men | 66% | 233% | 115% | 57.4 |

*Source:* Author's calculations based on the results of respective national TUS.

**TABLE 3.4** Gender, Work, and Time Allocation in Eight African Countries (urban and rural areas)

| Country | Year | Total Work Time (minutes per day) | | Female Work Time (% of male) | Time Allocation (%) | | | | | |
| | | Women | Men | | Total Work Time | | Time Spent by Women | | Time Spent by Men | |
| | | | | | SNA Activities | Non-SNA Activities | SNA Activities | Non-SNA Activities | SNA Activities | Non-SNA Activities |
|---|---|---|---|---|---|---|---|---|---|---|
| **National** | | | | | | | | | | |
| Benin | 1998 | 478 | 339 | 141 | 67 | 33 | 58 | 42 | 81 | 19% |
| South Africa | 2000 | 343 | 265 | 129 | 48 | 52 | 34 | 66 | 72 | 28% |
| Madagascar | 2001 | 437 | 383 | 114 | 68 | 32 | 51 | 49 | 88 | 12% |
| Mauritius | 2003 | 393 | 369 | 107 | 54 | 46 | 30 | 70 | 80 | 20% |
| Tunisia | 2005–6 | 408 | 296 | 138 | 50 | 50 | 23 | 77 | 87 | 13% |
| Tanzania | 2006 | 418 | 348 | 120 | 62 | 38 | 49 | 51 | 79 | 21% |
| Mali | 2008 | 467 | 324 | 144 | 68 | 32 | 48 | 52 | 96 | 4% |
| Ghana | 2009 | 455 | 378 | 120 | 67 | 33 | 54 | 46 | 82 | 18% |
| Ethiopia | 2013 | 491 | 426 | 115 | 55 | 45 | 41 | 59 | 71 | 29% |
| **Urban** | | | | | | | | | | |
| Benin | 1998 | 428 | 323 | 133 | 64 | 36 | 55 | 45 | 79 | 21% |
| Madagascar | 2001 | 400 | 344 | 116 | 61 | 39 | 44 | 56 | 84 | 16% |
| Tunisia | 2005–6 | 387 | 290 | 133 | 62 | 38 | 20 | 80 | 87 | 13% |
| Mali | 2008 | 374 | 309 | 121 | 62 | 38 | 37 | 63 | 91 | 9% |
| Ghana | 2009 | 442 | 361 | 122 | 66 | 34 | 54 | 46 | 80 | 20% |
| Ethiopia | 2013 | 422 | 384 | 110 | 61 | 39 | 42 | 58 | 83 | 17% |

(Cont'd)

**TABLE 3.4** (*Cont'd*)

| Country | Year | Total Work Time (minutes per day) | | Female Work Time (% of male) | Total Work Time | | Time Allocation (%) | | | |
|---|---|---|---|---|---|---|---|---|---|---|
| | | | | | | | Time Spent by Women | | Time Spent by Men | |
| | | Women | Men | | SNA Activities | Non-SNA Activities | SNA Activities | Non-SNA Activities | SNA Activities | Non-SNA Activities |
| **Rural** | | | | | | | | | | |
| Benin | 1998 | 508 | 348 | 146 | 69 | 31 | 61 | 39 | 82 | 18% |
| Madagascar | 2001 | 451 | 398 | 113 | 70 | 30 | 53 | 47 | 90 | 10% |
| Tunisia | 2005–6 | 448 | 310 | 145 | 51 | 49 | 26 | 74 | 86 | 14% |
| Mali | 2008 | 508 | 340 | 149 | 69 | 31 | 52 | 48 | 96 | 4% |
| Ghana | 2009 | 469 | 396 | 118 | 67 | 33 | 54 | 46 | 83 | 17% |
| Ethiopia | 2013 | 510 | 437 | 117 | 53 | 47 | 40 | 60 | 68 | 32% |

*Source:* Author's calculations based on the results of the respective national TUS.

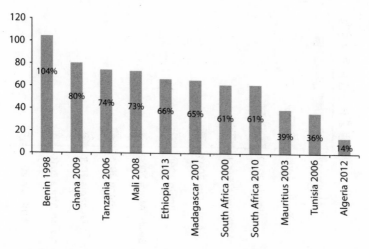

**FIGURE 3.1** SNA Production of Women and Men (%)
*Source:* Based on Table 3.3.

measurement of GDP) as much as men (and even a little bit more): 4 hours 37 minutes per day against 4 hours and 26 minutes per day for men (or 104 per cent). In the other 10 countries, the participation of women in SNA economic activities is far lower: from 80 per cent of men's time in Ghana (2009), 74 per cent in Tanzania (2006), 73 per cent in Mali (2008), 66 per cent in Ethiopia (2013), 65 per cent in Madagascar (2001), 61 per cent in South Africa (2000), down to 39 per cent in Mauritius (2003), 36 per cent in Tunisia (2005–6) and only 14 per cent in Algeria (2012).

However, it is in the contribution to domestic activities and care work (corresponding to the general production boundary in the SNA) that the differences in statuses and roles become most striking. According to Table 3.3 and Figure 3.2, women's contribution is three times higher than men's in Tanzania, Ghana, South Africa, Ethiopia, and Benin; 3.8 times in Mauritius; 4.9 times in Madagascar; up to 7.5 times in Tunisia and 18 times in Mali. This implies that of the 11 countries, Mali is the one where the status of women has remained the most embedded in customs and religion.

Regarding total work (Table 3.3 and Figure 3.3), Benin, Mali, Ghana, and Ethiopia are the four countries where the burden of women is the

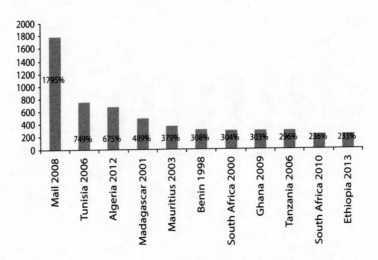

**FIGURE 3.2**  Extended SNA Production of Women and Men (%)
*Source*: Based on Table 3.3.

heaviest, with 7–8 work hours per day; in South Africa and Algeria, it is least heavy, with 5–6 work hours per day. However, the workday is around 7–8 hours for women in 7 countries (Benin, Mali, Ghana, Madagascar, Tanzania, Ethiopia, and Tunisia), whereas it is around or

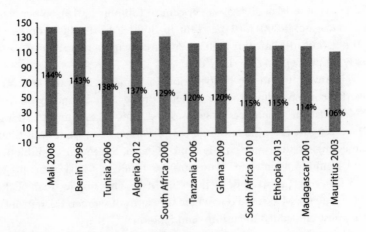

**FIGURE 3.3**  Total Work: Women/Men (%)
*Source*: Based on Table 3.3.

above 6 hours for men in 4 countries only (Mauritius, Ghana, Ethiopia, and Madagascar).

SNA economic activities represent between one-third (in Mauritius [30 per cent] and South Africa [34 per cent]) and one-fourth (in Tunisia [22 per cent]) of total women's work (see Table 3.4). They represent between 40 per cent and 50 per cent of total women's work in three countries (41 per cent in Ethiopia, 48 per cent in Mali, and 49 per cent in Tanzania), and more than 50 per cent of total women's work in three other countries, (51 per cent in Madagascar, 54 per cent in Ghana, and 58 per cent in Benin).

In rural areas (as shown in Table 3.4) where women's burden is generally (but not always) much higher than men's than in urban areas—146 per cent against 133 per cent in Benin, 145 per cent against 133 per cent in Tunisia, and 149 per cent against 121 per cent in Mali—the share of SNA activities in total women's work is also more important than in urban areas, but at the cost of longer hours.

Mali is exceptionally remarkable in that men's contribution to household work is nearly non-existent, with only 4 per cent of men's work time devoted to household care in rural areas and 9 per cent in urban areas. Even in Madagascar where gender inequalities are less strik-ing than in the other countries under review (wood and water fetching are more equally shared, for instance), men devote only 12 per cent of their work time to household duties. Tunisia is also remarkable by the low contribution of men to domestic and care activities (13 per cent).

When interpreting these figures, it must be kept in mind that they are averages, including all the population of all ages, all active and inactive persons. Should the analyses be restricted to the adult active population, the figures would be much higher. As a matter of fact, micro-level analyses can be conducted on the basis of TUS, given that many sub-categories of population can be distinguished, if only the sample size is large enough to allow it.

Figures 3.1, 3.2, and 3.3 represent the values of a parity index, which compares the time spent by women with the time spent by men in SNA activities that is included: in the GDP (Figure 3.1), in extended SNA activities or the unpaid work of the household production estimated in the satellite accounts (Figure 3.2), and in total work or SNA + extended SNA activities (Figure 3.3).

Regarding SNA activities (Figure 3.1), the maxima are observed in Benin (104 per cent) and in Ghana (80 per cent) and the minima in Algeria (14 per cent) and Tunisia (36 per cent). Intermediate indices are observed in South Africa (61 per cent), Madagascar (65 per cent), Mali (73 per cent), and Tanzania (74 per cent).

It is for extended SNA activities or unpaid work (Figure 3.2) that the disparities are the highest: women spend nearly 18 times more time than men in household chores and care work in Mali, nearly 7.5 times in Tunisia, and 6.7 times in Algeria. In four countries (Tanzania, Ghana, South Africa, and Benin), women spend around three times more time than men in those activities, and 3.8 times in Mauritius, and 4.9 times in Madagascar. It can be noted that the parity index has decreased between 2000 and 2010 in South Africa, in favour of women (from 3.04 to 2.36 times).

Figure 3.3 summarizes the results for the 10 African countries by adding up work time in SNA activities and in unpaid work. The total burden of women is the heaviest in Mali, Benin, Tunisia, and Algeria (with parity indices at 1.44, 1.43, 1.38, and 1.37 respectively). In all countries, women work longer hours than men.

For comparison purposes, Figure 3.4 shows the number of minutes spent in unpaid work by women and men in certain OECD countries: in average women spend approximately two times more time than men in unpaid work in the 26 countries of OECD, from 1.5 times in Norway to 3.4 times in Portugal, and 3.25 times in Turkey. China is at 2.6 and France at 1.9. On an average, disparities are much higher in Africa, where the lowest index was measured at 2.96 in Tanzania.

Table 3.5 compares the results of two surveys in Ghana: the GLSS fifth round, which is the second type of TUS (short set of questions in a multipurpose household survey) and the GTUS 2009, which is a standalone TUS. The time in minutes spent by the household members significantly diverges in the two surveys.

The comparisons are made difficult because of the characteristics of the two surveys for the following reasons:

1.  The minimum age is 7 years in the GLSS and 10 years in the GTUS.

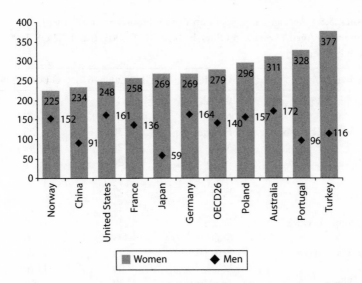

**FIGURE 3.4**   Time Spent in Unpaid Work by Women and Men in OECD
Countries (minutes)

*Source*: Organisation for Economic Co-operation and Development (OECD)
Gender Initiative, available at http://www.oecd.org/gender/data/timespentinun-
paidpaidandtotalworkbysex.htm, data accessed as of 5 April 2013.

*Notes*: (a) Countries are ordered on the increasing workload of women. (b) OECD26
represents the 26 member countries of OECD (of which only 10 are taken here).

2.   The period of the year is different: a whole year from September
     2005 to September 2006 for the GLSS, June to August 2009 for
     the GTUS.
3.   The classification is different in the two surveys.

However, these variations cannot explain the huge difference in values
and gender gaps for the two activities of 'childcare' and 'cooking'. While
females spend 2 hours and 44 minutes per day in childcare in the GTUS,
against only 16 minutes for males, the time spent as per GLSS is only
2 hours and 9 minutes, against a stark value of 1 hour and 7 minutes
for males. A possible explanation can be found in the method of data
collection: while the involved persons are responding for the day before
the survey in the GTUS 2009, proxy respondents (especially men) may
respond for the other members (especially women) and for the period

**TABLE 3.5**　Average Time Spent on Various Housekeeping Activities by Population Aged 7 Years and Older, by Sex: GLSS 2005–6 and GTUS 2009 (minutes per day)

| Activity | Gender | GLSS 2005–6 | GTUS 2009 |
|---|---|---|---|
| Fetching Water | Females | 31 | 35 |
| | Males | 23 | 27 |
| Collecting Firewood | Females | 30 | 25 |
| | Males | 25 | 42 |
| Washing Clothes | Females | 26 | N.A. |
| | Males | 17 | N.A. |
| Cleaning | Females | 27 | 22 |
| | Males | 21 | 10 |
| Running Errands | Females | 30 | 9 |
| | Males | 35 | 6 |
| Washing Dishes | Females | 24 | N.A. |
| | Males | 20 | N.A. |
| Childcare | Females | 129 | 164 |
| | Males | 67 | 16 |
| Cooking | Females | 82 | 98 |
| | Males | 46 | 27 |

*Sources*: Ghana Statistical Service (2008): GLSS fifth round; Ghana Statistical Service (2013): GTUS 2009.
*Note*: N.A. - Not available

of a week in the GLSS. Consequently men may exaggerate the time they spend in these activities and understate the time spent by women.

Another interesting observation is that the gender gap remains the same for the activity of fetching water in the two surveys, but at a higher level in the GTUS, while the gender gap is reversed for the activity of collecting firewood, where males devote more time to this activity than females in the GTUS. For these reasons, the results of short time-use modules in multi-purpose household surveys should be used with caution.

## Problems and Prospects

Time-use surveys are on the rise in Africa and the fact that the gender gaps in time use have been included as indicators of the African Gender and Development Index (AGDI) by the African Centre for

Gender and Social Development (ACGSD) of the UNECA and are applied to 12 countries (UNECA 2009) is a good news, all the more so, as 23 more countries have compiled the AGDI in the second round of this programme (2012).

As in other parts of the developing world, these surveys have to face several challenges in Africa. First, since 1998, most African surveys have been conducted without considering their usability by the policymakers and this lack of use has definitely got to change for the next generation of surveys. Second, quality concern should focus on higher response rates at an individual level and on seasonal variations. Third, the major concern of improvement of labour force statistics through time-use statistics should become a priority, especially in countries where female activity rates remain low. Fourth, harmonization issues continue to arise despite efforts made towards generalization of international classifications. Last, simultaneous activities are not given the importance they should have and their capture and analysis remain secondary. In fact, all these concerns are equally important in other regions, even though they are not always given priority.

## USEFULNESS OF TIME-USE DATA FOR POLICYMAKERS

Until now, and maybe with the exception of South Africa, economists and gender analysts have not really tried or succeeded in making data a sufficiently convincing tool for policymakers in charge of designing policy measures. Gender equality and women's empowerment are certainly not the central concerns in most African countries. Even though certain gender-based focal points have been put in place in many ministries in many countries, they have not been given the leading role they should have. The AGDI has been a positive step in this direction by generalizing the exercise of inter-ministerial committees, which have been discussing the materials collected and recognizing the measures of gender gaps in various dimensions of gender inequalities, in particular the importance and necessity of conducting TUS and the potential use of them.

Recent preparatory works for future TUS have convened all stakeholders, beyond the Ministries of Women Affairs and the National

Statistical Offices in order to sensitize all potential users of time-use statistics. These exercises show that there is still a huge lack of knowledge of what it is about and what it could be used for. By involving all stakeholders in the preparation of the surveys and the design of their questionnaires, statistical agencies pave the way for a better use of TUS findings by policymakers. Such better understanding of the potential uses of TUS is all the more important so that countries that have conducted a TUS are now willing to repeat it. Future projects in this area should then be accompanied by a sound and sustained component of dissemination and communication, likely to be translated into political commitment.

## Quality in Terms of Response Rates and Seasonal Variations

As all other household surveys, TUS publish and provide details about response rates of sampled households. In this regard, they are not facing higher non-response rates than other household surveys. But TUS (and this is not only the case in Africa) rarely explicit non-response rates for individuals and even more rarely explain to which extent the individual non-response rate impacts the characteristics of the surveyed population.

It has already been stressed that the diaries do not allow proxy respondents to fill the questionnaires, given the details and precisions required. Consequently, the quality of responses is higher than in other household surveys where proxy responses are widely used. But the downside of this advantage is the risk of high non-response rates. In a typical LFS or living conditions survey, the interviewer tries to fill the questionnaire with the person most likely to be aware of all the characteristics of the household and of its members, in general the household head or his spouse, and the interviewer will come back to the household several times until he/she meets such a person.

This task is much more difficult in the case of a TUS where the interviewer has to meet each member above a certain age or each member randomly selected in the household: the risk is high that many of these persons will be absent when the interviewer visits the household and after several unsuccessful visits, the member will be replaced by another one or treated as a non-respondent. Consequently, the missing categories of the sampled population are likely to be the persons who are usually at work or away from home during daytime and there is a risk of underrepresentation of employed adult males or a concentration of them during weekends. The right way of dealing with this issue would be to present a table of the distribution of characteristics (gender, age group, work status, etc.) of the sampled population according to the household members section of the questionnaire and a table of the same characteristics of the sample for the diaries. Few TUS, if any, have made such tables available, and not only in Africa. Yet, too large distortions would require an adjustment of the sample.

Seasonal variations are another issue to be dealt with. Among the standalone surveys, Tunisia (2005–6) and Morocco (2011-12) were based on rotating samples or samples distributed across the country for each month of the year. Surveys conducted in South Africa (2000), Mauritius (2003), and Tanzania (2006) organized the data collection in three rounds over the year for the first country and in four quarters for the two others. However, South Africa gave up the three rounds in its 2010 survey, which was conducted during the fourth quarter.

In the case of complete time-use modules attached to another household survey (living conditions, labour force, or multipurpose), the capture of seasonal variations is tightly related to the methodology of the household survey—four quarters in Mauritius (2003) and in Tanzania (2006). In all other countries, the period of the survey was limited to the period of data collection and seasonal variations were not taken into account, neither for time use nor for any other variable. Efforts should be made in this regard, but they are dependent on the financial resources available.

## Use of Time-use Data for Improving Labour Force Statistics

Although female labour participation rates are rather high in sub-Saharan Africa, the measurement of female activities is an important issue, especially in Northern African countries, where female participation rates are among the lowest in the world (with countries of Western

**TABLE 3.6** Labour Force Participation Rates of Population Aged 15 Years and Above (%), 2010

| Regions | Both Sexes | Male | Female |
|---|---|---|---|
| World | 64.1 | 77.2 | 51.2 |
| Africa | 65.1 | 75.6 | 54.9 |
| Asia | 64.8 | 79.8 | 49.3 |
| Europe | 58.5 | 66.2 | 51.6 |
| Latin America and Caribbean | 66.2 | 79.8 | 53.2 |
| Northern America | 64.0 | 70.3 | 57.9 |
| Northern Africa | 49.0 | 74.2 | 24.2 |
| Western Asia | 51.1 | 72.9 | 27.5 |
| South Central Asia | 56.8 | 80.7 | 31.8 |

*Source*: ILO (2013), Economically-active population estimates and projections 1990–2020, http://laborsta.ilo.org/applv8/data/EAPEP/eapep_E.html, accessed in 2011.

Asia and South-Central Asia) as the data in the grey highlighted part of Table 3.6 shows.

Moreover, even in countries where female participation rates are among the highest (Benin, Ghana), findings of the TUS clearly show that female activities as well as male activities are underestimated in LFS. Table 3.7 shows that 19 per cent of the inactive females (according to the section of the questionnaire on employment) and as many of the inactive males were engaged in some kinds of activities in the formal sector (work for corporations, non-profit institutions, or government) for nearly 2 hours per day (110 minutes for females, 107 minutes for males). Similarly, 66 per cent of the inactive females were performing some kinds of activities in primary production (1.5 hours), 15 per cent in non-primary production for more than 4 hours (276 minutes) per day, 7 per cent in construction activities for nearly one hour (58 minutes), and finally 25 per cent in provision of services for income, for approximately 4 hours per day (221 minutes for females). As for males, they were 72 per cent among the inactive to perform some activities in primary production (for 2.5 hours), 7 per cent in non-primary production (for more than 3 hours—219 minutes exactly—per day), 7 per cent in construction activities (for nearly 4 hours or 223 minutes), and 16 per cent in provision of services for income for nearly 4 hours (216 minutes).

**TABLE 3.7** Participation Rate, Time Spent by Persons Involved, and Average Time Spent in Various SNA Activities, for Population Aged 10 Years and Older by Work Status in Ghana (2009)

| Attributes | Work for Corporations/Quasi corporations, Non-profit Institutions and Government (formal sector work) | | Work for Household in Primary Production Activities | | Work for Household in Non-primary Production Activities | | Work for Household in Construction Activities | | Work for Household Providing Services for Income | |
|---|---|---|---|---|---|---|---|---|---|---|
| | Male | Female | Male | Female | Male | Female | Male | Female | Male | Female |
| **Participation Rates (%)** | | | | | | | | | | |
| **Total** | **22** | **18** | **69** | **62** | **10** | **20** | **4** | **3** | **25** | **39** |
| Employed | 23 | 17 | 69 | 62 | 11 | 21 | 4 | 2 | 27 | 42 |
| Unemployed | 9 | 36 | 52 | 57 | 25 | 11 | 7 | 4 | 25 | 27 |
| Not economically active | 19 | 19 | 72 | 66 | 7 | 15 | 7 | 7 | 16 | 25 |
| **Time Spent by Persons Involved** | | | | | | | | | | |
| **Total** | **412** | **228** | **367** | **250** | **351** | **327** | **379** | **67** | **412** | **384** |
| Employed | 454 | 269 | 419 | 288 | 388 | 339 | 426 | 83 | 437 | 405 |
| Unemployed | 228 | 49 | 255 | 132 | 214 | 53 | 89 | 45 | 245 | 147 |
| Not economically active | 107 | 110 | 148 | 99 | 219 | 276 | 223 | 58 | 216 | 221 |
| **Average Time (minutes)** | | | | | | | | | | |
| **Total** | **65** | **23** | **121** | **70** | **21** | **33** | **10** | **1** | **71** | **103** |
| Employed | 95 | 31 | 167 | 96 | 28 | 44 | 14 | 1 | 100 | 147 |
| Unemployed | 9 | 5 | 28 | 15 | 15 | 1 | 1 | 1 | 18 | 8 |
| Not economically active | 7 | 7 | 32 | 18 | 8 | 14 | 4 | 2 | 14 | 21 |

*Source:* Ghana Statistical Service (2012), GTUS 2009.

The unemployed also filled diaries showing that they were active in the formal sector: 36 per cent of the unemployed females and 9 per cent of males for 110 and 107 minutes respectively per day; 57 per cent of the unemployed females were working in primary production (for more than 2 hours or 132 minutes), 11 per cent in non-primary production (for nearly 1.5 hours), and 27 per cent in provision of services for income (for nearly 2.5 hours or 147 minutes). For males this breakup was as follows: 52 per cent in primary production (more than 4 hours or 245 minutes), 25 per cent in non-primary production (nearly one hour), and 25 per cent in provision of services for income (for more than 4 hours or 245 minutes). At the macro-economic level, on multiplying the average time in minutes by 365 days per year and by the number of the inactive and of the unemployed, the result is far from negligible, all the more so, as these corrections are dealing with the SNA production boundary and not with the general production boundary.

However, the comparisons between time-use data and labour force data raise some difficulties in terms of concepts, periods, and classifications (Charmes 2011). In particular, the ICATUS does not allow a re-classification of the unemployed and the inactive who have actually worked during the period of the survey, unless the questionnaires provide for the capture of the detailed industry, occupation, and status in employment.

## Harmonization in Concepts and Survey Methods as well as Tabulation of Data

Most sub-Saharan countries have adopted the ICATUS with the notable exception of Northern African countries, which preferred an adaptation of the HETUS. Although the comparisons between the two classifications are made easier by a special table, one can regret such a divergence, all the more so, as many female productive activities, which are usually underestimated by LFS in these countries (see Table 3.6) are classified in the HETUS as belonging to the extended non-SNA productive work (introducing confusion, for example, between animal husbandry of cows or sheep and caring of pets, or occasionally preparing cakes and pastries, and a more regular and traditional activity in this domain).

With the support of the ACGSD of UNECA, harmonization is recommended in terms of the adoption and adaptation of the ICATUS, but also of other classifications, such as age groupings, composition of households, and, furthermore, tabulations in order to make international comparisons easier. Also, most countries are adopting a harmonized diary with 4–5 activities each for one-hour slots, with complementary contextual questions (with whom, for whom, and where) facilitating the classification of the activity.

A special mention needs to be made of the absence of harmonization of time-use activities in the short modules included in the multipurpose household surveys, which certainly could allow data collection on a large scale and through time series, but that, as they stand now, are rather misleading and unreliable.

## Simultaneous Activities

In many aspects, the capture of simultaneous activities seems to be neglected and remains to be treated seriously, in order to be used for advocacy purposes (in terms of intensity or overburden, for example). Not many tables (in certain cases, none at all), are devoted to simultaneous activities in the survey reports, probably because of an absence of reliability in the findings. While simultaneous activities are widespread, the recorded number of hours is generally small, and sometimes in unexpected sectors of activity. For instance, it is in primary production activities that simultaneous activities are the most frequent in Ghana (2009): while minding the herd, the shepherd can simultaneously cut grass or fetch firewood to bring back home. But few care activities were recorded simultaneously with other domestic duties. Probing questions asked after the diary is filled are generalized in order to come back, check, and complete the diary, if necessary. But one wonders whether columns should be added to the diary to systematize a question on simultaneous activities for each recorded principal activity.

The decade of the 2010s will probably be a decade of intense data collection on time use in Africa, with new surveys in many countries and repetition of TUS in a certain number of countries. This is not surprising given the intense efforts of UNECA, through both the ACGSD and the African Center for Statistics The ACGSD has conducted a programme on TUS and the elaboration of satellite accounts of household production, gender budgets and gender-aware modelling (UNECA 2004b), and designed in parallel the AGDI as a tool that makes use of TUS data (UNECA 2004a, 2009), while the ACS prepared a compendium of gender statistics (Charmes 2012) and a toolkit for gender statistics, emphasizing and encouraging the leading role of national statistical offices (NSOs) in producing and disseminating gender-disaggregated data and supporting gender focal points in line ministries. Contrary to the previous decade, it can be taken for granted that African TUS will lead to national time accounts and detailed satellite accounts of household production as well as gender-aware modelling. Policymakers should then be more sensitive to the challenges towards gender equality and empowerment of women and more open to designing policy measures to these aims.

## REFERENCES

Central Statistical Agency. 2014. *How Women and Men Spend Their Time, Ethiopian Time Use Survey 2013, Main Report.* Addis Ababa: Central Statistical Agency.

Charmes, Jacques. 2005. 'Gender and Time Poverty in Sub-Saharan Africa, A Review of Empirical Evidence', in M. Blackden and Q. Wodon (eds), *Gender, Time-Use and Poverty in Sub-Saharan Africa,* pp. 39–72, World Bank Working Paper no. 73, Washington (pp. 39–72).

———. 2009. 'Issues in Time-Use Measurement and Valuation: Lessons from African Experience on Technical and Analytical Issues' in Rania Antonopoulos and Indira Hirway (eds), *Unpaid Work and the Economy: Gender, Time-Use and Poverty in Developing Countries.* London: Palgrave-Macmillan.

———. 2011. 'Understanding Informal Employment Through Time-Use Surveys', paper presented at the international workshop 'Towards Harmonization of Time Use Surveys at the Global Level with Special Reference to Developing Countries' , 6–8 April 2011, Delhi.

———. 2012. *Compendium of Gender Statistics in Africa,* UNECA, African Centre of Statistics.

———. 2015. 'Time Use Across The World: Findings of a World Compilation of Time-Use Surveys', background paper for the *Human Development Report 2015*, UNDP/HDRO, New York.

Ghana Statistical Service (GSS). 2008. *Ghana Living Standard Survey, Report of the 5th Round (GLSS 5)*, Accra: GSS.

———. 2012. 'How Ghanaian Women and Men Spend their Time', *Ghana Time-Use Survey 2009*, Main Report. Accra: GSS-UNECA.

INSAE/PNUD. 1998. *Enquête emploi du temps au Bénin, Méthodologie et resultants* (Time use survey in Benin, Methodology and Results), Cotonou.

INSTAT. 2001. *EPM 2001 Module Emploi du Temps* (Periodical Survey of Households, Time Use Module), Antananarivo, INSTAT-DSM/PNUD-MAG/97/007.

———. 2009. *Rapport de l'enquête malienne sur l'utilisation du temps (EMUT 2008)* (Report of Time Use Survey of Mali), Bamako.

Ky, Barbara. 2013. *Time Use Surveys in Africa, Assessment and Policy Recommendations*. Addis Ababa: UNECA-ACGSD.

Office National des Statistiques. 2013. *Enquête Nationale Emploi du Temps ENET 2012* (National Survey on Time Use). Alger: Office National des Statistiques.

République Tunisienne, Ministère des Affaires de la Femme. 2011. *Budget temps des femmes et des hommes en Tunisie, 2005–06* (Time Budget of Women and Men in Tunisia). Tunis: République Tunisienne.

Republic of Mauritius, Central Statistics Office. 2004. *Continuous Multi-Purpose Household Survey 2003*, main Results of the time-use study. Mauritius: Republic of Mauritius, Central Statistics Office.

System of National Accounts (SNA). 2008. *System of National Accounts*, Commission of the European Communities, IMF, OECD, UN, WB.

Statistics South Africa (SSA). 2001. *How South African Women and Men Spend Their Time, A Survey of Time Use*. Pretoria: SSA.

———. 2013. *A Survey of Time Use 2010*. Pretoria: SSA.

Uganda Bureau of Statistics. 2006. *Uganda National Household Survey 2005–06, Report of the Socio-Economic Module*. Kampala: Uganda Bureau of Statistics.

United Nations Development Programme (UNDP). 2008. *Human Development Report*. New York: UNDP.

United Nations Economic Commission for Africa (UNECA). 2004a. *The African Gender and Development Index (AGDI)*. Addis Ababa: UNECA.

———. 2004b. *A Guidebook For Mainstreaming Gender Perspectives and Household Production into National Statistics, Budgets and Policies in Africa*. Addis Ababa: UNECA.

———. 2009. *African Women Report 2009*. Addis Ababa: UNECA.

United Republic of Tanzania, National Bureau of Statistics. 2007. *Analytical Report for Integrated Labour Force Survey ILFS 2006*. Dar es Salaam: National Bureau of Statistics.

# 4 Measurement of Total Working Time with a Gender Perspective

## *Development of Time-use Surveys in Latin America*

Sonia Montaño[*]

Time-use surveys (TUS) have come a long way in a short period in Latin America. A number of countries, or at least representatives from governments and civil society, went to Beijing indicating the progress made. Of particular interest was the Italian survey, which was widely distributed there: it inspired the significant enthusiasm towards the measurement of what was considered the fundamental basis of gender discrimination. It was now possible to understand and validate the sexual division of labour through the surveys that would contribute information for better policymaking.

It took Latin America longer than Europe to incorporate and make progress with gender policies and TUS because the road towards recognizing women's rights was slower to navigate. Even though this recognition started globally with a social movement in the 1960s, with

[*] The source document of this chapter has been written in collaboration with Vivian Milosavljevic, Paulina Pavez, Ana Ferigra Stafanovic, Alvaro Zapata, and Patricio Olivera. The views expressed in this chapter are those of the author and do not necessarily reflect the views of the Economic Commission for Latin America and the Caribbean (ECLAC).

the exception of Brazil that was a pioneer in the region (Montaño, Pitanguy, and Lobos 2003), it was not until the 1990s that governments took action.

When countries started to develop policies, these policies dealt mainly with poverty and democracy issues. Social protection was not even talked about. The notion of welfare states was unimaginable and not part of the political agenda. Latin America's most significant contribution addressed democratic issues and women's political representation. It is around the regional processes, which were inspired by Beijing, and particularly with the 11 Regional Conferences on Women in Latin America and the Caribbean (or RCWLAC),[1] that the issue of unpaid work, its measurement, and its incorporation into public policies by governments began to develop.

A turning point was the adoption of the Quito Consensus at the tenth RCWLAC (Quito, Ecuador, 6–9 August 2007), which recognized parity as 'one of the key driving forces of democracy, that its aim is to achieve equality in the exercise of power, in decision-making, in mechanisms of social and political participation and representation, in diverse types of family relations, and in social, economic, political, and cultural relations, and that it constitutes a goal for the eradication of women's structural exclusion' (Economic Commission for Latin America and the Caribbean [ECLAC] 2007: 3).

In this context, in many countries of Latin America and the Caribbean, policymaking has become a matter of social concern and an object of institutional reforms to promote informed participation by citizens in decision-making, to anticipate risks through timely analysis of social processes, and to strengthen confidence in public institutions. In the area of gender policy, a number of countries have combined the need for the gender perspective to be mainstreamed with efforts to create systems for accountability and transparency in policy execution. To this end, in the Quito Consensus, the ECLAC member states, together

---

[1] http://www.eclac.cl/mujer/conferencia/default.asp, last accessed on 8 July 2016. The Regional Conference is a subsidiary body of ECLAC that convenes regularly to identify regional needs. Governmental representatives meet every three years to present recommendations and undertake periodic assessment of activities carried out in compliance with the international agreements.

with other organizations in the UN system, requested the Commission to 'collaborate with member States that request them to do so in following up on the fulfilment of the agreements that have been adopted through the creation of a gender equality observatory that will help strengthen national gender mechanisms'.

The Gender Equality Observatory,[2] which was created under the coordination of ECLAC, was conceived as a tool to support governments in analysing regional realities, monitoring gender policy and international agreements, and providing technical support and training to national mechanisms for the advancement of women and to national statistical agencies in countries that request such aid.

Data from TUS in Mexico and Ecuador confirm the hypothesis that women's participation in anti-poverty cash transfer programmes increases the time that women spend in doing unpaid work. Interaction to poverty refers to the fact that, poor women devote a large part of their time to unpaid work which consists of caring for others, keeping a house, and activities associated with the day-to-day reproduction of the family. Rural women also often add food production to this burden. Conversely, men devote most of their time to paid work and very little to unpaid work.

Independent TUS are considered the most appropriate source of information to construct the indicators for showing the uneven distribution of time between men and women. Nonetheless, while there has been extensive promotion and dissemination of the importance of TUS, the number of independent surveys that have actually been carried out in the region[3] and the quality of these surveys are still negligible. Till date, the experiences of Ecuador, Mexico, and Uruguay stand out. Due to institutional considerations and scarce resources available, many countries have instead opted for a module on time use as part of regular household surveys. While this is considered to be a more minimalist approach that does not allow for the same level of analysis, it has permitted more countries to reach the principal objective of measuring women's unpaid work. Of key importance is the

---

[2] http://www.eclac.org/oig/, last accessed on 8 July 2016.

[3] Between 1998 and 2012, 18 out of 33 countries of Latin America and the Caribbean have undertaken an activity to measure time use from a gender perspective.

need to ensure that efforts to measure time use are fully integrated into national statistics and are undertaken with a certain periodicity that allows for comparison across time.

In practice, efforts to measure time use that have been carried out to date are incomplete. They have not incorporated all of the activities that define and cover unpaid work and the amount of time people spend doing various activities, such as household activities, childcare, volunteering, and personal work. This problem is further compounded by the difficulty of including additional questions at relevant times and maximize response rates, in the meantime, within a tight budget.

Producers of information on time use are confronted with big challenges. They lack a sufficient conceptual understanding of issues and face a rigorous methodological challenge under tremendous pressure. They have a very limited budget and little understanding of how to incorporate a gender perspective in collecting information. They also lack models or prototypes to follow that are similar in circumstances to the reality of their country. This problem is faced by most of the statistical systems in the region, where there are too many variables to fit into an equation, making it difficult to reach a common solution. Agencies of UN, specialists in the field, and other experts have held many meetings, training seminars, and technical assistance and horizontal cooperation missions; prepared publications; and promoted other actions with and between countries in order to propose guidelines for action and standardization and to refine the measurement objective for defining the key indicator that guides the entire research process.

The key indicator for measuring the working time from a gender perspective is defined as: Total working time = time for paid work + time for unpaid domestic work. This simple expression implies recognition of household activities as work and requires a clear specification of the nature of each daily activity, avoiding overlap, and delimiting its expression in such a way that each activity is present in a hierarchical order within a systematized conceptual framework. This requires a time-use classification of activities that is appropriate to the regional settings and, at the same time, adaptable to the countries of the region.

In 2015, the Conference of Statisticians adapted the Classification of Time-use Activities for Latin America and the Caribbean (CAUTAL), which was developed by Maria Eugenia Gómez Luna in 2009.[4] CAUTAL, with its identification and definition of key indicators, together with all the experience and recommendations that have been collected in order to carry out TUS, will expand opportunities in the region so that in the near future, surveys become harmonized and indicators comparable among countries.

The present chapter aims at describing a part of this process by presenting the state of the art of measurement through TUS and other means and identifying the main differences which present challenges for comparability between countries at present. In addition, it gives attention to the activities and process that are followed in proposing and developing a classification of time use adapted to the realities in Latin America, which aims towards comparability between countries.

The second section of this chapter presents some of the trends that emerge from an analysis of efforts to measure time use in the region, and thus aims at addressing the most common concerns of users and producers of statistics regarding the analysis of the data once results of the surveys are obtained, and their usefulness in giving visibility to gender inequalities in this area.

As noted earlier, the surveys carried out till date are not comparable in design, implementation, and processing of information, thereby making it impossible to compare the magnitudes between countries. Nonetheless, the indicators calculated from a common analysis plan show a high coincidence in behaviour patterns of women and men facing certain situations, which illustrates the potential of this information and its essential character for guiding public policy.

## MEASURING TIME USE IN LATIN AMERICA AND THE CARIBBEAN

The value of measuring time use, to clarify and, in a quantitative way, render visible the unequal distribution of work that affects both men and women, is unquestionable. Regional and international conferences

---

[4] See  http://repositorio.cepal.org/bitstream/handle/11362/39260/S150 1054_es.pdf?sequence=1&isAllowed=y, last accessed on 8 July 2016. See the section 'Measuring Time Use in Latin America and the Caribbean' for a more elaborate discussion of the formation of CAUTAL.

repeatedly highlight the usefulness of this source and call on national statistical institutes to measure the time spent by women and men on work as well as on other activities in the domestic sphere, including care activities. A significant number of countries in Latin America have collected information on time use, in accordance with recommendations and mandates of the international and Regional Conferences on Women in Latin America and the Caribbean. Between 1998 and 2012, at least 18 countries took one or more measurement initiatives (which are summarized in Table 4.1).

These countries have employed various methods and instruments to collect information. One modality for collecting information on time use is through the use of a diary where all the activities carried out during the day are recorded in chronological order, specifying in each case, whether the activity was carried out in conjunction with another activity (so as to capture simultaneous activities), identifying where the activity took place (that is, within or outside the home), and whether others (member of household or other) were involved, etc., whereby the diary is filled out by the respondent. Another way has been to incorporate a general question, or a set of questions on time invested in domestic work, in the household surveys. Nonetheless, the most widely used methodology has been to add a module on time use to multipurpose household surveys already in existence. Thus, there has been an attempt to configure an estimate of time dedicated to household and care work through a limited number of questions.

These initiatives to measure time have shown gender gaps in the distribution, demonstrating empirically the difficulties that women face in reconciling participation in economic life and the labour market with family responsibilities. This shows that men, in general, do not have a significant presence in household and care activities, and that the factors affecting the time utilized by women generally are not the same as those impacting men's behaviour.

The lack of comparability between the surveys carried out is evident in aspects, such as the reference time, the age of the interviewee, the type of questionnaire used, the recording of simultaneous activities, the breakdown of activities or thematic coverage, the length of the questionnaire, geographic coverage, and other methodological issues related to field work and the subsequent treatment for consistency and validation of the results. Furthermore, the greatest challenge in

**TABLE 4.1** Overview of Efforts to Measure Time Use in Latin America and the Caribbean

| Country | Latest Year of Survey | Geographic Coverage | Executing Institution | Type of Survey | Instrument | Period | Sample | Previous Experiences |
|---|---|---|---|---|---|---|---|---|
| Argentina | 2010 | 1 state | Universidad Nacional de Rosario | Independent | Diary | Day | 1,000 HHs | 2005 (Buenos Aires) |
| Bolivia, Plurinational State of | 2010–11 (pilots) | National | INE | | Diary (10 mins) | Day | 5,744 HHs | 2001 (Module) |
| Brazil | 2011 | National | IBGE | Questionnaire | | Week | | 2001, 2005, 2008 2009–10, Pilot TUS in 5 states |
| Chile | 2009 | Metropolitan area | INE | Independent | Diary (30 mins) | Day | 1,571 HHs | |
| Colombia | 2012 | National | DANE | Independent | List of activities | Week | 54,000 surveys | 2007, 2008, 2009, 2010 Module in National Household Survey |
| Costa Rica | 2011 | Metropolitan area | INEC/UNA/ INAMU | Independent | List of activities | Week | 2,520 HHs | 2004 pilot TUS |
| Cuba | 2001 | 5 states | ONE | Independent | | Day | 2,520 HHs and 6,469 persons | |

| Country | Year | Coverage | Institution | Type | Method | Period | Sample | Previous surveys |
|---|---|---|---|---|---|---|---|---|
| Dominican Republic | 2007 | National | CESDEM | Module | List of activities | | 32,431 HHs; 27,195 women; 27,975 men | 2006 |
| Ecuador | 2012 | National | INEC | Independent | List of activities | Week | 22,968 HHs | 2005, 2007, 2010 (TUS) 2011 (Questions in Labour Force survey) |
| El Salvador | 2011 | National | DIGESTYC | Module | List of activities | Day | 3,728 HHs | 2005 |
| Guatemala | 2011 | National | INE | Module | List of activities | Day | 14,337 HHs | 2000, 2006 |
| Honduras | 2011 | National | INE | Module | List of activities | Day | 21,330 HHs | 2009 (Module) |
| Mexico | 2009 | National | INEGI/ INMUJERES | Independent | List of activities | Week | 17,000 HHs | 1996 (TUS), 1998 (TUS), 2002, 2010 (Module) |
| Nicaragua | 1998 | 7 macro areas | INEC | Module | List of activities | Day | 2,325 HHs | |
| Panama | 2011 | National— urban | INEC | Independent | List of activities | Week | 3,720 HHs | 2006 (Module) |
| Peru | 2010 | National | INEI | Independent | List of activities | Week | 4,580 HHs | 2006 |
| Uruguay | 2007 | National | INE | Module | List of activities | Week | 4,100 HHs and 8,973 persons | 2003 (TUS in metropolitan area) |
| Venezuela, Bolivarian Republic of | 2011 | National | INE | Independent | Diary | Day | 10,500 HHs and 32,500 persons | 2008 |

*Source*: ECLAC, prepared by the author on the basis of TUS or modules within household surveys.

creating a basis for comparison is the lack of a standard classification of activities of time use to identify, enumerate, and classify in a uniform way activities in the different surveys employed.

Although many of the surveys carried out were initiated on the basis of the United Nations trial International Classification of Activities for Time-Use Statistics (ICATUS), during the process the classification was adapted to each country's reality, such as Cuba (2001), Mexico (2002), Argentina (2005), Chile (2009), Peru (2010), Brazil (2009), Venezuela (Bolivarian Republic) (2011), and Colombia (2012), with the use of fewer codes and more flexibility to record the measurement of specific objectives targeted by each country.

It is widely recognized that TUS implies a high level of complexity, with both conceptual as well as methodological aspects, while, at the same time, requiring the initiation of actions conducive to its comparability, including the common budgetary limitations that restrict carrying out of independent surveys. Various meetings have been held at the international level, such as:

1. The Annual Meeting on Time-Use Statistics, held by the Working Group on Gender Statistics, which was created in 2007 at the fourth meeting of the Statistical Conference of the Americas of the ECLAC, which serves as a mechanism for intergovernmental coordination on international statistical activities in the region. This group promotes the production, development, and systematization of statistics and gender indicators among national statistical institutes, as well as the distribution and use of the data in public policies in all the countries of the region.

2. The Annual International Statistical Meeting on Time Use, which held its tenth session in 2012, is organized by the National Women's Institute and the National Institute on Statistics and Geography of Mexico, along with UN Women and ECLAC, and has become the main forum for exchange and dissemination of experiences of TUS in the region.

Participants at these meetings include representatives of national statistical institutes as well as national women's offices, thereby allowing for dialogue between users and producers to reflect on the use of information in research and in the formulation of public policy with a gender perspective. Results of these regional efforts formed the base for the 'Guidelines to harmonize time-use surveys in Latin America and the Caribbean', from which CAUTAL has been developed.

In 2009, a technical meeting to refine the CAUTAL took place in Mexico prior to the seventh International Experts' Meeting on Time-Use Surveys. The purpose of that meeting was to respond to the needs of countries of the region for a conceptual framework and methodology, as well as for a classification to contribute to the strengthening and harmonization of surveys, statistics, and indicators on time use that have the total work time, both paid and unpaid, as a central objective. At this meeting, a group of specialists analysed accumulated regional experience on TUS, based on a working document (Gómez Luna 2009). They reviewed the conceptual and methodological highlights of these surveys, the international classification of activities on time use, the expanded conceptualization of production and work, the referential concepts and methodological guidelines to harmonize the TUS in the region, and the proposed CAUTAL. The group came up with a set of recommendations and guidelines to consolidate the proposal for a regional classification.

The trial ICATUS, which is currently being updated, remains a key international reference for TUS. Nonetheless, the latest version of the CAUTAL has a more marked dimension than the ICATUS and is specially oriented to the collection of data on time use through sample surveys, with questionnaires. Its language is simplified, it has a more synthetic and versatile structure, and while the structure of ICATUS is more extensive in its hierarchy, the CAUTAL is more limited. Table 4.2

**TABLE 4.2**     CAUTAL versus ICATUS versus Eurostat

| Aggregation Levels | Codes | CAUTAL | ICATUS | Eurostat |
| --- | --- | --- | --- | --- |
| Major divisions | Letter Codes | 3 | – | – |
| Divisions | One Digit | 9 | 10 | 10 |
| Groups | Two Digits | 28 | 54 | 31 |
| Sub-groups | Three Digits | 82 | 92 | 166 |
| Classes | Four Digits | 29 | 200 | – |
| Sub-classes | Five Digits | – | 363 | – |

*Source*: ECLAC, prepared by the author on the basis of TUS or modules within household surveys.

compares the classification schemes under CAUTAL, ICATUS, and the Eurostat (Statistical Office of the European Communities), which are used for harmonization of TUS within the European community.

## ANALYSIS OF TIME–USE SURVEYS: A CASE STUDY

This section aims to analyse the overburden of work among economically active women and the lack of time as an expression of female poverty. For the purpose of this section, female poverty is understood in the context of the following assumptions:

1. Women are not free to choose to enter the paid workforce if they have no alternatives for care and domestic activities within their households.

2. Men can delegate domestic work to their female partners, which permits them to have more options to develop professionally and opt for better wages or income. In the case of women, in order to develop professionally, they usually have to seek paid domestic help.

3. The quality of life of women is affected by the extended working day that leaves women exhausted, stressed, and depressed due to the lack of possibilities for rest, leisure time, and recreation.

4. It is impossible to remove oneself from the time required for domestic work, which, in turn, leaves women with a certain level of isolation that keeps them from establishing and participating in networks to access better jobs or participate in other activities for their personal development.

5. The adverse conditions under which women live, such as the household characteristics or restrictions they face related to social class, education, age, etc., affect them in a significant way, where they constantly have to adjust their working day, in terms of both paid activities and domestic responsibilities, to these unfavourable conditions—a problem that does not require changes in a man's working day.

6. In addition to the restrictions imposed by care responsibilities and domestic work, once women gain access to the labour market, they earn about one-third less than men.

7. The prospect of becoming independent or achieving entrepreneurship comes with a high cost in terms of hours worked, from which it is difficult to remove oneself from.

The sources of information for this study are TUS or specific questions contained in household surveys, which measure time designated to remunerated and non-remunerated activities. Specifically, we rely on data from five countries: Brazil (2011), Colombia (2011), Ecuador (2011), Mexico (2011), and Peru (2010).[5]

Additional Details:

**Unit of analysis**: Employed population, ages 15 years and above
**Unit of time**: Some countries have used the previous day or the week prior to the day of the survey as a unit of time. Brazil, Colombia, Ecuador, Mexico, and Peru have used the prior week as the unit of time. This study only analyses countries that employ the prior week as a unit of time
**Database**: Configured at the country level, to permit analysis of the variables considered between countries (and not within). Each registry corresponds to a country with the specified measurement in each category of the variables studied
**Study variables**: Condition of poverty, zone of residence, age, marital status, occupational group, presence in the household of minors under the age of 6 years, type of household, availability of water within the dwelling, access to healthcare, and electrical energy
**Comparability between countries**: There are wide variations between the surveys consulted due to a lack of comparable definitions and calculations across countries. This means that magnitudes are not based on common criteria, mainly due to an absence of a common classifier of activities, in addition to differences in definitions, units of analysis, age limit, reference period, geographical coverage, etc. Nonetheless, it is important to note that regardless of the methodology used, all the results exhibit a similar pattern of behaviour of women and men towards time allocation and their level of participation in paid

---

[5] Brazil 2011: Pesquisa Nacional por Amostra de Domicilios; Colombia 2011: Encuesta Integrada de Hogares, Departamento Administrativo Nacional de Estadística (DANE) de Colombia; Ecuador 2011: Encuesta de Empleo, Desempleo y Subempleo, Instituto Nacional de Estadística y Censos (INEC) de Ecuador; Mexico 2010: Encuesta Nacional de Ingresos y Gastos de los Hogares, (INEGI); and Peru 2010: Encuesta Nacional de Uso del Tiempo.

and unpaid work. The results suggest a level of homogeneity in the manifestations of unpaid domestic work. This forms the basis for the hypothesis and conclusions provided.

## Total Time for Paid Work and Unpaid Domestic Work

Figure 4.1 shows that in the five countries, the total work time is greater for women, which suggests a negative impact on their quality of life, and, therefore, little time for rest.

The official working day for men is greater than that of women by 13 to 20 hours weekly. Nevertheless, the time dedicated to unpaid domestic work is greater for women, with a wider difference noted. Women dedicate between 15 and 20 hours more than men on a weekly basis to unpaid domestic work. Women who wish to become entrepreneurs face a difficult situation, with the cost being strenuous working hours in order to attend to paid work and unpaid domestic work.

An analysis of the different categories of work (Figure 4.2) highlights the facts that employed women put longer working hours in terms of total time of work, an important factor that explains the

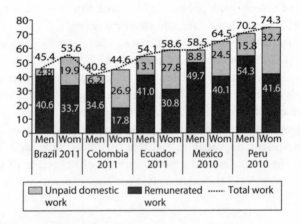

**FIGURE 4.1** Total Working Time, Paid and Unpaid Working Time, and Employed Population by Sex (population 15 years and above; time in hours per week)

*Source*: ECLAC, prepared by the author on the basis of TUS or modules within household surveys.

lower percentage of female entrepreneurship. Surveys that use the weekly work time as the unit of analysis show with little variation that women employers dedicate 44 hours per week to paid work, followed by 41 hours per week for salary earners and 34 hours per week—the shortest work day—for own-account workers. Given these circumstances, it should come as no surprise that many women carry out independent work as a way of complementing both types of works and gaining access to income. Women own-account workers are also the ones who dedicate more time to unpaid domestic work (averaging 30 hours) followed closely by unpaid family workers—the factor that influences the hours they can dedicate to paid work.

### Time Use Based on Type of Household

When there is no woman to handle domestic work, single men are faced with having to dedicate more time to these activities, as shown in Figure 4.3. On the other hand, women who live in households with more members are more likely to bear the burden and dedicate more time to domestic work.

Without exception, it is the women who live in two-parent households that dedicate more time to domestic work. In single-parent households and extended households, similar averages and variations are observed. Unlike men, women who live alone (as compared to other women) dedicate less time to domestic work, given that they have only to care for one person. However, the differential range is still wide, thereby indicating that within this group, diverse situations exist.

In comparison to other men, the majority of men who live alone handle their own domestic activities and dedicate more time to household work. It is important to highlight that almost no variation exists with respect to the average of men who do not live alone. They spend no more than nine hours weekly on household work, illustrating that women carry out the brunt of domestic work, and men are visibly absent. Gender equity is manifested in both men and women who live alone, where the total work time is similar. Men who live alone are able to dedicate more time to paid work.

Brazil 2011

| | Salary earners | | Employers | | Own-account workers | | Unpaid family workers | |
|---|---|---|---|---|---|---|---|---|
| | Wom | Men | Wom | Men | Wom | Men | Wom | Men |
| | 55.7 | 47.5 | 59.1 | 51.0 | 57.5 | 47.0 | 26.6 | 4.4 |
| | 16.6 | 4.7 | 15.8 | 3.4 | 24.3 | 4.9 | 26.6 | 4.4 |
| | 39.1 | 42.8 | 43.8 | 47.6 | 33.2 | 42.1 | | |

Colombia 2011

| | Domestic employm. | | Salary earners | | Employers | | Own-account workers | | Unpaid family workers | |
|---|---|---|---|---|---|---|---|---|---|---|
| | Wom | Men | Wom | Men | Wom | Men | Wom | Men | Wom | Men |
| | 57.1 | 48.9 | 63.5 | 56.2 | 64.9 | 52.9 | 61.6 | 51.9 | 28.5 | 6.3 |
| | 22.2 | 7.7 | 18.7 | 5.5 | 19.2 | 4.9 | 27.2 | 6.2 | 28.5 | 6.3 |
| | 34.8 | 41.2 | 44.8 | 50.7 | 45.8 | 48.0 | 34.5 | 45.7 | | |

Ecuador 2011

| | Domestic employm. | | Salary earners | | Employers | | Own-account workers | | Unpaid family workers | | Domestic employm. | |
|---|---|---|---|---|---|---|---|---|---|---|---|---|
| | Wom | Men | Wom | Men | Wom | Men | Wom | Men | Wom | Men | Wom | Men |
| | 64.1 | 58.3 | 64.5 | 56.3 | 70.9 | 56.8 | 62.7 | 55.1 | 28.8 | 12.8 | 66.5 | 57.2 |
| | 18.8 | 7.5 | 24.4 | 12.4 | 25.9 | 12.0 | 31.3 | 14.5 | 28.8 | 12.8 | 25.7 | 12.0 |
| | 45.3 | 50.8 | 40.1 | 44.0 | 44.9 | 44.8 | 31.4 | 40.7 | | | 40.9 | 45.2 |

*Cont'd* →

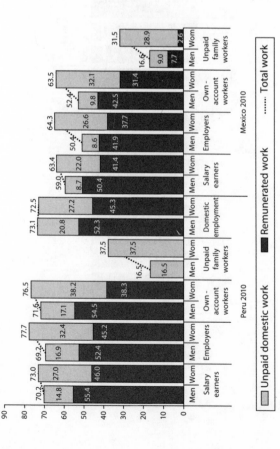

**FIGURE 4.2** Total Working Time, Paid and Unpaid Work Time, and Employed Population by Sex and Occupational Category (Population 15 years and above; time hours per week)

*Source:* ECLAC, prepared by the author on the basis of TUS or modules within household surveys.

*Note:* At the time of going to print, data for 'Domestic Employment' for Mexico was not available, and therefore is not part of the figure.

Brazil 2011

| | Extendend or composite | | Two-parent nuclear | | Single parent nuclear | | Single person | |
|---|---|---|---|---|---|---|---|---|
| | Men | Wom | Men | Wom | Men | Wom | Men | Wom |
| | 43.4 | 51.9 | 44.9 | 54.7 | 45.5 | 54.1 | 52.9 | 52.8 |
| | 3.9 | 17.9 | 5.6 | 18.1 | 4.4 | 21.4 | 12.1 | 17.5 |
| | 39.5 | 34.1 | 39.3 | 36.6 | 41.1 | 32.7 | 40.8 | 35.2 |

Colombia 2011

| | Extendend or composite | | Two-parent nuclear | | Single parent nuclear | | Single person | |
|---|---|---|---|---|---|---|---|---|
| | Men | Wom | Men | Wom | Men | Wom | Men | Wom |
| | 51.2 | 59.3 | 48.8 | 61.1 | 52.2 | 59.5 | 56.0 | 53.4 |
| | 5.4 | 22.1 | 5.8 | 21.1 | 5.7 | 25.4 | 8.1 | 12.9 |
| | 45.8 | 37.3 | 43.0 | 40.0 | 46.6 | 34.2 | 47.9 | 40.5 |

Ecuador 2011

| | Extendend or composite | | Two-parent nuclear | | Single parent nuclear | | Single person | |
|---|---|---|---|---|---|---|---|---|
| | Men | Wom | Men | Wom | Men | Wom | Men | Wom |
| | 54.6 | 58.7 | 52.4 | 62.1 | 53.7 | 57.1 | 59.6 | 56.9 |
| | 11.9 | 27.2 | 13.7 | 26.8 | 12.5 | 28.6 | 19.7 | 24.2 |
| | 42.7 | 31.5 | 38.7 | 35.3 | 41.2 | 28.4 | 39.9 | 32.7 |

*Cont'd* →

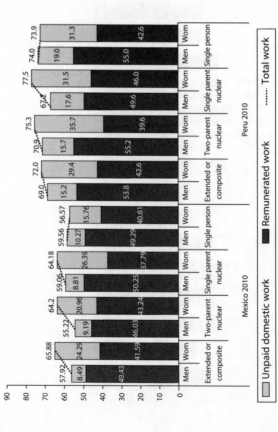

**FIGURE 4.3** Total Working Time, Paid and Unpaid Work Time, Employed Population by Type of Household (population 15 years and above; time in hours per week)

*Source:* ECLAC, prepared by the author on the basis of TUS and modules within household surveys.

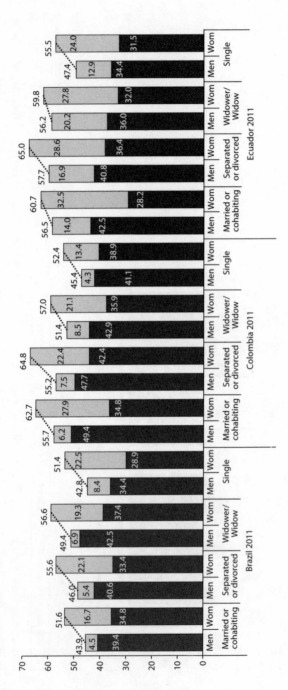

*Cont'd* →

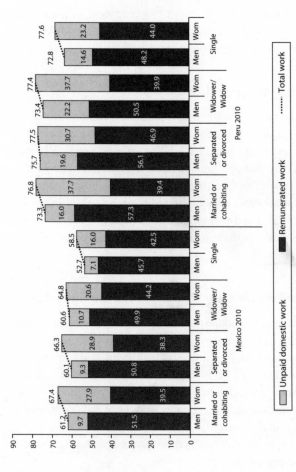

**FIGURE 4.4** Total Working Time, Paid and Unpaid Work Time, and Employed Population by Sex and Marital Status (population 15 years and above; time in hours per week)

*Source:* ECLAC, prepared by the author on the basis of TUS and modules within household surveys.

## Time Use Based on Marital Status

Women who live with a partner will face more difficulties and higher levels of stress and exhaustion, due to the need to carry out both paid and unpaid work, as shown in Figure 4.4. Married women and those with live-in partners have the highest average in total work time, of all the characteristics analysed in this chapter.

For women who live with a partner, little variation in the working day is observed, with about 35 hours weekly dedicated to paid work. These women are of productive age (between the ages of 25 and 59 years) and they face major difficulties in coordinating both paid and unpaid work, and consequently, in gaining access to jobs and positions that require longer working hours. Married men, on the other hand, do not face this dichotomy when it comes to occupation, because of the support provided by their wives in the area of domestic work, which enables them to dedicate themselves almost exclusively to paid work.

## Time Use Based on Age and Life Cycle

Women of productive age who wish to enter the labour market face a great challenge. Data shows that on a weekly basis, they face about 27 hours of domestic work and 37 hours of paid work, as shown in Figure 4.5. These women tend towards a higher average of time dedicated to total work and, compared to women in other age groups, they also demonstrate more time dedicated to paid work and domestic work. Public policies need to pay special attention to the characteristics of this age group, as they usually constitute the women who are raising their children.

## Time Use Based on Living with Minors of Pre-school Age

The presence of younger children in the household shows that women dedicate six hours more per week to domestic activities and care, as compared to women who do not live with children. It also means that employed women work a total of four hours more than women who do not share a home with children of this age group. Figure 4.6 illustrates that this increase is due to a greater amount of time dedicated to domestic work or, in this case, care.

In the case of men, an increase is also observed, with an average of three hours more per week.

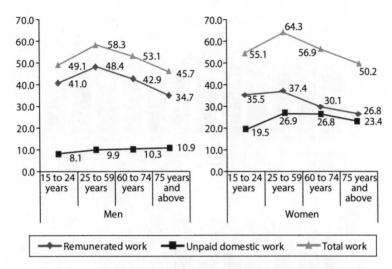

**FIGURE 4.5**     Total Working Time, Paid and Unpaid Working Time, and Employed Population by Sex and Age Group (population 15 years and above; time hours per week)
*Source:* ECLAC, prepared by the authors on the basis of TUS and modules within household surveys.

## Time Use Based on Household Poverty

Men who live in indigent households tend to have fewer paid working hours compared to poor and non-poor men. This situation is not strongly defined for women, although indigent women do demonstrate shorter days. Nonetheless, indigent women dedicated between 27 and 34 hours in a week to unpaid domestic work. In the case of men, the dedication to unpaid domestic work is between 7 and 17 hours (as demonstrated in Figure 4.7).

## LESSONS FROM THE STUDY

The above analysis of regional trends in Latin America and the Caribbean demonstrates the crucial role of TUS for public policies aimed at gender equality. Nonetheless, the short review of the process through which gender has been mainstreamed into the work of the Statistical Conference of the Americas of the ECLAC, which has been presented in this chapter, highlights to what extent this is a long and complex process, based on continuous analysis and exchange of expe-

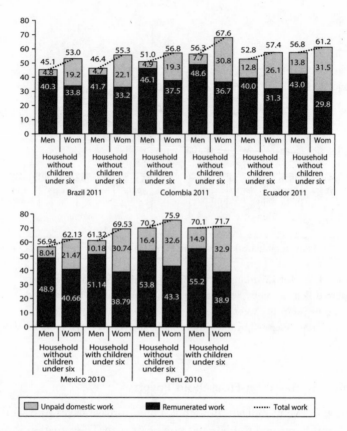

**FIGURE 4.6** Total Working Time, Paid and Unpaid Working Time, and Employed Population by Sex and Household Presence of Children under Six Years (population 15 years and above, time in hours per week)
*Source*: ECLAC, prepared by the authors on the basis of TUS and modules within household surveys.

rience and lessons learned among countries. In this process, there are no immediate solutions; instead, the specific path is shaped through an interplay of juridical, political, and social variables and realities.

A first step in this process requires national statistical institutes to look at the available data. As a subsequent step, methodological issues are explored with a particular view to the challenges encountered in attempting to compare data among countries. It is from the analysis

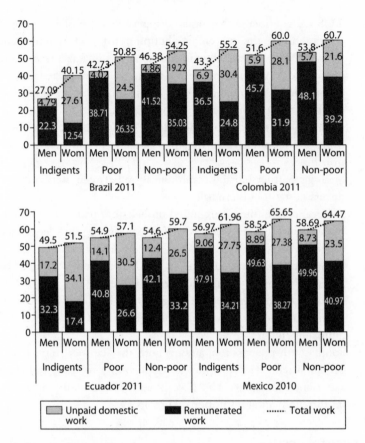

**FIGURE 4.7**    Total Working Time, Paid and Unpaid Working Time, and Employed Population by Sex, Poverty, and Indigence Status (population 15 years and above; time in hours per week)

*Source*: ECLAC, prepared by the authors on the basis of modules within household surveys.

*Note*: Data for Peru was unavailable at the time of going to print.

of these processes and continued exchanges among countries that harmonization of TUS emerges as a tool and as a challenge to resolve the methodological issues and ensure comparability in the future.

One can draw the following set of recommendations for the international level from the experience of Latin America and the Caribbean:

1. TUS are considered the most appropriate source of information to demonstrate the uneven distribution of time between men and women. Nonetheless, when institutional and financial restrictions do not allow for an independent survey, a well-constructed module within multipurpose household surveys can be an important source of information, as this chapter shows.
2. Efforts to measure time use need to be integrated into official statistics and should have a standard periodicity to allow comparison over time.
3. Strategic partnership and communication between users and producers of statistics is crucial.
4. Political commitment is required on behalf of national and international institutions, backed by the experience, knowledge, and support of academia and non-governmental organizations.
5. Coordination among countries is needed, including through the provision of forums to exchange experience.
6. In this context, increased transparency on behalf of countries is required, to allow for an exchange of information that provides for mutual learning.
7. South-south cooperation, among both the statistical bureau and gender machineries, provides an opportunity to learn from the experiences of others who have gone through similar processes, thus strengthening institutional knowledge.

## REFERENCES

Aguirre, Rosario, Cristina García Sainz, and Cristina Carrasco. 2005. 'El tiempo, los tiempos, una vara de desigualdad', *Mujer y desarrollo series*, No. 65 (LC/L.2324-P), Santiago, Chile, Economic Commission for Latin America and the Caribbean (ECLAC), July [online] http://www.eclac.cl/publicaciones/xml/7/22367/lcl2324e.pdf, last accessed on 8 July 2016.

Araya, María José. 2003. 'Un acercamiento a las encuestas sobre el uso del tiempo con orientación de género', *Mujer y desarrollo series,* No. 50 (LC/L.2022-P), Santiago, Chile, Economic Commission for Latin America and the Caribbean (ECLAC), November [online] http://www.eclac.cl/publicaciones/xml/7/13907/lcl2022e.pdf, last accessed on 8 July 2016.

Economic Commission for Latin America and the Caribbean (ECLAC). 2004. *Report of the Meeting of Experts on Time-Use Surveys*, Santiago, Chile, 11 and 12 December 2003 (LC/L.2058) [online]http://www.eclac.cl/publicaciones/xml/9/15229/lcl2058i.pdf, last accessed on 8 July 2016.

————. 2005. Regional meeting: 'Las Encuestas del Uso del Tiempo: Su Diseño y Aplicación', Santiago, Chile, 21–23 November 2005.

————. 2007. 'Quito Consensus' (DSC/1), tenth session of the Regional Conference on Women in Latin America and the Caribbean, Quito, 6–9 August [online] http://www.eclac.cl/publicaciones/xml/9/29489/dsc1i. pdf, last accessed on 8 July 2016.

————. 2009. 'Reunión Técnica para el desarrollo del Clasificador de Actividades de Uso del Tiempo para América Latina y el Caribe (CAUTAL)', Technical meeting document, Mexico D.F., 4–5 August 2009. Meeting agenda available at http://www.eclac.cl/mujer/noticias/ noticias/5/38415/Reuni%C3%B3nTecnicaClasificadorRegional.pdf, last accessed on 8 July 2016.

————. 2010. 'Tiempo total de trabajo (remunerado y no remunerado). Recopilación de experiencias de encuestas de uso del tiempo en los países', *Observatory of Gender Equality of Latin America and the Caribbean*, ECLAC División de Asuntos de Género [online] http://www.cepal.org/ oig/noticias/paginas/3/38403/TiempoTotalTrabajo.pdf, last accessed on 8 July 2016.

Gómez Luna, María Eugenia. 2009. 'Documento de Trabajo, Directrices y referentes conceptuales para armonizar las encuestas sobre uso del tiempo en América Latina y el Caribe' (Guidelines to Harmonize Time-use Surveys in Latin America and the Caribbean), unpublished.

Milosavljevic, Vivian and Odette Tacla. 2007. 'Incorporando un módulo de uso del tiempo a las encuestas de hogares: restricciones y potencialidades', *Mujer y desarrollo series*, No. 83 (LC/L.2709-P), Santiago, Chile, ECLAC, April [online] http://www.eclac.cl/publicaciones/xml/1/28541/lcl2709e. pdf, last accessed on 8 July 2016.

Montaño, Sonia, Jacqueline Pitanguy, and Thereza Lobo. 'Las políticas públicas de género: un modelo para armar: El caso de Brasil', Serie mujer y desarrollo N 45. LC/L.1920-P/E.

# PART TWO

## Analytical Tools for Addressing Critical Concerns

# 5 Challenges to Measuring Workforce/Labour Force in Global South

Indira Hirway

Labour force surveys (LFS) do not appear to be adequate to estimate 'workforce' and 'labour force' and to understand their characteristics in most economies today. This is because of the changing labour market structures in most economies on the one hand, and the recent groundbreaking resolution on statistics on work of the International Labour Organization (ILO) on the other hand. Therefore, there is a need to look for additional sources of data on work and labour force. This chapter examines, conceptually as well as empirically, how these developments have made it difficult for LFS to estimate correctly and understand comprehensively the workforce and labour force in an economy and how far these difficulties can be addressed by using time-use surveys (TUS).

The first section discusses the challenges to measurement emerging after the 19th International Conference of Labour Statistics (ICLS) resolution on statistics on work, while the second section presents the challenges emerging from the structural changes that have taken in the labour market during the past decades. The third section talks about how and how far time-use statistics can address these challenges. It is to be noted that this chapter does not discuss the role of time-use statistics in implementing the resolution on work statistics (ILO 2013). It is a limited discussion on the role of time-use statistics in the context of expanding production boundary and certain structural changes in the labour market.

## CHALLENGES EMERGING FROM STRUCTURAL CHANGES IN THE LABOUR MARKET

Labour force surveys or household-based surveys that collect work-related statistics are expected to be the main source of collecting information on workforce and labour force. Over the years, however, several limitations of LFS are coming to the fore. These limitations have emerged from several relatively recent developments, namely: (a) changes in the production boundary of the UN System of National Accounts (SNA) that have made it difficult to capture workforce statistics adequately; (b) changes in the labour market structures and in the characteristics of workforce and labour force over the years that call for some innovative approaches to estimate and understand the flexibilities of work; and (c) the new classification of SNA work under the resolution (unpaid trainee work and voluntary work of certain kinds) that calls for modification in the workforce/labour force classifications. In addition, there is also an acceptance that the causes of the inferior status of women, as compared to men, in the labour market lie in the unequal sharing of unpaid work by men and women.

### Changes in Production Boundary

The SNA presents the internationally agreed standard set of recommendations to compile measures of economic activity. It describes a coherent, consistent, and integrated set of macroeconomic accounts in the context of a set of globally accepted concepts, definitions, classifications, and accounting rules.[1] The broad objective of SNA is to

---

[1] The first SNA was designed in 1947 by the Sub-committee on National Income Statistics of the League of the National Committee of Statistical Experts. In 1953, the SNA was published under the auspices of UN Statistical Commission with a limited coverage of SNA. The SNA has been revised periodically thereafter in 1960, 1964, 1968, 1993, and 2008. The 1993 revision of SNA as well as the 2008 revision, which is an update of SNA 1993,

provide a comprehensive conceptual and accounting framework that can be used to create a macroeconomic database suitable for analysing the performance of an economy.[2] The production boundary defines the kind of goods and services to be covered under national income accounts.

Over the years, however, the production boundary has expanded to include several non-market activities. In addition to goods and services which have a monetary transaction, bartered for other goods and services, or provided free as transfers in kind, the production boundary now includes: (a) production of goods (which can potentially be sold in the market) for self-consumption, as the decision whether the goods are to be retained for own use can be made even after they are produced;[3] (b) construction of own dwellings or production of housing services for own final consumption; (c) collection of free goods, such as fuel wood, water, fish, vegetables, fruits and wood; and (d) voluntary work in market and non-market units, and voluntary work in household production of goods.[4] The LFS find it difficult to capture some of these additions either because it is difficult to collect this data or because they are not really equipped to do so.

---

have addressed several new issues, brought about by changes in the economic environment, advances in methodological research and the needs of users (UN 1993, 2008).

[2] The UNSNA (or Intersecretariat Working Group on National Accounts [ISWGNA]) enhances cooperation among international organizations working in the same field, namely, European Commission, IMF, OECD, UN, and the World Bank (ISWGNA 2008).

[3] This includes production of agricultural goods for self-consumption, production of food staffs, clothing craft goods, etc., for own consumption, production of mats, baskets, clothes, etc.

[4] Not all countries have fully adopted these changes to the production boundary. For example, in India, processing of primary production for own consumption (for example, husking of paddy, grinding foodgrains, manufacturing of jaggery, and preservation of fish, meat), manufacturing of goods of own consumption (for example, production of mats and baskets, etc.) are excluded from SNA in India. Also, some non-market activities related to agricultural production (such as kitchen garden, free collection of fish, vegetables) are excluded on the ground that these activities are 'insignificant'/negligible.

To start with, LFS find it difficult to capture informal work and subsistence work. Informal employment is difficult to capture largely because it is highly heterogeneous, and is frequently scattered, sporadic, irregular, seasonal, or unstable. Some countries have (a) tried to ask probing questions to non-workers (like housewives, students, retired persons) to find out whether they are engaged in any gainful SNA activities and (b) have employed establishment surveys to net economic activities in small family business enterprises; and/or used 'mixed surveys', that is, household-cum-establishment surveys to net all informal scattered workers, particularly women workers located in households and/or working in small informal enterprises. However, the overall results have not been always satisfactory. Jacques Charmes (2004) prepared an in-depth and comprehensive review of all these efforts made by different countries. He observed that: (a) there are large inconsistencies in the concepts and methods used by different countries leading to non-comparability of data; (b) compilation and calculation of harmonized indicators and estimates remains difficult and hazardous in the sense that the data leads to wrong conclusions; and (c) neither probing questions, nor modified LFS or 'mixed' surveys give reliable and comparable results. There is a need to look for innovative methods to improve the datasets on workforce and labour force (Hirway 2012).

Labour force surveys are also not equipped to collect data on subsistence work, multiple jobs, and work performed as simultaneous activities.[5] They usually collect data on one or two secondary activities, but not on 3–4 or 5 activities frequently performed by men and particularly women in some countries. Considering the fact that people in the Global South undertake multiple jobs, this is a serious limitation of these surveys. These surveys are also not equipped to

---

[5] Although LFS are expected to collect data on non-market work such as, goods for self-consumption, subsistence agriculture, and self-consumption of own dwelling, in reality these surveys are not able to collect on all production of goods for self-consumption (such as pickles and jams, or mats produced on a small scale only for the consumption of own family). While these surveys do collect data on secondary jobs and may be one additional job performed by a person, they are not equipped to collect data for more than three jobs and their scattered nature. These surveys are not designed to collect data on activities performed simultaneously.

collect data on simultaneous activities, that is, activities performed simultaneously, such as animal grazing and collecting fodder at the same time, or to collect information on subsistence work, production of goods for own use and not for sale, or collection of a range of free goods for own consumption. Clearly, there is a need to use other innovative tools (such as TUS) to capture the data.

## Changing Labour Market Structures

Another major challenge is the fast expanding flexibility in the labour market. One observes increasing flexibility of both production structure and labour. In the context of growing competition and uncertainties arising from it, production units are sub-contracting and outsourcing their production to smaller units, including home-based/home work. Many small units have emerged on the scene and many of them are not even stable or registered. It is not easy to collect data on workers working in these very small scattered units. The labour also has become increasingly flexible as a result of increased flexibility of production. New types of work arrangements (such as part-time work, weekend work, and compressed work) are spreading fast. In the case of home-based work and home work, the timings are very irregular—starting from early morning to late evening—depending on the convenience of workers. People who work from home in the formal sector also have irregular timings. LFS find it difficult to collect data on these multiple work arrangements and flexible timings.

LFS do not provide data on the time spent by workers on work. Though data is made available on part-time work (one to four hours of work) and full-time work (more than four hours of work), there is no exact information on the workers who work for less than four hours or who work more than four but less than eight hours. The recent ILO Resolution (ILO 2013) on statistics on work has recommended data collection on 'measures of labour underutilization'. However, LFS are not equipped to collect this data. Also, LFS do not collect data on what workers do during 'working hours' or 'office time'—how many formal and informal breaks they take during working hours. This 'black box' of work remains a puzzle under LFS (Hoffmann and Mata 2003). Finally, these surveys are not equipped to provide information on the unemployed or underemployed in terms of the hours and timings of unemployment.

## Understanding Inferior Status of Women in the Labour Market

There is a growing realization that the inferior status of women in the labour market (in terms of their overcrowding in low productivity activities and in home-based work, inferior employment status, lower wages, poorer chances for upward mobility in the labour market, etc.) is rooted in the nature and extent of their unpaid domestic services. When women enter the labour market, they do it with a burden of responsibilities of domestic services and care on their shoulder, with the result that they do not enjoy a level playing field with men right from the entry. The unequal sharing of unpaid domestic services (that is, household upkeep and care of children, old, sick, and differently abled persons) by men and women and the social norms associated with this sharing (that strengthen patriarchy) tend to put many constraints on women workers in the labour market. Women get less time and less encouragement to acquire education and skills, have limited mobility, and have time stress, which results in depletion of their productivity. All these factors adversely affect their prospects in the labour market. It is necessary, therefore, to understand the nature and extent of women's unpaid work responsibilities in order to analyse the status of women in the labour market.

Therefore, LFS are not equipped to provide all these newly needed information that is taking place in labour market structures, including flexibility of work and work intensity. There is, therefore, an urgent need to develop approaches to address the limitations of these surveys by appropriate measures.

## RESOLUTION ON STATISTICS ON WORK BY ILO

The recent resolution on statistics of work, employment, and labour underutilization passed by the 19th ICLS (ILO 2013) sets new standards for work statistics.[6] It defines the statistical concept of work for reference purposes and provides operational concepts, definitions,

---

[6] This section refers to several parts of another study (ILO 2013) done by the author on the subject for the ILO, Bangkok. The author is thankful to Sikti Dasgupta for sponsoring the study.

and guidelines for forms of work, labour force status, and measures of labour underutilization. Labour underutilization refers to mismatches between labour supply and demand, which translate into an unmet need for employment among the population.

Although LFS (modified)[7] is going to be the main source of the data to implement this new resolution, this will need many other additional sources of data and, among these sources, time-use statistics will be a dominant source. LFS will not be able to collect data on the new conceptual framework of work,[8] the new classification labour force status, and labour underutilization.

This groundbreaking resolution, passed in 2013, has radically changed the concept of work. Earlier the term 'work' included only those activities that were included in the production boundary and counted in national accounts. However, according to this resolution, 'work' is defined as 'any activity performed by persons of any sex and age to produce goods or to provide services for use by others or for own use'. This definition recognizes all production activities—legal, illegal, formal, and informal—as work. This definition is consistent with the concept of general production boundary under the SNA (ILO 2013), and excludes those activities that do not satisfy the third-person criterion (non-delegable activities) and activities that do not produce goods or services (such as begging, theft): the concept of work has been expanded to include all 'economic activities', that is, all forms of work.

The resolution defines five distinguished forms of work: (a) own-use production work, that is, activities to produce goods and services for own use by households; (b) employment work, that is, activities to produce goods and services for pay or profit or for exchange/barter; (c) unpaid trainee work, that is, work that produces goods and services for others, is without pay, and is done to acquire workplace experience

---

[7] 'Modified' LFS refers to the surveys which tap the full potential of the surveys and collect data on different categories of work as defined in the resolution.

[8] The new conceptual framework of work includes unpaid work that includes unpaid household upkeep and care of own household members. It also measures under employment of employed persons in terms of time. LFS are not designed to collect this information.

on skills in that trade or profession by a person of working age; (d) volunteer work, that is, non-compulsory activities performed without pay to produce goods and services for others; and (e) other work activities, that is, compulsory activities performed without pay to produce goods and services for others. Apart from presenting a new conceptual framework on work, the resolution also presents new labour force status classification and measures of labour underutilization. Both require additional methods of data collection.

In this chapter, we discuss the SNA work, that is, the work that is included within the production boundary and in national income accounts as per the UN SNA (ISWGNA 2008). In the terminology of the 19th ICLS resolution, SNA work includes: (a) employment; (b) own-use production of goods; (c) unpaid trainee work; (d) other work that is, compulsory activities performed without pay to produce goods and services for others; (e) voluntary work in market and non-market units; and (f) voluntary work in household production of goods. Own-use provision of services and the remaining part of voluntary work fall in the general production boundary but outside the production boundary.

Persons in employment are defined as all those of working age who, during a short reference period, were engaged in any activity to produce goods or provide services for pay or profit. They comprise employed persons 'at work', that is, those who worked at a job for at least one hour, and employed persons who are 'not at work' due to temporary absence from a job or to other working time arrangements (such as shift work, flexible time, and compensatory leave for overtime). An activity here is recognized as own production work if the total time spent on it is at least one hour.

Own-use production of goods (within the 2008 SNA production boundary) covers producing and/or processing for storage agricultural, fishing, hunting, and gathering products; collecting and/or processing for storage mining and forestry products, including firewood and other fuels; fetching water from natural and other sources; manufacturing household goods (such as furniture, textiles, clothing, footwear, pottery or other durables, including boats and canoes); and building or conducting major repairs on one's own dwelling, farm buildings, etc. Subsistence foodstuff producers, which constitute an important subgroup of persons in own-use production of goods, includes producers of goods from agriculture, fishing, hunting, or gathering that contribute to the livelihood of the household or family. However, it excludes persons engaged in such production for recreational or leisure purpose (for example, fishing as a hobby). For operational purposes, an important test to verify the subsistence nature of an activity is that such activity is carried out without workers hired for pay or profit.

Unpaid trainee work is work that produces goods and services for others, is without pay, and is done to acquire workplace experience on skills in a trade or profession by persons of working age. An activity here is recognized as unpaid trainee work if the total time spent on it is at least one hour. Unpaid trainee work includes persons in: (a) traineeships, apprenticeships, internships, or other types of programmes, when their engagement in the production process of the economic unit is unpaid and (b) unpaid skills training or retraining schemes within employment promotion programmes, when engaged in the production process of the economic unit. However, the activities excluded from unpaid trainee work are periods of probation associated with the start of job, general on-the-job or lifelong learning while in employment, including in market and non-market units owned by household or family members, orientation and learning while engaged in volunteer work, and learning while engaged in own-use production work.

Voluntary work in market and non-market units, and voluntary work in household production of goods is also work that is unpaid. 'Unpaid' here is the absence of remuneration in cash or in kind for work done or hours worked. Nevertheless, these workers may receive some form of support, such as education stipends or grants, occasional in cash or in kind support (for example, meal, drinks).

Based on the resolution, 'workforce' in a country should include all the six categories of workers (it is not yet clear whether the concept of workforce changes radically after the resolution). However, we stick to the earlier definition of workforce, that is, workforce in a country essentially consists of all those who contribute to the production of goods and services, the value of which is counted in national income accounts. There is, therefore, a correspondence between the workforce and the national income of an economy: what goes into national income is determined by the production boundary of the globally accepted SNA. Although not all the countries have adopted this boundary fully, it is the main guiding force in determining the coverage of national income accounts. Labour force of an economy consists of the workforce and those who are unemployed, that is, those who are looking for work, are available for work, and are willing to work at the market rates of remuneration.

## Measures of Labour Underutilization

The resolution has also presented a new concept, 'measuring labour underutilization'. Measures of labour underutilization include, but may not be restricted to: (a) time-related underemployment, when the working time of persons in employment is insufficient in relation to alternative employment situations in which they are willing and available to engage; (b) unemployment, reflecting an active job search by persons not in employment who are available for this form of work; and (c) potential labour force, referring to persons not in employment who express an interest in this form of work but for whom existing conditions limit their active job search and/or their availability. The potential labour force can be further subcategorized as those involved in activities (a) carried out to 'seek employment' were not 'currently available' but would become available within a short subsequent period established in the light of national circumstances (that is, unavailable jobseekers) or (b) did not carry out activities to seek employment but wanted employment and were 'currently available', that is available potential jobseekers.

The composite measures of labour underutilization are of four categories:

LU1: Unemployed

LU2: Time-related Underemployed + Unemployed

LU3: Unemployed + Potential Labour Force

LU4: Time-related Underemployed + Unemployed + Potential Labour Force

(As seen here, potential labour force includes 'seeking not available' + 'available not seeking').

The composite measures of labour underutilization can be translated into the following rates of labour underutilization:

$$\textbf{LU1} = Unemployment\ Rate = \frac{Persons\ in\ Unemployment}{Labour\ Force} \times 100$$

$\mathbf{LU2} = Combined\ Rate\ of\ Time\text{-}related\ Underemployment\ and\ Unemployment$

$$= \frac{Persons\ in\ Time\text{-}related\ Underemployment + Persons\ in\ Unemployment}{Labour\ Force} \times 100$$

$\mathbf{LU3} = Combined\ Rate\ of\ Unemployment\ and\ Potential\ Labour\ Force$

$$= \frac{Persons\ in\ Unemployment\ +\ Potential\ Labour\ Force}{Extended\ Labour\ Force} \times 100$$

$\mathbf{LU4} = Composite\ Measure\ of\ Labour\ Underutilization$

$$= \frac{\begin{array}{c} Persons\ in\ time\text{-}related\ Underemployed\ + \\ Persons\ Unemployed + Potential\ Labour\ Force \end{array}}{Extended\ Labour\ Force} \times 100$$

## Practical Implications of New Standards

An implication of the new standards under the resolution will be to investigate all forms of work so as (a) to identify all forms of work for all persons of the working age and (b) to measure working hours in all forms. This will also imply review of LFS: (a) questionnaires, manuals, and training; (b) new indicators; (c) calculations in parallel, (d) dissemination of the changes and justification; and (e) frequency of collection: intra/year/3–5 years.

There are some questions, however, that remains unanswered: given the narrower activity scope of employment and its implications for measurement of unemployment, will the link between labour supply and the SNA production boundary be broken? Also, is the comparability of employment statistics from the past series broken? Again, if the concept of employment is restricted to paid work (in exchange for pay or profit), it will: (a) reduce the size of the labour force and the participation rate in the labour force; (b) reduce level and rate of employment; (c) may increase level and rate of unemployment; and (d) may reduce level and rate of underemployment (because employment is lower). Can we assume that the new standards will change these basic concepts?

However, without delving into these questions, we proceed to the discussion on the required database of the resolution and the role of time-use statistics in the new database.

## TIME–USE SURVEYS

TUS have the potential to address the limitations of the LFS as discussed earlier, and they need to complement and supplement LFS. In this section, we discuss how far TUS help in addressing the recent structural changes in the labour market.

The main strength of TUS is that they provide comprehensive information on how individuals spend their time, daily or weekly, on SNA activities, non-SNA activities that fall within the general production boundary, and personal activities that are non-delegable activities.[9] There are three major components of a TUS: (a) information on major socio-economic characteristics of households and individuals (for whom time-use data is collected) through a background schedule or through the main schedule in case TUS is a module in a major survey; (b) data on the time spent by individuals on different activities; and (c) the context in which activities are carried out.[10] Additionally, time-use statistics can also be used with other data (such as LFS) to enhance the value of the data (Hirway and Charmes 2006).

### Subsistence Work

As discussed earlier, subsistence employment (production of goods for own use) is excluded from workforce estimates in most economies, mainly due to the availability of data. Time-use surveys, however, can capture this information, with the help of appropriate contextual variables. For example, the context variable, whether the activity/production is for sale or is for self-consumption, can help in identifying production of goods for self-consumption. Also, collection of free goods like water, fuel wood, fodder, etc., is an important activity in many developing countries (Charmes 2004; Hirway 2003). A TUS can provide information on the time spent on these activities. Although some LFS collect data on how many persons collect water, fuel wood,

---

[9] Personal services are non-delegable services, that is, the services that cannot be delegated to others. For example, sleeping, watching TV, etc.

[10] The context variables in time-use statistics usually refer to the location where the activity took place (where), the presence of other people when the activity took place (with whom), the beneficiary, person, or institution of the activity (for whom the activity was carried out), the motivation of the activity (for example, whether the activity was paid or unpaid), etc.

fodder, etc., the coverage is usually inadequate and no information is available on how much time is spent on these activities. Considering the fact that the poor in developing countries are forced to spend long hours on these activities, it is necessary to collect data on the time spent (Hirway and Charmes 2006).

The Organization for Economic Co-operation and Development's (OECD's) handbook on *Measuring the Non-Observed Economy* (2002) has pointed out that TUS need to be used for estimating the sub-sistence sector, particularly when labour is the main input in their production process. The time spent on these activities will capture the work (worker) and also help in valuation of the output—which will be calculated by multiplying the time spent to the prevailing wages (2002).

## Informal Work

It has been observed in the context of several countries in the Global South that all work (including SNA work) is underreported by women, or even the poor, as they frequently perceive their SNA work as household work. Even investigators have been observed to have this bias. As a result, SNA work in household enterprises, self-employment, or in informal work in general tends to get underestimated. In the case of TUS, however, no question is asked to respondents as to whether they are 'workers' or are engaged in any 'economically productive activity'. Instead, comprehensive information is collected on how respondents spend their time on different activities without bothering about whether the activity is 'work' or 'non-work'. This information is then coded systematically and, with the help of a relevant set of context variables and a well-designed activity classification, classified as per their characteristics. This information, therefore, is likely to have less bias in terms of identifying 'work' and 'workers'. Time-use data is also likely to capture all short-term, sporadic, scattered, or temporary SNA activities of the population (Hirway and Charmes 2006).

Since TUS collect complete information on how people spend their time, they are able to give full details about the multiple activities performed in a scattered manner by people. They can provide detailed data on the number of hours spent by workers on work as well as on the scattered nature of their work. The data can also be used in esti-mating, seasonal, temporary, part-time and short-time work. Similarly, TUS can provide data on multitasking or on simultaneous activities performed by men and women.

## Women's Status in Labour Market

In addition to the preceding elements, time-use data also provides improved understanding of gender gaps in the status of workers in the labour market. This is because this data provides information on the burden of unpaid domestic services and unpaid care work on men and women. As seen earlier, the burden of unpaid work on women is observed to be one of the major constraints which do not allow women a level playing field with men in the labour market. The highly unequal distribution of unpaid domestic work between men and women in the household, along with the socio-cultural norms emanating from it, tends to restrict human capital formation among women and reduce their participation, their mobility, as well as their choice of work in the labour market.

Therefore, TUS have considerable potential to get over some of the problems and limitations of LFS in terms of estimating and understanding informal and subsistence work of men and women in an economy.

## EMPIRICAL ANALYSIS

This section aims to see how far TUS can actually help in improving workforce/labour force estimates and how much additional insight they provide on their characteristics. We have, therefore, compared the results of an LFS with that of a TUS.

The National Sample Survey Office (NSSO) in India conducts an all-India employment and unemployment survey (EUS) every five years. Since the year of the TUS that was conducted in 1998–9 matched with the EUS in 1999–2000, we decided to compare the results of the two surveys. As both the years are close to each other and are 'normal years', the data can be treated as comparable. The comparison was made for the six states covered under the TUS as well as all-India estimates of the EUS and the 'combined state' estimates of the time-use statistics.[11]

---

[11] The analysis has used data for 'combined states', that is, weighted averages of the six states, because the six states represent the all-India situation in most of the parameters, such as age and sex composition of population, rural–urban distribution of the population, literacy rates, per capita income (Pandey 2000). As Pandey has explained, this indicates that the six states selected for

India's first national TUS was conducted on a pilot basis in 1998–9 (Hirway 2003).[12] The survey covered six major states: Haryana from north, Madhya Pradesh from centre, Tamil Nadu from south, Gujarat from west, Orissa (now Odisha) from east, and Meghalaya from north-east. The survey covered both rural and urban areas, and was conducted in four rounds to capture seasonal changes in the time use. In all, 18,591 households and 77,593 individuals (all members above six years of age from the selected households) were selected for the survey (Government of India 2000a).

Keeping in mind the specific conditions in India, the following innovative ideas were adopted (Hirway 2003):

1. Since the level of literacy in India is low, it was not possible to use established self-reported 24-hour time diary with a 10-minute slot, India used face-to-face interviews with one-day recall to fill in the diary. Also, as timepieces and clocks are not followed religiously by people in India, particularly in remote, rural areas, India went for a 30-minute time slot.
2. Fearing a hurdle in getting the right responses from women due to cultural factors, women investigators were employed in many parts.
3. As agriculture is a major occupation in India, it was decided to conduct the survey in all four seasons of a year.
4. Keeping in mind the existence of child labour in India, the minimum age for selecting individuals was kept at six years.

The Central Statistical Office (CSO) set up a Technical Committee[13] to design, plan, and decide related matters leading to conducting a TUS, and to suggest appropriate definitions and concepts, schedule of inquiry, and a suitable reference period for the purpose of data

---

the survey together represent the all-India situation. Though we have presented state-wise differences in the relevant parameters, we have also used estimates for 'combined states' for the analysis (2000).

[12] The present author headed the technical advisory committee set up for the purpose.

[13] Since the proposed TUS was a methodological survey, the government invited academics, concerned government officials, and representatives from civil society organizations as members to the committee.

collection. The technical committee in its first meeting decided the following as the objectives of the TUS:

- to collect and analyse time-use patterns of men and women to understand the time spent on marketed and non-marketed economic activities
- to generate more a reliable estimate of workforce
- to estimate and value unpaid work
- to develop a conceptual framework and a suitable methodology for designing and conducting TUS in India

Time-use surveys usually collect data for two days—a weekday and another weekly variant day (a few countries collect data on one day or three days). As the days are distributed systematically in a random manner across the different days of a week, and as the survey is carried out throughout the year (in three or four quarters), one can compile weekly estimates that can be considered comparable with the estimates compiled based on the LFS (or any other household survey). Estimates of any kind of work based on TUS can be treated as comparable with the estimates of the same category of work based on a household survey. Both the surveys use the criterion of at least one hour of work in the last week. To repeat, this is because each day of the week gets equal chance of getting selected (random selection) under the TUS. This is valid theoretically, and is found valid in the case of India where the efforts are made to compare the two sets of estimates (Hirway and Jose 2011).

Using an ILO concept of worker (a person who spends at least one hour on work during the reference week is a worker) estimates were made of workers and workforce participation rates of the sample population.[14]

Though the above argument is valid at the macro level, the TUS-based estimates cannot allow unit-level analysis, because one compares the two sets of data of specific individuals in a unit-level analysis. How can they conduct unit-level analysis under TUS? Experts on time-use studies have recommended several approaches. Jonathan Gershuny

---

[14] However, it was observed that the concept of weekly holiday does not exist in most places (people work throughout the week), with the result the weekly estimates of the time-use pattern were made by using 6.5 normal days and 0.5 weekly variant day in the reference week.

(University of Oxford), for example, has recommended conducting TUS for all days of the week from selected individuals (International Association for Time Use Research [IATUR] 2012). It is argued that the seven-day data will not miss out on work performed on any day of the reference week, and, therefore, it will provide comparable estimates (with the estimates based on LFS). The solution appears to be valid. However, it is not easy to get response from people on their time use for seven consecutive days. In the case of Nigeria, time diaries were collected for this period, but the response was very poor (Hirway 2010). What Gershuny recommends, however, is to select willing respondents only, who are prepared to fill in a time diary for consecutive seven days. The question, however, is even if data quality is good, (a) whether the selected sample of willing persons is representative of the reference population and (b) whether this approach can work at the national level.

In the case of the NSSO, on the other hand, there are three reference periods, namely, one year, one week, and each day of the week, and workforce estimates are made for each of the reference periods. For classification of persons according to current weekly status approach, they are assigned a unique activity status with reference to a period of seven days preceding the date of the survey. This is an easy task in the case of persons having only one status during the reference week. But for the persons pursuing more than one activity, a priority-cum-major time rule is applied to obtain a unique activity status. Under the priority rule, the status of 'working' gets a priority over the status of 'not working but seeking/available for work'. Within the broad category of working and non-working, the detailed activity category is assigned by the major time spent criterion. Using this procedure in the current weekly status, a person is considered working or employed if the person was engaged for at least one hour a day on any one of the days of the previous week in any economic activity. A person who has not worked for even one hour on any day of the week, but had been seeking or had been available for work any time for at least one hour during the week was considered as seeking/available for work. Others were considered 'not available for work' or 'out of labour force' (NSSO 2000).

The analysis here primarily deals with: (a) workforce participation rates of men and women as estimated under NSSO and TUS databases; (b) diversification of SNA work of men and women as per the NSSO and TUS databases, in terms of participation rates as well as the time spent on different activities; (c) specific characteristics of women's SNA work, such as their multiple jobs, subsistence work; and (d) the sharing of total work, that is, SNA and non-SNA work by men and women and the likely impact of the sharing on women's status in the labour market.

## Workforce Participation Rates under NSSO and TUS Databases

Table 5.1[15] presents weekly workforce participation rates (WPRs) of men and women for rural and urban areas from NSSO (1999–2000) and from the TUS (1998–9). Some of the striking observations from the table are as follows:

1.  The TUS-based estimates of WPRs are higher than the NSSO-based WPRs for men and women in both rural and urban areas. The WPRs of women under the TUS are double or more than the corresponding WPRs under the NSSO.
2.  The gap between the NSSO-based rates and TUS-based rates is much higher for women than for men. This indicates greater under-reporting of women's work than of men's work under the NSSO. The highest gap between the NSSO-based WPRs and TUS-based WPRs is observed in the case of urban women. This indicates that the most underestimated WPRs under the NSSO are WPRs of urban women.
3.  Although there are interstate differences, the above two observations are applicable to all the states.

However, there are still two problems with the comparability of the two datasets:

1.  There are differences in the concepts of work between the two surveys: TUS-based rates include subsistence work and travel time, while the other survey does not.
2.  Since the TUS-based rates are only for the selected two days and not for all days, as is done under the NSSO survey, even those workers whose attachment to the labour market is negligible are considered as workers.

---

[15] Unless otherwise specified, tables in this chapter have been borrowed from the special issue of *Feminist Economics* 2011. The author is thankful to *Feminist Economics* for the permission to reproduce these.

**TABLE 5.1** Estimated WPRs from NSSO and TUS (%)

| State | NSSO 1999–2000 | | | | | | TUS 1998–9 | | | | | |
|---|---|---|---|---|---|---|---|---|---|---|---|---|
| | Rural | | | Urban | | | Rural | | | Urban | | |
| | Male | Female | Person | Male | Female | Person | Male | Female | Person | Male | Female | Person |
| Haryana | 46.2 | 17.7 | 32.8 | 50.2 | 10.0 | 31.3 | 58.7 | 61.47 | 59.96 | 54.5 | 39.08 | 47.55 |
| Madhya Pradesh | 51.2 | 30.7 | 41.3 | 47.3 | 12.1 | 30.5 | 61.8 | 54.92 | 58.58 | 57.5 | 30.68 | 44.98 |
| Gujarat | 57.1 | 35.5 | 46.4 | 52.9 | 12.5 | 33.6 | 63.4 | 58.48 | 61.05 | 56.9 | 25.78 | 42.34 |
| Odisha | 52.7 | 23.3 | 37.9 | 45.7 | 11.6 | 29.3 | 61.7 | 58.34 | 60 | 58.4 | 30.97 | 45.77 |
| Tamil Nadu | 56.6 | 38.1 | 47.4 | 55.2 | 20.1 | 38.1 | 68.4 | 60.62 | 64.52 | 63.8 | 34.21 | 48.88 |
| Meghalaya | 55.6 | 42.0 | 48.7 | 39.3 | 19.7 | 29.7 | 58.6 | 59.35 | 58.91 | 53.8 | 35.06 | 43.84 |
| Combined States | 51.0 | 25.3 | 38.4 | 50.9 | 12.8 | 32.7 | 63.3 | 58.2 | 60.82 | 59.3 | 30.89 | 45.69 |

*Source*: Indian TUS 1998–9 and Employment and Unemployment Survey 1999–2000.

New WPRs were, therefore, calculated by making the two concepts of work comparable by subtracting time spent on subsistence work and travel time and by defining attachment to the labour market in terms of periods of four hours or more and eight hours or more.

Table 5.2 shows that even when four or eight hours are taken as criterion for 'work', and comparable definitions of 'work' are used, the TUS-based estimates show higher WPRs.

**TABLE 5.2**   Modified TUS-based WPR as per Weekly Hours Spent on SNA Work (%)

| State | Rural | | | Urban | | |
|---|---|---|---|---|---|---|
| | Men | Women | Total | Men | Women | Total |
| **Haryana** | | | | | | |
| 4 hours or more | 54.77 | 52.70 | 53.83 | 52.98 | 31.00 | 43.08 |
| 8 hours or more | 51.78 | 47.23 | 49.72 | 52.07 | 28.06 | 41.25 |
| **Madhya Pradesh** | | | | | | |
| 4 hours or more | 59.41 | 49.28 | 54.63 | 54.28 | 23.53 | 39.92 |
| 8 hours or more | 57.23 | 43.42 | 50.72 | 53.16 | 18.15 | 36.81 |
| **Gujarat** | | | | | | |
| 4 hours or more | 61.10 | 53.82 | 57.61 | 55.98 | 20.93 | 39.58 |
| 8 hours or more | 60.01 | 48.93 | 54.71 | 55.42 | 16.67 | 37.29 |
| **Odisha** | | | | | | |
| 4 hours or more | 60.29 | 53.52 | 56.92 | 57.62 | 25.56 | 42.88 |
| 8 hours or more | 59.00 | 45.00 | 52.03 | 57.22 | 20.73 | 40.44 |
| **Tamil Nadu** | | | | | | |
| 4 hours or more | 66.09 | 49.40 | 57.78 | 61.39 | 22.00 | 41.50 |
| 8 hours or more | 65.02 | 44.53 | 54.82 | 60.43 | 19.09 | 39.56 |
| **Meghalaya** | | | | | | |
| 4 hours or more | 55.69 | 51.23 | 53.46 | 48.29 | 23.98 | 35.31 |
| 8 hours or more | 54.90 | 46.99 | 50.97 | 48.06 | 21.99 | 34.13 |
| **All States** | | | | | | |
| 4 hours or more | 60.93 | 51.31 | 56.29 | 57.41 | 22.74 | 40.80 |
| 8 hours or more | 59.32 | 45.42 | 52.62 | 56.61 | 18.78 | 38.49 |

*Source*: Government of India (2000a).
*Note*: Hours worked includes all paid work activities—primary, secondary, and tertiary.

Another interesting finding is that time-use-data-based WPRs of men and women show much lower gender gaps (Table 5.3). Also, interstate gaps in WPRs are also much lower as per the time-use based estimates of WPRs.

The table shows that both the gaps, that is, gender gaps as well as variations across the states, are much lower for the WPRs based on the TUS data. For example, in the case of Haryana, the gender gaps in the WPRs are 31.39 points as per the NSSO data, but it is 0.39 for the TUS-based WPRs. This is because Haryana has well-developed agriculture and animal husbandry (dairy industry) where women's participation as unpaid family workers is predominant. However, the gender gap is the highest in Gujarat among the six states, perhaps because there are several social constraints against women's participation in workforce in certain castes in Saurashtra and Kachchh—the two major regions in the state.

Scholars in India have frequently observed that women's labour market participation is very low, and have tried to explain this through various theories. But the TUS data shows that the gaps are not very large. For the combined states, the gender gap in WPR is 11.41 points under the TUS estimates, and 28.88 in the cases of NSSO. This clearly indicates that the large gender gaps discussed by scholars are not really so large in reality, and the gaps are mainly due to the inability of the conventional sources to capture SNA work of women.

Similarly, one does not observe wide variations in the WPRs across the states in the WPRs based on TUS data. The coefficient of variations

**TABLE 5.3** Gender Gap in WPRs in India (%)

| States | TUS, 1998–9 | | | NSSO, 1999–2000 | | |
|---|---|---|---|---|---|---|
| | Male | Female | Gap | Male | Female | Gap |
| Haryana | 57.98 | 57.59 | 0.39 | 47.19 | 15.80 | 31.39 |
| Meghalaya | 57.77 | 55.05 | 2.72 | 52.57 | 37.85 | 14.72 |
| Odisha | 61.02 | 53.68 | 7.34 | 51.76 | 21.73 | 30.03 |
| Tamil Nadu | 66.76 | 51.04 | 15.72 | 56.12 | 31.95 | 24.17 |
| Madhya Pradesh | 60.99 | 50.26 | 10.73 | 50.30 | 26.39 | 23.91 |
| Gujarat | 60.96 | 46.55 | 14.41 | 55.65 | 27.57 | 28.08 |
| Combined States/All India | 62.16 | 50.75 | 11.41 | 50.97 | 22.09 | 28.88 |
| Coefficient of Variation | 0.07 | 0.11 | – | 0.09 | 0.41 | – |

*Source*: Indian TUS 1998–9 and Employment and Unemployment Survey 1999–2000.

in the WPRs across the six states is much lower in the case of the TUS-based rates, for men as well as women workers. In the case of women's WPR, the coefficient of variation is 0.11 for TUS-based WPRs, while it is 0.41 for NSSO-based ones. It appears that the wide variations in the conventional WPRs across the states in India are more due to the limitations of the methods to capture SNA work of women and less due to socio-economic variations.

### WPRs for Different Age Groups

To study the gaps in the WPRs age-wise, the WPRs of men and women by age groups as per the NSSO and the TUS are analysed for the six states together. As far as WPRs of men are concerned, the gap between the NSSO-based WPRs and TUS-based WPRs is the minimum for the age group 30–50 (that is, 30–34, 35–39, 40–44, 45–50 age groups). This gap is less than 3 points in both rural and urban areas with the TUS-based rates being higher than the NSSO-based ones. The gap in the age group 51–60 years is slightly higher, between 5 to 7 points (Figure 5.1). However, the gaps in other age groups are much higher, particularly in the age groups 5–24 years and 60+ years. It seems that the work of those who are outside the working age groups, that is, below 14 years and 60+ years is underestimated in the NSSO survey. This could be because their work is mostly in informal sector and in family enterprises.

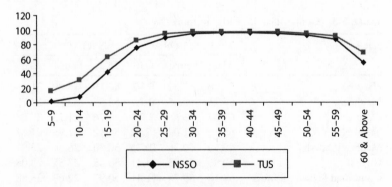

**FIGURE 5.1**   NSSO- and TUS-based WPRs by Age Groups: Male
*Source*: Indian TUS 1998–9 and Employment and Unemployment Survey 1999–2000.

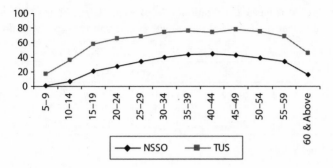

**FIGURE 5.2**     NSSO- and TUS-based WPRs by Age Groups: Female
*Source*: Indian TUS 1998–9 and Employment and Unemployment Survey 1999–2000.

In the case of female WPRs, the gaps between the NSSO- and the TUS-based rates are large for all age groups. Even in the working-age groups, that is, 15–60 years, the gaps are very high (see Figure 5.2). The overall WPR is higher for TUS than the corresponding rates based on the NSSO data for all age groups. An important implication is that women's workforce participation is underestimated in all age groups, starting from the 5–9 age group to the 60 years and above age group. Men's workforce participation is underestimated mainly for specific age groups.

It should be noted here that the two figures have used the 1993 SNA definition of 'work' and not the NSSO definition. The gaps, therefore, are due to the differences in the definition as well as due to the TUS capturing 'work' more effectively. The figures also show that if you define 'work' properly as per the norms of the global SNA, then (a) the participation of men and women in 'work' is much higher and (b) the underestimation of 'work' by the NSSO is applicable to all age groups in the case of women workers. Women's participation in subsistence work is indeed significant and it needs to be considered while designing policies for interventions to the labour market.

## Diversification of SNA Activities

Table 5.4 presents percentage distribution of workers as per time-use data and the NSSO data by industrial categories with comparable concepts of work. The NSSO estimates are for combined states, while the NSSO estimates are all-India.

**TABLE 5.4**   Percentage Distribution of Workers in TUS and NSSO by Industrial Categories (combined states with comparable concepts of work)

| Industrial Category | TUS 1998–9 | | | NSSO 1999–2000 | | |
|---|---|---|---|---|---|---|
| | Male | Female | Average | Male | Female | Average |
| Primary | 56.13 | 77.45 | 66.00 | 47.00 | 70.00 | 53.80 |
| Secondary | 15.11 | 9.97 | 12.00 | 20.20 | 13.50 | 18.40 |
| Tertiary | 28.75 | 12.59 | 22.00 | 32.80 | 16.50 | 27.80 |

*Source:* Pandey 2000.

The table shows that the workforce is less diversified for NSSO-based WPRs. While the time–use-based male WPR in the primary sector is 56.13 per cent, the NSSO-based WPR in the primary sector is 47 per cent. Again, the time–use-based male WPR in the non-primary sector is 43.86 per cent, the corresponding rate for NSSO is 53 per cent. Both estimates show predominance of the tertiary sector over the secondary sector, with the TUS-based estimates showing much lower values. Overall, it appears that the TUS has been able to capture the primary sector work of men and women more effectively. This could be because the share of organized/formal employment is relatively low in the sector.

As expected, men's work is more diversified than that of women. As against 56.13 per cent male workers in the primary sector, 77.45 per cent female workers are working in the primary sector. The percentage of workers in the secondary and tertiary sectors is much less: 15.11 per cent and 28.75 per cent for men and 9.97 per cent and 12.59 per cent for women, respectively.

Table 5.5 gives detailed information on the participation of men and women in the different activities in the three sectors as well as the time spent by them in these activities. Within the primary sector, women are predominant in collection of free goods, animal husbandry, and crop farming, while men are mainly in crop farming and animal husbandry. In the secondary sector, women are mainly in the manufacturing activities, while in the tertiary sector they are mainly in services. Men's work is also significant in construction and trade. In short, men have better opportunities in the non-primary sectors as compared to women. In terms of the time spent on SNA activities, men spend 54.65 hours per week as against 30.04 hours by women. That is, men

**TABLE 5.5** Diversification of SNA Activities for Men and Women Workforce (%)

| SNA Activity Type | WPR | | Weekly Time Spent | |
|---|---|---|---|---|
| | Male | Female | Male | Female |
| **Primary Activities** | **56.13** | **77.45** | **28.31** | **17.29** |
| Crop farming, kitchen gardening, etc. | 37.00 | 29.54 | 45.61 | 34.81 |
| Animal husbandry | 23.36 | 30.33 | 15.79 | 12.80 |
| Fishing, forestry, horticulture, gardening | 4.06 | 4.03 | 23.35 | 12.14 |
| Fetching of fruits, water, plants, etc.; storing and hunting | 8.40 | 39.08 | 11.48 | 9.62 |
| Processing and storage | 1.14 | 5.46 | 21.19 | 8.37 |
| Mining, quarrying, digging, cutting, etc. | 1.57 | 0.66 | 48.2 | 34.73 |
| **Secondary Activities** | **15.11** | **9.97** | **8.13** | **2.16** |
| Construction activities | 4.96 | 1.56 | 44.76 | 29.54 |
| Manufacturing activities | 8.38 | 8.48 | 49.48 | 24.81 |
| **Tertiary Activities** | **28.75** | **12.59** | **16.28** | **2.70** |
| Trade and business | 10.30 | 2.72 | 53.62 | 22.00 |
| Services | 20.62 | 12.06 | 42.11 | 21.07 |
| Community-organized constructions and repairs | 0.07 | 0.13 | 7.24 | 7.52 |
| **SNA Activities Combined** | **100.00** | **100.00** | **54.65** | **30.04** |

*Source:* Indian TUS 1998–9.

spend around 8 hours per day (including Sundays) and women spend 4.5 hours per day (including Sundays) on SNA work. Clearly, women carry a larger burden of SNA work.

It is important to note that women are predominantly involved in collection of free goods (which includes water, fuel wood, vegetables, fruits, and leaves) for meeting basic needs of the household, fodder, wood, and raw material for family business, etc. from common lands, common forests, and other common property resources. These activities are time-consuming, and more so with the increasing depletion and degradation of common property resources in most developing countries. For rural and urban areas combined, 35.56 per cent of women, which is more than one-third of total women, participate in these activities, as against only 5 per cent of men. The total time spent on these activities also is much longer (3.11 hours per week) for participant women than for participant men (0.97 hours per week). The most time-consuming activities for women are collection of water (WPR 12.87), followed by collection of vegetables, fruits, etc. (WPR 11.61), and collection of fodder and raw material for crafts, etc. (WPR 5.74). Women's participation in these activities is seven times more than that of men. On an average, women spend 3.11 hours per week on collection of free goods, which is more than three times the time spent by men (Hirway and Jose 2011).

Table 5.7 shows that 7.23 per cent of men and 9.27 per cent of women participate in some additional activities of the same type, namely, animal grazing; making cow dung; collecting, storing, and stocking of fruits; woodcutting; and stocking of firewood. These activities, like the activities listed in Table 5.7 have low productivity and they are time-consuming drudgery. Men (mainly young boys) participate in animal grazing, while women participate in making dung cakes, grazing animals, and chopping and storing firewood. Once again, participant women spend more time per day (70.43 minutes) on these activities than the time spent by participating men (66.40 minutes). Similarly, men and women spend significant time on making dung cakes, grazing animals, and cutting and chopping wood for fuel. These time-consuming activities do not do not leave much time for women to participate in the productive activities in the labour market.

## Multiple Activities of Men and Women Workers

An important characteristic of workforce in developing countries is that a significant percentage of the workforce is employed in multiple activities (see Table 5.6 for data on India). For example, a man may work on his farm for some time or during a crop season, and then may work as hired labour on other farms, may migrate to an urban area and work on construction of roads, or may work in a brick kiln or in a small factory. Similarly, a woman may tend animals at home, work on the family farm, work as hired labour on other farms, or may work as domestic servant at a rich man's house. These multiple jobs are taken up because: (a) one job does not provide enough employment (for example, a small field does not need more than one full-time worker, or a cow or two do not need full-time work); (b) one job does not earn enough income for survival; (c) there are not enough skills or

**TABLE 5.6**  Multiple SNA Activities, Men and Women (%)

| State | Number of Activities-Male | | | | Number of Activities-Female | | | |
|---|---|---|---|---|---|---|---|---|
| | 1 | 2 | 3 to 5 | Above 5 | 1 | 2 | 3 to 5 | Above 5 |
| Haryana | 10.78 | 45.69 | 38.55 | 4.99 | 17.97 | 19.30 | 42.51 | 20.22 |
| Madhya Pradesh | 8.94 | 40.34 | 45.70 | 5.02 | 25.66 | 37.09 | 34.53 | 2.72 |
| Gujarat | 13.59 | 55.03 | 28.73 | 2.66 | 23.58 | 29.40 | 39.74 | 7.28 |
| Odisha | 26.59 | 45.00 | 27.60 | 0.81 | 32.81 | 34.42 | 32.18 | 0.60 |
| Tamil Nadu | 17.27 | 56.13 | 24.77 | 1.83 | 36.76 | 34.25 | 27.59 | 1.40 |
| Meghalaya | 8.50 | 25.82 | 61.27 | 4.41 | 23.05 | 28.93 | 43.47 | 4.55 |
| Combined States | 15.17 | 49.00 | 32.89 | 2.94 | 28.85 | 30.71 | 35.06 | 5.37 |

*Source:* Government of India (2000a).

education to access a full-time job; or (d) there are not enough funds or access to funds to expand the present activity into a full-time activity.

Some of the disadvantages of undertaking multiple jobs are that (a) performing multiple jobs does not help the person acquire specialization or skills in any one job; (b) the persons performing multiple jobs remain in low productivity and low wage/earning activities; and (c) they find it difficult to move upward in the labour market due to their pre-occupation with too many activities.

Table 5.7 shows that the percentage of workers performing one SNA activity is small—15.17 per cent for men workers and 28.85 per cent for women workers. Performing two activities is, however, very common with half of men workers and 30 per cent of women workers. However, women's share is much higher in performing three, four, and more activities. 5.37 per cent women workers perform more than five SNA activities against 2.94 per cent of men workers. The different activities are perhaps performed at different times and at different locations.

## Unpaid Non-SNA Work, a Major Constraint of Women Workers

The burden of unpaid non-SNA work is shared highly unequally between men and women. Table 5.7 shows that women, on an average, spend 28.96 hours per week on household management, that is,

**TABLE 5.7** Weekly Time Spent by Men and Women on Household Management and on Care Activities (hours)

| Activity Type | Male | Female | Total |
|---|---|---|---|
| **Household Management Activities** | | | |
| Cooking food items, beverages, and serving | 0.49 | 14.59 | 7.33 |
| Cleaning and upkeep of dwelling and surroundings | 0.22 | 4.59 | 2.34 |
| Cleaning of utensils | 0.09 | 3.30 | 1.65 |
| Care of textiles: sorting, mending, washing, ironing, and ordering clothes and linen | 0.16 | 2.31 | 1.21 |
| Shopping for goods and non-personal services: capital goods, household appliances, equipment, food, and various household supplies | 0.35 | 0.41 | 0.38 |
| Household management: planning, supervising, paying bills, etc. | 0.05 | 0.13 | 0.09 |
| Do-it-yourself home improvements and maintenance, installation, servicing, and repair of personal and household goods | 0.21 | 1.21 | 0.69 |
| Pet care | 0.03 | 0.06 | 0.04 |
| Travel related to household maintenance, management, and shopping | 0.22 | 0.21 | 0.22 |
| Household maintenance, management, and shopping not elsewhere classified | 0.29 | 2.14 | 1.18 |
| **Total** | **2.11** | **28.96** | **15.14** |
| **Care-related Activities** | | | |
| Physical care of children: washing, dressing, feeding | 0.31 | 3.09 | 1.66 |
| Teaching, training, and instruction of own children | 0.12 | 0.11 | 0.11 |
| Accompanying children to places: school, sports, lessons, etc. /PHC/doctor | 0.09 | 0.08 | 0.09 |
| Physical care of sick, disabled, elderly household members; washing, dressing, feeding, helping | 0.03 | 0.16 | 0.09 |
| Accompanying adults to receive personal care services, such as hairdresser's therapy sessions, temple, religious places | 0.00 | 0.01 | 0.01 |
| Supervising children, needing care with or without other activity | 0.27 | 0.84 | 0.55 |
| Supervising adults, needing care with or without other activity | 0.00 | 0.05 | 0.03 |
| Travel related to care of children | 0.01 | 0.03 | 0.02 |
| Travel related to care of adults and others | 0.01 | 0.01 | 0.01 |
| Taking care of guests/visitors | 0.01 | 0.03 | 0.02 |
| Any other activity not mentioned above | 0.03 | 0.07 | 0.05 |
| **Total** | **0.88** | **4.47** | **2.62** |

*Source*: Indian TUS 1998–9.

taking care of the household. The maximum time is spent on cooking (14.59 hours), followed by cleaning and washing (7.89 hours), care of textiles (2.31 hours), and household maintenance, shopping, etc. (2.14 hours). Men, on an average, spend less than one hour per week on each of these activities. As regards childcare and care of the old, sick, or disabled in the household, women spend 4.47 hours per week against 0.88 hours per week by men. Women spend maximum time on physical care of children (3.09 hours), followed by non-physical care of children (that is, teaching and training children, accompanying them to places, etc.). Women also spend more time on other care activities than men. On an average, men spend 2.17 per cent of their total time on non-SNA work as against 20.61 per cent by women. Clearly, this is a major constraint for women who want to participate in the labour market.

## Unequal Sharing of Total Work by Men and Women

The time-use data indicates a highly unequal sharing of total work, including SNA and non-SNA work, by men and women. While men spend more time in SNA work, women spend more time on non-SNA work. However, the gender gap is much more in non-SNA work, with the result that women carry much higher burden of total work. Table 5.8 indicates that women spend an average 69.03 hours on total work, while men spend about 62.71 hours. As a result, women get much less time for personal activities, such as rest, sleep, recreation, etc., as compared to men. Women also get less time for studying, skill formation, etc.

**TABLE 5.8**  Participation and Average Weekly Time Spent by Men and Women on SNA and Non-SNA Activities

| Activity | WPR | | Average Weekly Time Spent | | Male/ Female Ratio (WPR) | Male/Female Ratio (Time Spent) |
|---|---|---|---|---|---|---|
| | Male | Female | Male | Female | | |
| SNA | 62.16 | 50.75 | 54.65 | 30.04 | 1.29 | 2.38 |
| Non-SNA | 24.81 | 84.17 | 8.40 | 39.79 | 0.37 | 0.09 |
| Personal | 99.65 | 99.69 | 111.28 | 105.55 | 1.00 | 1.05 |

*Source*: Indian TUS 1998–9.

If we include all men and women, and not just participants, men spend about 27 per cent of their time on SNA and non–SNA work put together, while women spend about 38 per cent of their time on this total work. As regards sharing of the SNA work, men share 67.89 per cent of work (in total person hours of SNA work), while women share 32.11 per cent of SNA work. It appears that though the gender gap in WPR is not very high, the gap in work intensity is significant (Hirway and Jose 2011).

## INFERENCES FROM THE STUDY

This chapter has shown, conceptually as well as empirically, that LFS are not adequate to estimate and understand workforce and labour force in an economy. It also showed that TUS can throw useful light not only on the size but also on the characteristics of workforce and labour force in an economy. In other words, TUS can complement LFS to design realistic and relevant labour–market interventions.

In the Indian context, the data underlines the fact that women's participation in SNA work is not as low as is seen from the conventional surveys, though it is commonly observed that the WPR of women in the country is very low due to socio–cultural. The Indian time–use data shows that the gap between the WPRs of men and women is not as big as revealed by LFS. The major difference between men and women's WPR is that women participate, on an average, for four hours a day or less, as compared to men who participate full–time, in SNA work, which is mostly because of their domestic responsibilities. They are constrained heavily by the high burden of unpaid work, which leaves them with less time and energy to participate in productive work in the labour market. This burden is also reflected in women's low capabilities and low human capital formation as well as low mobility in the labour market.

Another major constraint of women is their high participation in collection of free goods for meeting basic needs of the household. The lack of basic infrastructure like water, fuel wood/energy, etc., keeps women busy in acquiring these needs, which takes away a lot of time and energy of women. Free collection of raw material for family business (that is, fodder, wood, and raw material for craft) is another form of drudgery for women. The preoccupation of women in unpaid SNA and non-SNA work leaves little scope for women to move into productive activities in the labour market. Poor diversification and crowding in low-productivity, stereotypical activities is a consequence of the overall pattern of use of women's labour in SNA and non-SNA work.

It will not be out of place here to mention that the working group for the 68th round on employment and unemployment in India has recognized the advantages of TUS and accepted its role in enriching the household survey (NSSO 2013).

## REFERENCES

Charmes, Jacques. 2004. 'Data Collection on the Informal Sector: A Review of Concepts and Methods Use since the Adoption of an International Definition Towards a Better Comparability of Available Statistics', Delhi Group on Informal Sector Statistics, International Labour Organization (ILO) Bangkok, February.

Gershuny, Jonathan. 2012. 'Conducting Time Use Survey for Seven Consecutive Days', presentation made at the Annual Conference of the International Association for Time Use Research (IATUR), Turku, Finland.

Government of India. 2000a. *Report of the Indian Time Use Survey 1998–99*, Central Statistical Organization, Ministry of Statistics and Programme Implementation, Government of India, New Delhi

————. 2000b. 'Hours worked includes all paid work activities—primary, secondary and tertiary', in *Estimating Workforce participation Rates Using Time Survey Data and Its Comparisons with the Usual Labour Force Survey: Indian Experiences*, New Delhi: Central Statistical Organization, Ministry of Statistics and Programme Implementation.

Hirway, Indira. 2003. 'Using Time Use Data for Estimating Informal Sector in Developing Countries: Conceptual and Methodological Issues with Reference to South Asia', paper presented at the IATUR Conference at Brussels.

————. 2010. 'Time Use Surveys in Developing Countries: An Assessment', in Rania Antonopoulos and Indira Hirway (eds), *Unpaid Work and the Economy: Gender, Time Use and Poverty in Developing Countries*. London: Palgrave Macmillan.

————. 2012. 'Missing Labour Force: An Explanation', *Economic and Political Weekly*, 47(37): 67–72.

Hirway, Indira and Jacques Charmes. 2006. 'Estimating and Understanding Informal Employment through Time Use Studies', paper presented at Delhi Group Meeting, New Delhi.

Hirway, Indira and Sunny Jose. 2011. 'Understanding Women's SNA Work Using Time-Use Statistics: The Case of India', Special Issue of *Feminist Economics*.

Hoffmann, Eivind and Adriana Mata. 2003. 'Statistics on Working Time Arrangements: An Overview of Issues', *Statistical Journal of the United Nations Economic Commission for Europe*, 18(1): 25–41.

International Labour Organization (ILO). 2013. Resolution on Statistics on Work, Employment, and Labour Underutilization passed by the 19th International Conference on Labour Statistics (ICLS) of the ILO.

Inter-secretariat Working Group on National Accounts ISWGNA. 2008. Systems of National Accounts, UN, New York.

National Sample Survey Organization (NSSO). 2000. *Report of the 1999–2000 Round of Survey of Employment and Unemployment*. New Delhi: NSSO and Ministry of Statistics and Programme Implementation.

———. 2013. *Report of the Employment and Unemployment Survey*, NSSO 68th Round. New Delhi: NSSO and Ministry of Statistics and Programme Implementation.

Organisation for Economic Co-operation and Development (OECD). 2002. *Measuring the Non-Observed Economy*, a handbook. Geneva: ILO.

Pandey, R.N. 2000. 'Estimating Workforce Participation Rates Using Time Survey Data and Its Comparisons with the Usual Labour Force Survey: Indian Experiences', NSSO and Ministry of Statistics and Programme Implementation, New Delhi.

# 6 Time Use and Job Search among the Unemployed and Underemployed

Maria Sagrario Floro and Hitomi Komatsu

The persistence of high unemployment in South Africa has generated a number of debates and puzzles among academics and policymakers. These range from issues regarding the reliability of the measurement and estimate of unemployment levels to underlying causes and explanations of their trends and patterns. Questions have also been raised about how several unemployed persons manage to survive and cope. Given the severity of the problem, the issue of searching for employment and the ability of the unemployed to become employed has become an important topic of study. However, the use of time-use data for exploring the issue of job search among the unemployed and underemployed has received little attention in economic analysis.

In this chapter, we examine South Africa's labour market situation through the lens of people's time use, which is obtained through the data from the 2000 South Africa National Time-Use Survey (TUS). Though not designed to focus on the labour market, the TUS offers useful information for exploring labour market participation of women and men and for examining their time constraints, especially since the TUS combines information on both the labour market and unpaid work activities.[1] The chapter argues that an understanding of how

---

[1] See Floro and Komatsu (2011), for example.

individuals organize their daily life can provide additional insight into the factors influencing a person's engagement in job search. More specifically, the chapter hypothesizes that individuals who are constrained by gender-assigned roles of performing household maintenance and care work will likely find their employment prospects to be persistently below that of other groups due to lack of time and are, therefore, likely to face higher unemployment rates. Gender norms reflected in household division of labour can pose greater hurdles for women in search of jobs, as compared to men. Our study shows that gender roles have implications on the dynamics of job search. Women's unpaid work activities, such as gathering water and fuel; domestic chores; and caring for children, sick, and the elderly in the household are critical, and often neglected, elements of this debate.

The objectives of this chapter are twofold: the first is to examine the time-use patterns and incidence of employment search among the 10,465 adult respondents, aged between 16 and 64 years, as a means of assessing search cost in terms of time by their labour force status. Given that looking for work or for additional work and that starting a new enterprise activity takes time and involves transaction costs, time-use data can provide useful information on the extent of search intensity. The second is to examine pertinent gender-based constraints as well as other household-level and community-level factors that may affect a person's search for wage employment or for starting an enterprise activity. In particular, we want to explore time-use dimensions in order to better understand any differences in labour market situations of women and men. By means of probit and tobit analyses, we examine the relationship between time spent in job search and gender roles among unemployed and underemployed women and men, controlling for economic, social, and demographic factors, such as race, marital status, household lifecycle, education, household composition, as well as community characteristics (for example, access to government transfers and social services).

The chapter differs from previous labour force or employment studies in several respects. First, we analyse the incidence and intensity in job search of women and men by their labour force status using TUS data. This is conducted by measuring the incidence and average time spent which is conditional on participation in job search. Second, we focus on the unemployed female and male survey respondents and explore how they allocate their time among different activities, such as labour market work, household and care work, and leisure. Given that the so-called leisure and social activities can involve spending with non-family friends that can lead to networking and making informal job contacts, we distinguish leisure by self or with family members and leisure with non-family. Third, we examine the likelihood that unemployed and underemployed persons spend time in job search using both probit and tobit analyses, controlling for economic, social, and demographic factors. The significance of this approach will be justified in later part of the chapter.

The chapter is organized as follows: the next section gives an overview of the literature on job search. The second discusses the data used in our empirical analysis, and the method of classifying the individuals' labour force status. The third examines the time-use patterns of men and women by their labour force categories. Probit and tobit models are used to assess the incidence of job search and time spent in job search respectively in the fourth section. The last section summarizes the main points and policy considerations.

## UNEMPLOYMENT IN SOUTH AFRICA

The challenges of South Africa's labour market are starkly represented by its very high unemployment rate and the fact that there are millions of underemployed people. This section briefly describes the labour force participation, employment, and unemployment trends in South Africa. Studies on labour markets routinely make use of two different concepts of unemployment, namely, the official (or strict) definition and the expanded or broad definition.[2] The difference between these definitions lies in the treatment of discouraged workers. The official definition requires that those without work must be actively seeking work and, therefore, treats discouraged jobseekers as part of the not-economically-active population (also referred to as 'not in the labour force' or NLF). The expanded definition includes those not actively seeking employment because they have given up finding work. In a fundamental sense, the situation of the non-searching unemployed individuals is more

---

[2] These are defined by Statistics South Africa (henceforth Stats SA), which is the government agency responsible for collecting and publishing the Labour Force Survey (LFS) (Stats SA 2001a).

disadvantaged and deprived compared to the actively seeking unemployed.[3] For purposes of this study, however, we use the official (or strict) definition, thus focus on those who are actively seeking work.

Table 6.1 shows the participation, employment, and unemployment rates of men and women in South Africa over the period 1995–2010 using Labour Force Survey (LFS) data. It is evident that male labour force participation rate (LFPR) grew from 62.1 per cent in 1995 to 65.2 per cent in 2005 and then declined to 54.2 per cent in 2010. During the same period, their unemployment rate more than doubled, with an increase from 12.3 per cent to 25.3 per cent. Table 6.1 also shows that gender is an important marker of labour market outcomes in South Africa. Fewer women are employed, while more remain unemployed as is evident from the rise of unemployment rate from 20.5 per cent in 1995 to 31.7 per cent in 2005, then declining to 28.0 per cent in 2010 even as female LFPR increased from 41.1 per cent to 47.1 per cent over the same period. A number of studies have examined the factors that may explain these trends. First, as Casale and Posel (2002), Kingdon and Knight (2005), Klasen and Woolard (2009), and Rodrik (2008) point out, the rising unemployment has likely been a result of increased labour supply, particularly among coloured Africans, at a rate much faster than the growth of new employment opportunities.[4] Casale and Posel (2002: 13) argue that this is particularly striking among women such that the feminization of the labour force has been associated with rising rates of female unemployment and the predominance of women in generally insecure forms of employment.

---

[3] Kingdon and Knight (2005) give empirical evidence that the non-searching unemployed are not any happier than the searching employed and question the validity that their labour market status is due to tastes (or lack of desire to work).

[4] The inability of the economy, especially the formal sector, to create jobs and absorb the expanding labour force participation has been linked to the trade policies and global competition. Rodrik (2008) identifies the manufacturing industry's poor performance relative to skill-intensive services as the main cause behind rising unemployment, especially among lower-skilled jobseekers. He argues that the manufacturing industry's decline since the end of apartheid can largely be attributed to low profitability caused by rising import competition.

**TABLE 6.1** Men and Women's Participation, Employment, and Unemployment Rates, 1995–2005 (using strict definition of unemployment)

| Year | Men | | | Women | | |
|------|---------------|--------------|------------|---------------|--------------|------------|
|      | Participation | Unemployment | Employment | Participation | Unemployment | Employment |
| 1995 | 62.1 | 12.3 | 54.5 | 41.1 | 20.5 | 32.7 |
| 1997 | 57.9 | 17.7 | 47.7 | 39.2 | 28.1 | 28.2 |
| 1999 | 63.3 | 20.7 | 50.2 | 48.1 | 29.7 | 33.8 |
| 2001 | 66.5 | 26.7 | 48.7 | 53.0 | 34.4 | 34.8 |
| 2003 | 64.2 | 25.6 | 47.7 | 50.3 | 31.9 | 34.2 |
| 2005 | 65.2 | 22.6 | 50.5 | 49.8 | 31.7 | 34.0 |
| 2010 | 54.2 | 25.3 | 40.5 | 47.1 | 28.0 | 33.9 |

*Source:* Banerjee et al. (2007) for 1995–2005; Stats SA (2010).

*Note:* All figures are for the third quarter.

Among unemployed Africans, especially coloured Africans, the lack of or limited access to capital as well as insufficient entrepreneurial skills pose additional barriers to job creation in the form of business enterprise (Davies and Thurlow 2009; Kingdon and Knight 2005). The evolving demographic changes and changes in household arrangements in the post-apartheid era also affected the labour market situation in South Africa. Casale, Muller, and Posel (2004) argue that the increase in female headship of households and the erosion of male income support have contributed to the significant increase in women's LFPR. The number of women of working age and living at least with one employed male in the household had decreased substantially, particularly during the 1995–9 post-apartheid period.

The problem of unemployment, however, is only one dimension of the labour market problems that South Africans face. A number of studies on poverty and employment have drawn attention to the growing problem of underemployment. Michael Aliber's (2003) study of chronic poverty, for example, points out that jobs, such as self-employment, tend to be precarious and finds that half of those who were engaged in self-employment ended up either underemployed, unemployed, or out of the labour force. Questions on how the unemployed and underemployed manage to survive are raised, since South Africa has few social safety nets (for example, the old-aged pension and child support grant) and social programmes aimed specifically at providing support to the long-term unemployed are non-existent.[5] Thus, the unemployed have to seek out whatever work opportunities they can find, however inadequate or unstable.

## UNDERSTANDING THE PROCESS OF JOB SEARCH

There is, by now, a growing recognition of the importance of understanding job search in the context of rising job insecurity and trend in the growth of joblessness. A number of studies, including Devine

---

[5] The Unemployment Insurance Fund does provide a short-term (six months) safety net for those in cyclical unemployment. There is evidence, however, that safety nets, such as old-aged pensions, are pooled inside the household and provide support for the structurally unemployed (see Ardington and Lund 1995; Klasen and Woolard 2009; Lund and Ardington 2006).

and Kiefer (1993), Mortensen and Pissarides (1999), and Wittenberg (2002) provide a review of the varied approaches to job search. One key observation provided by these reviews is the existence of intrinsic search frictions that prevent labour markets from clearing, even if there are large shifts in 'labour price' or wage. These search frictions have to do with the significant transaction costs due to information asymmetry between jobseekers and employers, screening, and the fact that any contract requires bringing the job applicant and employer into spatial and temporal proximity (Wittenberg 2002: 1164). Using non-parametric analysis on the 1995 October Household Survey data, Wittenberg (2002) explored labour market flows in South Africa, particularly youth unemployment and long-term unemployment. His findings indicate that education has little impact in determining access to employment. Rather, it is the set of 'contacts' and networks of friends, relatives, and neighbours that plays a crucial role in the informal methods of recruitment and for the screening process that are typically used by employers.

Dinkelman's and Pirouz's (2003) study of unemployment and labour force participation in South Africa highlights another point, namely, that job search is a continuous or graded activity involving different intensities of searching and different degrees of responsiveness to changes in labour market conditions. Using South Africa's October Household Surveys 1997 and 1999, they examined varied factors that influence a person's job search intensity. These range from expected benefits (that is, those with higher education are likely to actively seek work) to the cost of obtaining information (that is, those with no previous work experience face higher information costs), as well as having resources to meet job search-related expenses (that is, those living in households with a pensioner or migrant worker are likely to increase search intensity).

The study by Kingdon and Knight (2000) considers several factors that may influence the extent of search intensity among unemployed and underemployed. One factor has to do with the prevailing labour market conditions that lead to discouragement in terms of low prospects of finding work. The results of the 1997 Statistics South Africa's Special Retrospective Survey among the unemployed and underemployed support this view. These results indicate the general loss of hope of finding work and the high levels of unemployment in the communities where they reside as the main reason. A second factor has to do with the cost of job search. Seeking work involves taking the time to meet with friends and relatives and/or going in person to workplaces and asking for work. Among the unemployed and underemployed living far from workplaces, the travel time as well as transportation costs of job search can be prohibitive.

A third factor has to do with both the recruitment and job-search methods used by employers and job seekers respectively (Kingdon and Knight 2000: 5), which echoes the findings of Wittenberg (2002). Such methods typically rely on social networks of friends and relatives, who act as go-betweens or informants, as well as on personal contacts. The work of Aldrich and Zimmer (1986), Holzer (1988), and Montgomery (1991), for example, demonstrate the importance of informal networks of friends, relatives, and neighbours that jointly provide economic opportunities and information flows regarding possible jobs, etc. Network members can potentially broker job openings and jobseekers. Holzer (1988) and Montgomery (1991) developed adverse selection and job search analytical models to explain why workers prefer to conduct job search through informal ties and, thus, fare better than poorly-connected ones. Social networks also play a crucial role among the self-employed. Aldrich and Zimmer (1986) develop the 'network approach to entrepreneurship' framework and argue that network resources and activities are heavily used to establish new firms and that those with a broad and diverse social network are likely to have more successful enterprises. Their findings are corroborated by studies on the relationship between social networks and job-search behaviour—such as those by Franzen and Hangartner (2006) and Nicodemo and García (2015)—conducted among workers in the US and Germany, and in Colombia, respectively.

The role of social networks is particularly important among low-wage and unskilled workers. This is because of the limited employment opportunities and the large supply of jobseekers that characterize the labour market in which they operate. Under such conditions, it is more likely that employers will search for workers using an informal referral method, instead of the more costly formal recruitment methods, such as advertising. Corcoran, Datcher, and Duncan (1980), for example, provide evidence about the importance of informal channels in finding jobs among low-skilled jobs and among less educated workers in the United States. Similarly, Johnson, Bienenstock, and Farrell (1999), in their study of female labour force participation in the poor areas of Los Angeles, show the likelihood of employment to be significantly affected by the presence of social networks. Munshi (2003) has reached a similar conclusion through his study among Mexican migrant workers. Topa (2001) explores the manner in which agents exchange information about job openings within their social networks. Using US Census tract data for Chicago, his empirical investigation shows not only the significance of social interactions, but also the importance of these in areas with less educated workers.

The specific characteristics of social networks and their impact on job information gathering are further explored by Kingdon and Knight (2000) and Calvo-Armengol and Jackson (2004). Calvo-Armengol and Jackson (2004) observe that the unemployed make use of the network for job opportunities, while the employed (especially underemployed and part-timers) gather information on more attractive jobs. Kingdon and Knight (2000) suggest that job searches can be also passive. For example, an on-the-spot recruitment method for hiring unskilled labour involves a truck or van arriving in a rural area or remote, 'formerly homeland' areas.[6] Given the distance from towns and urban centres, individuals in these areas would wait either for word of a job or for recruiters to visit. These jobs, however, tend to be either casual or very short-term in nature.

Although the gender dimensions in job search are recognized in the literature, the relation between gender roles and job search has yet to be empirically investigated. Unemployed women are likely to experience the same strains and stresses in their search for jobs as those faced by men: in addition they continue to perform their socially ascribed roles. Given the fact that time is a significant cost of job search, the demands of household and care work are likely to influence not only women's availability for paid work, but also their ability to search for jobs and to participate in associated activities. The latter includes having time to take up learning and skills acquisition and to socialize, develop networks, and meet 'contacts'. Domestic work and care responsibilities can also limit the range of job-search methods that can be used. For example, women are less likely to take advantage of on-the-spot recruitment methods used by some employers. Given women's household obligations, job search can involve an added process, which

---

[6] A homeland area, referred to as *Bantustan*, was a territory set aside for coloured population of South Africa during the apartheid regime.

serves as an added 'hurdle', namely, finding a replacement or substitute person(s) who can perform these care and household work obligations for both the duration of job search and the duration of employment.

It is not surprising, therefore, that women find their labour market options to be less that of men's and are likely to face higher unemployment rates. This brings about a vicious cycle as higher female unemployment rates lead to even greater discouragement and lower hopes of finding work among women. Those that are successful in finding work and are able to benefit from labour market opportunities may find themselves facing the dilemma of balancing paid work and family life. Some employed women may have their well-being compromised if they experience an increase in total work burden (paid and unpaid) and in stress levels. These labour market outcomes are likely to influence the search intensity of female jobseekers. Thus, an examination of the allocation of time spent in job search alongside household and care work responsibilities is crucial for a comprehensive assessment of the gender inequalities in the labour market.

## TIME-USE PATTERNS OF MEN AND WOMEN BY LABOUR FORCE STATUS

The data we use in the study is a subset of the 2000 South Africa TUS collected by Statistics South Africa (or Stats SA) (2001a). The sub-sample includes 10,465 respondents with complete time-use diaries and who are between the ages of 16 and 64 years. Those who did not have a complete record of time-use diaries were excluded from the sub-sample. For the time-use module, a recall method was employed where respondents answered open-ended questions about what they did the previous day, and where up to three simultaneous activities could be recorded in 30-minute slots over a 24-hour period. The respondents were then asked to clarify whether these activities occurred simultaneously or subsequently. Within each household, up to two individuals aged 10 or above were selected as respondents. The United Nations System of National Accounts (SNA) activity classification system was used to classify the recorded activities (Stats SA 2001).

More than a third of the households have young children aged 0–6 years and about 60 per cent have access to a health clinic (Table 6.2). Nearly two-thirds of the households live in the urban (formal and

**TABLE 6.2** Selected Household Characteristics as per South African TUS (2001)

| Characteristic | Number of Households | Percentage of Total |
|---|---|---|
| **By Presence of Children** | | |
| Households with Children 0–6 Years of Age | 2,452 | 36.3 |
| Households with Children 7–17 Years of Age | 3,305 | 49.0 |
| **By Access to Services** | | |
| With Easy Access to Bus, Taxi, or Train | 5,782 | 85.6 |
| With Easy Access to Health Clinic | 4,138 | 61.3 |
| **Geographic Location** | | |
| Urban Formal | 2,780 | 41.2 |
| Urban Informal | 1,676 | 24.8 |
| Rural | 1,018 | 15.1 |
| Commercial Farming | 1,278 | 18.91 |
| **Total** | **6,752** | **100.00** |
| Household Receiving Money from State Grants | 896 | 13.3 |
| Household Receiving Remittances | 992 | 14.7 |
| **Monthly Household Income (rand)** | | |
| 0–R399 | 1,540 | 22.8 |
| R400–799 | 1,694 | 25.1 |
| R800–1,199 | 970 | 14.4 |
| R1,200–1,799 | 755 | 11.2 |
| R1,800–2,499 | 426 | 6.3 |
| R2,500–4,999 | 540 | 8.0 |
| R5,000–9,999 | 342 | 5.1 |
| R10,000 | 142 | 2.1 |
| No Answer, In Kind | 343 | 5.1 |
| **Total** | **6,752** | **100.00** |

*Source:* Floro and Komatsu 2011. Reproduced with permission from *Feminist Economics*, http://www.feministeconomics.org. © IAFFE 2006.

informal) areas, while 15 per cent live in rural areas. Forty-eight per cent of the households earn a monthly income of R799 (about USD 59 equivalent) or less, while over 7.3 per cent earn at least R5,000

**TABLE 6.3** Selected Individual Survey Respondent Characteristics

| | Number of Men | Percentage of Total | Number of Women | Percentage of Total |
|---|---|---|---|---|
| **Age** | | | | |
| 16–19 | 489 | 9.67 | 512 | 9.47 |
| 20–24 | 832 | 16.45 | 892 | 16.49 |
| 25–34 | 1,405 | 27.78 | 1,494 | 27.63 |
| 35–44 | 1,123 | 22.21 | 1,196 | 22.12 |
| 45–59 | 1,022 | 20.21 | 1,072 | 19.82 |
| 60–64 | 186 | 3.68 | 242 | 4.47 |
| **Total** | **5,057** | **100%** | **5,408** | **100%** |
| **Highest Educational Attainment** | | | | |
| No qualification[a] | 446 | 8.82 | 582 | 10.76 |
| 1–7 years | 1,528 | 30.22 | 1,538 | 28.44 |
| Primary School Completion | 1,872 | 37.02 | 1,969 | 36.41 |
| Secondary School, or Higher | 1,211 | 23.95 | 1,319 | 24.39 |
| **Total** | **5,057** | **100%** | **5,408** | **100%** |
| **Marital Status** | | | | |
| Never Married | 2,314 | 45.76 | 2,303 | 42.59 |
| Married or Living Together | 2,466 | 48.76 | 2,448 | 45.27 |
| Widowed | 77 | 1.52 | 341 | 6.31 |
| Divorced or Separated | 185 | 3.66 | 302 | 5.58 |
| Not Indicated | 15 | 0.30 | 14 | 0.26 |
| **Total** | **5,057** | **100%** | **5,408** | **100%** |
| **Race** | | | | |
| African | 3,884 | 76.80 | 4,088 | 75.59 |
| Indian or Asian | 141 | 2.79 | 145 | 2.68 |
| Coloured | 519 | 10.26 | 635 | 11.74 |
| White | 513 | 10.14 | 540 | 9.99 |
| **Total** | **5,057** | **100%** | **5,408** | **100%** |

*Source*: Floro and Komatsu 2011. Reproduced with permission from *Feminist Economics*, http://www.feministeconomics.org. © IAFFE 2006.

*Note*: [a] This group includes those who have not received qualifications in any of the above categories.

(or USD 368).[7] Slightly over half (52 per cent) of the respondents are women, about 45 per cent of whom are married, compared to 49 per cent among men (Table 6.3). The mean ages of men and women in the sample are similar, about 34.5 and 34.8 years, respectively. Men have slightly higher mean years of schooling compared to women—almost 11 per cent of women have no schooling compared to about 9 per cent of men. More than three-fourths (76 per cent) of the total respondents are Africans, while 11 per cent are coloured. Whites represent 10 per cent of the sample, while Indian and other Asians represent 2.7 per cent of the sample.

There are some limitations of the survey data that need to be acknowledged. First, educational attainment categories include only up to grade 12. Therefore, we are unable to distinguish between respondents who have completed high school and those with college, university, or higher degrees. Second, there are likely to be problems of misreporting on time spent in different activities, including household work, care work, and job search activities, given that not everyone has a watch. This suggests that time spent on a particular activity may be influenced by the respondent's perception or notion of time itself. Moreover, some respondents, women in particular, may have been acculturated into and/ or have adopted the performance of two or more activities simultaneously without being conscious of it. These factors are likely to result in the underestimation of multiple work activities, especially those involving childcare or care for the sick, sometimes referred to as multitasking.

An unemployed person is defined as someone who did not do any labour market work in the last seven days, but is available to accept work in the next week, and has taken action to look for work in the last four weeks. Consistent with South Africa's LFS, this is called a strict definition of unemployment, as it excludes discouraged work seekers who are available to work in the next week but have given up looking for employment because they do not believe they would find it (Stats SA 2001b).[8] An employed person is someone who reported that they did any work in the last seven days. They are also classified as employed

---

[7] This is at 13.6R = 1 USD exchange rate, as of August 2016.

[8] Discouraged work seekers are classified as not in the labour force in the strict definition. However, in the broad definition of unemployment, they are classified as being unemployed (Stats SA 2001).

**TABLE 6.4** Labour Force Status of Respondents in 2000 TUS (using strict definition of unemployment), in Percentage of Total Sample

| Labour Force Status | Total TUS N = 10,465 | Women TUS N = 5,408 | Men TUS N = 5,057 |
|---|---|---|---|
| Not in Labour Force | 35.8 | 43.1 | 27.8 |
| Unemployed (strict definition) | 10.3 | 10.8 | 9.8 |
| Underemployed | 6.9 | 5.9 | 7.9 |
| Fully Employed | 47.0 | 40.2 | 54.5 |
| Total | 100% | 100% | 100% |
| Strict Unemployment Rate[a] | 16.0% | 18.9% | 13.5% |

*Source:* Authors' calculation using data from Statistics South Africa (Stats SA) (2001a).
*Notes:* Data was collected in 2000 for the TUS 2001. We used person weights.
[a] We based the employment status classification on respondents' answer to question 2.11: 'Did you do any of the following activities in the last seven days?', in the demographic part of the TUS questionnaire.

if they did not work in the last seven days, but have a job to return to, or they did not look for work because they are satisfied with their current work.

Work is defined as running a business, helping a family business without payment, working for a wage, salary, piecework pay, commission, or payment in kind, working as a paid domestic worker, growing crops and vegetables on a family farm, raising animals, catching fish, or performing any construction or repair work (Stats SA 2001a). A person is defined as being underemployed if they are employed but worked in the labour market for less than 4.4 hours on the reference day of the TUS, and they looked for work in the last four weeks. This classification follows the International Labour Organization's (ILO's) definition of underemployment (ILO 1998).[9] A person is defined as fully employed if they are employed but not underemployed.

Table 6.4 shows the estimates for the labour force status of respondents aged 16–64 years with complete time-use diaries in the 2000

---

[9] The ILO defines underemployment as a person willing and available to work in the labour market for more hours and has worked in the labour market less than a threshold (ILO 1998). We define the threshold as 22 hours per week based on the South Africa labour legislation that specifies part-time work for the service sector.

time-use data. The distribution of labour force status of the sample shows that women (43.1 per cent of the sample) are more likely to be classified as not in the labour force than men (27.8 per cent of the sample). Using the narrow or official definition of unemployment rate, calculated as the number of unemployed persons (excluding discouraged work seekers) as a percentage of the economically active population, women's unemployment rate is 18.9 per cent which is higher than men's at 13.5 per cent. Men are more likely to be fully employed (54.5 per cent) and underemployed (7.9 per cent) than women (40.2 per cent and 5.9 per cent respectively).

Our study now explores the incidence and time spent in job search activities by unemployed and underemployed men and women. It analyses the time spent in job-seeking activities that are reported as first activity as well as those that occurred simultaneously with or sequentially after the first activity.[10]

Table 6.5a shows the percentage of respondents who spent at least 30 minutes seeking employment and in activities related to seeking employment in the 24-hour period. Table 6.5b presents the mean time spent (in minutes) in job-seeking activities, and Table 6.5c presents the mean time spent (in minutes) in job-seeking activities among those who spent at least 30 minutes. All three tables disaggregate the results by sex.

Statistics of the TUS show that women (unemployed and underemployed) are engaged in job-search activities to a lesser extent than men, in terms of the incidence, average time spent, and average time spent conditional on participation in that particular activity. Only 3.2 per cent of unemployed and 1.4 per cent of underemployed women did some job search compared to their male counterparts (19.9 per cent and 6.7 per cent of unemployed and underemployed men respectively). The gender difference is also stark in terms of the mean time spent on job-search activities: unemployed and underemployed men on average

---

[10] Stats SA (2001b) used two different methods of assigning minutes to multiple activities. When there were two or three activities in a half hour that were performed sequentially, each activity was assigned 10 or 15 minutes. However, when two or more activities were performed simultaneously, it assigned 30 minutes to each of the three activities in order to show a more accurate duration of a particular activity.

**TABLE 6.5A**   Incidence of those who did some Job Search Activities Among Unemployed and Underemployed by Sex

|  | Unemployed | Underemployed |
|---|---|---|
| All | 10.8% | 4.3% |
| Men | 19.9% | 6.7% |
| Women | 3.2% | 1.4% |

**TABLE 6.5B**   Mean Time Spent (minutes) in Job Search Activities Among Unemployed and Underemployed by Sex

|  | Unemployed | Underemployed |
|---|---|---|
| All | 30.33 | 5.61 |
| Men | 58.91 | 9.19 |
| Women | 6.55 | 1.24 |

**TABLE 6.5C**   Mean Time Spent (minutes) in Job Search Conditional on Participation Among Unemployed and Underemployed by Sex

|  | Unemployed | Underemployed |
|---|---|---|
| All | 280.99 | 130.93 |
| Men | 296.02 | 138.06 |
| Women | 203.57 | 89.30 |

*Source:* Authors' calculation using data from Statistics South Africa (Stats SA) (2001a).

spent about 59 minutes and 9.19 minutes a day, respectively, while unemployed and underemployed women spent 6.55 minutes and 1.24 minutes, respectively. Among those that spent some time in looking for work, unemployed men spent more time (about 296 minutes) in job search compared to unemployed women (nearly 204 minutes) as shown in Table 6.5c. A similar trend is observed among underemployed jobseekers, with women spending less time (89.3 minutes) compared to men (138.06 minutes).

If the likelihood of getting employed is positively correlated with time spent in seeking jobs, contacting friends and relatives, and/or developing networks through social activities, then the relative lack of time among unemployed and underemployed women compared to men could contribute to this trend. Gender-based responsibilities in household maintenance and care work reduce women's time to look for work, placing them at a disadvantage compared to men and, thus, adversely affecting their ability to transition to being employed. In the following paragraphs, we examine how women and men aged between 16 and 64 years, in different labour force status, spend their time in labour market work, household work, volunteer and community service, leisure and social activities, and personal care and self-maintenance.

In estimating the time allocation of NLF, unemployed, underemployed, and fully employed, we use a modified SNA-based activity classification. First, we reclassified the 'collecting fuel and water' activity as part of non-SNA production activities (namely, household work), instead of classifying it as part of SNA production activities, which are wage employment, primary production, and home-based and domestic services. Second, we distinguish between leisure activity with non-family and leisure activity with family or self since the former may be an important component of networking and finding labour market work. Hence, the following activity classification is used: (a) labour market work (SNA production activities, excluding fuel and water collecting); (b) household work, including fuel and water gathering, domestic chores, childcare, and shopping; (c) volunteer and community service; (d) leisure with non-family and social activities; (e) leisure activities with family or self; and (f) personal care and other activities, including sleep, personal hygiene, learning, and doing nothing. The average time spent in minutes in both first and second activities is shown in Table 6.6.

Unemployed and NLF men spent just over 45 minutes and 30 minutes, respectively, a day in activities classified as labour market work even though they said they did not work in the last seven days, while unemployed and NLF women spent 18 minutes and 16 minutes, respectively.[11] Among the fully employed, men spent about 356 minutes per day on average in labour market work, which is 65 minutes (or 1 hour) more per day than women. Underemployed men and women spent about the same amount of time in this activity (28 minutes and 33 minutes, respectively). Hence, in all categories except the

---

[11] For a study on why unemployed and NLF men and women may have spent time in labour market work even though they said they did not work in the last seven days, please see Floro and Komatsu (2011).

TABLE 6.6 Mean Time of Unemployed Women and Men Spent in First and Secondary Activities (minutes per day)

| | Not in labour force | | Unemployed | | Underemployed | | Fully employed | |
|---|---|---|---|---|---|---|---|---|
| | Women | Men | Women | Men | Women | Men | Women | Men |
| *I. Labour Force Participation* | | | | | | | | |
| Labour Market Work[a] | 16 | 32 | 18 | 47 | 33 | 28 | 291 | 356 |
| Job Search Activities[b] | 1 | 5 | 7 | 59 | 1 | 9 | 2 | 5 |
| *II. Household Work* | 315 | 128 | 400 | 146 | 391 | 162 | 228 | 91 |
| Fuel and Water Collection, Stone Cutting | 17 | 11 | 22 | 6 | 19 | 2 | 9 | 4 |
| Domestic Chores and Care Work[c] | 298 | 118 | 378 | 140 | 372 | 160 | 220 | 87 |
| *III. Volunteer and Community Service[d]* | 4 | 7 | 5 | 8 | 16 | 7 | 5 | 8 |
| *IV. Leisure and Social Activities* | 393 | 481 | 412 | 549 | 418 | 601 | 329 | 381 |
| Leisure with Non-family and Social Activities[e] | 123 | 184 | 110 | 243 | 130 | 285 | 103 | 148 |
| Leisure with Family or Alone[f] | 270 | 297 | 302 | 306 | 288 | 316 | 226 | 233 |
| *V. Personal Care and Self-maintenance* | 947 | 1006 | 798 | 844 | 829 | 878 | 768 | 773 |
| Learning[g] | 122 | 195 | 9 | 19 | 11 | 19 | 18 | 24 |
| Personal Care[h] | 772 | 766 | 744 | 776 | 764 | 791 | 722 | 721 |
| Doing Nothing | 53 | 45 | 46 | 49 | 54 | 67 | 29 | 29 |

*Source:* Authors' calculation using data from Statistics South Africa (Stats SA) (2001a).

*Notes:*

[a] These activities include wage and salary work, home-based work, unpaid family work, domestic and personal service, self-employed work, subsistence farming, animal husbandry, fishing, food processing and selling, textile, leather and other craft-making, construction, petty trading, tools and machinery making, and other personal services. Labour market work here excludes travel to and from work and travel for seeking employment and job search and related activities. The latter is given as a separate category.

[b] These include seeking employment and activities related to seeking employment.

[c] These are largely unpaid work activities. They include food preparation and clean up, laundry, ironing, care of clothing and other house-work, animal care, home maintenance and repair, household management, transporting household members, and travel associated with any of the above activities. They also include physical care and minding of own and other children, care for sick or disabled child, teaching own and other children, playing with own and other children, and travel associated with childcare, shopping, and accessing government services.

[d] These refer to all unpaid community services, including civic responsibilities, helping or caring for disabled adults, unpaid services for children, and travel connected with these activities.

[e] These activities include participating in cultural activities, weddings, funerals, religious activities, socializing with non-family members, and travel related to these activities.

[f] These include socializing with family, spending time in arts, hobbies, sports, games and being a spectator to sports, cinema, and other events, reading, watching TV, listening to music, or other mass media use.

[g] These include attending school or training workshops and doing homework.

[h] These include sleeping, eating, drinking, dressing, and washing.

underemployed, men spent considerably more time in SNA production activities than women.

Women, on the other hand, were engaged in household work, fuel
and water gathering, and care work to a much larger extent than men
in every labour force category. For example, NLF, unemployed, and
underemployed women spent over six hours a day in these activities
(315 minutes, 400 minutes, and 391 minutes respectively), compared to
men who are NLF, unemployed, and underemployed who spent about
2.5 hours a day. In fact, unemployed women spent the most amount
of time in housework than any other category. Even women who are
fully employed spent approximately four hours a day in these activities,
while fully employed men spent 1.5 hours. These results indicate that
the burden of care work and household maintenance fall much more
heavily on women, regardless of their labour force status. Whether
they are unemployed, underemployed, NLF, or fully employed, women
spend about three times the amount of time spent by men on these
unpaid work activities.

We disaggregate leisure in our study between: (a) activities that
occurred with non-family members and social activities, such as
participating in weddings, funerals, religious activities and (b) activities that took place with family or self, such as spending time in art,
hobbies, sports, games, cinema, reading, watching TV, listening to
music, or other mass media use. In doing so, we make a distinction
between the former type of non-economic activities, which provide
individuals the opportunity to contact friends and develop networks
with acquaintances for possible employment, and the latter, which are
mainly activities for entertainment.

Men who are unemployed and underemployed spent over four
hours a day (243 minutes and 285 minutes respectively) on average
in non-family leisure and social activities; these figures are about two
hours longer than those spent by unemployed and underemployed
women. At 110 minutes and 103 minutes, respectively, unemployed
and fully employed women spent the least amount of time in this
type of leisure. For NLF category, men spent three hours compared
to women who spent two hours in these activities. When it comes to
leisure activity with family or self, however, there is little gender difference. Men and women who are NLF, unemployed, or underemployed
spent about five hours a day in this type of leisure activity, while fully
employed men and women spent almost four hours a day.

The above trends in time-use allocation indicate that because women bear a considerably larger burden of household work, fuel and water collection, and care for others, they have relatively less time available than men for job-search activities and for those social/leisure activities with non-family members that could help them expand their social networks and find a job. This is particularly true for unemployed women who spent the longest time doing housework and care work and the least amount of time in leisure activities with non-family members and social activities. The average time unemployed and underemployed women spent in job search activities (7 minutes and 1 minute, respectively) is only a very small proportion of what unemployed and underemployed men spent (59 minutes and 9 minutes, respectively). Time-use data can, therefore, provide useful information and evidence on the relationship between the gender-assigned roles and responsibilities, that is, time constraints that women face, and their ability to undertake job search and make potential job contacts. They indicate the extent to which gender norms contribute to higher unemployment of women.

## RELATION BETWEEN JOB SEARCH AND GENDER ROLES: AN EMPIRICAL ANALYSIS

In this section, we explore the impact of gender role indicators on the incidence and extent of job-search intensity using a sample of 1,800 women and men who are unemployed and underemployed between the ages of 16 and 64 years. In particular, we investigate the determinants of who are actively seeking work and the extent of their search intensity. Only the estimates using the strict definition of unemployed are reported in the study since the incidence of discouraged workers in job search is very small (only one woman and six men engaged in job search).[12] The sub-sample excludes those respondents who are unable to account at least two hours of their total time on a given day.

The extent to which an unemployed and underemployed individual is likely to spend time in job search activities depends on a variety of economic, demographic, and household factors. These include

[12] Estimates using the broad definition are available upon request from authors.

sex, race, marital status, household lifecycle, and composition. Living in rural or less developed areas makes informal job search even more prevalent. Given that job search costs involve investing time for job information gathering and developing potential job contacts, we expect that those who are time constrained are less likely to invest time in such activities.

Market work is still perceived to be the primary role of men, and household maintenance and childcare to be women's principal work domain. These distinct social constructs have a number of implications. First, they influence the sexual division of labour within the household, thereby creating time pressure for many women, regardless of their labour force status, as indicated by the long hours of work spent in unpaid household work activities. This likely restricts them from engaging in job-search activities. Second, there may be high unemployment rates and/or patterns of sex discrimination in areas where they live that cause women to give up looking for work, or be discouraged from searching.

Demographic factors also influence the time spent in job search. Persons who are older and those who belong in single-adult-headed households tend to experience greater pressure to seek employment and, thus, are likely to engage in job search. At the same time, some unemployed as well as underemployed persons may have less time available, given the presence of dependents and the demands of caring work. Household composition, particularly the presence of young children, elderly, and sick people plays an important role. Given the intensive nature of childcare and care of elderly and sick, demands on caregivers' time are high, reducing the intensity of job search. The age of children in the household also sets the parameters by which these individuals can perform other tasks. Pre-school-aged children place a higher demand on adults' primary time than older children, increasing the conflict between time spent in job search and childcare. As one moves into a later stage (for example, older children, retirement, etc.), time pressure is expected to decline.

The probability that an unemployed or underemploye individual $i$ spends time in job search is first estimated by using the probit model below:

$$Y_i^* = X_i\,\beta + u_i, \tag{1}$$

where $Y_i^\star = 1$ if they spent time in job search, and $Y_i^\star = 0$ otherwise. $X_i$ is a $1 \times k$ vector that is uncorrelated with an error term, $u_i$ where k refers to a list of pertinent individual and household characteristics such as demographic and household factors, access to services. $\beta$ is a $k \times 1$ vector of parameters to be estimated.

The demand for time spent in job search (measured in minutes per day), $S_i^\star$ by individual $i$ is next estimated using the equation below:

$$S_i^* = X_i \, \beta + u_i, \tag{2}$$

where $S_i^\star$ is the time spent in job search, and $X_i$ is a $1 \times k$ matrix of variables (such as, demographic and household factors) uncorrelated with an error term $u_i$. Since $S_i$ is censored, a tobit model is used to estimate equation (2). One should note that the above Tobit model imposes the same economic structure on both the decision to seek paid work actively and the length of time spent in such activity. Hence, it uses the same regressors and parameters. Thus, for estimation purposes, the equation that determines the time spent by individual $i$ on job search becomes a function of the same set of exogenous household and individual characteristics that determine whether that person will seek paid work.

We include the following individual and household characteristics in the both probit and tobit models: lifecycle stage (represented by the age and age$^2$ of the individual), a woman dummy variable, race variables, educational attainment, marital status, household size and composition, wealth, rural area, and access to government grants. We define education attainment as dummy variables indicating low level (less than 8 years of schooling) and moderate level (8–11 years of schooling) to high level (12 years or more). Educational attainment is likely to increase the probability of actively engaging in job search. The household and composition variables are represented by two variables: the number of young children under 7 years of age and the number of household members aged 10 years and above. The dummy variable for women is interacted with marital status and the number of children under 7 years of age since women's gender-assigned responsibilities to care for their families and young children could reduce their ability to spend time in job search. Two additional interaction variables are includes as well: marital status (married) dummy and number of children under 7 years on one hand, and woman dummy and number of children under 7 years on the other.

Two probit and tobit models are estimated, each differing in the sub-sample of jobseekers who are included. First, we estimate the model for the unemployed to examine pertinent individual, household, and area-level factors that may influence the dependent variable (that is, the probability of undertaking job search in the probit model and the intensity of job-search activity as measured by the amount of time spent in active job search). Next, we extend the sample to include the underemployed as well to test the robustness of the regression results.

The results of the probit model estimates are given in Table 6.7, which shows that unemployed women are 16 per cent less likely to engage in job search on the day the TUS was conducted. When underemployed women are included, the marginal effects are slightly lower—about 11.4 per cent. The dummy variable for being married, by itself, is not statistically significant; it is only significant when inter-acted with the woman dummy variable. Our estimates show that the probability of seeking work is lower if the unemployed women are married (58 per cent less likely to undertake job search). It should be noted, however, that the interaction variable effect is statistically insig-nificant when underemployed women are included in the sample. This suggests that unemployed women's marital status affects their ability to spend time in job search, but not among the underemployed. Our results also indicate that having young children in the household does not affect the likelihood of spending time in looking for work.

Older people face a higher probability of spending time in job search. Unemployed Africans are 5.3 per cent more likely to engage in searching for work compared to those who are white, coloured, or others, while there is no difference between Indians and the reference categories. Although race does not seem to influence the probability of seeking work when underemployed are included in the sample, hav-ing a moderate level of education seems to increase the likelihood of both unemployed and underemployed to search for job. Living in a rural area makes job search more difficult also for both unemployed and underemployed, where we find that they are 8.4 per cent (for unemployed) and 7.1 per cent (for both unemployed and underem-ployed) less likely to undertake job search.

The tobit model results for exploring the determinants of degree of search intensity (length of time spent in seeking work) among the unemployed sub-sample and the combined unemployed and

**TABLE 6.7** Probability that Unemployed or Underemployed Persons Conducted Some Job Market Search (marginal effects at mean)

| Variables | Unemployed | Unemployed or Underemployed |
|---|---|---|
| Woman | −0.161★★★ | −0.114★★★ |
| | (0.0206) | (0.0139) |
| Number of Children under 7 Years | −0.0048 | 0.0039 |
| of Age | (0.0152) | (0.0100) |
| Married | −0.274 | −0.0206 |
| | (0.229) | (0.0149) |
| Woman × Number of Children | 0.0259 | 0.0303 |
| under 7 Years old | (0.372) | (0.0193) |
| Woman × Married | −0.144★★ | −0.0287 |
| | (0.0488) | (0.03067) |
| Married × Number of Children | −0.0278 | −0.0038 |
| under 7 Years of Age | (0.267) | (0.0169) |
| Woman × Married × Number of | −0.064 | −0.0176 |
| Children under 7 Years of Age | (0.226) | (0.0353) |
| Age | 0.0101★ | 0.00391 |
| | (0.00574) | (0.00380) |
| $Age^2$ | −0.000129★ | −4.87e-05 |
| | (7.62e-05) | (5.05e-05) |
| African Dummy | 0.0533★★★ | 0.0227 |
| | (0.0205) | (0.0162) |
| Indian or Coloured Dummy | −0.0242 | −0.0437 |
| | (0.0781) | (0.0313) |
| Single Head of Household | 0.0499 | 0.0253 |
| | (0.0369) | (0.0221) |
| Number of Household Members | 0.00415 | 0.00359 |
| Aged 10 Years or Above | (0.00467) | (0.00320) |
| Low Education Dummy | −0.00107 | 0.00668 |
| | (0.0268) | (0.0190) |
| Moderate Education Dummy | 0.0198 | 0.0317★★ |
| | (0.0203) | (0.0143) |
| State Grants Recipient | −0.0344★ | −0.0167 |
| | (0.0206) | (0.0150) |
| Household Receives Remittances | −0.00922 | 0.0237 |
| | (0.0208) | (0.0167) |
| Rural | −0.0843★★★ | −0.0711★★★ |
| | (0.0170) | (0.0107) |
| Easy Access to Health Centre or | −0.0126 | −0.00845 |
| Clinic | (0.0187) | (0.0126) |

*(Cont'd)*

**TABLE 6.7**    (*Cont'd*)

| Variables | Unemployed | Unemployed or Underemployed |
|---|---|---|
| Gautung | −0.0153 | −0.0191 |
|  | (0.0218) | (0.0138) |
| Observations | 1,060 | 1,734 |
| Correctly classified | 86.6% | 90.1% |
| Pseudo-$R^2$ | 0.1392 | 0.1115 |

*Source*: Authors' calculation using data from Statistics South Africa (Stats SA) (2001a).
*Notes*: Robust standard errors in parentheses. We used person weights. We report marginal effects at the mean (standard errors in parenthesis). ★★★, ★★, ★ denote statistical significance at the 1, 5, and 10 per cent levels, respectively.

underemployed sub-sample are presented in Table 6.8. It gives the marginal effects at the mean from the regressions using time spent in both primary and secondary job search activities. Unemployed women on average spend much less time (312.9 minutes) than men in job search, and if they are married, they spend even less time (444.5 minutes) in this activity. When underemployed are included in the sample, the gender-based difference increases to 354 minutes. If unemployed women are married and there are young children in the house, they spend 578.8 minutes less time and even fewer minutes for each additional child. On the other hand, married unemployed men spend 114.9 minutes more in job search, and if there is one child under 7 years in the household, they spend 164.5 more minutes—this increases with each additional child. When underemployed married women with young children are included in the sample, the time spent on job search is about 473.1 minutes less than their male counterparts.

A person is likely to spend less time in job search at a younger age, if he/she is not married, and/or if he/she has few or no young children. These results confirm that women are more likely to be constrained by gender-assigned roles of shouldering the bulk of housework, which inhibits their ability to network or to travel in person to workplaces and, therefore, to get a job. Being an unemployed African increases the time spent in job search by 163.2 minutes, although the race dummy effect is statistically insignificant when the underemployed is included in the model estimation. Not surprisingly, we also find that living in rural areas reduces the amount of time spent in job search by 273 minutes.

**TABLE 6.8** Tobit Minutes that Unemployed or Underemployed Persons Spent Doing Job Market Search (marginal effects at mean)

| Variables | Unemployed | Unemployed or Underemployed |
|---|---|---|
| Woman | −312.9★★★ | −354.0★★★ |
| | (68.28) | (61.97) |
| Number of Children under 7 Years of Age | −46.86 | −40.68 |
| | (50.50) | (41.15) |
| Married | 114.9★ | 18.46 |
| | (66.64) | (57.79) |
| Woman × Number of Children under 7 Years of Age | 131.7★★ | 119.1★★ |
| | (61.35) | (53.73) |
| Woman × Married | −246.5★ | −139.9 |
| | (126.8) | (123.1) |
| Married × Number of Children under 7 Years of Age | 49.57 | 20.54 |
| | (65.63) | (60.34) |
| Woman × Married × Number of Children under 7 Years of Age | −268.7★★ | −75.71 |
| | (134.0) | (114.4) |
| Age | 22.55★ | 11.17 |
| | (13.44) | (11.48) |
| Age$^2$ | −0.286 | −0.137 |
| | (0.181) | (0.154) |
| African dummy | 163.2★★ | 85.01 |
| | (71.56) | (60.78) |
| Indian or Coloured Dummy | −31.02 | −156.8 |
| | (246.4) | (210.9) |
| Single Head of Household | 92.07 | 58.36 |
| | (67.44) | (55.57) |
| Number of Household Members Aged 10 years or Above | 10.40 | 11.11 |
| | (10.97) | (9.709) |
| Low Education Dummy | −1.474 | 22.86 |
| | (63.12) | (55.72) |
| Moderate Education Dummy | 51.10 | 93.88★★ |
| | (46.22) | (39.87) |
| State Grants Recipient | −106.7★ | −64.16 |
| | (59.56) | (51.95) |
| Household Receives Remittances | −32.50 | 60.89 |
| | (50.79) | (43.16) |
| Rural | −273.0★★★ | −309.5★★★ |
| | (82.99) | (73.38) |
| Easy Access to Health Centre or Clinic | −32.48 | −24.59 |
| | (43.07) | (37.47) |

*(Cont'd)*

**TABLE 6.8**    (*Cont'd*)

| Variables | Unemployed | Unemployed or Underemployed |
|---|---|---|
| Gautung | −39.67 | −62.42 |
|  | (55.18) | (48.29) |
| Observations | 1,060 | 1,734 |

*Source:* Authors' calculation using data from Statistics South Africa (Stats SA) (2001a).
*Notes:* Robust standard errors in parentheses. We used person weights. We report marginal effects at the mean (standard errors in parenthesis). ★★★, ★★, ★ denote statistical significance at the 1, 5, and 10 per cent levels, respectively.

This chapter examined the time-use patterns and incidence of job search among unemployed and underemployed persons aged between 16 and 64 years as a means of assessing their ability to find work. In particular, the chapter explored its time dimensions to understand better any differences in women's and men's situations. Hence, we examine the determinants that likely influence the unemployed or underemployed person's ability to look for work, including gender-based constraints as well as household-level and community-level factors that may affect search for wage employment or the development of a new enterprise activity.

The study findings indicate that the male unemployed and underemployed are more likely to spend more time in job search than unemployed or underemployed women. Using a sub-sample drawn from the 2000 National South African TUS, the study illuminates the relationship between gender roles in the form of household and care work assignation, as proxied by gender, marital status, and presence of young children interaction variables, and the intensity of job search undertaken by unemployed and underemployed men and women. Since time is a significant cost of job search, our findings indicate that there are crucial gender dimensions regarding the time constraints faced by participants in the labour market that policymakers cannot ignore. As the estimates of probit and tobit models suggest, women's ability (or lack thereof) to find work is linked to the amount of unpaid work for household maintenance and care work that they perform. Thus, any effort to lower unemployment rates should include programmes and strategies that reduce the unpaid work burden of women.

The significance of these results lies in the fact that time-use data is now receiving greater attention among policymakers and researchers worldwide concerned with measurement and analysis of policy impacts as well as with formulation of economic and social policies. They provide a more comprehensive picture of the unemployed and underemployed individual's use of time and, thus, the linkage between the time he/she spends in job search and in the performance of unpaid work activities. This factor also explain why women in South Africa find their labour market options to be less than that of men's and why they face higher unemployment rates. Thus, an examination of the allocation of time is crucial for a comprehensive assessment of the gender inequalities in the labour market.

## REFERENCES

Aldrich, Howard and Catherine Zimmer. 1986. 'Entrepreneurship Through Social Networks', in Donald Sexton and Raymond Smilor (eds), *The Art and Science of Entrepreneurship*, pp. 3–23. New York: Ballinger.

Aliber, Michael. 2003. 'Chronic Poverty in South Africa: Incidence, Causes and Policies,' *World Development*, 31(3): 473–90.

Ardington, E. and F. Lund. 1995. 'Pensions and Development: Social Security as Complementary to Programmes of Reconstruction and Development', *Development Southern Africa,* 12(4): 557–77.

Banerjee, A., Sebastian Galiani, Jim Levinsohn, Zoe McLaren, and Ingrid Woolard. 2007. 'Why Has Unemployment Risen in the New South Africa?', *NBER Working Paper 13167*, Washington DC: National Bureau of Economic Research.

Calvo-Armengol, A. and M.O. Jackson. 2004. 'The Effects of Social Networks on Employment and Inequality.', *The American Economic Review,* 94(3): 426–54.

Casale, Daniela and Dorrit Posel. 2002. 'The Continued Feminisation of the Labour Force in South Africa: An Analysis of Recent Data and Trends.', *South African Journal of Economics,* 70(1): 156–84.

Casale, Daniela, Colette Muller, and Dorrit Posel. 2004. 'Two Million Net New Jobs: A Reconsideration of the Rise in Employment in South Africa, 1995–2003', *South African Journal of Economics,* 72(5): 978–1002.

Corcoran, Mary, Linda Datcher, and Greg Duncan. 1980. 'Information and Influence Networks in Labour Markets', in Greg Duncan and James Morgan (eds), *Five Thousand American Families: Patterns of Economic Progress*, Vol. 7. Ann Arbor, MI: Institute for Social Research, pp. 1–37.

Davies, Rob and James Thurlow. 2009. 'Formal–Informal Economy Linkages and Unemployment in South Africa.' Discussion Paper 00943, International Food Policy Research Institute (IFPRI), Washington, DC.

Devine, T.J. and N.M. Kiefer. 1993. 'The Empirical Status of Job Search Theory', *Labour Economics*, 1(1): 3–24.

Dinkelman, T. and F. Pirouz. 2003. 'Unemployment and Labour Force Participation in South Africa: A Focus on the Supply-Side.' Working Paper, Econometric Research Southern Africa, University of Witwatersrand. Available at http://www.econrsa.org/system/files/publications/working_papers_interest/wp28_interest.pdf, last accessed on 19 August 2013.

Floro, M.S. and H. Komatsu. 2011. 'Gender and Work in South Africa: What can Time-Use Data Reveal?', *Feminist Economics*, 17(4), 33–66.

Franzen, A. and D. Hangartner. 2006. 'Social Networks and Labour Market Outcomes: The Non-Monetary Benefits of Social Capital', *European Sociological Review*, 22(4), 353–68.

Holzer, Harry. 1988. 'Search Method Use by Unemployed Youth', *Journal of Labor Economics*, 6(1): 1–20.

International Labour Office (ILO). 1998. *Resolution Concerning the Measurement of Underemployment and Inadequate Employment Situations, adopted by the Sixteenth International Conference of Labor Statisticians*. Geneva: ILO.

Johnson, J., E.J. Bienenstock, and W.C. Farrell, Jr. 1999. 'Bridging Social Networks and Female Labour Force Participation in a Multi-Ethnic Metropolis', *Urban Geography*, 20(1): 3–30.

Kingdon, Geeta and John Knight. 2000. 'Are Searching and Non-searching Unemployment Distinct States When Unemployment is High? The Case of South Africa'. Centre for the Study of African Economies, Oxford University.

————. 2005. 'Unemployment in South Africa 1995–2003: Causes, Problems and Policies'. Working Paper Series WPS 010, Economic and Social Research Council, Global Poverty Research Group, Oxford, UK.

Klasen, Stephan and Ingrid Woolard. 2009. 'Surviving Unemployment Without State Support: Unemployment and Household Formation in South Africa', *Journal of African Economies*, 18(1): 1–51.

Lund, Francie and Cally Ardington. 2006. 'Employment Status, Security And The Management Of Risk: A Study of Workers in Kwamsane, KwaZulu-Natal', Working Paper 24/2006, SALDRU, Cape Town: University of Cape Town.

Montgomery, James. 1991. 'Social Networks and Labor Market Outcomes: Towards an Economic Analysis', *American Economic Review*, 81(5): 1408–18.

Mortensen, D.T. and C.A. Pissarides. 1999. 'Job Reallocation, Employment Fluctuations and Unemployment', in J.B. Taylor (ed.), *Handbook of Macroeconomics*, Volume 1, pp. 1171–228. North-Holland: Elsevier.

Munshi, Kaivan. 2003. 'Networks in the Modern Economy: Mexican Migrants in the US Labor Market', *The Quarterly Journal of Economics*, 118(2): 549–99.

Nicodemo, C. and G.A. García. 2015. 'Job Search Channels, Neighborhood Effects, and Wages Inequality in Developing Countries: The Colombian Case', *The Developing Economies*, 53(2): 75–99.

Rodrik, D. 2008. 'Understanding South Africa's Economic Puzzles', *Economics of Transition*, 16(4): 769–97.

Statistics South Africa (Stats SA). 2001a. *A Survey of Time Use*. Pretoria: Stats SA.

_____. 2001b. *Labour Force Survey, September 2001*. Pretoria: *Stats SA*.

_____. 2010. *Quarterly Labour Force Survey*, September. Pretoria: *Stats SA*.

Topa, G. 2001. 'Social Interactions, Local Spillovers and Unemployment', *Review of Economic Studies*, 68(2): 261–95.

Wittenberg, M. 2002. 'Job Search in South Africa: A Nonparametric Analysis', *South African Journal of Economics*, 70(8): 1163–96.

# 7 Measurement of Time and Income Poverty

Ajit Zacharias

The purpose of this chapter is to represent the major existing approaches to time and income poverty within a unified framework. As will be obvious, this purpose has compromised certain subtle aspects of the various approaches. However, I hope that the framework captures the essential aspects of the different contributions. I also propose a modification to the standard time and income poverty measures to account for intra-household disparities.

## A TWO-DIMENSIONAL MEASURE OF POVERTY

We choose week as the unit of time so that the total number of hours is fixed at 168 (= 24×7). We also restrict the attention to a household with a single worker so as to avoid dealing with intra-household allocation of time. We begin by defining the time available to the household $^{(A)}$ for income generation[1] and 'leisure',[2] after setting aside:

---

[1] Income-generating activities can involve working for wage and own-account work.

[2] We put the term leisure in quotes because it is used here as a catch-all for the time available for all activities other than income generation, household production, and personal care. Such activities can include, in addition to 'pure leisure', learning, community activities, and political/social activism.

(a) the minimum required amount of time for personal care ($C-$); (b) the minimum required amount of non-substitutable time for household production ($D-$); and (c) the amount of essential substitutable household production time ($R-$) required to subsist at the poverty level of income. Substitutable time represents the time that can be replaced by the purchase of market substitutes by the household.

$$A = 168 - \bar{C} - \bar{D} - \bar{R} \tag{1}$$

The symbols on the right hand side (RHS) of the equation have a bar (-) because they represent the 'norms' for the group that the household belongs to rather than the actual observed values for the household. They are the time allocation parameters for the household, which, in principle, are similar to the parameters (such as, minimum expenditures on food and non-food items) used in the construction of income/consumption poverty measures.

Time deficit or surplus ($X$) is defined as the excess or deficiency of hours of income-generating activity ($L$) in relation to available time:

$$X = A - L \tag{2}$$

The Vickery modification to the standard income-poverty threshold is based on the notion that the time deficit represents an uncompensated loss in necessary household production for employed individuals (Vickery 1977). The time deficit is valued using the unit price ($p$) of market substitutes for household production. Denoting the standard poverty threshold for the household as and the $\tilde{y}$ Vickery threshold as $y^\circ$ one can write:

$$y^\circ = \tilde{y} - \min(0, X) p \tag{3}$$

To attain the poverty level of consumption, the household has to combine a certain amount of money with a certain amount of time spent on the household production. Consider two households that are identical in all respects, $A$ and $B$, who also happen to have an identical amount of money income. Suppose that one household, $A$, does not have enough time available to devote to the necessary amount of household production, while the other household, $B$, has the necessary available time. To treat the two households as equally income-poor would be inequitable towards *B*. The latter's money income (or its poverty threshold) will have to be adjusted by an amount that represents the replacement cost of the foregone household production associated with its time deficit.

The standard and Vickery poverty thresholds coincide if the household has no time deficit. The two-dimensional poverty measure would classify the household as poor if its income, denoted as $y$, is less than the Vickery threshold $y°$ or if the household has a time deficit. That is:

$$y < y° \text{ or } X < 0 \tag{4}$$

## FULL-TIME WORK

Vickery (1977) chose to evaluate poverty under the hypothetical scenario where all individuals could work full time and income consisted only of wage income, that is:

$$L = L^f, \tag{5}$$

where $L^f$ indicates hours of full-time work. The time deficit associated with full-time work is:

$$X = X^f = A - L^f. \tag{6}$$

The equation for income is:

$$y = y^f = wL^f, \tag{7}$$

where the superscript $f$ indicates full-time work and $w$ the hourly wage rate.[3] Under these assumptions, the household is considered poor if:

$$y^f < y° \text{ or } X^f < 0. \tag{8}$$

An advantage of the framework is that it helps identify individuals who would be poor even if they could work full-time.

---

[3] We leave aside here questions related to the determination of the wage rate associated with full-time work for those who are currently working and not working.

## ACTUAL WORKING TIME AND ACTUAL INCOME

Harvey and Mukhopadhyay (2007) evaluated poverty under the actually observed working time and income, known as the Harvey and Mukhopadhyay (HM) method, which is,

$$L = L^a, \tag{9}$$

where $L^a$ indicates actual hours of employment. The associated time deficit is:

$$X = X^a = A - L^a. \tag{10}$$

The equation for income is simply:

$$y = y^a, \tag{11}$$

where the superscript $a$ indicates the actual value. Under these assumptions, the household is considered poor if:

$$y^a < y^\circ \text{ or } X^a < 0. \tag{12}$$

## VICKERY AND HARVEY AND MUKHOPADHYAY METHODS: A COMPARISON

Suppose that the point labelled '$Z$' represents the observed situation of the household, as can be seen in Figure 7.1. The HM method will tell us that the household is income-poor according to the standard income threshold ($y^\circ$) and time non-poor because their actual hours of employment are less than their available time ($A$). The Vickery method would show, on the basis of the assumed wage rate, that the household would be at point $D$ if it was employed full-time ($Lf$)—a situation in which they are time poor, but income non-poor according to the standard income threshold. However, their income poverty status according to the Vickery threshold (equation 3) depends on the replacement cost of household production relative to their wage. If the replacement cost is higher than the wage, they would be income poor. This situation can be seen by comparing the line segments *CD1*

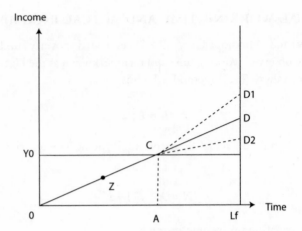

**FIGURE 7.1** Time and Income Poverty with Actual and Full-time Hours of Employment
*Source:* Author's own compilation.

(representing the Vickery threshold) and *CD*. The household cannot work itself out of poverty because the additional income that it earns by working an additional hour beyond *A* is less than the replacement cost of the foregone amount of household production. Comparison of the line segments *CD2* (representing the Vickery threshold) and *CD* shows the opposite situation, where the replacement cost is lower than the wage.

## POTENTIAL TIME DEFICIT/SURPLUS WITH NO INCOME DEFICIT

There are several studies that measure and discuss the 'time-crunch' phenomenon. In an influential contribution, Goodin et al. (2005) argued that most of that literature is somewhat misguided because it fails to compare the actual amounts of time spent by individuals on unpaid work, paid work, and personal care against their respective thresholds. We interpret these thresholds (see equation 1) as representing, at least in spirit, the thresholds for personal care and household production postulated by Goodin et al., referred to as the Goodin approach. Analogously, the Goodin approach defines the amount of necessary time in employment as 'putting in enough paid hours to get your income up to the poverty-level' (Goodin et al. 2005: 50), that is,

$$L = L' = \tilde{y} / w, \tag{13}$$

where $L'$ indicates the hours of employment required to earn the poverty level of income.[4] The associated time deficit, which corresponds to the definition of 'discretionary time', as given by Goodin et al., is:

$$X = X' = A - L'. \tag{14}$$

Income is, by assumption, set equal to the standard poverty threshold:

$$y = \tilde{y}. \tag{15}$$

The household is considered time-poor or under time crunch if:

$$X' < 0. \tag{16}$$

Unlike the earlier two scenarios, this approach does not yield a two-dimensional measure. Instead, what emerges from the analysis is a time-poverty measure that seeks to adjust for differential wage rates.[5]

## POTENTIAL INCOME WITH NO TIME DEFICIT

Instead of asking what the amount of discretionary time would be if the household's hours of employment were just enough hours to earn the poverty level of income, one could ask what the amount of income would be if the household with a time deficit cuts back its hours of employment to eliminate such deficit. If the household has

[4] Goodin et al. (2005) estimated a regression equation for the wage, conditional on the hours of employment and demographics, to account for the potential dependence of wage on the hours of employment. The threshold values for the wage and hours of employment were determined using an iterative procedure.

[5] Goodin et al. (2005) defined discretionary time as the residual time left after subtracting the necessary time for paid work, personal care, and household production. Poverty in discretionary time was defined in purely relative terms.

no time deficit, its income would be calculated using its actual hours of employment. Thus, the hours of employment are given by:

$$L = L'' \begin{cases} = A \text{ if } X^a < 0 \\ = L^a \text{ if } X^a \geq 0 \end{cases} \tag{17}$$

The associated (labour) income is:

$$y = y'' = wL''. \tag{18}$$

The household is considered time poor if:

$$y'' < \tilde{y} \text{ and } X^a < 0. \tag{19}$$

This definition of time poverty captures the spirit of the notion of Bardasi and Wodon (BW) (2009) that the time poor are those with a time deficit and 'belong to households that are poor or would be poor if individuals were to reduce their working hours up to the time poverty line' (2009: 7).[6]

## GOODIN AND BW APPROACHES: A COMPARISON

Suppose that the actual situation of the household is at point $M$. The hours of employment, $L$, exceed the available time, $A$, and hence the household is time poor (see Figure 7.2). However, their income at that level of employment is above the standard poverty line, and hence the household is income non-poor. The Goodin approach involves a thought experiment in which we find the hours of employment that is just enough to earn a poverty level of income: point $M1$ in the figure represents such a situation for the household, accompanied by a time deficit (negative 'discretionary time'). In contrast, the BW approach calculates the hypothetical level of income consistent without any time deficit and compares it against the income poverty threshold. The point $M2$ represents such a situation, where the household has reduced its hours of employment from $L$ to $A$. However, such a reduction makes it income poor, thus, making it time poor as per the BW definition (see equation 19).

[6] Bardasi and Wodon defined (unadjusted) time poverty in terms of total (sum of paid and unpaid) work time. The definition that the author discusses here is a version of this definition, focusing only on paid work.

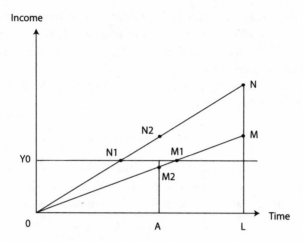

**FIGURE 7.2**    Discretionary Time and Income Poverty
*Source:* Author's own compilation.

To illustrate the role of the wage in determining the outcomes under both approaches, let us consider the scenario under a higher wage rate. Compared to the actual situation, now assumed to be represented by the point *N*, the Goodin method would indicate that the household could reduce its hours of employment (point *N1*) and avail a positive amount of discretionary time, while the BW approach would, by comparing points *N2* and *N*, conclude that the household is not time poor.

Figure 7.2 also illustrates the similarity between the two approaches. The 'critical' wage in both is the wage that would allow the household to earn the poverty-level income by being employed for just the time available (*A*). Geometrically, the critical wage is represented by the slope of the line that passes through the intersection of *A* and *Y0* (income-poverty threshold). The household that is time poor according to the HM definition would be considered time poor (or non-poor) by BW and Goodin et al. if the wage faced by the household is lower (or higher) than the critical wage.

## POTENTIAL FREE TIME AND INCOME

Burchardt (2008) modified the standard time deficit equation that has been used so far by incorporating the consideration that households with sufficient income can replace the necessary amount of household production associated with $R$ (equation 1) with market substitutes, irrespective of whether they have a time deficit, thus enhancing the amount of free time that they can obtain.[7] A fuller treatment of Burchardt's approach has been provided in Appendix 7A. Denoting the amount of time replaced by market substitutes as $B$, the free time $S$, can be written as:

$$S = X + B = A - L + B. \tag{20}$$

The amount of time that can be replaced cannot, obviously, exceed $R$. It also makes sense to assume that the expenses of replacement are incurred after meeting the poverty-level consumption needs. Hence:

$$B \begin{cases} = \min(R,(\gamma - \tilde{\gamma})) / p \text{ if } \gamma \geq \tilde{\gamma} \\ = 0 \text{ if } \gamma < \tilde{\gamma} \end{cases}. \tag{21}$$

Income available to the household is expressed net of the replacement cost of household production:

$$\gamma' = \gamma - pB. \tag{22}$$

The associated two-dimensional poverty measure would classify the household as poor if the income net of the replacement cost of household production is below the standard income threshold or if the free time is negative:

$$\gamma' < \tilde{\gamma} \text{ or } S < 0. \tag{23}$$

Alternatively, a composite index that may be called the 'time-income capability index' ($TI$), could be defined as:[8]

$$TI = f(\gamma', S). \tag{24}$$

---

[7] Burchardt also included the possibility of help from outside of the household and government-provided help, issues that are considered later.

[8] Burchardt took into account the potential of being employed for alternative number of hours (that is, alternative values of $L$) and replacing different amounts of household production (alternative values of $B$) in defining the index. We present a simpler version of her approach that facilitates a straightforward comparison with the other approaches.

The contrast between this approach and that of BW and Goodin et al. can be seen by considering the situation when the household is time poor but income-non-poor. Both BW and Goodin approaches would consider the household as time poor only if its potential income from working available hours (*A*) falls below the standard income threshold. Our adaptation of the Burchardt approach would consider the same household as time poor only if its current income does not allow the household to 'buy out' the time deficit without falling into income poverty. The replacement cost of household production plays no role in the analysis of BW and Goodin approaches; the time-poverty status of the household depends only on its wage rate. Burchardt's approach, as in the earlier Vickery and HM approaches, conceptualizes the time poverty (and income poverty) status as dependent on the household's income (wage rate) and the replacement cost of household production.

The relationship between income (wage rate) and replacement cost is illustrated in Figure 7.3. Suppose that the actually observed situation of the household is that of time poverty, the extent of which is indicated

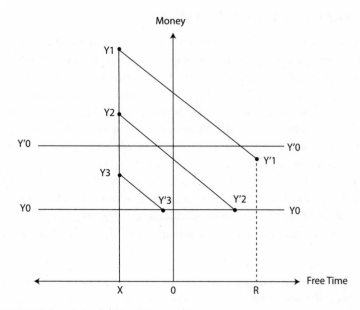

**FIGURE 7.3**    Potential Free Time and Income
*Source*: Author's own compilation.

by the distance on the horizontal axis between 0 and $X$. Hypothetical income levels associated with that extent of time poverty are shown by the points labelled as $Y1$, $Y2$, and $Y3$, where the higher income levels are assumed to result from higher wage rates.[9] All income levels shown are above the standard income-poverty threshold, indicated by the line $Y0Y0$, but the lowest income level is below the Vickery threshold indicated by the line $Y'0Y'0$. The distance between the two thresholds is the monetized value of the time deficit, $|pX|$.

At the lowest level of income (wage rate), the maximum amount of time deficit that can be 'bought off' by the household without falling below the standard income poverty threshold would still leave it in a situation of time poverty. Instead, if the household were to have the intermediate level of income (wage rate), it would, according to the logic of equations 20 to 22, end up in the situation labelled $(Y'2)$ with the poverty level of income and some amount of free time. The highest level of income (wage rate), shown in Figure 7.3, would allow the household to enjoy the maximum free time possible $(R)$ and a higher-than-poverty-level income, as represented by point $(Y'3)$.

## INTRA-HOUSEHOLD DISPARITIES

The discussion so far has been confined to the household consisting of a single person (or, more precisely, a single employable individual). Admittedly, the concept of poverty becomes more complicated in a multi-person household, especially because there are well-entrenched social and economic inequalities between the persons. These considerations introduce both theoretical and practical difficulties in terms of the measurement of income poverty. They revolve around the definitions of the income available to the person and the person's ability to attain the poverty level of consumption. A household is, by definition, a unit in which there is pooling of income and sharing of consumption among its members, though the degrees of pooling and sharing are hard to determine unambiguously.[10] It is difficult to justify,

---

[9] Here we are assuming a positive and monotonic relationship between the wage rate and income.

[10] A voluminous body of work exists on this topic. For a recent overview and references, see Quisumbing (2004: Chapter 1 and Part 1).

in principle, why we would consider a single woman with an annual income of Rs 4 million to be richer than a married, non-working wife with zero personal income, but a household income of Rs 10 million. On the other hand, the wives in two married-couple households with a poverty level of income may not be equally non-poor if the wife in one household is systematically deprived, for example, of food that is required to attain the nutritional intake specified in the poverty line. The inability to categorically define the income and consumption available to each person in a household has, for better or worse, favoured the choice of the household or family as the unit of analysis in the measurement of income poverty.

Curiously, Vickery (and, later Douthitt [2000] and HM) accepted the household as the unit of analysis in the development of the two-dimensional measure of poverty. The type of difficulties that prevented the choice of the person as the unit of analysis in the measurement of income poverty does not apply in the measurement of time poverty. Unlike income or consumption, the individuals in the household cannot pool or share their time. It is perfectly feasible to choose the household as the unit of analysis in the income dimension and the individual as the unit of analysis in the time dimension. The two-dimensional poverty measure constructed in such a manner can be presented in terms of individuals and households.[11]

Inter-household comparisons of time poverty that do not take into account the intra-household disparities in the division of domestic labour and paid labour can be fundamentally inequitable toward the individuals in the households. The equity argument here is identical to how the neglect of intra-household inequality in consumption or income biases the measurement of poverty. Consider two households that are identical in all respects, *A* and *B*, which also happen to possess

[11] A generally accepted definition of the unit of analysis is the group of 'people whose economic resources are to be pooled in determining poverty status' as provided by the report of the Citro and Michael (1995: 301). The report also makes the distinction between the unit of analysis and the unit of presentation. The latter refers to the unit in terms of which poverty statistics can be presented. Thus, though the unit of analysis in poverty measurement may be the household, poverty rates can be presented for different groups of persons, such as children.

the same amount of money income and the same amount of available time. Household *A* is 'egalitarian' in the sense that the division of domestic labour and paid labour among its members does not result in time deficit for any of its members. On the other hand, household *B* is non–egalitarian and at least one of its members ends up with a time deficit, defined as the amount by which their hours of employment exceed the time that they have available. Defining the two households as equally time non-poor is inequitable toward the individuals in household *B* who actually face the time deficit.

The adoption of the household as the unit of measurement in the Vickery-type measure obfuscates the disparities in the division of available time among the members of the household. Consider the situation, as depicted in Figure 7.4, for a household that is on the time poverty threshold according to the household-level definition, that is, their available hours is exactly equal to the hours of employment ($L=A$). The household is assumed to consist of two employable adults, a man and a woman. The hours of employment and income for each of them, as well as for the household as a whole, are shown by the distinct markers in the time-income space.[12] The hours available to the woman

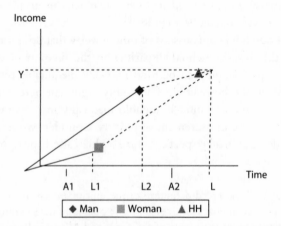

**FIGURE 7.4**    Time Non-poor Household with a Time Poor Woman
*Source*: Author's own compilation.

---

[12] As before, we are assuming that wages are the only source of income.

($L1$) is less than her hours of employment ($A1$) and she is, therefore, time poor, according to the individual-level definition of time poverty. On the other hand, the man is employed for an amount of time ($L2$) that does not exceed the time available to him ($A2$) and is, therefore, time non-poor.

An example could be constructed for the household depicted in Figure 7.4 to show the case of the time non-poor household with a time poor man. In this case, perfect equality in the division of available time is assumed, but the hours of employment for the man are supposed to exceed the time available to him. Such a situation can be visualized using Figure 7.4, by switching the positions of $A1$ and $A2$ on the horizontal axis and making the necessary revisions to the coordinates of the parallelogram. Both examples illustrate the problem with the household-level measure of time deficit constructed, according to the Vickery approach. It can hide the time deficits faced by individuals because it fails to take into account the intra-household disparities in the division of domestic and paid labour.

The shift from the household to the individual as the unit of analysis in the measurement of time poverty necessitates a change in the Vickery definition of time poverty. Instead of designating the household as time poor if its hours of employment exceed the available time, we should designate the household as time poor if the hours of employment exceed the available time for at least one of its members. The modified definition can be stated formally with minor modifications to equations 1 and 2. As before, the minimum required time for household production ($\bar{D}$) and time for household production required for subsistence at the poverty level of income ($\bar{R}$) are considered as household-level parameters. He also assumes that the minimum time required for personal care ($\bar{C}$) is the same for all employable adults. The time available to adult $i$ in the household is:

$$A_i = 168 - \bar{C} - \alpha_i \bar{D} - \gamma_i \bar{R}, \tag{25}$$

where the parameters $\alpha$ and $\gamma$ indicate the shares of the individual in, respectively, the minimum required time for household production and time for household production required for subsistence at the poverty level of income. Time deficit or surplus for the individual is given by:

$$X_i = A_i - L_i, \tag{26}$$

where $L_i$ indicates the individual's hours of employment. The modified definition of the time deficit faced by the household with $n$ individuals is:

$$X' = \sum_{i=1}^{n} \min(0, X_i). \qquad (27)$$

Unlike the earlier specification, the above equation sets the value of time deficit for time non-poor households to zero, thereby ignoring the disparities that would exist among such households in the free time available to them. However, such disparities did not play any role in the definition of the Vickery threshold for income poverty. Neither do such disparities matter in drawing the line between the time poor and the time non-poor.

A logical corollary of the new definition of time poverty is that the Vickery threshold for income poverty would have to be modified. The modification takes into account the replacement cost of the foregone amount of household production that accompanies the time deficit of the individual(s) in the household. Instead of the earlier definition of time poverty, we should now use the definition that takes into account intra-household time deficits (equation 27):

$$y' = \tilde{y} - X'p. \qquad (28)$$

When revised to account for the intra-household disparities, the two-dimensional poverty measure would designate the household as poor if its income is less than the modified Vickery threshold $y'$ or if any of its members have a time deficit, that is:

$$y < y' \text{ or } X' < 0. \qquad (29)$$

For the individual in the household, the two-dimensional poverty measure would deem him/her as poor if the income of the household that he/she belongs to is less than the modified Vickery threshold $y'$ or if he/she has a time deficit:

$$y < y' \text{ or } X_i' < 0. \qquad (30)$$

The revised two-dimensional measure can be presented in terms of individuals and households.

## POLICY IMPLICATIONS

The standard approach of poverty alleviation via income transfers can be applied in the context of the household that is income poor, according to the Vickery threshold (see equation 3). All that is required is an income transfer equal to or greater than the poverty gap $(y°-y)$ to enable the household to escape income poverty. However, such a policy might not be effective or desirable by itself.

The effectiveness of the income-transfer policy depends on the ability of the household to obtain the market substitutes with the amount that it receives. This is possible only if the relevant market exists in an accessible manner for the household. In other instances, the market might exist, but it may be impossible for the household to obtain the requisite amount of substitutes at the price that is implicit in the transfer. The problems of missing and imperfect markets can compromise the effectiveness of an anti-poverty strategy that relies solely on income transfers. Such problems are likely to be quite significant in several situations; for example, the rural developing world and segregated pockets of poverty with relatively high levels of social exclusion in the industrialized world. Direct public provisioning or publicly financed community provisioning of the wants, which are currently met through self-provisioning, would be a far more effective anti-poverty strategy in these contexts.

An implicit assumption behind relying solely on the income-transfer strategy is that the observed level of the household's hours of employment and its wage rate should be 'left alone', irrespective of whether it is acceptable to the household itself or socially. Consider the situation depicted in Figure 7.5 of three hypothetical households, all of them income and time poor. For simplicity, let us assume that they have the same wage rate and the identical amount of time available, labelled $A$, as in the previous figures. Suppose that the household, which is employed full time $(Lf)$, is doing exactly the desired amount of paid work. An income transfer that is at least equal to the vertical distance between the lines $Y$ and $Y^{ro}$ at $Lf$ should, in principle, allow it to escape time and income poverty because the transfer enables it to purchase the requisite market substitutes.

Now, suppose that the other two households are employed (a) less than full-time, that is, underemployed $(L1)$, and (b) working overtime

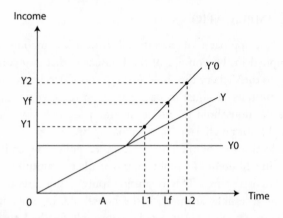

**FIGURE 7.5**   Potential Inadequacies of Income Transfers
*Source:* Author's own compilation.

(L2), and are not working the number of hours that is desirable. While it is true that the appropriate amount of income transfers can eliminate the time and income poverty faced by the two households, this may not represent the desirable policy in itself. Underemployment and overwork impose their own human, economic, and social costs. The two-dimensional measure of poverty discussed here can be used to identify the households that may suffer such vulnerabilities and encourage a closer examination of the causes of underemployment and overwork. Nevertheless, an essential component of anti-poverty strategy for such vulnerable households would be the creation of jobs that pay living wages.

The Vickery (1977) and HM (2007) approaches appear to be the most pertinent for examining the income–time nexus for the segment of the population that is below or near the income-poverty threshold. The use of the Vickery threshold enables the identification of the 'hidden poor'—those who might be income non-poor according to the standard threshold, but actually poor when the necessary replacement costs of household production are taken into account. The approaches of both Goodin et al. (2005) and Bardasi and Wodon (2009) result in modified measures of time poverty alone, with no implications for rethinking income poverty or the time constraints faced by the working poor. Income poverty rate, as measured by the modified Burchardt model, will also be identical to the income poverty rate calculated using the standard income threshold and lower than the rate implied by the Vickery threshold. Consider a household that is time poor and income poor according to the Vickery threshold, but not income poor according to the standard threshold. This household will not be income poor in the modified Burchardt model because the household can spend only the amount left after meeting the poverty-level consumption needs on buying out the time deficit. It will, however, remain time poor because it does not have enough disposable income to buy out the time deficit.

These considerations do not imply that modified measures of time poverty are useless. Comparing the alternatives presented earlier, it seems that the argument—that the notion of time poverty should reflect the differential capacity of households to remedy such poverty by purchasing market substitutes (as recognized by Burchardt)—is stronger than the argument that the notion of time poverty should reflect the 'capacity' of households to choose its hours of employment (as in Goodin et al. and Bardasi and Wodon). Typically, in a capitalist economy, workers have more freedom to spend their money in the manner they choose than to choose the hours of employment of their liking. This suggests that the Burchardt model or some variant thereof may be fruitfully used in identifying the 'genuinely' time-poor households among the income-non-poor households.

## APPENDIX 7A

The purpose of this appendix is to propose a formal framework for the time-income capability measure put forward by Tania Burchardt (2008). Since our aim is to translate the core ideas into a tractable form, we have not dealt with issues can that complicate matters significantly but not radically alter the basic model sketched below.

There are three key assumptions made in what follows. First, wages are the only source of household income. Second, the wage remains constant, irrespective of hours worked. Third, the replacement cost of household production remains constant, irrespective of the hours replaced and the income of the household. We consider the household with a single adult in order to abstract from issues related to the intra-household allocation of time.

## Time–income Capability Set

The time–income capability set of the household is the list of all potential pairs of free time and income denoted as $Z = \{S_{ij}, y_{ij}\}$, where the subscript $i$ is used to denote elements of the set of possible hours of employment (paid work) and the subscript $j$ is used to denote the elements of the set of possible hours of household production that can be 'bought off', that is, replaced by market substitutes (for example, by hiring a maid). The idea here is that the free time ($S$) and income ($y$) that may be obtained by the household depends on both the hours of employment and the hours of household production that they replace with market substitutes. Increasing the hours of employment reduces free time, but enhances the capacity to purchase market substitutes, which, if feasible, increases free time.

Below, we denote the hours of employment as $L$, hours of household production replaced by market substitutes as $B$, the wage rate of the household as $w$, and the price of market substitute as $p$. In addition, the time available to the household after setting aside: (a) the minimum required amount of time for personal care and household production and (b) the amount of household production time required to subsist at the poverty level of income, is denoted as $A$. This is the amount of time available to the household that can be split between employment and free time. The maximum number of hours household production that can be replaced are denoted as $R$. The equations for free time and income are:

$$S_{ij} = A - L_i + B_{ij};$$  (A1)

$$y_{ij} = wL_i - pB_{ij}.$$  (A2)

Note that the potential interval for $B_{ij}$ is $\left(0, B_i^{\max}\right)$ and that $B_i^{\max} = \min(R, wL_i/p)$. The *potential* interval for $L_i$ is $(0, L'')$, where $L''$ represents the maximum hours of employment that are assumed to be available.

The set $Z$ can be constructed for the household using the equations above for the specified intervals of $B$ and $L$.

## Time–income Capability Index

The time–income capability index for the household is derived from the set of all 'feasible' pairs of free time and income, $F = \{S_{ij}, y_{ij}\}$. 'Feasible' combinations are the combinations in which $S_{ij} \geq 0$ and $y_{ij} \geq y^{\circ}$, where $y^{\circ}$ is the income poverty threshold for the household. It should be noted that the first requirement, that is, the non–negativity of free time (or no time deficit), implies that for the combinations in which $A < L_i$, the wage income of the household, is sufficiently large to 'buy out' the time deficit $(A - L_i)$. If the household has only allocations (that is, the division of hours between employment and free time) that yield below-poverty income, the time–income capability index is not defined for that household.[13] Similarly, allocations that yield income below the poverty threshold are not taken for the determination of the index for the household that also happen to have feasible allocations.

The relative wage and time available to the household play a central role in constructing the feasible set, for which it is necessary to redefine the intervals of the values that $L$ and $B$ can take. The starting point for determining the minimum feasible hours of employment is the hours of employment that, given the wage, will be just sufficient to earn the poverty level of income:

$$L^{\circ} = \frac{y^{\circ}}{w}. \qquad (A3)$$

If the time available to the household $(A)$ is equal to or greater than the hours of employment required to earn the poverty level of income, $L^{\circ}$ would serve as the minimum feasible hours of employment. But the hours of employment required to earn the poverty level of income may exceed the time available to the household either because of its relatively low wage or relatively high burden of household production.

---

[13] This is conceptually distinct from the case when the index takes a value of zero that can occur for borderline allocations—allocations with zero free time or poverty-level income.

In this case, the household would have to work beyond $L°$ to earn a poverty level of income. The extra hours required are denoted as:

$$L' = \frac{w(L° - A) - p(L° - A)}{w}. \qquad (A4)$$

The numerator of the equation is the difference between the amount that the household earns by working for hours beyond what is available to it and the amount that the household has to spend on the market substitutes replacing the uncompensated portion of the household production foregone to facilitate the extra work. Dividing this difference by the wage yields the additional hours required, over and above $L°$, to earn the poverty level of income for the household that faces a time deficit when working for $L°$ hours.

However, working for the extra hours to attain the poverty threshold is not an option if the extra wage income is less than the extra costs of replacing the uncompensated portion of the household production, that is, if the first term is less than the second term in the numerator of equation A4. This would be the case if the household wage is less than the price of the market substitutes. Under this scenario, the household with a time deficit at $L°$ hours will have no feasible allocations.

Thus, one can express the minimum hours of employment that would support the set of feasible allocations as:

$$L_i^{min} \begin{cases} = L°, \text{ if } A \geq L° \\ = L° + L', \\ \text{if } A < L° \text{ and } w > p \end{cases} \qquad (A5)$$

Turning to the maximum hours of employment, it is evident that if the minimum is given by the second line of the above equation, the maximum would simply be the maximum hours of employment that is assumed to be available ($L''$). On the other hand, if the minimum is $L°$, then the maximum would depend on difference between the wage of the household and the price of the market substitutes. If the wage is less than the price, working beyond the time available will not be feasible because, as discussed earlier, the extra income from working will not be sufficient to replace the uncompensated amount of the foregone household production. Otherwise, the household can potentially work up to the maximum hours of employment that are assumed to be available.

To sum up, there are four possible scenarios for the household, depending on its relative wage and available time:

**TABLE 7A.1**   Possible Scenarios for Hours of Employment

| Condition | Minimum | Maximum |
|---|---|---|
| $A \geq L°$ and $w \geq p$ | $L°$ | $L''$ |
| $A < L°$ and $w \geq p$ | $L° + L'$ | $L''$ |
| $A \geq L°$ and $w < p$ | $L°$ | $A$ |
| $A < L°$ and $w < p$ | No feasible hours of employment★ | |

*Source:* Author's own compilation.
*Note:* ★ The feasible set is not defined for the household under the specified condition.

The quantity of time spent on household production that the market substitutes would replace ($B$), also would fall in a narrower interval under feasible allocations than under all possible allocations. For any given hours of employment (and the associated income), the minimum quantity of $B$ should rule out time deficits:

$$B_i^{min} \begin{cases} = 0, \text{ if } A - L_i \geq 0 \\ = |A - L_i|, \\ \text{ if } A - L_i < 0 \end{cases} \qquad (A6)$$

The maximum value that $B$ can take has to be lowered to ensure that the household has enough income left to meet other, poverty-level expenses:

$$B_i^{max} = \min\left( R, \frac{wL_i - y°}{p} \right). \qquad (A7)$$

The set F can be constructed for the household using the equations A1 and A2 for the newly specified intervals of $L$ and $B$. The time-income capability index is defined as an area measure. Its derivation relies on the fact that for any given level of employment, the relationship between $y_{ij}$ and $S_{ij}$ is linear, with the slope equal to the replacement cost of household production. Replacing for $B_{ij}$ in equation A2 using A1 yields:

$$y_{ij} = wL_i - p\left(S_{ij} + L_i - A\right). \qquad (A8)$$

The two ends of the line segment defined by equation A8 for a given level of $L$ is given by the pairs $\left(y_i^{max}, S_i^{min}\right)$ and $\left(y_i^{min}, S_i^{max}\right)$, calculated as follows:

$$y_i^{max} = wL_i - pB_i^{min};$$
$$S_i^{min} = A - L_i + B_i^{min};$$
$$y_i^{min} = wL_i - pB_i^{max}; \text{ and}$$
$$S_i^{max} = A - L_i + B_i^{max}.$$

(A9)

An illustration is shown below: in Figure 7A.1.

Once the set F has been computed, the pairs are ordered in such manner that $S_1^{max} \leq S_2^{max} \leq S_3^{max} ... \leq S_k^{max}$, where the subscripts 1, 2, 3, ....., $k$ indicate various hours of employment in descending order, with 1 indicating the highest number of hours, 2 indicating the second highest number, and $k$ indicating the lowest. In order to avoid double counting of the areas under the line segments, from the set of ordered pairs, the pair in which the maximum free time is less than the maximum free time in the pairs that preceded it (for example, the maximum free time-income pair associated with six hours of employment in Figure A7.1),

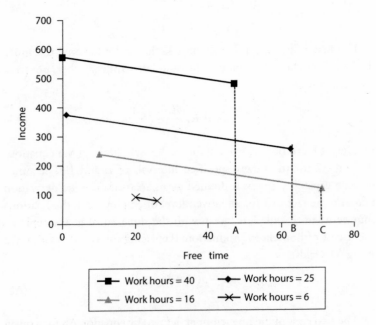

**FIGURE 7A.1**  Example of Time–Income Capability Index
*Source*: Author's own compilation.

is omitted.[14] Several such pairs may exist for the household. The time-income capability index is the sum of the non-overlapping areas under the line segments defined by equation A8 for various hours of employment, 1, 2, 3, ....., $k$:

$$TI = \int_{S_1^{min}}^{S_1^{max}} f\left(S_{1j}| L_1\right)dS + \int_{S_1^{max}}^{S_2^{max}} f\left(S_{2j}| L_2\right)dS$$

$$+ \cdots + \int_{S_{k-1}^{max}}^{S_k^{max}} f\left(S_{kj}| L_k\right)dS, \tag{A10}$$

where $f(.)$ indicates the equation for the line segment. In the example shown in Figure A7.1, the limits of integration are given by 0, $A$, $B$, and, $C$.

## REFERENCES

Bardasi, Elena and Quentin Wodon. 2009. 'Working Long Hours and Having No Choice: Time Poverty In Guinea', Policy Research Working Paper Series 4961. Washington, DC: The World Bank. Available at http://ideas. repec.org/p/wbk/wbrwps/4961.html, last accessed on 8 March 2010.

Burchardt, Tania. 2008. *Time and Income Poverty*. London: Centre for Analysis of Social Exclusion, London School of Economics. Available at http:// sticerd.lse.ac.uk/dps/case/cr/CASEreport57.pdf, last accessed on 10 April 2010.

Citro, Constance F. and Robert T. Michael (eds). 1995. *Measuring Poverty: A New Approach*. Washington, DC: National Academy Press.

Douthitt, Robin. A. 2000. '"Time to Do the Chores?" Factoring Home-Production Needs into Measures of Poverty', *Journal of Family and Economic Issues*, 21(7): 7–22.

Goodin, Robert E., James Mahmud Rice, Michael Bittman, and Peter Saunders. 2005. 'The Time Pressure Illusion: Discretionary Time Versus Free Time', *Social Indicators Research*, 73(1): 43–70.

Harvey, Andrew S. and Arun K. Mukhopadhyay. 2007. 'When Twenty-Four Hours is not Enough: Time-Poverty of Working Parents', *Social Indicators Research*, 82(1): 57–77.

---

[14] Alternatively, we could set their contribution to the index equal to zero. The equation below assumes this to be the case to simplify notation.

Quisumbing, Agnes R. 2004. *Household Decisions, Gender, and Development: A Synthesis of Recent Research*. Washington, DC: International Food Policy Research Institute.

Vickery, Clair. 1977. 'The Time-Poor: A New Look at Poverty', *The Journal of Human Resources*, 12(1): 27–48.

# 8 Time Poverty: A Contributor to Women's Poverty?

*Analysis of Time-Use Data in Africa*

Omar Ismael Abdourahman

Inequality is a major challenge to development and an obstacle to achieving the millennium development goals (MDGs). It takes many different forms, including income inequality, inequality in access to and control over property, inequality in access to civil and political rights, and unequal access to social, cultural, and economic rights. All these forms of inequality possess inherent gender dimensions. One form of inequality that has received much less analysis but has adverse implications for accessing economic rights is that relating to time. The allocation of time between women and men in the household and in the economy is a major gender issue in the evolving discourse on time poverty. This chapter, in analysing the allocation of social roles between men and women, shows first how this allocation leads to time poverty among women, and second, how this has an impact on achievement of the MDGs.

It is well known that patriarchal systems that still prevail in many regions of the world, including Africa, have defined and perpetuated gender roles that allow men to control women's time and labour. In most African societies, women and girls are allocated critically important and time-consuming responsibilities, which overburden them with work in the reproduction, production, household, and community spheres.

An analysis of who does what and when, within the household, shows that women and girls are responsible for collecting water and firewood; cooking; cleaning; taking care of the children, infirm, and the sick; producing food; and marketing any surpluses. They also dedicate a lot of their time to maintaining social cohesion within the community. All these tasks are considered as low-status activities, and are unremunerated and unrecognized in the national statistics. Women who spend most of their time performing these tasks are often considered as 'not working'.

## TIME–USE DATA: HOW TO MAKE WOMEN'S UNRECOGNIZED CONTRIBUTION TO THE ECONOMY VISIBLE

Traditional concepts and theories on how to measure economies are largely designed to consider only the market economy and the remunerated work, and then offer limited guidance and indication for policies to promote women's empowerment and gender justice. That is why the unpaid and invisible women's work has been identified as a key source of policy intervention by United Nations through its Platform for Action of Beijing (PFA), 1995. The PFA has called for developing 'suitable statistical means to recognize and make visible the full extent of the work of women and all their contributions to the national economy including their contribution in the unremunerated and domestic sectors'.

The 1995 Human Development Report (United Nations Development Programme [UNDP] 1995) used time–use data from 31 countries to show up women's status in the world and to measure their contributions to economies. The main finding of this report was that if both the paid and unpaid work were considered, women did a larger share of work in developing and developed countries. This women's work, which is important for human well-being, is largely unpaid and not considered in national accounting systems. The conclusion of that report was that 'much of women's work remains unrecognized and unvalued. This has an impact on the status of women in society, their opportunities in public life and the gender blindness of development policy' (UNDP 1995).

The time–use survey (TUS) is identified as one of the most appropriate methods to estimate and value the non-market work (NMW) and the household care services and to develop national satellite accounts of household production. The TUS are designed to account for the nature, duration, and location of all activities that are carried out by the population during a reference period.

The entry point of this approach is the widespread recognition of the fact that time is the ultimate resource, which should, in principle, be equally shared by everyone. Time can be converted into money, goods, and services through work. Additionally, time is also required for the consumption of goods and services, community work, and even leisure activities. This is why time-use analysis can offer an overview of all human activities (market work and NMW, consumption, community, and leisure activities).

Basically TUS plays an essential role to improve the current vision of the economy and of the statistical system and three reasons can explain this: (a) TUS helps to show a more complete presentation of the economy and society by providing vital information on those areas that are presently invisible in national accounts; (b) TUS contributes for better information on informal sectors in order to improve the estimation of economic activities (System of National Accounts [SNA] work) in national accounts; (c) TUS highlights the importance of the NMW, for maintaining the labour force and the human capital: it also allows an estimation of its contribution to the economy and long-term growth.

## THE CONCEPTUAL FRAMEWORK: PROMOTING TIME POVERTY ANALYSIS

A promising way to re-enforce women's economic rights and to increase accountability for various international development initiatives, such as millenium development goals (MDGs), is to include time poverty analysis into poverty reduction strategies and assessment and monitoring of MDGs. This approach, using time-use data to analyse gender inequality in the allocation of unremunerated work, is a field of research that is still nascent and insufficiently explored, especially within Africa.

The concept of 'time poverty' is not new, and in many research papers it is basically defined by two main elements: (a) the lack of spare time for leisure and rest and (b) being under pressure to complete usual daily activities. According to the literature, Clair Vickery was, in 1977, the first to use the concept of time poverty into the measurement of poverty and well-being. She set up the two interdependent dimensions of poverty (income and time poverty) by developing the idea that if the minimal non-poor level of consumption requires both money and time to perform household activities, the official poverty measurement standards, which consider only the monetary aspect, do not correctly measure household needs. She argued that any poverty alleviation programmes that aim to reduce income differences without taking into account the time-use differences across households will have discriminatory effects against households with only one adult.

Bardasi and Wodon (2006) defined time poverty as the lack of enough time for rest and leisure after considering the time spent performing productive and paid activities as much as on time spent on unpaid household activities and other related activities as fetching water and wood. As time is a limited resource, the more time you spend on paid and unpaid household work, the less time you will have for rest and leisure and, therefore, higher 'time poverty'.

Burchardt's 2008 study considers time and money as two of the main constraints on what people can achieve in their lives. She emphasized that if the income constraint is widely recognized by policymakers in their concern with poverty, analysis of the time constraint and its direct link to the income constraint is more limited. Taking into account analysis of time and income linkages reveals the situation of those who are missed by traditional poverty measures, for example, those who have to work long hours to keep their families above the poverty line, and some who are classified as time poor can hardly reduce their work hours without the risk of falling into income poverty. This is usually the case with women in poor families who are forced to increase the unpaid household activities by extending their working time in order to save money and provide goods and services to other family members.

This is true in Africa where time is a major resource available for poor families to fight against deprivations and vulnerability related to poverty. Women in poor families have to work for long hours and they have no choice to do otherwise without increasing the level of poverty due to the loss in income or consumption associated with the reduction of working time.

Of course, both men and women play different roles in society (productive, reproductive, and community). However, compared to men, the unpaid household activities are a kind of 'tax' that women have to pay before undertaking any market or remunerated work. They have to respond simultaneously to the competing and time-consuming demands related to their different roles in the society. In addition, women, more often than men, tend to engage in simultaneous activities and combining activities help women reduce their time poverty by allowing them to perform more activities in a given time. This has, of course, a cost in terms of stress and health. This is why a main concern in collecting time-use data is the invisibility of women's economic contribution through the household activity.

## TIME–USE ANALYSIS AND ACHIEVEMENT OF THE MDGs

Existing data in relation to gender inequality, including the *South Africa Time-use Report 2000*, the *Madagascar Time-use Report 2002*, the *Tanzanian Time-use Report 2006*, the *Tunisian Time-use Report 2006*, and the *Draft Ghana Time-use Report 2009*, shows that time itself is a prerequisite and an essential resource for undertaking activities that allow people to free themselves from poverty.

The first MDG aims to reduce the proportion of people living on less than a dollar a day by half, targeting eradication of extreme poverty and hunger. Since income is the ultimate resource that most governments take into account when measuring poverty and national poverty levels, governments have to consider the amount of income people should generate in order to acquire basic food items sufficient to feed families of different sizes. In measuring poverty rates, it is necessary to consider the incomes of families and the number of people in them. However, governments must also recognize that escaping poverty first requires expenditure of time towards remunerated or income-generating activities. It goes without saying that if a poor person devotes time only to unremunerated activities, it is very unlikely that he/she will not be able to pull out of the cycle of poverty without substantial assistance.

The data for Africa, when it comes to paid and unpaid work (see Tables 8.1 and 8.2), shows that women work longer hours per day than men. In rural areas especially, most of women's time is spent on household and subsistence activities. Less time is dedicated to market-related and remunerated activities and little time is left for rest

**TABLE 8.1**    Time Spent per Day on Paid and Unpaid Work (minutes)

| Country | Male | Female |
|---|---|---|
| Tanzania TUS 2006 | 458 | 543 |
| (18–49 year olds) | | |
| South Africa TUS 2000 | 273 | 332 |
| (Mean time per day) | | |
| Ghana TUS 2009 | 557 | 601 |
| Madagascar TUS 2002 | 435 | 530 |
| Tunisia TUS 2006 | 295 | 405 |

*Source:* Author's own compilation from the respective countries' surveys.

and leisure. Compared to men, women have heavy time loads due to the need to balance the demands of their multiple roles: productive, reproductive, social, and community. The patriarchal foundation of distribution of roles by gender is the major cause of gender inequality, the time-burden on women and girls, and ultimately, the feminization of poverty.

In South Africa, women's contribution in non-market production to the national economy was found to be almost double that of men. Women had 30–40 per cent less time for personal care and leisure than men at the household level. According to the 2000 South African TUS, males between the ages of 15 and 65 years spent an average of only 84 minutes per day on unpaid work, while females, on average, spent 215 minutes on unpaid work. Furthermore, men, on average, spent a larger proportion of their day than women on SNA production activities, while women spent longer on non-SNA production. The gender differences were least stark for the relatively small group of people aged 60 years and above. In all age groups, women, on average, spent less time on non-productive activities than men.

In Tanzania, women's workload is much heavier than men's. For example, among the persons aged between 18 and 49 years, women do nearly one-fifth more work than men, at 543 minutes per day for women and 458 minutes per day for men. This allows men of this age to spend an average of 110 minutes—nearly two hours—on socializing each day, compared to only 65 minutes spent socializing by women. The situation is the same in Madagascar, where women spend an average of 530 minutes on productive activities, both paid and unpaid,

**TABLE 8.2**   Time Spent per Day on Unpaid Work (minutes)

| Country | Male | Female |
|---|---|---|
| Tanzania TUS 2006 | 85 | 248 |
| South Africa TUS 2000 | 82 | 210 |
| Ghana TUS 2009 | 111 | 229 |
| Madagascar TUS 2002 | 40 | 210 |
| Tunisia TUS 2006 | 40 | 315 |

*Source:* Author's own compilation from the respective countries' surveys.

while men spend only 435 minutes. The difference is even greater in Tunisia, where women spend 405 minutes against 295 for men on paid and unpaid productive activities.

When it comes to paid versus unpaid work, men, on average, spent a larger proportion of their time than women on paid activities while women spent longer on unpaid productive activities. In South Africa, males spent an average of only 82 minutes per day on unpaid work, while females, on average, spent 210 minutes per day. The average time spent by men on unpaid work in Tanzania, is 85 minutes, while women spend 248 minutes. In Tunisia, women spend an average of 315 minutes on unpaid household work, which is almost eight times of the average time spent by men (40 minutes) on the same activities. The same situation is in Madagascar where women spend 210 minutes on unpaid work, while men spend five times less (40 minutes).

Childcare and care of elders represent another important form of women's unpaid workload. Women in each of the studied countries spent much more time than men on care activities. The time difference tends to increase when there is a child, an elder, and/or an ill person in the household. In South Africa, women with children under 7 years living with them spent an average of 80 minutes per day on childcare, compared to an average of 13 minutes for men.

In Tanzania, males spend a total of 5 per cent of their day on unpaid care work (less than 1.5 hours), compared to 14 per cent for females (3.5 hours). If we multiply the unpaid care work done by males and females by the number of males and females in the population, 71.3 million hours are spent on unpaid care work each day, compared to 117.2 million hours on SNA work. Women do more than three-quarters of the volume of unpaid care work, and 45 per cent of the

SNA work. Care of persons of the household accounts for only 1 per cent of the day for the average male, compared to 2 per cent of the day for the average female. So females do far more unpaid care work than males. In Tunisia, married women allocate an average of 43 minutes to the care of dependants, while for their partners this task is almost non-existent in their daily activities. In Ghana, women are more likely to be involved in unpaid household work (92 per cent) and unpaid care-giving services to household members (50 per cent) than men (at 50 per cent and 19 per cent, respectively).

Several analyses have shown the negative impact of time poverty and, correspondingly, the positive impact of time-saving technologies and activities on female labour force participation. Oropesa (1993) illustrated this quite well. A study by Barrett and Browne (1994) also investigated the results of the introduction of village cereal mills in Gambia on the lives of women and their communities. The study concentrated on women's access to technology, the time and energy this saved, its sustainability, and their level of control. It was found that the energy saved was of great significance to rural women, enabling them to contribute more effectively to village life. A field study on Bangladeshi villages by Biswas, Bryce, and Bryce (2001) tested the contextual relevance of applying renewable energy technologies. Cooking was found to be the major activity where the transfer of a time-saving technology offered practical opportunities for major lifestyle improvements. This saved time could be spent on income-generation activities, without affecting the time allocated for other daily activities, including resting hours.

Encouraging research in Africa can only be useful in further documenting and addressing the impact of women's time burden, both on the household economy, and the market and public service economies. This analysis should particularly examine the linkage between time poverty, monetary poverty, and gender equity and address the adverse impact of unduly heavy time burdens on the lives of women as human beings.

The second and third MDGs target the promotion of gender equality through girls' education, that is, ensuring that all boys and girls complete a full course of primary schooling, thereby eliminating gender disparity in primary and secondary education by 2005, and at all levels by 2015.

**TABLE 8.3** Average Time per Day Spent by Boys and Girls on Unpaid Work (minutes)

| Country | Male | Female |
|---|---|---|
| Tanzania TUS 2000 (5–17 years old) | 68 | 126 |
| South Africa TUS 2000 (10–19 years old) | 61 | 129 |
| Ghana TUS 2009 (10–17 years old) | 78 | 162 |
| Madagascar TUS 2002 (14–16 years old) | 41 | 86 |
| Tunisia TUS 2006 (15–17 years old) | 21 | 133 |

*Source:* Author's own compilation from the respective countries' surveys.

Time poverty is again one of the main barriers to girls' education, especially in rural areas, where the social tradition and practices assume that girls rather than boys should assist their mothers in performing household chores (UNICEF 2003). That is why around the world, and especially in Africa, girls face multiple social and economic barriers to enrolling and staying in schools. The figures in Table 8.3 show that in Ghana, Madagascar, South Africa, and Tanzania, time spent by girls on unpaid household work is the double of the time spent by boys. The highest difference is seen in Tunisia, where girls spend 133 minutes and boys only 21 minutes on unpaid household work.

Several studies have also revealed the impact of gender differences in education and employment on growth (Ellis, Manuel, and Blackden 2006; Klasen 1988). Between 1960 and 1992, the limited education and employment opportunities in Sub-Saharan Africa reduced annual per capita growth for women by 0.8 per cent. This is significant, as a boost of 0.8 per cent a year would have doubled economic growth over the past 30 years. The analysis suggests that gender inequality appears to account for about 15–20 per cent of the difference in growth performance between Sub-Saharan Africa and East Asia. This gives credence to the argument that one important element in Africa's low growth may be the high level of gender inequality in education and employment. Gender inequality is an important element in accounting for the region's poor economic performance. Although growth regressions must be interpreted with caution, these results are striking and suggest that economic growth in Sub-Saharan Africa could increase significantly if gender-based obstacles to growth were eliminated, a point made forcefully in World Bank (2000). In Swaziland, enrolment of girls is estimated to have fallen by 36 per cent as a result of their having to provide home-based care, while their mothers or grandmothers seek waged employment (United Nations Economic Commission for Africa [UNECA] 2009).

In many African societies, parents see limited economic benefits to educating daughters, compared to the convenience of the unremunerated labour they provide. According to the available literature,[1] one of the main barriers that girls face is lack of time to attend school regularly. The priority is elsewhere, as they are needed more for domestic work at home or on the farm during school hours. This lack of time is a serious root cause of lower enrolment and high dropout rates of girls. More systematic research through time-use data analysis should be encouraged on the specific linkages between girls' time poverty, their enrolment in school, and success rates in various personal, household, and community activities in later life.

The fourth and fifth MDGs target reduced child mortality and improved maternal health. In these areas also, time-use analysis is an entry point to inform policies and programmes. Child and maternal health present very distinct challenges that are inextricably linked to time use. Research has proven that extreme fatigue and weakness that women suffer due to work overload (lack of time devoted to resting and/or leisure activities), especially while they are pregnant, aggravated by difficult access to healthcare services, are among the factors that cause maternal and neonatal mortality.

The time-use data from Africa shows as well that women have less time for rest and leisure activities, which are important for humans' well-being. In Ghana, men spend 15 minutes on hobbies, games, and other activities to pass their time, while women dedicate only 4 minutes for the same activities. In Tunisia, time spent on leisure is 8 minutes for women

---

[1] See the report 'Because I am a Girl: The State of the World's Girls 2012: Learning for Life', available on http://becauseiamagirl.org, last accessed in August 2016.

against 27 minutes for men. In Madagascar, compared to men, women in urban areas dedicate 15 per cent less time to leisure and 27 per cent less in rural areas. In South Africa, the mean time spent on social and cultural activities is 218 minutes for men and 171 minutes for women.

Several studies have also found a positive correlation between education, lower fertility, and lower infant mortality. This means that where girls are given the chance to use their time to gain an education, it translates into gains for their future families by reducing fertility and leading to a healthier family.

The sixth MDG targets elimination of HIV/AIDS and it is important to incorporate the gender dimension and the time-use aspect in designing, planning, and implementing support programmes. While it is widely recognized that Africa is severely affected by this pandemic, and that women and young girls are the ones who carry the heavy burden of looking after the children as well as those family members who are HIV-infected, most HIV/AIDS-support programmes have not considered the time-use dimension. Country experiences in Africa show that in families affected with HIV/AIDS and communities, the responsibilities of women and girls towards caregiving for the family and community can increase as they are required to meet the demand for care that exceed the capacities of health systems. Under normal circumstances, these activities limit women's participation in productive economic activities (such as, farming, school attendance, and income generation). The burden on women and young girls in the care economy is increasing.

The seventh MDG aims at ensuring environmental sustainability, as the survival of communities depends on access to natural resources—land, water, forests, and plots. Women and girls spend a lot of time

**TABLE 8.4** Time Spent per Day on Collecting Fuel, Wood, and Water

|  | Male | Female |
| --- | --- | --- |
| Tanzania TUS 2006 | 43% Participation rate | 78% Participation rate |
| South Africa TUS 2000 | 87 minutes | 224 minutes |
| Ghana TUS 2009 | 83 minutes | 216 minutes |
| Madagascar TUS 2002 | 60 minutes | 50 minutes |
| Tunisia TUS 2006 | 1 minute | 6 minutes |

*Source:* Author's own compilation from the respective countries' surveys.

walking long distances to bring water, wood, and fuel to their families (see Table 8.4). Women are the primary collectors and transporters of these utilities, and have developed in-depth knowledge on how to manage them to ensure their preservation for future use and future generations. One way to improve women's access to and control over natural resources is to reduce time spent and distance travelled to obtain these resources.

## CRITICAL METHODOLOGICAL ISSUES IN CONDUCTING TIME-USE SURVEYS: COMPARISON BETWEEN EUROPE AND AFRICA

It is important to briefly analyse the way in which the surveys have been conducted because it deeply affects the quality and quantity of data collected: it shows how comprehensive and reliable the findings are. The basic methodological issues are almost common to all TUS, and they can be addressed through the different themes and questions discussed in the following paragraphs.

### Methods for Sample Design

#### EUROPEAN COUNTRIES

TUS have been conducted in most European countries, but due to national variants in the survey design, the international comparability of the results was very low. To rectify this situation, the European countries expressed the need to increase comparability between national TUS, and gave a mandate to Eurostat (the statistical office of the European Union) to develop recommendations for harmonized methodologies, which will ensure that the results will be comparable in time and between countries. The harmonized method was finalized in 2000.

For the sample design, the main recommendations of the 'Methodological Guidelines on Harmonized European Time-Use Surveys' are:

1. The survey will consider, as the reference population, the persons resident at domestic addresses and to exclude from the survey, the persons living in institutions (military service, hospitals, prisons, etc.).

2. The sampled households must be representative of the whole population in its diversity.
3. The household approach is the unit of study, meaning that all
   individuals (10 years and older) of the sampled households will be
   included in the survey.
4. The surveys will use the population registers to draw samples of
   individuals and then the households of the sampled individuals to
   achieve the sample of the population.

Some European countries did not follow these recommendations
and introduced modifications. In Sweden and Norway, individuals were
chosen from the population register. Portugal did not use the household
as the sample unit as well and decided to choose one or two members
of the household to be interviewed. Concerning the minimum age,
the lowest age was in Portugal, where all persons from six years and
above were surveyed. In France, the minimum age was 15 years, and in
Sweden, persons aged 20 years and above were interviewed.

AFRICAN COUNTRIES

The five countries—South Africa, Ghana, Tanzania, Tunisia, and
Madagascar, have tried to ensure that the sampled population is representative of the whole population in its diversity by gender, age, and
type and area of settlement. In South Africa, the sample population was
8,564 households and 14,553 respondents chosen from all the nine
provinces constituting the country. Within each province, they were
chosen from four different types of settlement areas (formal urban
settlement, informal urban settlement, commercial farming areas, and
other rural areas). Persons living in institutions like prisons, hospitals,
hotels, and boarding schools were excluded from the survey. The survey has adopted the individual approach, which is why information
was collected from two respondents aged 10 years and above from each
selected household.

In Madagascar, the sample population was based on the frame
prepared for the 2001 Household survey, where 2,663 households
and 7,743 respondents, chosen from the urban and rural areas of each
province constituting the country, were interviewed. The survey
has adopted the household approach, meaning that information was

collected from all respondents aged between 6 and 65 years from each selected household.

In Tunisia, the survey covered a representative sample of 4,464 households from each governorate. From each household, all members aged 15 years and above were interviewed. In Tanzania, the TUS, which was part of the national Integrated Labour Force Survey (ILFS), covered more than 3,000 households all over the country. All members of the sampled households who were aged 5 years and above were interviewed, giving a total sample of more than 10,500 individuals. The data was 'weighted' so that they could give a picture of the country's total population aged 5 years and above.

The sample population for the Ghanaian TUS was designed to provide estimates of key indicators at the national and regional level as well as for urban and rural areas in Ghana. A representative sample of 4,800 households was selected and in the selected households all individuals aged 10 years and above were interviewed.

It should be noted here that in some other countries, the sample population was not very representative of the whole population. For example, in Morocco, the 1998 TUS had the particularity to focus only on women activities, which did not allow a comparison of the time spent by women and men and in Nigeria in 1999, it was applied on a very small sample of 100 private households selected from the General Household Survey's sample. The survey was conducted only in five states (four states plus Lagos) of the federation.

## The Time Diary Approach

### EUROPEAN COUNTRIES

The recommendations of the 'Methodological Guidelines on Harmonized European Time-Use surveys' are:

1. The surveys will use the self-completed diary to record the daily activities.
2. They will use at least two diary days, one weekday (Monday to Friday) and one weekend day (Saturday or Sunday).
3. Separate diaries will be used for an adult and for a child.
4. The surveys will use fixed 10-minute time slots.

5. They will record the secondary activities.
6. The surveys will mention to whom and with whom the activity is performed.
7. The survey fieldwork would be spread over a full 12-month period in order to take into the effect of seasonal variation on various activities.
8. The diary days and dates would be allocated to households and individuals by a controlled random procedure, in order to minimize the postponing and the non-response rate.

In Denmark, respondents were asked to complete two diaries, one on a weekday, and one on a weekend day. Diaries covered full 24-hour periods and were divided into 10-minute time slots. Sampled respondents and their spouses or partners were asked to complete the diaries.

Here again certain European countries deviated from the harmonized recommendations: for example, instead of using two diary days, countries like Belgium, France, and Portugal used a one-day diary. Romania, Denmark, and Portugal have not covered, as recommended, the whole year, but undertook the survey only over two or three months.

AFRICAN COUNTRIES

In Africa, as in other developing countries, the respondents' daily activities were recorded through the face-to-face interview, rather than asking them to fill a diary. This methodology was used because of the high level of illiteracy in the continent. The questionnaire was administrated in different local languages. The use of at least two diary days with fixed 10-minute time slots in Africa was found to be very difficult because (a) there is a constraint of budget limitations and (b) as time schedules and clocks are not used vigorously by Africans, particularly in rural areas, it is impossible to respect the 10-minute slots. Most African countries used a one-day diary with a half hour or an hour's time slot.

South Africa used the one-day 24-hour diary, which was divided into half-hour slots and a maximum of three activities could be recorded in each slot. Madagascar and Tunisia also used the one-day 24-hour diary, but it was divided into 15-minute slots. In each slot, respondents were asked to report if they performed more than one activity. However, there were no specifications on which of the simultaneous activities were primary or secondary. Tanzania and Ghana used the one-day 24-hour diary, which was divided into one-hour slots, and in each slot, a maximum of five activities could be recorded.

In addition, instead of covering a whole year, some African surveys, except for Tunisia where the fieldwork was conducted for a year, were carried out over three or four months at different periods of the year (South Africa and Madagascar) in order to catch seasonal variations. For some others, the survey was carried out one time (Ghana and Tanzania).

## The Survey Forms

### EUROPEAN COUNTRIES

Concerning these tools, the 'Methodological Guidelines on Harmonized European Time-Use Surveys' have proposed the directions for the survey forms as the guidance for the design of household and individual questionnaires and also for the diary. The household questionnaire provides valuable information about the household stocks of capital (domestic appliances, etc.) and about the consumption of market services that substitute for the household's own labour (maids, childcare centres, nursing, etc.). In many European countries, inventories of domestic appliances have formed part of this questionnaire. The household and the individual questionnaires are used in face-to-face or telephone interviews. The diary is left behind to be filled further by the household members.

### AFRICAN COUNTRIES

Each country has built its own survey instruments (questionnaires), which are largely based on those developed by the European countries and on its own experience related to other surveys, such as the household surveys or labour force surveys (LFS). The most important is that the instruments contain adequate and pertinent questions to measure non-market household work. The social and cultural contexts of women's behaviours or activities belonging, for example, to ethnic or religious origin are not taken into account in those questionnaires.

Usually the three main tools used for collecting time-use and con-textual data are: (a) the household questionnaire, providing information about the household on its composition, housing and living conditions, and income; (b) the individual questionnaire, providing demographic information about the sampled individuals, such as status in employ-ment, level of education; (c) the diary, which records information on the individual's main and secondary activities, the duration, and the location of these activities.

The first two questionnaires contained many standard questions from other surveys, such as household surveys or LFS. The third is the one focusing on time use with a diary, which permitted the inter-viewer to record the activities performed by the first person selected. The TUS can be administrated as a standalone one as in South Africa and Ghana or along with the household survey as in Madagascar and Tunisia and with the LFS as in Tanzania.

## The Activity Classification System

### EUROPEAN COUNTRIES

The Eurostat classification system, used by more than 18 European countries, proposes a coding scheme at one and two-digit levels while maintaining the opportunity for country-specific adaptations at the third digit level. The first level contains 10 categories, and at the third level there are more than 100 activity categories. The diary contained three variables coded, which were main activity, secondary activity, and location.

The activities under the first level of 10 categories are:

0  Personal Care
1  Employment
2  Study
3  Household and Family Care
4  Volunteer Work and Meetings
5  Social Life and Entertainment
6  Sport and Outdoors Activities
7  Hobbies and Games
8  Mass Media
9  Travel and Unspecified Time Use

## AFRICAN COUNTRIES

Some African countries (Ghana, Madagascar, South Africa, and Tanzania) have used a modified version of the UN trial system, International Classification of Activities for Time Use Statistics (ICATUS). This differs from the Eurostat classification mainly in three ways:

1. The basic framework for distinguishing the economic nature of activities is the SNA.
2. The entire non-market production has been brought together into a single one-digit category and is further classified at the two-digit and three-digit levels.
3. Paid work activities that are undefined at the two- and three-digit levels have been given more detailed breakdown.

This classification emphasizes productive activities, not only in the formal sector but also in the household and informal sectors. These distinctions are essential in understanding and recording the full range of work, both in developed and developing countries. In this classification system, activities that represent production within the SNA production boundary are classified in groups 1–3. Activities that fall predominantly within the general production boundary but outside the SNA, are classified in groups 4–6, and groups 7–10 cover non-production activities.

Tunisia used a three-digit nomenclature based on the general nomenclature used in time-budget surveys in Europe and adapted to the national reality. For the purposes of processing the survey, 182 activities were grouped into 51 groups and in 10 major business groups.

This chapter has questioned the enduring patriarchal allocation of gender roles by recognizing that alleviating women's time poverty not only benefits women and their communities, but also contributes to achievement of the MDGs. Reducing women's workload of household activities, among other things, can save time that could otherwise be allocated for other productive work, reducing poverty, enabling girls to receive an education (a factor proven to lead to reduction in maternal and child mortality), and for enabling women to better claim their right to participate in decision-making and in management of natural resources.

The ability of women and girls to escape from poverty, participate in decision-making and educate themselves by going to school, and engaging in productive and remunerated activities is often limited by their responsibility for every day unpaid household and care activities. For poor women and girls, this burden is even greater because of the under-investment in public infrastructure and the effect of wars and conflicts on infrastructure. The time women and girls spend on routine tasks can be reduced dramatically if the appropriate infrastructure is in place, efficient sources of energy (especially, newer forms of fuel for cooking and heating), transport systems, and water and sanitation systems are accessible to women (UNECA Guidebook 2005).

Investments in such infrastructure to relieve women's time burdens are essential to maximize the impact of the strategic priorities within poverty reduction strategies and MDGs. Providing infrastructure in both rural and urban areas benefits poor men and women. But lack of adequate physical facilities (such as roads, utility supply systems, communication systems, water and waste disposal systems) and the under-provision of services flowing from those facilities typically results in a far greater time burden on women than on men because of a gender-based household division of labour.

Increased participation due to reduced workloads will greatly boost overall achievement of the MDGs. Time-use data is an efficient means to provide valuable information for mainstreaming gender in poverty alleviation strategies and achievement of MDGs.

At the macroeconomic level, it is clear that cutbacks in national budgets through cutbacks in social services increase unpaid time spent on care work. Available data in developing countries under structural adjustment programmes also showed that cuts in health, family planning, and other social services, such as subsidies, increase the burden of unpaid home care and services on women. Thus, what may be seen as an increase in productivity or efficiency in the market economy is actually a shift of costs from the market to the household economy. These include the time costs of those who provide the unpaid work and their loss of education, health, and well-being.

Household production is both complementary to and in competition with market production: meeting greater demands for household production may jeopardize ability to supply more paid work, and vice-versa. Unpaid labour usually assists in absorbing the shocks of adjustment. For example, unpaid labour may be substituted for paid labour in the production of food and clothing produced in the home instead of purchased from the market.

The TUS is, therefore, an innovative approach for integrating a gender perspective and particularly women's non-market work (unpaid work) into national accounting systems and national budgets. Many more countries in Africa will need to be encouraged to undertake TUS through strengthening the capacity of their National Statistical Offices to produce and analyse time-use survey data. Such data will be used to design and implement policies and programmes for the enforcement of women's economic and social rights and prevent the increasing feminization of poverty across the continent.

## REFERENCES

Bardasi, Elena and Quentin Wodon. 2006. 'Measuring Time Poverty and Analyzing Its Determinants: Concepts and Application to Guinea'. Available at https://mpra.ub.uni-muenchen.de/11082/1/MPRA_paper_11082.pdf, last accessed in August 2016.

Barrett, Hazel R.H.R. and Angela W. Browne. 1994. 'Women's Time, Labour-saving Saving Devices and Rural Development in Africa', *Community Development Journal*, 29(3): 203–14.

Biswas, W.K., D. Bryce, and P. Bryce. 2001. 'Technology in Context for Rural Bangladesh: The Options from an Improved Cooking Stove for Women', paper prepared for the International Solar Energy Society 2001, World Solar Congress, Adelaide. Available at www.isf.uts.edu.au/publications/WB_DB_ PB_2001.pdf, last accessed in August 2016.

Burchardt, Tania. 2008. 'Time and Income Poverty', LSE STICERD Research Paper No. CASEREPORT57, London School of Economics, Centre for Analysis of Social Exclusion, London.

Ellis A., C. Manuel, and C.M. Blackden. 2006. *Gender and Economic Growth in Uganda, Unleashing the Power of Women*. Washington, DC: The World Bank.

Eurostat. Methodological Guidelines on Harmonized European Time-Use Surveys (HETUS).

Institut National de la Statistique (INSTAT). 2002. 'L'emploi du temps de la femme et de l'homme malgache en 2001' (The time use of women and men in Madagascar in 2001).

Klasen, Stephan. 1999. 'Does Gender Inequality Reduce Growth and Development? Evidence from Cross-Country Regressions', Policy Research Report on Gender and Development Working Paper Series, No. 7, World Bank, Washington, DC.

Oropesa, Ralph Salvador. 1993. 'Female Labour Force Participation and Time Saving Household Technologies: A Case Study of the Microwave from 1978 to 1989', *Journal of Consumer Research*, 19: 567–79.

République du Bénin, UNDP. 1998. *Enquête Emploi du Temps au Bénin* (Time-use Survey in Benin).

Statistics Directorate, Morocco. 1999. Women's Time-Use in Morocco: 1997/98 National Survey on Women's Time-Budget.

*The Draft Ghana Time-use Report,* 2009.

*The Madagascar Time-use Report,* 2002.

*The South Africa Time-use Report,* 2000.

*The Tanzanian Time-use Report,* 2006.

*The Tunisian Time-use Report,* 2006.

UNECA. 2005. 'An "Africa-specific" Guidebook for Mainstreaming Gender Perspectives and Household Production in National Accounts, Budgets and Policies in Africa', Addis Ababa, Ethiopia, unpublished.

UNICEF. 2003. 'Barriers to Girls' Education: Strategies and Interventions', Working Paper, UNICEF.

United National Development Programme (UNDP). 1995. *Human Development Report.* New York: UNDP.

Vickery, Clair. 1977. 'The Time-Poor: A New Look at Poverty', *Journal of Human Resources*, 12(1): 27–48.

World Bank. 2000. *Can Africa Claim the 21st Century.* Washington, DC: World Bank.

# 9 Public Job Guarantee Programmes: The Economic Benefits of Investing in Social Care

## Case Studies in South Africa and The United States[*]

### Rania Antonopoulos and Kijong Kim

According to estimates by the World Bank, United Nations Development Programme (UNDP), and International Labour Organization (ILO), since the onset of the 2007 global financial and economic crisis (the Great Recession), at least 30 million more women and men joined the ranks of the unemployed—an astounding total of 200 million people out of work. In 2011, the eye of the storm hit several European countries as well and, by May 2012, to give an example, unemployment in Spain reached 25 per cent, with 51 per cent among the youth. Indeed, sudden declines in aggregate demand have

[*] This chapter's sections on South Africa are largely drawn from a research project titled 'Impact of Employment Guarantee Programs on Gender Equality and Pro-poor Economic Development in South Africa', which is financially supported by the United Nations Development Programme, Bureau for Development Policy, Gender Team. We appreciate their generous support. Sections on the US are largely drawn from Antonopoulos et al. (2010), which is the product of collaboration with Thomas Masterson and Ajit Zacharias at the Levy Economics Institute. We are grateful for their contributions.

always had serious repercussions for employment, and the evidence from previous financial crises shows that, despite stabilization of GDP growth, employment recovery in the aftermath of crises lags by five to seven years (Buvinic 2009).

Yet, thin employment opportunities, especially for the poor, are not exclusive to times of crisis. Most rural workers have access to agricultural work only seasonally and, therefore, despite large-scale annual distress migration patterns, the uncertainty of a job is daunting; other workers work under highly informal conditions, suffering from underemployment and unpredictable spells of no employment at all. Own-account workers also depend too often on unstable sources and levels of income, with earnings being highly volatile.[1] In addition, some countries experience deep-rooted structural unemployment. In South Africa, for example, entrenched structural factors have excluded about 25 per cent of the population[2] from access to work opportunities for more than a decade and a half. But lack of earnings has a human cost that goes beyond obvious material deprivations; people suffer from hopelessness, marginalization, social exclusion, exposure to increased violence, and inclination to suicides.

But even in countries that are counted among the success stories of the late 1990s and the early 2000s, inclusive growth has not taken sufficiently deep roots to lift the extremely and chronically deprived out of poverty. In the era of globalization, predictable and sufficiently well-paying work opportunities remain beyond the reach of 1.4 billion people living in extreme poverty, with half of this population having no access to paid work at all.

Public job creation programmes, alternatively known as public works (PW) and employment guarantee (EG) schemes, have emerged as government initiatives that aim to redress seasonal, cyclical, and structural joblessness for the poor by offering a minimum-pay job to those

---

[1] See Rodgers and Kuptsch (2008), particularly the following articles: J.A. Ocampo, 'The Links between Economic and Social Policies: A Conceptual Framework'; E. Kalula, 'The Decent Work Agenda: An African Perspective on Research Needs and Priorities'; and J. Ghosh, 'New Research Questions in the Decent Work Agenda, a View from Asia'. See also ILO (2010).

[2] Statistics South Africa (Stats SA) (1998–2009). The unemployment figures place the unemployment rate for the fourth quarter of 2009 at 24.3 per cent. See these statistics online at http://www.statssa.gov.za/keyindicators/keyindicators.asp.

who are ready and willing but are unable to find work. With a minimal wage effectively discouraging the better-off persons from taking
advantage of such programmes as beneficiaries, the work entitlement
and the income offered by these programmes provide a lifeline for the
low-skilled poor. In this regard, when all else fails, the state effectively
acts as the 'employer of last resort'. Though many such programme
initiatives have been introduced over the years,[3] the best-known and
largest in scale are the 'New Deal Programs' of the US (following the
Great Depression of 1929), and the more recent Expanded Public
Works Programme (EPWP) in South Africa and the Mahatma Gandhi
National Rural Employment Guarantee Act (MGNREGA) in India,
which were introduced in 2004–5 and 2005–6 respectively.

When countries consider direct job creation through PW and
EG programmes, meaningful work projects need to be identified,
and usually those prioritized are selected to bridge existing gaps in
physical infrastructure. This chapter argues that an additional target
for work-project consideration is that of social care delivery. Gaps exist
in care services for the young, elderly, sick, and the permanently ill
or severely disabled. The chapter shows that investing in mobilizing
unused domestic labour resources—that is, providing wage income
to previously unemployed job holders that serve the needs of their
communities—yields strong pro-poor income growth patterns, stronger than investment in other types of projects. But it also contributes to
another key developmental goal—that of promoting gender equality.
It does this in at least two ways: by reducing the burden of unpaid
work for women and girls, and by expanding and supplementing the
income-earning options for women, which is certain to increase the
labour force participation (LFP) of women who live in poverty.

Making progress in reaching development objectives points to the
extraordinary importance of public investment in areas traditionally
understood as women's work (which is usually unpaid). Time-use surveys (TUS) have long documented that unpaid forms of work, including unpaid care provisioning of families, falls disproportionately on

---

[3] For a comprehensive history of such initiatives, see Antonopoulos
(2009) and Kaboub (2007). As a 2007–9 crisis mitigation intervention, several
countries, including China, introduced or expanded previously smaller-scale
programmes.

women's shoulders and it is not necessary to reproduce this evidence here. It has also been convincingly argued that from better health outcomes to clean water and sanitation, public investment is necessary. What needs to be made evident is that, in addition to reducing unpaid work and woman's burden, and to contribute to human development, such spending makes good economic sense, both from the standpoint of enriching human capital resources and from the standpoint of pro-poor development and growth.

Closing the gaps today results in healthier, more educated citizens with higher productivity and income-earning potential tomorrow. The economics literature has highlighted, for instance, that early childhood development programmes spur the cognitive as well as the non-cognitive skills of children, which has positive economic impacts.[4] Caring for chronically ill patients at their homes has proved to be more cost-effective than providing similar care under alternative institutional settings. In addition, the relief of time from unpaid care provisioning improves the chances for engaging in paid work and/or the productivity of workers whose sick family members otherwise depend entirely on their care.[5] These social benefits, in and of themselves, warrant investment in public provisioning, but there exists a different and equally compelling argument, which is the focus of this chapter.

Shifting parts of unpaid care work to paid work[6] by expanding the domain of social services brings about powerful pro-poor

---

[4] See Dickens, Sawhill, and Tebbs (2006) and Heckman and Masterov (2007) for macroeconomic impacts of the early education through productivity growth. Golin, Mitchell, and Gault (2004) provide a concise summary of literature review on a series of research on estimating benefits of a high-quality, intensive pilot projects—the Abecedarian project in North Carolina, HighScope Perry Preschool Study, and Title I Chicago Child-Parent Centers. Additional references include Barnett et al. (2004) and Barnett, Lamy, and Jung (2005). Heckman et al. (2010) provide a new summary on the cost-benefit analysis of the Perry Preschool programme.

[5] The cost-effectiveness has been documented in the medical literature; see, for example, Casiro et al. (1993) and Fields et al. (1991). See MetLife (2006) on the potential gain in worker productivity from paid care relief.

[6] For a comprehensive discussion on the intersections of gender inequality, paid and unpaid work, and employment guarantee programmes, see Antonopoulos (2010).

and economy-wide employment outcomes that are superior, in fact, to those obtained in equally needed but less labour-intensive physical infrastructure investment. This is accomplished via the direct employment opportunities created, as well as indirect ones through inter-industry linkages and aggregate demand growth from the new jobs. Furthermore, there are distributional consequences of the job creation. We analyse, therefore, in what follows, the direct and indirect job creation and the distributional impacts of social care expansion through employment for two countries, South Africa and the US. This chapter's specific focus lies on the effects of labour demand adjustment on employment and income via expanding public service delivery. To the best of our knowledge, the topic has been overlooked in the literature.[7]

The chapter is organized as follows. The following section presents our methodology and data; the third section shows the employment impacts of the proposed interventions, while section four discusses the income distribution and poverty reduction results we obtain. The last section presents the concluding comments. But before moving to the next section, this section presents the economic and social contexts within which social care expansion's impacts are proposed and, subsequently, evaluated through an ex ante simulation exercise.

## UNEMPLOYMENT AND SOCIAL CARE INVESTMENT

### South Africa

The persistent high unemployment rates in South Africa in the aftermath of the apartheid era (see Figure 9.1) compelled the government to introduce the EPWP direct job creation initiative in 2004. The programme consists of job opportunities provided to unskilled, unemployed, poor individuals who work on projects that are labour intensive.

These individuals are hired at a minimum wage and, while receiving training and accreditation, they provide services for their communities.

---

[7] It should be noted, though, that we do not attempt to estimate the impact of social care on the changes in the labour force participation rates (LFPR) of mothers; see Bergemann and van den Berg (2006), Blau and Tekin (2007), Kimmel (1995), and Lefebvre and Merrigan (2008), among others. Also we do not endogenize the labour supply response of newly hired workers in the social care network whose family members are recipients of the care.

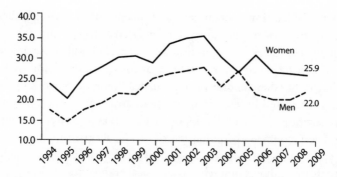

**FIGURE 9.1** Unemployment Rates in Africa, 1994–2009 (%)
*Source*: ILO 2009.

There are three main EPWP sectors designated for job creation: (a) labour-intensive physical infrastructure investments, including the building of roads, bridges, and irrigation systems; (b) environmental investments—creating work opportunities in public environmental improvement programmes; and (c) social service—creating work opportunities in public social programmes, with a focus on home- and community-based care (HCBC) and early childhood development (ECD).

The HCBC programme provides comprehensive services, including health and social services, by formal and informal caregivers in the home, aiming to restore and maintain a person's comfort, function, and health, including providing care toward a dignified death. The prevalence of HIV/AIDS, tuberculosis, and malaria has accentuated the need for expanding service delivery. As of 2003, there were 892 HCBC sites, mostly run by non-governmental organizations (NGOs) with the help of volunteers. As an employment programme, the EPWP-HCBC programme targeted the unpaid volunteers who were unemployed and often the adult dependents of the terminally ill and people living with the sick family members who were not in receipt of a state grant.

The ECD programme set out to provide temporary jobs, skills, and accreditation to 19,800 practitioners over five years, who would earn income but also would be involved in training, thereby improving the care and learning environment of children. The target workers were previously unpaid volunteers, unemployed and/or underemployed parents and caregivers in all ECD programmes. It was envisaged that they could be reached through: (a) learnerships, leading to various levels of educational attainment and qualifications corresponding to accreditation of teacher aides, kindergarten teachers, etc.; (b) work/employment/skills programmes for very low-skilled, unemployed people to be recruited and trained at sites designated for receiving indigent subsidies; (c) direct and immediate creation of work opportunities at targeted ECD sites in very poor areas; (d) on-the-job training and certification for ECD support staff, such as vegetable and legume gardeners, cooks, and administrators; and (e) short-term, three-month employment opportunities in auxiliary tasks for 3,000 unemployed parents through existing schools and local authorities.

Antonopoulos and Kim (2008) propose a massive scaling up of EPWP if the programme is to reduce unemployment, as the existing scale was incommensurate to the jobless problem at hand. Specifically, they propose the development of an ECD cadre that would extend the range, duration, and number of job opportunities to include two-year appointments for childcare workers, school nutrition workers, teachers' aides, school caretakers, school clerical workers, cooks, vegetable gardeners, and administrators for local ECD sites. The proposed expansion of the HCBC programme would create a cadre of community health workers, nutrition and food security workers, direct-observation therapy practitioners, and tuberculosis and malaria officers. The scale of the proposed expansion is 9.3 billion rand, roughly 1 per cent of GDP in 2000, the data year for simulation. This scale would cover the ECD of all children living in poor households and about 20 per cent of the population, mostly those in need of home-based care for patients of HIV/AIDS. Antonopoulos and Kim (2008) analysed ex ante policy impacts of expanding social care provisions under EPWP, using a multiplier analysis based on social accounting matrix (SAM).

## United States

The jobless recovery is a hallmark of the Great Recession. Figure 9.2 shows the trends in duration and severity of employment losses in the seven recessions since 1969. For each spell of recession, a seasonally adjusted non-farm payroll employment (PAYEM) level is indexed to be 100 at the start of the downturn and plotted to a period ranging 10 months before the onset to 50 months afterwards. The recession of 2007 (the line with red diamonds on the graph) started with a moderate

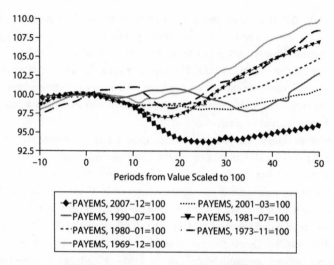

**FIGURE 9.2**   All Employees: Total Non-farm (PAYEMS)
*Source*: Current Employment Statistics, Bureau of Labor Statistics (BLS), via Federal Reserve Economic Data (FRED2) issued by the Federal Reserve Bank of St. Louis.

impact on employment for the first 12 months, but unleashed its full destructive force thereafter. It is obvious that hysteresis has settled into the US labour market.

Similar to the South African study, Antonopoulos et al. (2010) investigate the impacts of investing in localized community-based social care services; in particular, home-based healthcare (HBHC) and ECD as an effective employment policy. Instead of short-term public sector employment as a countercyclical measure, this proposal calls for a permanent expansion of public service delivery that, as it turns out, mostly hires women. Their stable earnings may dampen volatile income shocks from highly cyclical male-oriented jobs, such as construction. An ageing population and advances in medicine are extending life expectancy of the elderly and disabled patients for who HCBC can be cost-effective without compromising the quality of care. In 2007 alone, almost 1.5 million seniors and disabled persons received home-based care, according to the National Home Health Aide Survey. The ECD programmes for children from poor households—Head Start and Early Head Start—are not reaching the intended group, with merely 21 per cent of eligible kids participating (Iruka and Carver 2006).

Home-based care in the US consists of managed healthcare that deals with basic medical care for post-operative recuperation, managing chronic illness, and other non-invasive care performed by nurses and nursing assistants. The ECD programmes offer childcare with an educational component—for cognitive and non-cognitive growth— for children under the age of five years, before they enter a school-based educational system.

Most of the workers in these occupations are women. In home-based healthcare, 88 per cent of the care providers are women and minorities (52 per cent), especially African American women (30 per cent). Recent immigrants constitute 21 per cent of the workforce. The wage rate is low, at USD 10.31 per hour as of 2008 on average, and the annual mean earnings are USD 21,440 (King et al. 2009). The majority of jobs in ECD are preschool teachers and assistants and childcare workers, whose average wage rate is USD 11.32 per hour—much lower than private industry average of USD 18.08 (BLS 2009a).

Previous studies[8] assessing both long-term and short-term benefits of expanding social care did not take into account distributional impacts of employment in the sector: who would receive jobs from the expansion and how much income they would receive from the jobs. Employment opportunities created directly and indirectly from the expansion may or may not reach the disadvantaged groups in the labour market—women, the less educated, and poor households— depending on the occupations and industries in which these jobs are created. A job as an administrator in the healthcare industry is likely to be held by a highly educated male worker from an affluent household, while a less-educated woman from a middle-class household would be more likely to take a job as a childcare provider or preschool teacher. The individual characteristics of workers determine their likelihood of employment, and earnings vary across occupations and industries. We use a microsimulation method based on statistical matching techniques to analyse the distributional issues.

To highlight the employment effects of the investment in care, we compare the results to that of investing in infrastructure construction.

---

[8] See Blau and Tekin (2007); Heckman (2011); Peters and Sellick (2006); Sörensen et al. (2006), for example. Other such references can be found in Antonopoulos et al. (2010).

Our policy simulations consist of USD 50 billion on increasing final demand for social care versus for construction. We find that investment in care is a more cost-effective and equitable way to create jobs than infrastructure construction.

## METHODOLOGY

Input–output analysis depicting inter-industry linkages through which multiplicative processes generate employment seems an appropriate tool to assess the industry-specific, ex ante policy at the macro level. Absence of price changes in the analysis seems a secondary concern in a recessionary environment in which inflationary pressures from a large-scale policy intervention are negligible and slack conditions are prevalent in factor markets.

This section demonstrates two different methods to assign jobs created by the policy simulations. An SAM with various household types decomposed by relevant demographic and economic characteristics is used in the South African case study. The detailed decomposition makes it feasible to incorporate a flexible job-targeting scheme to maximize the poverty reduction effect.[9] The method is simple, and it is intuitively easy to grasp the underlying mechanism of job creation. A drawback, however, is that we cannot examine within-group heterogeneity that is a part of the ideal distributional impact analysis. A microsimulation technique enhances the distributional impact analyses. The statistical technique in the US case study is a propensity ranking system with multiple imputations, instead of estimating behavioural functions of labour supply and earnings of the population. The method emphasizes the effects of individual characteristics on each individual, rather than estimating the group-supply function by exploiting variations across individuals.

### South Africa: SAM-based Multiplier Analysis

Multiplier analysis based on the SAM provides an adequate simulation platform to analyse policy impacts on disaggregated sub-groups of households as well as industries. The method accounts for multiplicative

---

[9] See Appendix D of Antonopoulos and Kim (2008) for more on the job allocation formula.

direct and indirect impacts of an external demand stimulus. This method, however, rests on the supposition that the technical coefficients of production remain constant. Hence, modification of the SAM is necessary if an intended simulation exercise entails, in one form or another—a new technology requirement stemming from the labour intensity requirement of the EPWP, for instance.

An administrative requirement for intensive use of unskilled and poor workers with a large-scale intervention renders a new sector in terms of input composition and linkages to the rest of the economy. To incorporate the labour-intensity requirement of the EPWP, we develop a simple hypothetical integration method to circumvent a rebalancing of the SAM without sacrificing the accuracy of multiplier-effect analysis. A new hypothetical sector is simply inserted into the existing SAM, as shown in Table 9.1, with a scaled-down value of its gross output. The scaling down generates insignificant values for new accounts associated with the sector and, hence, may not violate an acceptable margin of error used in a conventional technical balancing. The insignificant values, however, preserve backward linkages that generate multiplicative effects of the intervention on the sector. The method is also flexible enough to incorporate policy

**TABLE 9.1** Employment Targeting: Shares of EPWP Unskilled Jobs

| Household Type | Shares of EPWP Unskilled Jobs (%) |
| --- | --- |
| Urban Formal African Poor | 3.5 |
| Urban Formal African Ultra-poor | 16.3 |
| Urban Formal Coloured Poor | 0.5 |
| Urban Formal Coloured Ultra-poor | 1.8 |
| Urban Informal African Poor | 2.5 |
| Urban Informal African Ultra-poor | 6.8 |
| Rural Commercial African Poor | 2.6 |
| Rural Commercial African Ultra-poor | 13.8 |
| Rural Commercial Coloured Poor | 0.1 |
| Rural Commercial Coloured Ultra-poor | 0.3 |
| Ex-homeland African Poor | 8.5 |
| Ex-homeland African Ultra-poor | 43.3 |

*Source*: Authors' own calculations.

*Note*: See Antonopoulos and Kim (2008) for details on the targeting formula.

exercises (in this study, employment targeting for the poor) into the SAM (Kim 2011).

The original South African SAM includes 26 productive sectors and 20 different household types, decomposed by location, residence type, race, and three-tiered income level. Construction of the hypothetical sector, called the EPWP social sector, relies on the data from Friedman et al. (2007). They describe detailed input costs for a social service initiative under the EPWP in South Africa. The initiative focuses on two projects: ECD and HCBC. The projects are more labour-intensive and employ more women and unskilled labour than the existing education and health sectors. Wage payments for unskilled labour account for 32 per cent of the total expenditure for the initiative, as compared to 4–7 per cent for relevant sectors in the economy. Wage payments for unskilled women account for 19 per cent of the total expenditure vis-à-vis 2–5 per cent from the relevant sectors. The total size of the injection for the simulation (9.3 billion rand) is equivalent to 1 per cent of the South African GDP at factor costs, or 8 per cent of the total value of output of the relevant sectors—namely, education and health—measured by total production costs. The policy simulation is to increase the final demand for social care services—EDC and HCBC.

For comparison purposes, we also simulate an infrastructure construction expansion of the same magnitude, 9.3 billion rand. Using administrative data on a water reticulation project—a water-main installation—we construct a new EPWP infrastructure sector.[10]

---

[10] The new sector is constructed from administrative data on a water-main installation contract under the EPWP. For the intermediate input composition, the authors examined the detailed expense records from the project and reclassified them according to the industry classifications used in the SAM. The wage payment records reveal the labour composition by skill level, and gender decomposition follows the existing pattern within the construction industry in the SAM. The new infrastructure sector may not be the best representation of all the infrastructure projects under the EPWP, but it represents the labour-intensity requirement. For instance, wages for male unskilled workers account for 19 per cent of total expenditures in the EPWP water project, but only 12 per cent in the construction sector. Moreover, unskilled job distribution in the existing structure is more biased toward non-poor workers than in the targeting scheme developed in this chapter.

We devise formula-based employment targeting for direct EPWP unskilled jobs to the poor, taking into account the unemployment rate, depth of poverty, and size of population by each poor household type. The formula is in no way a socially optimal allocation of jobs, but rather an attempt to incorporate the degree of hardship and a plain idea of fairness across various poor household types. Table 9.1 shows the resulting allocation of the direct unskilled jobs. African ultra-poor households (with household income below the 25th percentile) living in ex-homelands—rural tribal regions—receive the most jobs largely due to the relatively large number of households among the poor (23 per cent of all poor) and one of the lowest average household income among all household types, according to the South African National Household Survey in 2000.

## United States: Input–Output and Microsimulation

To analyse the employment impact of our proposed intervention, we combine two different quantitative methods: at the macro level we make use of input–output analysis and at the micro level we employ a microsimulation model. Input–output analysis allows for calculation of aggregate changes in employment, while the microsimulation distributes these jobs by matching them to individuals who are most likely to occupy them based on nationally representative survey data.

The employment multiplier matrix is computed from the US input–output table, which includes 201 detailed industries. The detailed classification allows distinction of specific industries under the care sector—HBHC and ECD.[11] The jobs created directly and indirectly from the multiplicative process are classified by industry and occupation based on the National Industry-Occupation Employment Matrix compiled by the BLS. This step produces a cross-tabulation

---

[11] The induced multiplier effects from household consumption of goods and services are not included in the study, as the multipliers seem too high to be relevant. Other studies—for instance, Pollin, Heintz, and Garrett-Peltier (2009)—econometrically estimate the induce effects separately. We chose to underestimate the total effects by dropping the induced effects, instead of the ad hoc treatment.

of jobs by industry and occupation that subsequently feeds into the microsimulation.

To assign jobs, we create a statistical ranking of occupations and industries for each individual by estimating the likelihood of their being employed in each job category. The method is to estimate a multinomial probit regression by industry and occupation and then predict probabilities for each.[12] For each individual, industries and occupations are ranked based on the highest propensity score. Then we estimate the likelihood of employment for each individual, using a probit regression and propensity score.[13] With these three sets of information, we then assign employment status to each individual in the employable pool using an iterative procedure, stepping through industry and occupation pairs, selecting those individuals most likely to be employed in that industry-occupation pair, in order of their likelihood to be employed, until all of the available jobs are assigned. Once we assign jobs, we allocate earnings to those individuals who receive a new job. The method was imputation by hot decking, a method often used to fill the missing values by transferring a value of a donor record that is statistically most similar to a recipient record with a missing value in the same data set.[14]

Our policy simulation assumes an investment of USD 50 billion on projects that increase social care provisioning. Divided equally between HBHC and ECD for children under the age of five years, this amount is equivalent to half of the total gross output of the two industries combined, in 2006. In input–output analysis, the spending is interpreted

[12] Independent variables for the industry and occupation multinomial logits were census division, metropolitan status, age, marital status, sex, educational attainment, and race.

[13] Independent variables for the employment probit were census division, metropolitan status, age, age squared, marital status, sex, educational attainment, and race.

[14] A three-stage Heckit model was used to predict imputed wage and usual hours for each individual in the pool, within age–sex cells. These, together with census division, metropolitan status, marital status, spouse's labour force status, industry and occupation of assigned job, and dummies for the age category of the youngest child and the number of children, were used in the imputation procedure.

as the increase in final demand of commodities by the amount. The increased final demand for child day care (North American Industry Classification System [NAICS] 6244) and HBHC services (NAICS 6216) leads to increasing labour demand in both industries, directly as well as in other industries that supply intermediate input to them. The injection of funds into the relevant private sectors, not to general government, reflects the current mechanism for the bulk of service delivery. In other words, although centres that act as service providers must meet certain state-level criteria, these entities do not act as government contractors whose activities otherwise would have fallen into the government production category.[15]

In the following sections, we analyse the results from the two case studies on employment, income distribution, and poverty reduction.

## EMPLOYMENT

Care provision by non-household institutions, public or private, can address unemployment and the poverty of women simultaneously, as women form the majority of workers in the relevant industries and earnings from their paid work contributes to their household income. The indirect employment generation from multiplier effects is not trivial, and the magnitude largely depends on the intensity and diversity of input sources—in other words, the strength of the backward linkages. This section focuses on the employment generation potential of bringing unpaid care work into the paid work domain.

### South Africa

Table 9.2 exhibits the number of full-year jobs created from the simulation. The increase in the final demand of social care by 1 per cent of the GDP in 2000 generates 571,505 direct jobs in the sector, while the linkages to other sectors and households generate 193,783 jobs.

---

[15] A small exception to this convention was made for preschool facilities under local school systems, which are counted as government activities under the current industry account convention, and thus may not suit the industry assumption. However, dominance of private providers allows us to use the 'private' assumption in the study, even if care comes from 'social' provisioning.

**TABLE 9.2** Direct and Indirect Job Creation by Gender and Skill Level from Social Sector Expansion and Infrastructure

| Social Care | Women Unskilled | Women Skilled | Men Unskilled | Men Skilled | Total | Unskilled Total | Skilled Total |
|---|---|---|---|---|---|---|---|
| Direct | 317,007 | 16,386 | 228,184 | 9,928 | 571,505 | 545,191 | 26,314 |
| Indirect | 66,149 | 22,638 | 71,789 | 33,207 | 193,783 | 137,938 | 55,845 |
| Total | 383,156 | 39,024 | 299,973 | 43,135 | 765,288 | 683,129 | 82,159 |

| Infra-structure | Women Unskilled | Women Skilled | Men Unskilled | Men Skilled | Total | Unskilled Total | Skilled Total |
|---|---|---|---|---|---|---|---|
| Direct | 5,201 | 2,306 | 218,224 | 36,674 | 262,405 | 223,425 | 38,980 |
| Indirect | 46,487 | 17,936 | 48,242 | 26,177 | 138,842 | 94,729 | 44,113 |
| Total | 51,688 | 20,242 | 266,466 | 62,851 | 401,247 | 318,154 | 83,093 |

*Source:* Antonopoulos and Kim (2008) and authors' calculations.

The requirement on labour intensity under the EPWP allocates the majority of direct EPWP jobs to unskilled workers (545,191), while only 26,314 jobs go to skilled workers, resulting in a 20.7 unskilled to one skilled job ratio. Overall, for every three jobs created due to the social care expansion, an additional job opens up within the economy. Job creation within the care sector turns out to be greater for women than for men across skilled and unskilled categories. The infrastructure expansion of the same scale yields 262,406 jobs within the new construction sector, as it generates 138,774 indirect jobs. The direct–indirect job ratio is 1.9, which is expected, as the exogenous wage rates for the sector are 1.5 to 1.7 times higher than they are in the social care sector.

Distribution of employment by household-level poverty status is illustrated in Table 9.3. There are over 11 million workers from non-poor households that comprise 62 per cent (or 11.2 million) of the total labour force. Meanwhile, 2.6 million out of 6.4 million unemployed are from the non-poor household type. The unemployment rate by poverty status reflects the inequality in the labour market: 23.1 per cent for the non-poor type, whereas 62.9 per cent of the ultra-poor type is unemployed. Ultra-poor workers receive most of EPWP direct jobs (78 per cent) as designed in the allocation formula. However, over 88 per cent of indirect jobs (170,287/193,783) belong to workers from

**TABLE 9.3** Labour Market Condition and Jobs Received, by Household Type

| Household Type | Base | | | Jobs Created: Social Care | | |
| --- | --- | --- | --- | --- | --- | --- |
| | Labour Force | Unemployed | Underemployed (%) | Direct | Indirect | Underemployed (%) |
| Non-poor | 11,282,393 | 2,604,134 | 23.1 | 26,028 | 170,287 | 21.3 |
| Poor | 3,875,849 | 1,910,895 | 49.3 | 96,776 | 17,190 | 46.4 |
| Ultra-poor | 3,084,604 | 1,940,813 | 62.9 | 448,701 | 5,416 | 48.2 |

| Household type | Base | | | Jobs Created: Infrastructure | | |
| --- | --- | --- | --- | --- | --- | --- |
| | Labour Force | Unemployed | Underemployed (%) | Direct | Indirect | Underemployed (%) |
| Non-poor | 11,282,393 | 2,604,134 | 23.1 | 3,8701 | 123,007 | 21.6 |
| Poor | 3,875,849 | 1,910,895 | 49.3 | 3,9808 | 12,039 | 48.0 |
| Ultra-poor | 3,084,604 | 1,940,813 | 62.9 | 183,897 | 3,796 | 56.8 |

*Source:* Antonopoulos and Kim (2008) and authors' calculations.

non-poor households, for the distribution follows the wage-income flow in the South African SAM.

As much as the highly unequal distribution reflects the selection of skill level of workers into poverty status, it demonstrates the need for a direct intervention in the labour market to ameliorate the perpetual inequality in the economy. The smaller number of EPWP unskilled jobs in the infrastructure sector means fewer jobs for poor and ultra-poor households than in the care sector. The shares of indirect jobs by household type follow an approximately identical distribution as in the care case, with 88 per cent of indirect jobs to the non-poor households and the remaining 9 per cent and 3 per cent to the poor and the ultra-poor, respectively.[16] The skill-intensive nature of infrastructure puts the workers from poor households at a disadvantage, and attributes to the higher unemployment rates ex post compared to social care.

## United States

A 50 per cent expansion of the social care sector (early childhood education and home-based care for elderly and chronically ill patients) in terms of gross output in 2006, which is equivalent to USD 50 billion, generates approximately 1.2 million jobs in the economy, of which 8 out of 10 new jobs (956,082/1,186,342) are within the care sector (Table 9.4). The same level of expansion in infrastructure construction and maintenance yields half a million jobs, with 6 out of 10 new jobs (345,955/555,942) in the construction sector.

Table 9.5 depicts the job distribution in absolute numbers and shares by various characteristics of the workers hired, including unemployed and few persons who are out of the labour force for reasons other than retirement or illness. A microsimulation based on propensity-score matching is used to assign the new jobs by matching potential workers' socio-economic characteristics to the job openings. The gender composition of job assignments shows almost exactly inverse ratios between social care and construction. Over 90 per cent of jobs go to

---

[16] This is true even with very different intermediate input compositions between the two cases. It implies that higher-order effects outweigh the secondary effects via backward linkages.

**TABLE 9.4** Total Employment Distribution across Industries

| Industry | Social Care | Infrastructure |
|---|---|---|
| Agriculture | 2,928 | 1,969 |
| Mining | 520 | 2,463 |
| Utilities | 773 | 1,808 |
| Construction | 4,489 | 345,955 |
| Manufacturing | 16,797 | 46,402 |
| Wholesale | 7,139 | 11,421 |
| Retail | 4,432 | 36,628 |
| Transportation and Warehousing | 7,020 | 12,715 |
| Information | 4,989 | 4,312 |
| Financial and Real Estate services | 13,621 | 11,474 |
| Professional and Business services | 57,672 | 55,675 |
| Education | 688 | 719 |
| Healthcare and Social Assistance | 21,046 | 675 |
| Social Care | 956,082 | 107 |
| Leisure and Hospitality | 15,650 | 6,509 |
| Other services | 3,113 | 5,009 |
| Government | 69,384 | 12,099 |
| Total | 1,186,342 | 555,942 |

*Source*: Antonopoulos et al. (2010).

women in social sector investment, as more than 80 per cent of jobs are created within the sector.

On the other hand, infrastructure construction generates over 88 per cent of jobs for men, as most jobs (almost 71 per cent) are created in male-dominated industries—construction and manufacturing. The decomposition of job assignments by educational attainment highlights the greater inclusiveness of social care investment. Over 42 per cent of jobs generated by social care investment go to people with less than a high school diploma, compared to only 14 per cent of jobs created by the infrastructure investment for this most disadvantaged group in the labour market. In the infrastructure case, the majority of jobs (62.6 per cent) are assigned to workers with high school diplomas. This fact is largely driven by the construction-related jobs typically held by men with high school diplomas.

Although social care investment more highly favours the group with less than a high school diploma, it also provides more opportunities

**TABLE 9.5** Distribution of Jobs Created by Public Investment on Social Care and Infrastructure in the United States

| Criterion | Jobs Assigned: Social Care | | Jobs Assigned: Infrastructure | |
|---|---|---|---|---|
| | Number | Per Cent | Number | Per Cent |
| *Gender* | | | | |
| Male | 116,525 | 9.9 | 489,814 | 88.6 |
| Female | 1,059,401 | 90.1 | 63,051 | 11.4 |
| *Education* | | | | |
| Less than High School | 500,959 | 42.6 | 77,482 | 14.0 |
| High School Graduate | 308,810 | 26.3 | 345,897 | 62.6 |
| Some College | 196,407 | 16.7 | 46,609 | 8.4 |
| College Graduate | 169,750 | 14.4 | 82,877 | 15.0 |
| *Household Income* | | | | |
| 1st–4th decile | 530,763 | 45.1 | 194,915 | 35.3 |
| 5th–8th decile | 395,846 | 33.7 | 279,438 | 50.5 |
| 9th–10th decile | 249,330 | 21.2 | 78,516 | 14.2 |
| Total | 1,175,939 | 100.0 | 552,869 | 100.0 |

*Source:* Antonopoulos et al. (2010).

to people with at least some higher education than does infrastructure investment (31.1 to 23.4 per cent respectively). This reflects the certificate requirement for preschool teachers and certain childcare providers that are under state or federal regulations for reimbursement purposes.

On the other hand, infrastructure investment raises the demand for engineers and architects, jobs the Standard Occupational Classification system identifies as a part of the 'professional and business services industry and professional occupations'. Typically, these occupations require a college-degree level of education, which accounts for the job assignment—in our simulation—to higher-education attainment groups.

The inclusive nature of social care investment is further reinforced by the job assignment by household annual income. Forty-five per cent of jobs go to workers from households with income below the 4th decile (approximately USD 39,000 a year). Home health aides, who comprise one of the major occupation groups in social care, are mainly women from low-income households: 45 per cent of the workers are from households under 200 per cent of the federal poverty line.[17] The social care expansion thus aids those workers specifically. The infrastructure case, on the other hand, provides half of the jobs created to workers from the middle-income group.

## EFFECTS ON INCOME, INEQUALITY, AND POVERTY REDUCTION

The large-scale employment policies pose consequences on household income and inequality. A method of job allotment, either by direct targeting or expanding private sector, influences overall income inequality. The composition of workers in affected industries, as well as the inter-industry linkages, largely shapes the outcome. The targeted nature of the EPWP contributes to the income growth of the poor and ultra-poor workers, although the total impacts are not as great as they would be under the more equitable labour market. The relatively low skill requirements tend to benefit the workers from poor households in the US.

This section examines the effects of the proposed policy intervention on income growth and inequality using the concept of 'pro-poor' growth as defined by Kakwani, Khandker, and Son (2004). Their study defines growth as being pro-poor only when income growth is higher for the poor than for the non-poor. As we will see below, even when we include indirect job creation in the calculations, EPWP job creation allocates jobs in a manner which results in pro-poor growth. In the case of the US, it is the very composition of workers in the care sector (mostly women from low-income households) that attributes to the pro-poor nature of the investment in social care. Poverty reduction follows naturally, as the wage earnings augment to the workers' household income. The depth of poverty predetermines the extent to which the external margin of poverty is reduced. Regardless, the investment attributes to the reduction in the internal margin of poverty.

---

[17] It is not clear whether the low skill requirements of care work attracts unskilled workers from low-income households or the low wage rates of care work cause workers to be in low-income households. It may be jointly determined, and thus a direction of causality is hard to establish.

## South Africa

Table 9.6 shows aggregated changes of income and distribution across non-poor, poor, and ultra-poor household groups. It is worthwhile to note that even with the targeted job distribution in favour of the poor and ultra-poor, most of the income growth goes to the non-poor, since they harness most of the highly paid skilled jobs and most of the unskilled jobs from indirect effects. The biased benefit distribution highlights the sharply skewed employment–income distribution to the non-poor. It may be the case that employment determines the poverty. Even within the argument of direction of causality, one cannot deny the strong evidence of the dependence on wage income overall and the lack of viable self-employment opportunities for the poor and ultra-poor in South Africa, in which total income of the bottom half is less than 8 per cent of the top half of the population. The skewed base income gives rise to the higher income growth rates for the poor and ultra-poor, which are 2.6 and 16.4 per cent growth, respectively, compared to a 1.3 per cent incline for the non-poor. Scaling up the social care sector at the level of 1 per cent of GDP may not make a large difference in terms of overall income distribution. However, it should be remembered that the participating households do receive significant benefits from the programme.

In the infrastructure expansion, the income changes reflect the skill-biased job creation that benefits non-poor households in that the income growth for the group remains similar. Meanwhile, total income growth for the poor and ultra-poor households is around half of the level in the social care expansion.

Table 9.7 displays the poverty reduction effects for participating households only. The income of participating households shows the opposite trends: the poor and ultra-poor households move further above the poverty line under the infrastructure expansion. The result is simply attributable to the higher wage rates (1.7 times higher) in the infrastructure case. Under the social care expansion, the programme wage rate for unskilled workers is exogenously set comparable to the near-poverty level, minimum wage rate to impose a certain degree of self-targeting. The higher participation rates of households in the EPWP programmes under the social care expansion are reflective of the lower wage rates and more labour-intensive nature of care provision.

**TABLE 9.6** Changes in Aggregate Income Level by Household Group

| Criterion | Social Sector | | | Infrastructure | | |
|---|---|---|---|---|---|---|
| | Non-poor | Poor | Ultra-poor | Non-poor | Poor | Ultra-poor |
| *Aggregate Income (million rand)* | | | | | | |
| Base (pre–intervention) | 640,846 | 38,410 | 15,986 | 640,846 | 38,410 | 15,986 |
| Increment | 8,496 | 983 | 2,620 | 8,396 | 611 | 1,153 |
| New | 649,342 | 39,393 | 18,606 | 649,239 | 39,494 | 16,666 |
| *Change (%)* | | | | | | |
| Base (pre–intervention) | 100 | 100 | 100 | 100 | 100 | 100 |
| Increment | 1.3 | 2.6 | 16.4 | 1.3 | 1.6 | 7.2 |
| New | 101.3 | 102.6 | 116.4 | 101.3 | 101.6 | 107.2 |
| *Income Distribution (%)* | | | | | | |
| Base (pre–intervention) | 92.2 | 5.5 | 2.3 | 92.2 | 5.5 | 2.3 |
| Increment | 70.2 | 8.1 | 21.7 | 82.6 | 6.0 | 11.3 |
| New | 91.8 | 5.6 | 2.6 | 92.0 | 5.5 | 2.4 |

*Source:* Antonopoulos and Kim (2008) and authors' own calculations.

**TABLE 9.7** Income Changes of Participating Households (rand, mean values)

| Household Type | Poverty Line (rand) Equivalency Scale Adjusted | Depth of Poverty Before | Depth of Poverty After Care | Depth of Poverty After Infrastructure | Participation Rate (as % of total households) Care | Participation Rate (as % of total households) Infrastructure |
|---|---|---|---|---|---|---|
| Urban Formal African Poor | 15,513 | −480 | 6,240 | 10,974 | 3.0 | 1.3 |
| Urban Formal African Ultra-poor | 18,770 | −10,952 | −4,232 | 502 | 29.2 | 12.0 |
| Urban Formal Coloured Poor | 16,458 | −429 | 6,291 | 11,026 | 2.8 | 1.1 |
| Urban Formal Coloured Ultra-poor | 16,277 | −8,861 | −2,141 | 2,594 | 24.2 | 9.9 |
| Urban Informal African Poor | 12,196 | −860 | 5,860 | 10,595 | 4.4 | 1.8 |
| Urban Informal African Ultra-poor | 14,630 | −8,496 | −1,776 | 2,958 | 23.2 | 9.5 |
| Rural Commercial African Poor | 13,801 | −1,051 | 5,669 | 10,403 | 4.6 | 1.9 |
| Rural Comm. African Ultra-poor | 18,595 | −10,794 | −4,074 | 661 | 26.6 | 10.9 |
| Rural Commercial Coloured Poor | 13,622 | −203 | 6,517 | 11,252 | 1.2 | 0.5 |
| Rural Commercial Coloured Ultra-poor | 15,833 | −8,100 | −1,380 | 3,355 | 19.7 | 8.1 |
| Ex-homeland African Poor | 14,079 | −1,333 | 5,387 | 10,121 | 5.6 | 2.3 |
| Ex-homeland African Ultra-poor | 17,375 | −10,354 | −3,634 | 1,101 | 25.5 | 10.5 |

*Source:* Antonopoulos and Kim (2008) and authors' own calculations.

**TABLE 9.8**  Impacts on Sectoral Gross Output and GDP Growth
(million rand)

|                            | Agriculture | Manufacturing | Services  | GDP (value added) |
|----------------------------|-------------|---------------|-----------|-------------------|
| Base                       | 241,457     | 1,132,106     | 1,040,440 | 835,651           |
| Increment (care)           | 9,850       | 12,087        | 14,696    | 15,167            |
| Growth Rate (%)            | 4.08        | 1.07          | 1.41      | 1.81              |
| Increment (infrastructure) | 2,562       | 13,148        | 12,316    | 14,078            |
| Growth Rate (%)            | 1.06        | 1.16          | 1.18      | 1.68              |

*Source*: Antonopoulos and Kim (2008) and authors' own calculations.

A closed system of the SAM enables us to examine the multiplier effects on macro-indicators. In the case of social care expansion, the 1 per cent spending on social care expansion produces an extra 0.8 per cent GDP growth, as Table 9.8 shows. Significant spending on food, a part of care services in Friedman et al. (2007), boosts the production in agriculture directly, while other sectors benefit from multiplier effects of indirect backward linkages as well. The infrastructure expansion benefits the manufacturing sector the most due to the heavy use of manufactured intermediate inputs. But the net GDP growth is lower, at 0.68 per cent, after deducting the original injection equivalent to 1 per cent of GDP. The lower GDP in level terms comes in part from the higher shares of intermediate input composition in the infrastructure case.

Table 9.9 shows the multiplier effects on tax revenue. Sales and indirect taxes are paid by the industries, while the 'direct tax' is another name for income taxes paid by the individuals. On average, the manufacturing sector pays higher share of their gross output on sales taxes (4–7 per cent with 22 per cent on petrol products, compared to 1–6 per cent on the service sector), according to the SAM. Non-poor households pay higher tax rates in terms of per cent of their income, and that contributes to the higher direct tax receipt in the case of infrastructure expansion. The social care expansion—effectively, aggregate demand stimulus—increases tax revenue by 1.5 per cent, or over 3 billion rand, equivalent to over a third of total spending on the social care expansion. The infrastructure expansion collects 2.9 billion

**TABLE 9.9** Multiplier Effects on Tax Revenue (million rand)

|  | Sales | Indirect | Direct | Total |
|---|---|---|---|---|
| Base | 83,933 | 18,529 | 121,085 | 223,548 |
| Increment (care) | 1,484 | 276 | 1,547 | 3,308 |
| Growth Rate (%) | 1.8 | 1.5 | 1.3 | 1.5 |
| Increment (infrastructure) | 1,037 | 253 | 1,642 | 2,932 |
| Growth Rate (%) | 1.2 | 1.4 | 1.4 | 1.3 |

*Source:* Antonopoulos and Kim (2008) and authors' own calculations.

rand, which raises the tax revenue growth by 1.3 per cent. The positive macroeconomic impacts prove that the social care expansion is a viable policy tool that not only addresses the unemployment among the poor but also improves macroeconomic conditions.

## United States

Tables 9.10a and 9.10b show the changes in individual median and mean earnings of those who are assigned jobs in social care and infrastructure construction. The comparison highlights the disparate distributional impacts of the two investments. It is noteworthy to mention that the mean–median earnings ratio decreases as the level of educational attainment increases among workers. It is more so for workers in social care than in infrastructure construction, which is indicative of the stronger equalizing effect of social care investment.

Workers with less than a high school diploma tend to benefit the most in relative terms from both of the simulated investments compared to workers with higher levels of educational attainment. Their median and mean earnings increase the most among all the groups. Infrastructure construction turns out to raise earnings of the least educated workers more than social care investment does. The result is attributable to much higher hourly wage rates of construction workers, which is USD 21.87 on average within the industry (BLS 2009b). Even unskilled construction labourers earn more than USD 14.30 per hour, significantly more than the USD 11.30 per hour that a preschool teacher earns on average. For the least-educated workers in social care, ex ante median earnings (USD 3,120) are less than half of mean earnings (USD 7,641), which suggests a highly skewed distribution of the least educated workers along their earnings level. Thus, the likely outcome of the social care investment would be close to the median earnings change for the workers.

For workers with higher educational attainment (some college or more), social care investment appears to raise median earnings relatively more than infrastructure construction investment does. The occupational composition of the jobs created by social care investment may

**TABLE 9.10A**   Changes in Median Earnings by Individual (USD)

| Criterion | Social Care | | | Infrastructure | | |
|---|---|---|---|---|---|---|
| | Before | After | Change (%) | Before | After | Change (%) |
| *Education* | | | | | | |
| Less than High School | 3,120 | 7,000 | 124.4 | 7,000 | 17,000 | 142.9 |
| High School Graduate | 15,000 | 26,500 | 76.7 | 18,000 | 30,000 | 66.7 |
| Some College | 14,000 | 30,000 | 114.3 | 15,000 | 30,002 | 100.0 |
| College Graduate | 26,000 | 55,000 | 111.5 | 28,000 | 52,000 | 85.7 |
| *Income* | | | | | | |
| 1st–4th decile | 7,000 | 22,029 | 214.7 | 8,060 | 27,500 | 241.2 |
| 5th–8th decile | 20,000 | 30,000 | 50.0 | 22,000 | 33,000 | 50.0 |
| 9th–10th decile | 30,000 | 34,002 | 13.3 | 35,000 | 38,000 | 8.6 |

*Source:* Authors' own calculations.

**TABLE 9.10B**   Changes in Mean Earnings by Individual (USD)

| Criterion | Social Care | | | Infrastructure | | |
|---|---|---|---|---|---|---|
| | Before | After | Change (%) | Before | After | Change (%) |
| *Education* | | | | | | |
| Less than High School | 7,641 | 12,893 | 68.7 | 11,583 | 21,900 | 89.1 |
| High School Grad | 21,654 | 31,382 | 44.9 | 23,163 | 35,304 | 52.4 |
| Some College | 22,950 | 33,169 | 44.5 | 23,994 | 33,960 | 41.5 |
| College Graduate | 44,475 | 67,694 | 52.2 | 45,693 | 69,284 | 51.6 |
| *Income* | | | | | | |
| 1st–4th decile | 9,940 | 29,862 | 200.4 | 10,863 | 33,787 | 211.0 |
| 5th–8th decile | 23,503 | 40,183 | 71.0 | 25,227 | 43,875 | 73.9 |
| 9th–10th decile | 50,810 | 46,903 | –7.7 | 55,879 | 51,569 | –7.7 |

*Source:* Authors' own calculations.

explain the difference: the sector hires more managers and professionals than infrastructure, and these jobs, unlike the lower-skilled occupations, usually offer wages comparable to similar jobs in the construction sector. Thus, social care investment appears to be more beneficial to highly educated workers than to those with the least education in terms of earnings. But one should note that social care investment generates many more jobs for workers with less than a high school diploma (500,959) than does infrastructure construction (77,482).

Workers from the poorest households (1st–4th decile) definitely receive the largest jump in earnings: a more than 200 per cent increase in all measures from both types of investment. The very-low initial earnings of the group are attributable to the jump. Earnings for workers from middle-income households (5th–8th decile) increase by more than 50 per cent, and the infrastructure investment seems to be a slightly better investment for that group. Workers from high-income households (9th–10th decile) show a moderate gain in median earnings but a moderate loss in mean earnings. This result implies that earnings from their new jobs are below the earnings from their previous jobs. It may be indicative of a downward transition of some of the newly hired workers from the high-income groups. Again, the infrastructure investment raises the earnings of all groups more than the social care investment does, simply due to relatively higher wage rates in construction industries.

★★★

The ex ante evaluation of social care expansion demonstrates that investment on caring for the elderly, chronically ill, and children under school age is an effective employment-generation policy. The labour-intensive nature of care giving is attributable to large employment multipliers in the care sector. Direct job creation within the sector accounts for 75 to 80 per cent of all jobs created within and across the sectors combined. The study also found that the investment on care is pro-poor, since workers from poor households take up the most of newly created jobs either by targeting design, as in the case of the EPWP, or by the market wage rates. The low wage rates in the sector do not deter pro-poor growth, in part because the initial income level of poor households is so low that even the small wage earnings are enough to lift their ex post income higher in relative terms. On the other hand, the lower wage rates discourage non-poor workers, who perhaps have higher reservation wage rates than the poor ones, to take up the job opportunities in the low-paying care sector. The microsimulation results for the US care expansion, compared to construction, confirm this view.

The social care expansion also contributes to the reduction of poverty directly through employment. The change in income from comparable expansion in construction seems to reduce income poverty more than that of the care sector. However, one should note that number of jobs for the low-income households (1st–4th decile) under the care expansion is more than 540,000, whereas less than 195,000 jobs go to the households in the case of infrastructure expansion. In other words, the internal margin of poverty for the participating households may be reduced more under the construction expansion, but the overall reduction of the external margin of poverty is much greater under the care expansion.

Aside from labour market analysis, we provide contextual evidence on the hidden demand for care. The insufficient coverage of Head Start and other ECD programmes is evident from the data. The distributional consequences of the short supply of care can be significant for the next generation, according to Heckman (2011). Ageing baby boomers imply higher demand for HBHC in the US. The prevalence of HIV/AIDS, tuberculosis, and malaria in South Africa warrants the wider establishment of an HCBC system.[18]

It should be reiterated that the methods used to compute aggregate job creation under labour-surplus conditions and low inflationary pressures does not require us to account for general equilibrium price effects. Input–output analysis, accordingly, is adequate and sufficient for the task at hand, and for both country case studies. Moreover, the detailed classification of industries in the analysis makes it possible to identify and utilize industry-level production technologies. The disaggregation and accurate representation of specifics in the key industries makes up for whatever loss there may be due to absence of price adjustments in the model.

---

[18] Hence, increasing life expectancy would have called for home-based care for the elderly in South Africa as well.

Distribution of jobs in the South African study may seem incomplete, since the unit of classification is still an aggregated group of households, whereas the US case study employs microsimulation. In defence of using the specific aggregated groups in the SAM, we invoke the detrimental effects of the apartheid era: strict segregation and unequal treatment in education and employment have left the majority of African population unskilled, poor, with low levels of education, and inexperienced as participants in forms of decent paid work. The great deal of in-group homogeneity, created by racialized segregation, among the majority of the unemployed and the bifurcation of those characteristics used in the statistical matching process across the whole population make the microsimulation technique based on propensity matching inadequate.

To generalize the framework developed in this chapter, it may be desirable to develop a computable general equilibrium model with detailed industry classifications that allows for supply bottlenecks and market failures in the sense of slack conditions and the underemployment of resources in factor markets. Furthermore, ex post programme evaluations of the EPWP, provided that necessary datasets are made widely available, could contribute to refinement of the ex ante methods discussed in the chapter.

## REFERENCES

Antonopoulos, R. 2008. 'The Unpaid Care Work-Paid Work Connection', Working Paper No. 86, Policy Integration and Statistics Department, International Labour Organization (ILO), Geneva.

———. 2009. 'Promoting Gender Equality through Stimulus Packages and Public Job Creation', Public Policy Brief No. 101, Levy Economics Institute of Bard College, New York.

———. 2010. 'Employment Guarantee Policies: A Gender Perspective', Policy Brief No. 2, Poverty Reduction and Gender Equality Series, United Nations Development Programme (UNDP), New York.

Antonopoulos, R. and K. Kim. 2008. 'The Impact of Employment Guarantee Programmes on Gender Equality and Pro-Poor Economic Development in South Africa: Scaling Up the Expanded Public Works Programme', Research Project No. 34, Levy Economics Institute of Bard College and United Nations Development Programme (UNDP), New York.

Antonopoulos, R., K. Kim, T. Masterson, and A. Zacharias. 2010. 'Investing in Care: A Strategy for Effective and Equitable Job Creation', Working Paper No. 610, Levy Economics Institute of Bard College, New York.

Barnett, W.S., J.T. Hustedt, K.B. Robin, and K.L. Schulman. 2004. 'The State of Preschool: 2004 State Preschool Yearbook', mimeo. New Brunswick, New Jersey: National Institute for Early Education Research.

Barnett, W.S., C. Lamy, and K. Jung. 2005. 'The Effects of State Prekinder-garten Programs on Young Children's School Readiness in Five States', mimeo. New Brunswick, New Jersey: National Institute for Early Education Research.

Bergemann, A. and G.J. van den Berg. 2006. 'Active Labor Market Policy Effects for Women in Europe: A Survey', IZA Discussion Paper No. 2365, Institute for the Study of Labor, Bonn, Germany.

Blau, D. and E. Tekin. 2007. 'The Determinants and Consequences of Childcare Subsidies for Single Mothers in the USA', *Journal of Population Economics*, 20(4): 719–41.

Bureau of Labor Statistics (BLS). 2009a. *Occupational Employment and Wages, 2008*. Washington, DC: BLS, Office of Occupational Statistics and Employment Projections.

————. 2009b. *Career Guide to Industries, 2010–2011 Edition*. Washington, DC: BLS, Office of Occupational Statistics and Employment Projections.

Buvinic, M. 2009. 'The Global Financial Crisis: Assessing Vulnerability for Women and Children, Identifying Policy Responses', *UN Commission on the Status of Women*, 53rd session, New York, 2–13 March.

Casiro, O.G., M.E. McKenzie, L. McFayden, C. Shapiro, M.M.K. Seshia, N. MacDonald, M. Moffat, and M.S. Cheang. 1993. 'Earlier Discharge with Community-Based Intervention for Low Birth Weight Infants: A Randomized Trial', *Pediatrics*, 92(1): 128–34.

Dickens, W., I. Sawhill, and J. Tebbs. 2006. 'The Effects of Investing in Early Education on Economic Growth', Policy Brief No. 153, Washington, DC: The Brookings Institution.

Fields, A.I., A. Rosenblatt, M.M. Pollack, and J. Kaufman. 1991. 'Home Care Cost-Effectiveness for Respiratory Technology-Dependent Children', *American Journal of Diseases of Children*, 145(7): 729–33.

Friedman, I., L. Bhengu, N. Mothibe, N. Reynolds, and A. Mafuleka. 2007. *Scaling up the EPWP*, vols. 1–4. Durban, South Africa: Health Systems Trust. Study commissioned by the Development Bank of South Africa and the EPWP.

Golin, S.C., A.W. Mitchell, and B. Gault. 2004. 'The Price of School Readiness: A Tool for Estimating the Cost of Universal Preschool in the States', Washington, DC: Institute for Women's Policy Research.

Heckman, J.J. 2011. 'The American Family in Black and White: A Post-Racial Strategy for Improving Skills to Promote Equality', IZA Discussion Paper 5495, Bonn, Germany: Institute for the Study of Labor.

Heckman, J.J. and D.V. Masterov. 2007. 'The Productivity Argument for Investing in Young Children', *Review of Agricultural Economics,* 29(3): 446–93.

Heckman, J.J., S.H. Moon, R. Pinto, P. Savelyev, and A. Yavitz. 2010. 'A New Cost-Benefit and Rate of Return Analysis for the Perry Preschool Program: A Summary', Working Paper No. 16180, Cambridge, Massachusetts: National Bureau of Economic Research.

International Labour Organization (ILO). 2009. *Key Indicators of the Labour Market,* 6th ed., Geneva: ILO.

———. 2010. *Global Employment Trends.* Geneva: ILO.

Iruka, I.U. and P.R. Carver. 2006. *Initial Results from the 2005 NHES Early Childhood Program Participation Survey* (NCES 2006–075), Washington, DC: National Center for Education Statistics.

Kaboub, F. 2007. 'Employment Guarantee Programs: A Survey of Theories and Policy Experiences', Working Paper No. 498. Annandale-on-Hudson, New York: Levy Economics Institute of Bard College.

Kakwani, N., S. Khandker, and H.H. Son. 2004. 'Pro-Poor Growth: Concepts and Measurement with Country Case Studies', Working Paper No. 1, Brasilia, Brazil: International Poverty Center, United Nations Development Programme.

Kim, K. 2011. 'Ex-Ante Evaluation of a Targeted Job Program: Hypothetical Integration in a Social Accounting Matrix of South Africa', *Economic Modelling,* 28, 2683–90.

Kimmel, J. 1995. 'The Effectiveness of Child-Care Subsidies in Encouraging the Welfare-To-Work Transition of Low-Income Single Mothers', *The American Economic Review,* 85(2), 271–5.

King, M., S. Ruggles, T. Alexander, D. Leicach, and M. Sobek. 2009. *Integrated Public Use Microdatas Series, Current Population Survey: Version 2.0.* [Machine-readable database]. Minneapolis: Minnesota Population Center.

Lefebvre, P. and P. Merrigan. 2008. 'Child-Care Policy and the Labor Supply of Mothers with Young Children: A Natural Experiment from Canada', *Journal of Labor Economics,* 26(3): 519–48.

MetLife. 2006. 'The MetLife Caregiving Cost Study: Productivity Losses to US Business'. New York: Metropolitan Life Insurance Company and National Alliance for Caregiving.

Peters, Louise and Ken Sellick. 2006. 'Quality of Life of Cancer Patients Receiving Inpatients and Home-based Palliative Care', *Journal of Advanced Nursing,* 53(5): 524–33.

Pollin, R., J. Heintz, and H. Garrett-Peltier. 2009. 'The Economic Benefits of Investing in Clean Energy: How the Economic Stimulus Program and New Legislation can Boost US Economic Growth and Employment', Amherst, Massachusetts: Department of Economics and Political Economy Research Institute.

Rodgers, G. and C. Kuptsch (eds) 2008. *Pursuing Decent Work Goals: Priorities for Research.* Geneva: ILO, International Institute for Labour Studies.

Sörensen, S., P. Duberstein, D. Gill, and M. Pinquart. 2006. 'Dementia Care: Mental Health Effects, Intervention Strategies, and Clinical Implications', *Lancet Neurology,* 5(11): 961–73.

Statistics South Africa (Stats SA). 2008–9. *Quarterly Labour Force Survey.* Issues 1–4.

# 10 Integrating Time Use in Gender Budgeting

## Lekha Chakraborty

Integrating the unpaid care sector in macro-level policymaking is an elusive area of research. Data paucity is often cited as a major constraint in undertaking research in unpaid care sectors. Time-use statistics, to a great extent, solves this problem by providing better workforce participation estimates in both paid and unpaid sectors, as well as in lifting the statistical invisibility of unpaid care work. However, despite the fact that gender budgeting is emerging as a significant socio-economic tool to analyse the budgetary policies for identifying its effect on gender equity, the integration of time-use statistics into this process remains partial or even nil across countries. Only a few countries have used time budgets in the process of gender budgeting. It is interesting to recall a paper by Becker (1965), where he notes:

> [T]hroughout history the amount of time spent at work has never consistently been much greater than that spent at other activities. Economic development has led to a large secular decline in the work week so that today time spent at work is less than a third of the total time available. Consequently, the allocation and efficiency of 'nonworking' time may now be more important to economic welfare than that of working time. Yet the attention paid by economists to the latter dwarfs any paid to the former.

The lack of integrating time budgets into gender budgeting is due to three primary reasons: One, the time-use survey (TUS) itself is not conducted at a macro level in many countries. Although these are conducted in a few countries, they remain as one-point surveys and lack time-series data, as in the case of Canada. Two, the process of gender budgeting itself is highly partial across countries focusing broadly on the market economy and does not incorporate the analysis of unpaid care economy. Although the conceptual discussions on gender budgeting highlighted the significance of giving thrust to the statistical invisibility of unpaid care economy in framing the policies related to gender budgeting, it is seldom translated at empirical levels. Three, gender budgeting is conducted across countries on a highly restricted assumption that 'all public expenditure cannot be gender partitioned', especially the mainstream infrastructure spending (both social and physical). This assumption is highly controversial.

Even the mainstream public expenditure, especially social and physical infrastructure, has gender-differential impacts. The results of limited benefit incidence analysis (BIA) conducted across income quintiles clearly shows the distributional impacts of public expenditure across class and gender. However, BIA exercises are not carried out for core public expenditure due to lack of data on 'units utilized'. The time-use budgets are a significant domain of 'unit-utilized data', which is hardly used by any researchers in BIA.

Gender budgeting has three significant components: (a) gender diagnosis; (b) analysis of the contribution of women not only in market economy, but also in unpaid care economy; and (c) analysis of the budgets for the gender-differential impacts of public expenditure. Time-use statistics play a significant role in each of these components, something that is highly neglected in the studies on gender budgeting. This chapter takes up these issues and analyses the scope and limitations of integrating time use in gender budgeting.

The chapter is organized as follows. The first section explains gender budgeting and its rationale. Section two deals with the analytical framework of gender budgeting and incorporating the time budgets. The next section discusses the scope of time-use statistics in gender diagnosis. Section four highlights the significance of time use in lifting the statistical invisibility of unpaid care sector and integrating in gender budgeting. Section five focuses on the use of time budgets in analysing the gender-differential impacts of public expenditure. The last section summarizes the arguments.

## WHAT IS GENDER BUDGETING AND ITS RATIONALE?

Gender budgeting neither makes separate budgets for women nor does it analyse the earmarking of funds for women-centric programmes in the budgets. It is simply an analysis of the entire budget through a gender lens to identify the gender-differential impacts and to translate gender commitments into budgetary commitments. Moreover, it enhances the transparency of and accountability for revenue and public expenditure. Prima facie, a budget may appear to be gender-neutral, but due to the differences in the socially determined systemic roles prescribed for men and women, the budgetary policies have differential impacts across gender. As a consequence, gender neutrality of budgetary policies can turn to gender blindness due to the fact that the men and women are at asymmetric levels of development on the socio-economic scale. Gender budgeting is not synonymous to women budgeting, rather it is an analysis of budgets to ascertain the relative benefits (and loss) derived by each gender from a particular fiscal programme/project. It is one among many macroeconomic policy tools to address the gender equity.

The existing budgets ignore the gender specific impacts of budgetary policies. Generally, budgeting involves four components: (a) the budgetary allocation of resources to various heads; (b) the actual government outlays on various heads; (c) an accounting of how resources are utilized for a particular purpose (for example, on administrative overheads and wages and salaries, operation, and maintenance); and (d) an evaluation of the effectiveness of the resources utilized in delivering the intended results. Gender budgeting involves looking at all the four components from the point of view of women as beneficiaries.

Can all public expenditure be gender partitioned? While it is a debate whether public goods and services, which are non-rival and non-excludable in nature, like defence, can be amenable to gender partitioning, many other public expenditures have differential impact on the two sexes. It is all the more relevant to note that the issues of being non-rival and non-excludable is an issue not just for any particular gender, but also for other disadvantaged sections of the population like aboriginals who cannot be segregated on a 'geographic area' basis. On the other hand, immunization has a public good aspect, but can be divided individually on the basis of girls and boys. In the same sense, poverty alleviation services may also have the characteristics for public good. It is generally held that all or most individuals across countries derive utility from less poverty; in that sense, benefits from poverty alleviation expenditure are fully non-excludable and non-rival, with gender-differential impacts.

Another point to be noted is that the public expenditure on infrastructure, such as roads, irrigation, energy, water and sanitation, and science and technology, has intrinsic gender dimensions. It is important to examine the infrastructure budgets like energy and technology and transport that are assumed to be gender-neutral. An analysis of infrastructure budgets not only reveals the differing needs of and constraints on women's and men's lives and productive roles, but also helps to reveal the inefficiency of existing allocations, which may not be adequately reaching women and men. A study by the International Food Policy Research Institute (IFPRI) showed that public expenditure on road infrastructure has the largest impact on poverty reduction (Fan, Hazell, and Thorat 1999). This generates debate on 'specifically targeted programmes for poor' versus 'infrastructure programmes', particularly in terms of gender-responsive budgeting (GRB). However, it is to be noted that women too have practical and strategic needs.[1] Investment in infrastructure can catalyse the fulfillment of practical needs of women. However, specifically targeted programmes for women are required to address the strategic needs of women.

---

[1] Practical gender needs are not aligned to any strategic goal, such as women's emancipation or gender equality. Practical gender needs include food, shelter, community-level requirements of basic services, or basic infrastructure like roads, water, and sanitation, which are required by the whole family, not women alone. Strategic gender needs are identified to overcome women's subordination, which, in turn, depends on a particular cultural and socio-political context. Strategic needs include abolition of sexual division of labour; alleviation of the burden of domestic labour, childcare; removal of institutional forms of discrimination such as rights to own land or property, access to credit, measures against domestic violence; and establishment of political equality.

Another example is that the outlays for augmenting the supply of safe drinking water can benefit women more than men in the care economy by cutting down on the time spent in fetching water from the river or ponds. The existing practice of budgeting across countries may not pay any special attention to the impact of budgets on women in the care economy. The Systems of National Accounts (SNA) 1993 recognizes unpaid work in the care economy as 'productive' and as 'work', however it is kept outside the purview of calculations of the GDP and kept as satellite accounts. The point to be noted is that despite the recognition of the care economy by SNA 1993, policymakers and economists have not yet satisfactorily integrated care economy into macro-level policy planning.

In many ways, government budgets are 'subsidized' by unpaid care economy work. For instance, when government cuts back public expenditure on health, it is women (caregivers) in households who bear the brunt of it. Moreover, to cope with the increasing demand for services generated by HIV/AIDS, many countries are opting for home-based care systems, where voluntary or low-paid workers, rather than hospitals, provide care to the patients. This can reduce the public expenditure on health by a considerable amount. Nevertheless, when a public expenditure policy on health is designed in any country, the policymakers take into consideration only the 'users' of health services, not the health providers (the care givers at the household level). The implications of this propensity on the GRB are tremendous.

The case for gender budgeting is based on a premise that ensures transparency in the budgetary allocation for women and it protects these provisions from being reappropriated and thereby enhances accountability ('voice'). The degree of accountability ('voice') in integrating gender in a federal fiscal setup is based on a dual conjecture: the accountability of the sub-national government to (a) the higher tier of government and (b) to the electorate. The former limits the latter, especially in cases where financial decisions are centralized, but the provision of public goods is decentralized. The dichotomy of finance from functional assignments can lead to inefficiencies, the most oft-cited problem being of unfunded mandates. On the other hand, the real autonomy of the feminization of governance (elected women representatives [EWR]) in playing a crucial role in integrating gender-specific needs in the fiscal policies and their accountability to the electorate gets constrained if the flow of funds is through deconcentrated intermediate levels with accountability to the central government. However, fiscal policy in a federal setting promotes government accountability, particularly in geographically or demographically large nations. However, the phenomenon of 'elite capture' can lead to aberrations in 'voice'. In all the aspects discussed above, time-use statistics have an important role to play, which this chapter discusses later.

## ANALYTICAL FRAMEWORK OF GENDER BUDGETING INCORPORATING TIME BUDGETS

An analytical framework to gender budgeting can be dichotomized into: (a) ex post gender budgeting, in which the existing budget is analysed through a gender lens and (b) ex ante gender budgeting, in which the needs of the women are identified first and then budgeting them. The ex ante gender budgeting is relatively easy at sub-national levels of government in which the identification of needs of women at the local level is relatively easy and they can then be budgeted for. This is usually referred in literature as 'bottom-up approach of gender budgeting'. In other words, the ex ante budgeting is basically what we aimed for in terms of gender budgeting, while ex post budgeting is towards a gender auditing process of the existing budgets. The ex post of the budget in period '*t*' can feed into the ex ante for the budget in period '*t* + 1' as well and ideally it would become the integral part of budget planning and allocation.[2]

---

[2] The South Australian women's budget in the mid-1980s used a trichotomy in classifying public expenditure, which includes: (a) women-specific expenditure; (b) equal opportunities in the public services; and (c) mainstream expenditure. In South Africa, a five-step approach towards GRB has been used, namely (a) situational analysis (gender); (b) assessment of policies, legislations, and programmes through a gender perspective; (c) assessment of the adequacy of budgetary allocations for the implementation of the policy; (d) monitoring whether the money is spent as planned; and (e) assessment of whether policy as implemented changed the situation described in the first step. The point to be noted here in the latter five-step approach is that the first two steps are mere gender analysis prelude to budget analysis through a gender lens.

Time-use statistics have a significant part in both ex ante and ex post analysis of gender budgeting. In the ex post analysis, the analysis of mainstream expenditure (assumption that all public spending has gender-differential impacts) can use time budgets to show gender differential effects of public spending. In ex ante gender budgeting, identifying gender needs and preferences before budgeting extracts data on preference revelation and demands mechanisms based on time-use statistics. Each of the methodology is described in detail in the following sub-sections.

## Analytical Framework for Ex Post Gender Budgeting

Ex post gender budget analysis begins with the identification of three categories of public expenditure: (a) specifically targeted expenditure to women and girls (100 per cent targeted for women); (b) pro-women allocations, which are the composite expenditure schemes with a women component (that is, a scale of 100 > expenditure ≥ 30; at least 30 per cent targeted for women, where exp. represents the expenditure);[3] and (c) residual public expenditures that have gender-differential impacts (that is, a scale of 0 ≥ expenditure > 30). It is relatively easy to identify the specifically targeted programmes for women across ministries from the expenditure budget documents. However, the challenge is that the information on the women component intrinsic in the composite programmes is not readily available in the budget documents.

---

[3] The criteria of 30 per cent cut-off has genesis in Women's Component Plan (where 30 per cent of development funds are earmarked for women) in the context of India. As other South Asian nations followed the National Institute of Public Finance and Policy (NIPFP) methodology of gender budgeting used in context of India, the 30 per cent cut-off has been practised per se, without any scientific backing. However, the point to be noted is that the Women's Component Plan of 30 per cent is also designed ad hoc. The other ad hoc fiscal policy measure was the fiscal rules based on fiscal deficit to GDP ratio by Maastricht Treaty at 3 per cent. The sanctity of cut-off points is not theoretical in both cases, that is, in case of rule-based fiscal policies as well as in gender budgeting policies, both cut-off points are arbitrary, which do not have any theoretical backing.

Within the analytical framework of gender budgeting, one can develop matrices to categorize the financial input from the gender perspective and can be sent to the identified ministries/government departments to obtain the gender budgeting allocations. Three matrices form a categorization of public expenditure on the scale of zero to hundred in terms of the proportions of beneficiaries who are women. In other words, the first matrix collates the specifically targeted programmes on women with 100 per cent of allocations on women, while the second matrix collates the public expenditure programmes with pro-women allocations, which is defined as at least 30 per cent of the budgetary allocations that benefit women (that is, a scale of 100 > exppenditure > 30). Pro-women allocation can be ex ante (if it is calculated on the basis of amounts 'earmarked' for women) or ex post (if it is based on the 'beneficiaries'). The third matrix collates the allocations, which are residual in nature, in the sense that the programmes do not come under the first and second matrices. This residual expenditure may have gendered impacts, if not proved otherwise. In the scale, the allocations come under the third category and form a range of gender-specific allocations of less than 30 to zero (that is, 0 > expenditure > 30).

It is important to note in this context that gender-sensitive analysis of budgets begins with categorizing expenditure, but it does not stop there. The categorization has to be followed by a number of exercises that examine the use of the expenditures and their impact (that is, from the financial input to the gendered output and impacts).

The attempts to incorporate time use in ex post gender budgeting belong to the second and third categories. Across the globe, particularly in India, only a limited number of the demand for grants in the second and third categories is analysed through a gender lens due to lack of unit utilized data on public provisioning. The point to be highlighted here is that time budgets provide a rare gamut of data on unit utilized.

## Analytical Framework for Ex Ante Gender Budgeting

The ex ante process of gender budgeting translates the goal towards gender equity in an iterative manner as follows: (a) identifying the spatial gender issues sector-wise and/or across socio-economic groups; (b) translating the gender concerns into relevant objectives to be included in the budget policy/programmes; (c) defining the gender strategies at the policy and programme levels with targets; (d) defining the gender-sensitive performance indicators; and (e) costing these indicators to form the gender budget and, subsequently identifying the budget heads.

Identifying spatial dimensions of ex ante gender budgeting is a critical step. The gender issues differ from region to region within a country. For instance, within India, the needs of women in a desert village in Rajasthan may differ from the needs of women in a coastal village in Kerala. The interface between gender and environment in Andaman and Nicobar Islands is different from the urbanized regions of Haryana with zero forest zones. This interface is also crucial when one talks about the spatial dimensions of gender budgeting. In the context of local level ex ante gender budgeting in one of the barangays of the Philippines, the interface between gender and environment has been clearly mapped out in the identification of gender and development budget (GAD) objectives like revamping irrigation facilities to lessen female migration and also against river quarrying to lessen the environmental hazards, which will be taken up later in the section on the Philippines.

Ex ante analysis of gender budgeting can extract data from time budgets for spatial mapping of gender needs. The patterns emerging from time budgets can give clues on preference revelations and demand mechanisms, which, in turn, can be used for the spatial mapping of gender needs.

## Gender-disaggregated Public Expenditure Benefit Incidence Analysis

Ex post gender budgeting can be extended incorporating a gender-disaggregated BIA.[4] Theoretically, there are two approaches to analysing the distributional impacts of public expenditure: benefit incidence

---

[4] In the mid-1990s, the Commonwealth Secretariat commissioned a study to develop tools for GRB analysis (Commonwealth 1999). The six tools suggested by Elson for GRB are the following: (a) a gender-aware policy appraisal; (b) beneficiary assessment; (c) gender disaggregated public expenditure incidence analysis; (d) analysis of impact of the budget on time use; (e) gender-aware,

studies and behavioural approaches. The behavioural approach is based on the notion that a rationed publicly provided good or service should be evaluated at the individual's own valuation of the good, which Demery (2000) called a 'virtual price'. Such prices will vary from individual to individual. This approach emphasizes the measurement of individual preferences for the publicly provided goods. The methodological complications in the valuation of revealed preferences based on the microeconomic theory and the paucity of unit record data related to the knowledge of the underlying demand functions of individuals or households led to less practicability of the behavioural approaches in estimating the distributional impact of public expenditure. However, time-use data can provide insights into the estimation of efficiency of public expenditure based on perceived measurement of individual preferences for publicly provided goods.

The other approach, BIA, is a relatively simple and practical method for estimating distributional impact of public expenditure across different demographic and socio-economic groups. The genesis of this approach lies in the path-breaking work on Malaysia by Jacob Meerman (1979) and on Colombia by Marcelo Selowsky (1979). A BIA involves allocating unit cost according to individual utilization rates of public services. A BIA can identify how well public services are targeted to certain groups in the population, across gender, income quintiles, and geographical units.

The studies on BIA revealed that a disproportionate share of the health budget benefits the elite in urban areas, or that the major part of education budget benefits schooling of boys rather than girls, which has

---

medium-term economic policy framework; and (f) GRB statements. Among these tools, the qualitative tools (a and b) are not sufficient to form an analytical framework to conduct GRB. These qualitative tools can provide the prelude information to begin GRB. However, tool (c) is relatively a sophisticated tool of analysis, which analyses the unit cost and unit utilized components in calculating the benefit incidence, at aggregate levels or by expenditure quintiles, which will be discussed in detail in the section. The gender-aware, medium-term framework and GRB statements are not an analytical framework of GRB per se; rather, these are specific tools to integrate gender in policy, through the appropriate logical entry points.

important policy implications. However, BIA studies have been largely confined to the education and health sectors due to the comparative richness of unit-utilized data from the secondary sources. To analyse the distributional impact of public expenditure on water supply and energy is difficult to undertake at a macro level due to paucity of data on units utilized. One must note that time-use statistics may provide this data on unit utilized of other social sector expenditure. There are four basic steps towards calculating benefit incidence (Demery 2000), as the following paragraphs discuss.

## ESTIMATING UNIT COST

The unit cost of a publicly provided good is estimated by dividing the total expenditure on that particular good by the total number of its users. This is synonymous to the notion of per capita expenditure, but the denominator is confined to the subset of population who are the users of the public good. For instance, the unit cost of the elementary education sector is total primary education spending per primary enrolment, while the unit cost of the health sector could be total outpatient hospital spending per outpatient visit.

Usually, information on the users of publicly provided goods is obtained from household surveys with the standard division of data into poor and non-poor, male- and female-headed households, rural and urban, and so on. Chakraborty (2008) attempted an illustrative calculation of gender-disaggregated BIA for water supply from unit-utilized data using a TUS, applying the time budget ratio of persons involved in fetching of water across gender to the rural and urban population separately.

## AGGREGATING USERS INTO GROUPS

It is important to aggregate individuals or households into groups to estimate how the benefits from public spending are distributed across the population. Empirical evidence has shown that the most frequent method of grouping is based on income quintiles or monthly per capita expenditure (MPCE) quintiles. The aggregation of users based on income or MPCE quintiles could reveal whether the distribution of public expenditure is progressive or regressive.

CALCULATING THE BENEFIT INCIDENCE

Benefit incidence is computed by combining information about the unit costs of provision of the publicly provided goods with information on the use of these goods. Mathematically, benefit incidence is estimated by the following formula:

$$X_j \equiv \sum_j U_{ij} \left( S_i / U_i \right) \equiv \sum_i \left( U_{ij} / U_j \right) S_i \equiv \sum_i e_{ij} S_i$$

where $X_j$ = sector specific subsidy enjoyed by group j;
   $U_{ij}$ = utilization of service i by group j;
   $U_i$ = utilization of service i by all groups combined;
   $S_i$ = government net expenditure on service i; and
   $e_{ij}$ = group j's share of utilization of service i.

An illustrative BIA analysis using sub-national time budgets and sub-national finance accounts is provided later in this chapter using data from India.

GENDER BUDGETING: TAX-SIDE ANALYSIS

Even though conceptual discussions on gender budgeting highlight the importance of constructing 'care tax' and analyse its co-movement along with other direct and indirect taxes, care tax has hardly been constructed across countries. Time-use budgets have a significant role in the construction of care tax but the unavailability of time budgets in many countries prevents its construction or analysis.

Empirical studies on gender-responsive tax policy, in particular gender-disaggregated tax incidence, are scarce. The literature on tax incidence is skewed towards looking at the distribution of tax burden in terms of income categories (Engel, Galetovic, and Raddatz 1999; Pechman 1985). There are only a few studies on gender and taxation in the context of Asian countries and Pacific—a study on tax incidence across gender in the context of India (Chakraborty, Chakraborty, and Karmakar 2008), and one on the impact of taxation on small enterprises through a gender lens in the context of Vietnam (Akram-Lodhi and van Staveren 2005). In some countries like India, greater tax concessions are given to women for reasons of gender equity. Studies on tax expenditure analysis (amount forgone by the government to meet the tax concessions for women) can also be attempted in the future.

The general analysis of impact of government revenues on women could be found in Barnett and Grown (2004).

In the context of developed countries like Australia, there was an early campaign about the 'dependant spouse rebate' paid primarily to male breadwinners, which the Federal Treasury eventually acknowledged in one of the early Federal Women's Budgets as a gender issue. In the context of developed countries, more recent work relates to the gender aspects of the interaction between the tax and welfare system in creating higher effective marginal tax rates for women. This has been a major criticism of the family assistance packages of recent federal budgets (Apps and Rees 2008). They argued that the recent reforms in the US, the UK, and Australia in lowering tax rates on high incomes and expanded tax credits and family transfer payments that are withdrawn on the joint income of a couple have led to high effective marginal rates across a wide middle band of earnings and to a shift towards joint taxation. They also argued that joint taxation results in high tax rates on secondary earners, with undesirable effects on both work incentive and fairness of the income distribution. The life-cycle analysis of time use and saving decisions applied in the study indicated strong negative effects on female labour supply and household saving. The study rightly highlighted that the debates related to direct taxes are yet to be inculcated in the tax policy debates in the context of most of the Asian countries.

This quick review showed that time-use statistics have hardly been used for any tax-side gender-budgeting papers across the globe.

## TIME BUDGETS IN GENDER DIAGNOSIS

Gender diagnosis is the basic premise for any gender-budgeting policy. Until 2010, the single most significant index used for identifying the gender diagnosis of any nation has been the gender development index (GDI) (see Box 10.1). This global index neutralizes or disregards many of the nation-specific gender inequality issues. For instance, the gender-disaggregated income component of GDI is constructed on the basis of market economy statistics. However, it is well known that women's work in non-market sector and the economic activity performed by them are highly unpaid or unremunerated in nature. Unless GDI is corrected for this component incorporating the time budgets, GDI remains partial in its construction.

**BOX 10.1**    Gender Development Index (until 2010)

The Human Development Index (HDI) is a gender-neutral measurement of the average achievements of a country as per three basic dimensions of human development: longevity, knowledge, and a decent standard of living. Longevity is measured by life expectancy at birth, knowledge by adult literacy and the combined gross primary, secondary and tertiary enrolment ratio, and standard of living by GDP per capita in US dollars in purchasing power parity (PPP) terms.

Let $L$ denote life expectancy at birth in years; $A$ denote adult literacy as per cent; $E$ denote combined gross primary, secondary, and tertiary enrolment ratio in per cent; and $Y$ denote per capita GDP in PPP USD terms. The value of each variable for a country is transformed into its deviation from the minimum possible value of the variable expressed as a proportion of the maximum deviation possible, that is, maximum − minimum. Thus, after transformation we have:

$$L^* = (L - 25)/(85 - 25), A^* = A/100, E^*$$
$$= E/100, \text{ and } Y^* = (Y - \min Y)(\max Y - \min Y).$$

Given that the minimum life expectancy for women and men is 27.5 years and 22.5 years, respectively, the average minimum life expectancy is taken as 25 [= (27.5 + 22.5)/2]. Similarly, maximum life expectancy is taken at 85. The maximum and minimum of both adult literacy and enrolment are taken as 100 and 0, respectively. The maximum and minimum for $Y$ are exogenously fixed. HDI is computed as:

$$\left\{ L^* + (2/3 \times A^* + 1/3 \times E^*) + Y^* \right\}/3.$$

The GDI uses the same variables as HDI, but adjusts for the degree of disparity in achievement across genders. The average value of each of the component variables is substituted by 'equally distributed equivalent' or 'ede' achievements. The equally distributed equivalent achievement for a variable is taken as that level of achievement that, if attained equally by women and men, would be judged to be exactly as valuable socially as the actually observed disparate achievements. Taking an additively separable, symmetric, and constant elasticity marginal valuation function with elasticity 2, the equally distributed equivalent achievement $X_{ede}$ for any variable $X$ turns out to be:

$$X_{ede} = \left[ n_f \left( 1 / X_f \right) + n_m \left( 1 / X_m \right) \right]^{-1},$$

where $X_f$ and $X_m$ are the values of the variable for females and males, and $n_f$ and $n_m$ are the population shares of females and males. $X_{ede}$ is a gender-equity-sensitive indicator (GESI).

Thus, for this chosen value of 2 for constant elasticity marginal valuation function, GDI is computed as:

$$\left\{ L_{ede} + \left( 2/3 \times A_{ede} + 1/3 \times E_{ede} \right) + Y_{ede} \right\} / 3.$$

*Source*: UNDP 1995.

If the partial construct of GDI is used as the optimal criteria for framing gender-budgeting policies in analysing the asymmetry in the socio-economic scale across gender, the gender-budgeting policy itself would reflect partial status of women with elements of elite capture.

The income component of GDI is partial, as it leaves apart the unpaid economic activity. It is a well-known that unpaid work remains significantly invisible in national accounts. In terms of time budgets, the income of any country captures only a part of the economic activity. This categorization of activities used in the TUS in India reveals how partial the GDP of a country is. Time budgets categorize activities into three types: SNA activities (that get included in GDP calculations), extended SNA activities (that do not get included in GDP but should be included in the satellite accounts), and residual non-SNA activities. The broad list of SNA, extended SNA and non-SNA activities of India is given in Table 10.1.

The global estimates suggest that USD 16 trillion of global output is invisible and USD 11 trillion was the non-monetized, invisible contribution of women (UNDP 1995). The attempts of the United Nations Statistical Division (UNSD) in extending the production boundary of the SNA, 1993, has led to the inclusion of the activities of unpaid work into the national accounting system as satellite accounts. This extension also provides a better understanding of women's contribution to the economy.

**TABLE 10.1**   Categorization of Work into SNA, Extended SNA, and Non-SNA

| SNA |
|---|

1  Crop farming, kitchen gardening
2  Animal husbandry
3  Fishing, forestry, horticulture, gardening
4  Fetching of water, fuel, edible goods like fruits, vegetables, minor forest produce, etc.
5  Processing and storage (husking, milling, sorting, grinding etc.)
6  Mining, quarrying, digging, cutting
7  Construction activities
8  Manufacturing activities (food processing and cooking for sale, butchering, drying and storing fish, meat, etc.; knitting, sewing, pottery, handicrafts for sale, etc.)
9  Trade and Business (buying and selling of consumer durables, consumer goods, petty trading, transporting, street or door-to-door vending, etc.)
10 Services (in government, NGO, private organizations, petty services like domestic servants, sweepers, gardener, private tuition, Xerox, parlours, saloons, plumbing, electrical, etc.)

| Extended SNA |
|---|

11 Household maintenance, management, and shopping for own household (cleaning utensils, house, textiles, etc.; paying bills; pet care; etc.)
12 Care for children, sick, elderly, disabled in the household (physical care of children like washing, dressing, feeding, teaching, training children in everyday activities and accompanying them to places; physical care of sick, disabled, and elderly household members, accompanying them to medical care, etc.)
13 Community services and help to the households (community-organized construction and repairs of dams, roads, wells, ponds, etc.), volunteer work, participation in local meetings, civic responsibilities like voting, attending Panchayat meetings, political parties, etc.
14 Learning (education, work-related training, non-formal education, etc.)
15 Social and cultural activities, mass media (social events such as marriages, funerals, births, religious activities; community functions such as dance, music, socializing at home and outside; watching TV; reading newspaper; spectator to sports, arts, cinema, mass media entertainment; etc.)

| Non-SNA |
|---|

16 Personal care and self-maintenance (sleep and related activities; eating, drinking, smoking, alcohol; personal hygiene; walking, exercise, rest, and relaxation; convalescing due to physical illness; etc.)

*Source*: Time-use Survey, India, 2000.

The 1993 SNA, however, limits economic production of households for their own consumption to the production of goods alone, and excludes the own-account production of personal and domestic services (except for the services produced by employing paid domestic staff and the own-account production of housing services produced by owner occupants). This allows the SNA to avoid valuing activities, such as eating, drinking, and sleeping, which are difficult for a person to obtain from another person. However, in the process, activities like fetching water from the river or the well, collecting fuel wood, washing clothes, house cleaning, preparation and serving of meals, care, training and instruction of children, and care of sick, infirm, or old people also get excluded from the definition of economic activity. These services are mostly performed by women, but can also be procured from other units. While these activities are excluded partly because of the inadequate price systems for valuing these services, this exclusion principle leads to the economic invisibility and a statistical underestimation of women's work.

## Gender Inequality Index

Since 2010, the HDI and GDI have undergone change in terms of variables used in calculating them as well as their methodology. Since 2010, HDI is the geometric mean of three dimensions: health, education, and income. The normalization procedure for these three dimensions is as follows. Normalization procedure is done by two steps: (a) to compute the deviation from the minimum values and (b) divide that, by value of (maximum − minimum).

- Normalization Procedure:
  - Life Expectancy Index = $[(LE - 20) / (82.3 - 20)]$
  - Education Index = [(root of $MYSE \times EYSI$)/0.978] as per 2001 HDR; where MYS: Mean years of schooling (years that a 25-year-old person or older has spent in schools) and EYS: Expected years of schooling (years that a 5-year-old child will spend with his/her education in his/her whole life)
  - − methodological details in NBER paper by Barro and Lee (2010)
  - INCOME = $[(l_n (Y) - l_n (Y_{max}) / (ln (Y_{max}) - l_n (Y_{min}))$ [in pc]

The plausibility of incorporating time use in the income component of HDI was missed out even in the reformulation of HDI in 2010.

When it comes to capturing the gender dimensions, health, empowerment, and labour are taken as the prioritized dimensions, where empowerment is captured through education and participation in governance. The variables used for each dimensions are as follows:

- Health
  (a) Maternal mortality rate (the number of maternal deaths per 1,000 women of reproductive age in the population, which is generally defined as 15–44 years of age).
  (b) Adolescent fertility rate (the number of births per 1,000 women aged 15–19 years).
- Empowerment
  (a) Education: Mean years of schooling (Barro and Lee 2010)
  (b) Governance/Political Participation
- Labour Market Participation.

The labour market participation is captured through the regular statistics instead of time use in this reformulation of gender index. There is immense scope for improving the index by incorporating the time-use statistics, which may be researched in the future.

## TIME USE IN QUANTIFYING UNPAID CARE COMPONENT OF GENDER BUDGETING

Ideally, gender budgeting should consider the aggregate contribution of women to the economy taking into consideration both the market economy and the care economy. However, across countries, gender budgeting procedure stops with looking into women's contribution to the market economy. The data, for instance, in India shows that only a minuscule number of women work in organized sector, which is as low as 4 per cent. If we consider women's contribution to the economy by only looking into the market economy, the analysis has high possibilities of getting skewed. Having said that, even the market-economy-related gender-budgeting policies are partial, as they have not come up with any social-security-related policies for women regarding their loss of work time in the care economy. A significant part of women's work is invisible, and carried out in the care economy.

Time-use surveys have been an effective tool in unfolding the statistical invisibility of unpaid work across countries. The time diary method is the most reliable way of obtaining time-use data, confined to a probability sample of all types of days (weekdays and weekends) and of different seasons of the year. The time diary is a retrospective method, in which the respondents are asked to keep an account of the recent 24-hour chronology of the use of time and the researchers then code the responses to a standard list of activities.

Time-use diaries are preferred over the other methods for they tend to be more comprehensive, enable respondents to report activities in their own terms, and have some form of built-in check that increases the reliability of the data (Juster and Stanford 1991). However, the time diary method also has certain deficiencies. The significant one is the presence of multitasking or omission of overlapping of activities. This results from the imposition of a rigid constraint of time use, namely, no person has either more or less time available than 24 hours per day (time constraint) and the set of activities capable of being measured, described, and analysed must add up to a fixed number of hours or days (Floro 1995).

Theoretically, the problems related to overlapping of activities can be solved by defining the new activity as a joint activity, but then the codes for possible diary activities would explode in number. The practical way of solving this problem is to indicate one activity as primary and the other as secondary. Another way to conceptualize secondary activities is to argue that there is really only one activity at any given time, but there are frequent switches between activities and if the time grid were fine enough, the issue of secondary activities would then effectively disappear.

Finally, it seems plausible that the issue of multiple or joint activities is the key source of the major failure of alternative recall methods. Recall accuracy falls when the respondents make primitive attempts to respond to questions about hours of an activity in the last week or month by engaging in a kind of temporal double counting, adding in periods when the activity was secondary to periods when it was central (Juster and Stanford 1991).

There is a growing recognition for TUS for getting better statistics on the size of the labour force of a country, as well as the contribution of women to the economy. A major finding of TUS across the globe is that women carry a disproportionately greater burden of work than men. Since women are responsible for a greater share of non-SNA work in the care economy, they enter the labour market already overburdened with work. This dual work burden or unequal sharing of work borne by women is neither recognized in the data nor considered adequately in socio-economic policymaking.

The major macro-level TUS was conducted in India in six major states, namely, Gujarat, Haryana, Madhya Pradesh, Meghalaya, Orissa (now Odisha), and Tamil Nadu, from July 1998 to June 1999 by the Central Statistical Organisation of India. It was a pioneering attempt not only in South Asia, but also among all developing countries. This large-scale survey of 18,591 households in India gave a better understanding of how time is allocated across gender in the economy and provides some insight into the extent of statistical invisibility of women's work in India. The TUS covered all members of the household aged six years and above.

In theoretical literature, there are two main approaches to the valuation of the unpaid work: (a) input-related method, which is based on imputing value to labour time spent on unpaid work and (b) output-related method, which is based on imputing market prices to goods and services produced (for example, imputing market price to the fuel wood collected, homemade utensils, etc.). The major problem related to input-related approach is to decide which value to impute to labour time.

Three methods have been used for this purpose: (a) the global substitute method, which uses the cost of a hired worker, who is paid to carry out the different tasks in the care economy; (b) the specialized substitute method, which uses the costs of a specialized worker, who would perform each specific task according to his/her specialization; and (c) the opportunity cost method, which is based on the wage, which the person carrying out the domestic work would receive if she/he worked in the market. Each method suffers from its own merits and demerits. The global substitute method tends to underestimate the unpaid work, as it uses the wages at the lower end of the wage category. On the contrary, the specialized substitute method tends to

**TABLE 10.2** Valuation of Unpaid Work using Sub-national Time-use Budgets (Rs crore)

| State | Men | Women | Total |
|---|---|---|---|
| Haryana | 928.74 | 10,209.30 | 11,138.04 |
| Madhya Pradesh | 4,466.03 | 29,034.09 | 33,500.12 |
| Gujarat | 2,209.55 | 22,577.63 | 24,787.18 |
| Odisha | 1,463.78 | 11,343.88 | 12,807.65 |
| Tamil Nadu | 3,073.37 | 19,922.04 | 22,995.40 |
| Meghalaya | 260.45 | 862.97 | 1,123.42 |

*Source*: NIPFP (2000).

*Note*: The estimates are fixed for the year of time-use statistics.

overestimate the unpaid work though they are more indicative of its market value. The opportunity cost method, on the other hand, tends to generate the widest range of estimates, depending on the skills and the opportunity wage of the individuals performing it (Beneria 1992).

From the perspective of accounting for unpaid work, input-related accounting is superior to output-related accounting. For example, if women have to walk longer to fetch water, input-related accounting will show an increase in the time input, though there is no increase in output. Thus, intensified effort of women is valued in input-related accounting. The results from the input-related global substitute method (improvised) for valuing the unpaid work in India are given in Table 10.2.

District-wise data on wage rates for agricultural labour and urban unskilled manual labour has been used for valuing unpaid work in rural and urban areas respectively. With this methodology, projecting the TUS results with age-wise and district-wise population and valuation of time spent on unpaid activities by females in Gujarat and Haryana indicates that the value of unpaid activities could be as much as 26 to 28 per cent of the relevant state domestic product (SDP). For example, the total value of such activities by women was Rs 22,578 crore and Rs 10,209 crore in Gujarat and Haryana, respectively, relative to SDP of Rs 86,609 crore and Rs 37,427 crore in these two states (Table 10.2). Compared to women, the valuation of unpaid activities by men was limited to only about 2–3 per cent of the SDP in these two states. The unpaid work, as a proportion of SDP (as shown in Table 10.3), is as high as 49.93 per cent in Meghalaya and 47 per cent in Madhya Pradesh.

**TABLE 10.3** Sub-national Estimates of Unpaid Care Work (as percentage of state income)

| State | Men (%) | Women (%) | Total (%) |
|---|---|---|---|
| Haryana | 2.48 | 27.28 | 29.76 |
| Madhya Pradesh | 6.31 | 40.99 | 47.30 |
| Gujarat | 2.55 | 26.07 | 28.62 |
| Odisha | 4.48 | 34.72 | 39.20 |
| Tamil Nadu | 3.52 | 22.80 | 26.31 |
| Meghalaya | 11.58 | 38.35 | 49.93 |

*Source*: NIPFP (2000).

*Note*: The estimates are fixed for the year of time-use statistics.

## GENDER-DIFFERENTIAL IMPACTS OF PUBLIC SPENDING: TIME-USE FINDINGS AT THE SUB-NATIONAL LEVEL

Gender budgeting usually looks into only specifically targeted pro-grammes for women, which is only around 1 per cent of the total budget. The challenging part of any gender-budgeting exercise is to look into mainstream expenditure through a gender lens. The par-titioning gender factor for mainstream public expenditure is highly unavailable and the data related to enrolment is used as a partition factor for education budgets, while morbidity statistics are used as a partition factor for analysing the distributional impact of health budgets. It is difficult to analyse mainstream budgets for their gender-differential impacts (other than education and health) due to unavail-ability of unit-utilized data. Time-use budgets are highly helpful in providing unit-utilized data, especially for water and energy budgets. Time budgets can also provide clues for framing care economy poli-cies as well.

For instance, the gender-differential impacts of water budget at the sub-national level can be analysed using time budgets. This sec-tion provides an illustrative exercise at sub-national government levels. Using finance accounts data, the public expenditure on water across rural and urban units are computed and Table 10.4 shows the percentage of public expenditure on water as a proportion of total expenditure of that state.

**TABLE 10.4** Disaggregating Plausible Public Expenditure on Water across Rural and Urban Sub-national Units (as percentage of total state budget)

| State | Rural (%) | Urban (%) |
|---|---|---|
| Meghalaya | 1.52 | 1.16 |
| Odisha | 0.37 | 0.44 |
| Haryana | 0.02 | 0.01 |
| Madhya Pradesh | 1.37 | 0.28 |
| Tamil Nadu | 0.98 | 0.79 |
| Gujarat | 1.55 | 0.07 |

*Source*: Finance Accounts (GoI) (various states, various years), corresponding years.
*Note*: The estimates are fixed for the year of time-use statistics.

**TABLE 10.5** Disaggregating Plausible Public Expenditure on Water across Sub-national Governments (as percentage of total state social sector budget)

| State | Rural (%) | Urban (%) |
|---|---|---|
| Meghalaya | 4.17 | 3.17 |
| Odisha | 2.21 | 2.64 |
| Haryana | 4.91 | 4.16 |
| Madhya Pradesh | 3.61 | 0.73 |
| Tamil Nadu | 2.61 | 2.09 |
| Gujarat | 4.72 | 0.20 |

*Source*: Finance Accounts (GoI) (various states, various years), corresponding years.
*Note*: The estimates are fixed for the year of time-use statistics.

The estimates provide only a part of water budgets at the state level, which were amenable for rural and urban partition of expenditure from the finance accounts. The plausible estimates given in Table 10.4 were disaggregated for rural and urban units and were based on revenue budgets, aggregating the rural and urban water supply schemes. The components are left out of calculation, which could not be partitioned into rural and urban components of the budget, such as water expenditure heads on direction and administration, survey and investigation, machinery and equipment, assistance to local bodies, sub-component plan for schedule castes, tribal area sub-plan, suspense, etc.

Table 10.5 shows the percentage of public expenditure in water as part of the total social sector spending. The rural component of

**TABLE 10.6** Per Capita Public Expenditure on Plausible Rural and Urban Expenditure on Water: Gender Disaggregation (Rs)

| State | Rural | | | Urban | | |
|---|---|---|---|---|---|---|
| | Men | Women | Total | Men | Women | Total |
| Meghalaya | 198.83 | 205.84 | 101.14 | 642.18 | 705.88 | 336.26 |
| Odisha | 43.53 | 44.06 | 21.90 | 316.42 | 365.26 | 169.54 |
| Haryana | 164.64 | 190.57 | 88.33 | 428.12 | 492.98 | 229.13 |
| Madhya Pradesh | 79.88 | 84.69 | 41.11 | 52.23 | 58.49 | 27.59 |
| Tamil Nadu | 99.92 | 101.86 | 50.44 | 152.85 | 159.15 | 77.97 |
| Gujarat | 200.01 | 210.71 | 102.61 | 15.96 | 17.60 | 8.37 |

*Source*: Finance Accounts (GoI) (various states), corresponding years and Population Census Data 2000.

*Note*: The estimates are fixed for the year of time-use statistics.

public spending on water is comparatively greater than in urban areas. However, the spending on water ranged from 2.21 per cent of the social sector spending in Odisha to 4.72 per cent in Gujarat.

If the allocation on water is increased across sub-national governments, then who would benefit from it? The *a priori* benefit could go to non-poor and women in rural geographical units. The per capita water spending disaggregated for gender is given in Table 10.6.

The figures in Table 10.6 have to be read with caution; the reporting of this table is primarily not to report that per capita expenditure on water for women is greater than men. The unit cost is assumed to be the same in this analysis, and, therefore, only the denominator (population disaggregated) made the difference in estimates.

Table 10.7 shows the proportion of gender-disaggregated population involved in the fetching of water. Gujarat has been taken out of analysis due to data constraints. The figures are revealing: in all states women are disproportionately higher than men. In definitive terms, the time-use statistics revealed that public expenditure on water schemes benefit women greater than men. In terms of time budgets, the utilization of time in fetching of water across selected states on the basis of gender and rural/urban is given in Table 10.8.

The time taken by women in fetching water is higher than men, and comparatively women in rural Haryana spent 2.31 hours per week

**TABLE 10.7** Population Proportion Involved in Fetching of Water using the TUS

| State | Rural | | | Urban | | | Total | | |
|---|---|---|---|---|---|---|---|---|---|
| | Men | Women | Total | Men | Women | Total | Men | Women | Total |
| Meghalaya | 31.08 | 68.92 | 100.00 | 40.00 | 60.00 | 100.00 | 33.08 | 66.92 | 100.00 |
| Odisha | 7.14 | 92.86 | 100.00 | 0.00 | 100.00 | 100.00 | 6.67 | 93.33 | 100.00 |
| Haryana | 6.58 | 93.42 | 100.00 | 7.69 | 92.31 | 100.00 | 6.71 | 93.29 | 100.00 |
| Madhya Pradesh | 16.17 | 83.83 | 100.00 | 14.63 | 85.37 | 100.00 | 15.99 | 84.01 | 100.00 |
| Tamil Nadu | 10.41 | 89.59 | 100.00 | 13.32 | 86.68 | 100.00 | 11.23 | 88.77 | 100.00 |
| Combined | 13.42 | 86.58 | 100.00 | 17.07 | 82.93 | 100.00 | 14.23 | 85.77 | 100.00 |

*Source:* CSO (2000) TUS.

*Note:* The estimates are fixed for the year of time-use statistics.

**TABLE 10.8** Weekly Average Time Spent on Fetching of Water: Gender Differentials (hours)

| State | Rural | | | Urban | | | Total | | |
|---|---|---|---|---|---|---|---|---|---|
| | Men | Women | Total | Men | Women | Total | Men | Women | Total |
| Haryana | 0.08 | 2.31 | 1.10 | 0.02 | 0.69 | 0.33 | 0.07 | 2.02 | 0.96 |
| Madhya Pradesh | 0.02 | 0.21 | 0.11 | 0.00 | 0.04 | 0.02 | 0.02 | 0.17 | 0.09 |
| Odisha | 0.00 | 0.05 | 0.03 | 0.00 | 0.00 | 0.00 | 0.00 | 0.04 | 0.02 |
| Tamil Nadu | 0.11 | 1.21 | 0.66 | 0.08 | 0.71 | 0.40 | 0.10 | 1.03 | 0.56 |
| Meghalaya | 1.33 | 2.82 | 2.09 | 1.94 | 1.26 | 1.58 | 1.44 | 2.53 | 2.00 |
| Combined | 0.05 | 0.58 | 0.31 | 0.04 | 0.31 | 0.17 | 0.05 | 0.50 | 0.27 |

*Source*: CSO (2000) Time-use Survey.

*Note*: The estimates are fixed for the year of time-use statistics.

**TABLE 10.9** Per Capita Benefit Incidence of Water Budgets Applying the Time Budget Data

| States | Rural | | Urban | |
|---|---|---|---|---|
| | Men | Women | Men | Women |
| Meghalaya | 73.92 | 170.71 | 291.90 | 485.70 |
| Odisha | 3.51 | 46.23 | – | 409.94 |
| Haryana | 12.49 | 206.30 | 37.30 | 517.11 |
| Madhya Pradesh | 15.00 | 82.84 | 8.67 | 57.06 |
| Tamil Nadu | 11.54 | 100.95 | 22.28 | 150.92 |

*Source*: Finance Accounts (GoI) (various states, various years), corresponding years and Population Census Data (GoI) 2000, and CSO (2000) TUS.

*Note*: The estimates are fixed for the year of time-use statistics.

in fetching water, while women in Meghalaya spent 2.82 hours per week (average). The women in urban areas spent comparatively less time in fetching water.

Applying the population proportion of time budget data, the benefit incidence of water expenditure is estimated. The figures are reported in Table 10.9, which clearly shows that women benefit more from public expenditure on water.

If gender budgeting is predominantly based on the index-based gender diagnosis, a reanalysis of the construction of the gender (inequality) index is necessary to avoid a partial capture of gender diagnosis in budget policymaking. The issue is even more revealing, as the available gender inequality index based on three dimensions—health, empowerment, and labour market participation—has, so far, not integrated time-use statistics in its calculations. From a public finance perspective, the gender-budgeting process often rests on the assumption that mainstream expenditure, such as public infrastructure, is non-rival in nature and applying a gender lens to these is not feasible. This argument is refuted by the time budget statistics. The time budget data revealed that this argument is often flawed, as there is intrinsic gender dimension to the non-rival expenditure. The time allocation in economic activities like fetching of water (and fuel) involves more girls and women and infrastructure investment with gender-sensitive water polices and energy policies can really benefit women.

## REFERENCES

Akram-Lodhi, Haroon and Irene van Staveren. 2005. 'A Gender Analysis of the Impact of Indirect Taxes on Small and Medium Enterprises in Vietnam', ISS Working Paper, International Institute of Social Studies, The Netherlands.

Apps, Patricia and Ray Rees, 2008. 'Taxation, Labour Supply and Saving', Discussion paper, ANU Centre for Economic Policy Research, Canberra.

Barnett, Kathleen and Caren Grown. 2004. *Gender Impacts of Government Revenue Collection: The Case of Taxation.* New York: United Nations Development Fund for Women (UNIFEM).

Barro, Robert J. and Jong-Wha Lee. 2010. A New Data Set of Educational Attainment in the World, 1950–2010, NBER Working Paper 15902, National Bureau of Economic Research, Cambridge, Massachusetts.

Becker, Gary S. 1965. 'A Theory of the Allocation of Time', *Economic Journal,* 75(299): 493–517.

Beneria, Lourdes. 1992. 'Accounting for Women's work: The Progress of Two Decades', *World Development,* 20(11): 1547–60.

Central Statistical Organisation (CSO) 2000. *Report of the Time Use Survey,* Ministry of Statistics and Programme Implementation. New Delhi: Government of India.

Chakraborty, Pinaki, Lekha Chakraborty, and Kishanu Karmakar. 2008. 'Gender and Incidence of Indirect Tax in India', mimeo. New Delhi: National Institute of Public Finance and Policy (NIPFP).

Chakraborty, Lekha. 2008. 'Deficient Public Infrastructure and Private Costs: Evidence for Water Sector', Levy Economics Institute Working Paper No. 536, Levy Economics Institute, New York.

Commonwealth Secretariat. 1999. *Tools for GRB*. London: Commonwealth Secretariat.

Demery, L. 2000. 'Benefit Incidence: A Practitioner's Guide', Poverty and Social Development Group, mimeo. Washington, DC: World Bank.

Engel, Eduardo M.R.A., Alexander Galetovic, and Claudio E. Raddatz. 1999. "Taxes and Income Distribution in Chile: Some Unpleasant Redistributive Arithmetic', *Journal of Development Economics*, 59(1): 155–92.

Fan, S., P. Hazell, and S. Thorat. 1999. 'Growth and Poverty in Rural India', *IFPRI Research Report*, Washington, DC: International Food Policy Research Institute (IFPRI).

Floro, Maria Sagrario. 1995. 'Economic Restructuring, Gender and the Allocation of Time', *World Development*, 23(11): 1913–29.

Government of India (GoI). 2000. Population Census Data, New Delhi: Government of India.

———. Various years. Finance Accounts. New Delhi: Government of India.

Juster, F.T. and F. Stanford. 1991. 'The Allocation of Time: Empirical Findings, Behavioral Models and Problems of Measurement', *Journal of Economic Literature*, 29 (2), 471–522.

Meerman, Jacob. 1979 *Public Expenditures in Malaysia: Who Benefits and Why?* New York: Oxford University Press.

National Institute of Public Finance and Policy (NIPFP). 2000. 'Women's Contribution to the Economy through Their Unpaid Household Work', Discussion Paper Series, New Delhi: NIPFP.

Pechman, Joseph A. 1985. *Who Paid the Taxes—1966–85?* Washington, DC: Brookings Institution.

Selowsky, Marcelo. 1979. *Who Benefits from Government Expenditure?* New York: Oxford University Press.

United Nations Development Programme (UNDP). 1995. *Human Development Report*, New York: Oxford University Press.

United Nations Statistical Division (UNSD). 1993. *Systems of National Accounts 1993*, New York: United Nations.

# 11 Trade Liberalization and Unpaid Work

*Integrating Unpaid Work into Macroeconomic Policies*

Indira Hirway

It is now widely accepted that the total economy consists of the work covered under national income accounts and unpaid domestic and voluntary services, which contribute to people's well-being but are excluded from the national income accounts (Inter-secretariat Working Group on National Accounts [ISWGNA] 2008). While the former is considered as the production boundary of the System of National Accounts (that is, SNA activities), the latter is covered under the general production boundary outside the production boundary (that is, non-SNA activities). This chapter argues that macroeconomic policies that are designed and monitored keeping in mind the SNA part of the total economy impact the non-SNA part of the economy also, as both their parts are closely interlinked. Consequently, macroeconomic policies are likely to go wrong if designed in isolation, without considering their impact on the non-SNA activities. This chapter, therefore, suggests that designing and monitoring macroeconomic policies in a broader framework makes the policies relevant and valid for the economy.

The chapter is divided into three sections. The first section presents a conceptual framework that shows how SNA and non-SNA activities are interlinked and why it is necessary to design macroeconomic policies addressing both the parts of the total economy. Section two shows how the major macroeconomic policy of trade liberalization impacts SNA and non-SNA activities. The third section, with the help of time-use data, shows how trade liberalization policy will be incorrect if non-SNA activities are neglected.

## LINKAGES BETWEEN SNA AND NON-SNA WORK

### Arbitrary Division of the Total Economy

It is important to note at the outset that both paid and unpaid work are viewed as a part of the total economy by UN SNA document (ISWGNA 2008). The five sectors that constitute the total economy are: (a) non-financial corporations; (b) financial corporations; (c) government sector, including social security funds; (d) non-profit institutions serving households (NPISH); and (e) the households (2008). The production boundary (SNA) includes the entire production of goods and services for sale or barter, and goods and services provided free to households or collectively to the community by government units or NPISH. Additionally, as seen in the chapter 'Introduction' it also includes production of agricultural goods by household enterprises for their own use, production of other goods for own final consumption by households (the construction of dwellings, the production of food stuff, clothing, etc.), and production of housing services for final self-consumption by owner occupiers (imputed rent). What is excluded from the production boundary is production of services for final self-consumption within households (excluding services of paid domestic staff) and voluntary unpaid services (that is, non-SNA work).

Unpaid services are arguably excluded from the production boundary because: (a) non-monetary flows have little relevance for macroeconomics; (b) inclusion of unpaid work will swamp away national accounts; and (c) inclusion will imply full employment condition—which does not make much sense (ISWGNA 2008) These arguments do not appear to be valid for several reasons. First, non-SNA or non-monetary flows have strong linkages with market flows, as the chapter shows later; macroeconomic forces have a significant influence on the size and characteristics of non-SNA activities. Second, unpaid work is important and, therefore, cannot be excluded from the total economy, irrespective of the fact that it swamps or does not swamp away national accounts. Third, inclusion of unpaid work needs modification of the concepts (such as, workforce, labour force), new analytical tools, and inclusion of unpaid work in the SNA boundary.

Luisella Goldschmidt-Clermont argues that the production process continues in both market and non-market spheres. For example, in food production, the process is crop farming, harvesting, processing, storing, processing, cooking, and consumption. Except for the last stage, all processes are part of production and value addition, and all should therefore be included in the SNA. Similarly, human capital formation starts with the nurturing of a child (taking care of the child's health and education, etc.) at home and continues thereafter in schools. However, human capital formation is recognized only after the child goes to school, and not before! Goldschmidt-Clermont, thus, calls this line of demarcation a patriarchal one that is not justifiable on any ground (Goldschmidt-Clermont 1987, 1989). This patriarchal demarcation divides the total economy arbitrarily and puts non-SNA into a cloak of invisibility and throws it outside the purview of economic policies, and, in the process, adds male bias in macroeconomics. In other words, this division forces policymakers to take a partial and biased view of the economy.

## Interlinkages between SNA and Non-SNA Work

It is important to add that there are no watertight compartments between SNA and non-SNA as different activities move from SNA to non-SNA and vice-versa. The level of development of the economy often influences such a division; for example, in wealthy economies there is a tendency to depend on the market economy for many of the goods and services that are usually produced within the household in relatively poor economies. Several care services (care for children, the elders, and the sick) are provided by the market or by the state. Also, governments in relatively better-off economies habitually spend more on public provisioning of goods and services, such as water and sanitation, nutrition and health services, and education. Conversely, in relatively poor countries, the burden on the household labour is considerably larger as they produce most of the goods and services within the household.

The status of the economy on the business cycles also affects the division of labour between the SNA and non-SNA work. In fact, one observes counter-business-cycles in the role of household labour during business cycles. During an upswing of a business cycle, when income, employment, and economic activities rise, the role of household labour declines. Conversely, during a downswing, the role of household labour increases, as the role of the market labour declines in terms of providing goods and services for the well-being of the population. In other words, unpaid work shows an anti-cyclical behaviour.

At the micro level, there are several household-level factors that influence the division of labour. These factors are household income, presence of young children, structure (presence of persons that can take up care responsibility), and socio-cultural notions that influence the role of household labour in providing goods and services to the household.

## Unpaid Work as Subsidy to (Conventional) Macroeconomy

The relationship between the non-SNA sector and the rest of the economy indicates that the latter subsidizes the macroeconomy in multiple ways (Antonopoulos and Hirway 2010). Household-level work (unpaid work) entails several services that the government is expected to provide to people such as care and basic public provisioning. Households take care of sick and chronically sick people, disabled, and elders as well as provide education, health, and nutrition to children.

Voluntary unpaid services also provide such services to people for which the state is supposed to be responsible. All these unpaid services, therefore, tend to reduce the burden on the state. In the absence of these unpaid services the state would have spent much more on their public provisioning. Unpaid work also fills in infrastructural gaps. For example, unpaid work is responsible for fetching drinking water, sometimes from long distances; it provides fuel wood, again from distant places when necessary; and it ensures access to distant basic services, such as health services. In short, it subsidizes the government by provisioning households. Similarly, households also subsidize the market and the business sector. Unpaid work lowers the cost of labour at the macro level. Private sector has to pay much less than what it would have paid to maintain the same standard of living of a worker (as their wear and tear—depreciation—is taken care of by unpaid household services). This raises profits at the macro level, leading to an increase in capital accumulated and in economic growth.

However, because of this engagement in unpaid work, work participation rates of unpaid workers (especially women) declines in the labour market, reducing the total workforce/labour force in the economy (Economic Commission for Latin America and the Caribbean [ECLAC] 2007; Hirway 2008). A significant number of women are observed to be not participating in the labour market because of their domestic duties. As this is not an optimum use of labour in the economy, it is a loss to the macroeconomy (International Monetary Fund [IMF] 2013).

## Unequal Distribution of Unpaid Work across Gender and Macroeconomic Losses

In spite of constituting nearly 50 per cent of the population, women's contribution to the conventional macroeconomy is very small—in terms of their labour force participation rate (LFPR) as well as their share in high productivity sectors. Women contribute much less than their potential to the economy (IMF 2013).

The unequal burden of unpaid work on women divides the labour market on gender lines (Esquivel 2008; Hirway 2008; IMF 2013). The burden of unpaid work, along with the social norms and traditions attached to it, results in lower acquisition of human capital (health, education, skills, etc.) by women thereby limiting women's performance in the labour market.

Most women enter the labour market with a great burden of unpaid household work on their shoulders that denies them a level playing field with men to start with. In most cases, lower education/skills along with lower mobility results in lower participation of women in the labour market, overcrowding in low-productivity occupations, lower wages, and higher unemployment rates. The segregation and discrimination against women tends to reduce significantly their prospects in the labour market. Women entrepreneurs are also inhibited due to their restricted access to resources, to credit, and to technology (IMF 2013). Thus, the sex-based division of the labour at home and in the market does not allow an economy to tap the full potential of its labour force. It is estimated by the IMF that the GDP of a country can increase considerably if the full potential of women labour force is tapped.

Unpaid work is also a subsidy to state provisioning: (a) since unpaid domestic services provide care for children, sick, elders, and other needy persons in the household, the burden of health services of the government declines to an extent; (b) unpaid domestic services providing, education, nutrition, transportation, water, sanitation, etc., have implications for lower cost of infrastructure and basic services of the government; and (c) voluntary services (which are outside the SNA) also contribute to basic services and infrastructure to people, thereby subsidizing state provisioning. If these domestic services were not available to people, the government would have been forced to spend more on basic services and infrastructure from the public exchequer. In short, labour engaged in non-SNA work reduces the burden of the market economy and government activities in different ways.

## Household as a Production Unit

Figure 11.1 shows how the household is one of the three sectors of the macroeconomy. Hence, it is not an add-on sector or an afterthought, but it is a fundamental building block, structurally interlinked with the other two sectors—public sector and the market.

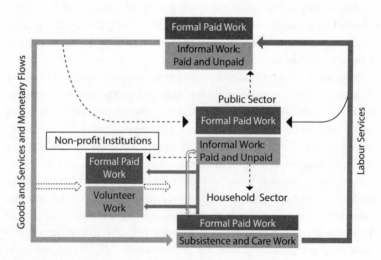

**FIGURE 11.1**  Business Sector: Agriculture, Industry, and Services
*Source*: Dian Elson (2008).

The figure shows that the household sector provides formal labour, informal labour, and unpaid labour to the economy in the form of workforce for both the business sector and the public sector. The household sector also provides formal paid work and voluntary work to non-profit institutions. Similarly, the business sector and the public sector provide goods and services to the household sector and to the non-profit institutions. The business sector also provides goods and services to the public sector. Finally, the public sector also provides services to the business sector, the household sector, and to the non-profit institutions. Figure 11.1 clearly depicts the linkage between the three fundamental sectors of the macroeconomy.

This figure implies that the way people divide their time between paid (SNA) and unpaid work (non-SNA) ought to be used to understand the impact of macro-level policies on those performing paid work as well as those performing unpaid work (Antonopoulos 2009).

An important characteristic of these linkages between SNA labour and non-SNA labour is in their hierarchy. Non-SNA labour in treated as inferior and it has several disadvantages in the economy. While the labour in the SNA work is recognized and visible (at least conceptually) and is covered under the purview of public policymaking, the labour in non-SNA work is neither recognized nor covered under by any policy or regulations. Since non-SNA is not visible and is unpaid (that is, free) in the sense that it does not receive any remuneration, it is treated as inferior. In fact, this division of labour and the consequent social norms developed around the division of work is at the root of power relations between men and women in the household and in the economy. In addition, labour in non-SNA work does not enjoy upward mobility or promotions, it does not receive pensions, its work is repetitive, it has poor exposure to the outside world, and it has limited human capital formation and overall poor prospects in the market economy. This labour, however, is neither visible (in most cases) nor covered under any policy or regulation.

## Concerns Related to Gender Inequalities in Sharing of Work

Predominance of women in the unpaid sector is a matter of concern because: (a) it implies sub-optimal use of the total labour force in an economy; (b) it results in the deficiency of 'care' in the economy causing not only loss of well-being of children, elders, disabled, sick, etc., but it also has an adverse impact on the development of future generations; and (c) it is unjust and unfair division of work that denies basic human rights to unpaid workers (mainly women).

The time-use surveys (TUS) of the Global South, though not universal, national, or regular in many countries,[1] clearly indicate that: (a) unpaid work is highly unequally distributed between men and women, with women sharing the main burden in terms of participation as well as the time spent;[2] (b) paid work is also distributed unequally with men carrying a somewhat higher burden; and (c) women carry a significantly higher burden of total work (paid and unpaid work) than men in the Global South (Antonopoulos 2011; Charmes 2008; Hirway 2010). Another reason for concern about this division of the total economy is that the work which contributes to the well-being of people is mostly invisible as time-use data has not yet become a regular feature of national statistical systems in many countries particularly in the Global South. Even when some time-use data is available, this unremunerated work is not yet recognized as important work to be covered under any economic policies.

In addition, such work is repetitive (performed daily) and boring, and frequently a drudgery.[3] Unpaid workers do not enjoy any upward mobility, no promotions and, therefore, it is a dead-end job. There is no retirement and no pensions in this work. These workers also have a limited exposure to the outside world and limited opportunities in life. This implies that a significant part of the total labour force available to an economy is locked up in low productivity inferior kind of work.

What is important to note is that the predominance of women in this work is not out of their free choice or their relative efficiency

[1] In all, about 40–60 per cent of the countries in the Global South have conducted at least one TUS. Of these, less that 3 per cent countries have mainstreamed TUS in their national statistical system.

[2] Time-use data shows that women spend 40 per cent to 500 per cent (or five times) more time on non-SNA unpaid work (Antonopoulos 2009; Hirway 2005).

[3] The drudgery part of work includes work that is strenuous and time-consuming. For example, women in most developing countries in Africa, Asia, and Latin America spend considerable time in fetching water, collecting fuel wood, collecting fodder and other free goods, or on petty urban work.

or inefficiency; the division of the work between men and women is largely a social construct, determined by patriarchal traditions and values. In fact, this highly unequal distribution is at the root of power relations between men and women, and all pervasive gender inequalities. As this type of work is outside the purview of economic policies, the drudgery of work along with the time stress of unpaid workers, the technology and the productivity of this work, their working conditions, etc., are also outside the purview of policymaking. Thus, unpaid work that contributes significantly to the economy is not addressed systematically in policymaking.

In other words, non-SNA work is a kind of time tax on women throughout their life cycle. This tends to reduce time for remunerative work, leisure time, and time for education and health of women. This time tax tends to trap women in poverty—of both, income and time (Hirway 2010).[4] This is, in a way, social and economic exclusion of women from the market, and from the mainstream economy. It is de facto segregation of women in the economy.

This can also be viewed as violation of basic human rights of women. The lop-sided distribution of paid and unpaid work between men and women violates women's rights to equal opportunities, to non-discrimination, to education and health, and to work. It also violates their rights to social security as unpaid workers, to enjoy benefits of scientific progress, and to participation. The last refers to the low level of participation of women in national level parliament to local-level governments and other important decision-making bodies due to less time available for this participation and patriarchal values. The report of the Special Rapporteur on Extreme Poverty and Human Rights points out that for women of extremely poor households, this unequal distribution also results in a violation of basic social, cultural, economic, and political rights (UN 2013).

The other major concern about this division of the total economy is the time stress and time poverty of the poor, especially women.

---

[4] Hirway's study has shown that due to the time stress caused by paid and unpaid work, the poor, and particularly poor women, do not have much time left for education/skill training, self-improvement, social networking, or even rest. As a result, there is limited scope for them to get out of the trap of poverty.

In underdeveloped countries, and particularly in poor households, where more time is needed in processing of food, cooking, cleaning, etc., and on fetching water and fuel wood (due to poor availability of basic infrastructure), the time spent on household upkeep is very high. Due to limited facilities available for childcare and care of the disabled, sick, and the elders, poor households, and particularly women, get limited time for resting, for acquiring human capital—education, skills—or for productive labour market work (Blackden and Wodon 2006; Hirway 2010). If the children of the household are also involved in this work, as is usually found in poor households, the future generation will also have to pay the cost of high household overhead time (HOT).[5]

Finally, this results in sub-optimal use of the total labour force of the economy. On the one hand, a part of the labour force is locked up in a low productivity sector (unpaid work) with poor scope for achieving their full potential, while on the other, those women who are able to enter the labour market also suffer from inferior status (overcrowding in low productivity sector, poor diversification, low wages, and higher unemployment rate). This is because women have low human capital formation, low upward and horizontal mobility, and other restrictions owing to an overarching patriarchy.

## RESTRUCTURING OF PRODUCTION AND LABOUR UNDER TRADE LIBERALIZATION

In this section, we examine the impact of a major macroeconomic policy—trade liberalization—on both men and women engaged in SNA and non-SNA work. This is based on our empirical study in India (Hirway 2012).

The global market at present is dominated by global production networks (GPN), which have now emerged as key players in the world trade for many commodities. The transnational corporations (TNC)

---

[5] Household overhead time (HOT) is defined as the minimum number of hours a household needs to maintain and manage the household, that is, the minimum number of hours needed to transform raw materials to consumable goods and to provide a clean and healthy environment (Harvey and Taylor 2000).

that control GPN now account for around two-thirds of the world trade. The widespread use of international outsourcing in GPN allows global producers to shed their non-core activities and focus on higher value-added activities like design, branding, and marketing (Hirway 2012). Developing countries compete with each other for outsourced production and, under pressure to meet the cost, quality, and delivery requirements of their clients as well as to handle fluctuating orders, they tend to restructure their production and then labour by using different methods of hiring workers (Hirway 2012).

Under the competitive environment after the repeal of the quotas (Multi Fibre Arrangement [MFA])[6] in the case of the textile and garment (T&G) industry. For example, it is observed that countries tried to cut costs in multiple ways: Philippines excluded the garment sector from the purview of the Minimum Wages Act; Dominican Republic and El Salvador exempted the wages of T&G workers from the cost of living index; Mauritius increased its working days to seven days a week without providing additional remuneration to its workers; and in China workers were reported to be working for 12–14 hours a day, seven days a week for low wages with limited labour rights (International Textile, Garment and Leather Workers Federation [ITGLWF] Press Release 2005). India also experienced similar changes.

In India, the process of globalization has opened up export markets to industries that can export their goods and services. Furthermore, trade liberalization has been backed by domestic policies in terms of reducing regulations and provision of incentives of different types to industries within the country. In the case of the T&G industry, the supportive policies of the Ministry of Textile and the positive interventions from the industry have given a big push to the industry and contributed towards its integration with the global market. The overall production of the industry has increased at an annual rate of more than 5 per cent in 1985–2005, while the exports have increased at a much higher rate, at more than 12 per cent annual average rate, indicating gradual integration of the industry with the global market. The exports increased from USD 212 billion in 1990, to USD 396 billion in 2003,

[6] A multi-fibre agreement is an agreement between some industrialized countries (the US, Canada, and the UK) and 65 developing countries under which export quotas have been given to the developing countries.

and to about USD 600 billion by 2010. India ranks seventh among the world exporters with a 3.8 per cent share in the world exports of T&G. The industry is doing fairly well even though it is suffering from several constraints and problems in the areas of credit, technological upgrade, infrastructure, etc., which will have to be addressed in the coming years.

The globalization of the industry, however, has put several pressures on the industry to restructure its production that is, in turn, pushing the industry to restructure its labour use. The major reasons for this are: (a) the need for technological upgrade in order to compete in the global market; (b) the need to expand the size of units and to increase the control over the value chains for better bargaining in the global market; (c) the need to acquire flexibility in production to address the fluctuating demand in the volatile global market; and (d) the need to minimize the cost of production to compete in the global market.

The large-scale units, especially the corporate ones, have gone for a rapid technological upgrade by investing in the newest machineries either by buying local machines or through inviting foreign direct investments (FDI) and foreign collaborations/licensing. They have also used backward and forward vertical integration to increase the size and control over complete value chains for better bargaining. Some units have opted for horizontal integration for the purpose. Along with increasing the size, large units are choosing a thin core and 'permanent' employment system. The rest of the workers are employed as contract workers on the factory premises or in outsourced small and household units as informal workers. There is, therefore, a wide and widening gap between the skilled and professional workers. These are core workers enjoying high salaries and secured employment, and semi-skilled and unskilled workers, who work mainly as casual, contractual, or temporary workers and earn low wages and low social protection.

The large units have increased sub-contracting of parts of their production to acquire flexibility in production in order to reduce risk on the one hand and to minimize the cost of production on the other. They have also adopted other ways to minimize the labour costs, apart from sub-contracting work, such as: (a) employing contract labour in the factory premises; (b) employing temporary and casual labour as and when possible; (c) depending on home-based workers directly or through contractors; and (d) minimizing the burden of social security and workers' welfare.

The small scale industry (SSI) units are also keen to access benefits of growth of production and growth of exports. Their major strategy is to strengthen their links with exports through large exporting units or through horizontal integration—through creating umbrella organizations or through linking with large exporters/businessmen. They have, therefore, gone for: (a) technological upgrade to improve quality and quantity of products; (b) taking up sub-contracting work from large units and also sub-contracting to small household units; and (c) expanding the size of production to earn higher incomes. Like large units, they also use labour in a way that minimizes the cost of labour.

The household units are basically of three types: (a) those who take up jobs or sub-contracted work from small and large units; (b) own-account independent workers who manage their own affairs; and (c) mixed units who take up sub-contracted work and are also independent workers. Keen to benefit from the liberalized environment, some of these units have adopted a strategy of upgrading their technology and expanding the size of their production. Some of the units are also buying new machines to improve their productivity and production capacity. However, most of them are happy to receive more sub-contracted work by large and medium units. When needed, they employ more of family members and in some cases hire a few workers. One observes that the process of integration with the global level is happening at two levels. At the high level, the units (particularly large and medium units) are producing high-value-added products and aiming at the top and middle ends of the market to earn higher profits, while, on the other hand, there are units that produce low- and medium-value-added products to integrate with the global market at the low end. These units want to acquire global markets mainly through low production costs.[7]

---

[7] Another mode through which some units in the industry get integrated with the global economy is diversification into non-clothing application of textiles, known as 'technical textiles', that is, non-woven textiles, which are used in specialized products in industries. This segment, which requires highly sophisticated machinery and highly skilled labour, tends to raise employment of skilled workers, mainly men workers. The low level of literacy and skills of women, on the one hand, and the low mobility and domestic constraints on women workers, on the other, act as a major restriction to women's entry into this new areas of development in the T&G industry.

### Employment and Labour

One major impact of the integration of the T&G industry with the global market is expansion of employment in this labour-intensive industry. According to an estimate by the Textile Committee in 2004, the increase in employment was to be of 25 million by 2010, bringing the total employment in the industry to about 60 million in 2010. Of the additional 25 million, more than 15 million were expected to be in the apparel sector (Textile Committee 2004).

In the organized sector, however, employment has not kept pace with the rapid growth of the industry in the post liberalization period. In spite of the capital growing at more than 13 per cent per year in the organized sector of both textiles and garments, the employment growth rate has been 0.21 per cent for textiles and 3.73 per cent for garments during the past 6–7 years. As against this, growth rates of employment are much higher in the unorganized sector, particularly in the last decade, around 14.44 per cent per year. This indicates that the organized sector is becoming more capital-intensive, while the unorganized sector is becoming more labour-intensive. The labour productivity is growing much faster in the organized sector than in the unorganized sector.

Again, the employment of women has increased at a much faster rate than that of men, in both the textile and garment industries. In the case of textiles, the employment of women has increased at an annual rate of 1.5 per cent during the period 1995–2005, as against a mere 0.1 per cent of men. The corresponding rates for the garment industry are 33.1 and 8.2 per cent for women and men, respectively. That is, the increase in employment of men and particularly women is largely in the unorganized informal sector.

Both textiles and garment industries show a rapid growth of unorganized and home-based work for women (see Table 11.1). In fact, women predominate as home-based workers, as compared to men, with their share increasing dramatically from 58.9 per cent in 1994–5 to 93.1 per cent in 2004–5. The share of home-based workers, including that of women, in the textile industry, however, declined during this period, indicating that the industry is shifting to non-home-based venues gradually, may be because there is a need to raise the size of production units to produce high-value-added textiles for the global market.

**TABLE 11.1**   Growth of Home-based Workers during 1993–4 to 2004–5

| Industry | Share of Home-based Workers (1994–5) | | | Share of Home-based Workers (2004–5) | | |
|---|---|---|---|---|---|---|
| | Men | Women | Total | Men | Women | Total |
| Textiles | 72.1 | 87.4 | 80.6 | 70.1 | 64.3 | 78.5 |
| Garments | 45.7 | 58.9 | 48.8 | 39.1 | 93.1 | 53.7 |
| All Manufacturing | 56.5 | 83.4 | 66.9 | 49.7 | 83.3 | 61.2 |

*Source*: NSSO Rounds.

Significant changes have taken place in the value addition and labour productivity of workers in the textile and garment industries, in both the organized and unorganized segments. Both textiles and garments show a higher growth rate in the value-added segment in the post-reform period as compared to the pre-reforms period: from –2.88 per cent in the pre-reform period to 6.26 per cent in the post-reform period in the case of textiles, and from 6.24 per cent to 14.40 per cent in the case of garments. However, the growth of employment has been much lower, –0.16 per cent. In the case of the textile industry, the increase in labour productivity has been much higher: 6.42 per cent during 1994–2000. This, once again, indicates that the textiles industry has acquired a higher capital intensity. It also indicates that industrial upgrade has taken place with limited social upgrade.

Women's employment shows peculiar behaviour in the organized and unorganized sectors. One observes a rapid increase in women's employment in the unorganized sector, compared to that of men's, especially in home-based work. There are several reasons for this. To start with, the burden of unpaid work and the social norms following this division of labour makes women choose flexible working hours, and preferably work from their home. They are willing to take up the lowest rung of garment work, such as stitching of cut fabrics, finishing of garments, or adding accessories to garments. Producers, sub-contractors, and traders find this very convenient, as women work at home without any money to spend on premises, electricity, etc. Second, women in this work do not need a lot of training as, traditionally, women are used to performing stitching and related work at home. Once again, this suits women as well as the employers. Third, women, in general, are docile and the women in home-based work system in particular are not likely to unionize and create any problem for the employers. Finally, since there are several such women available in cities, small towns, and large villages, employers are in a position to bargain for very low wages.

On the other hand, in the organized sector, women have a lower contribution, which is mainly in clerical and low-level administrative tasks, mostly as temporary employees. Several factors contribute to this: employers in the organized sector are less inclined to employ women as 'permanent' workers as they have to allow for special provisions such as separate toilets and rest rooms in the factory premises, additional facilities for pregnant women, maternity benefits, nursing breaks, and crèches, some of which may even have additional financial implications for the employers. Women are also perceived as less mobile and more absent from work (due to domestic responsibilities) and frequently less willing to take up responsible jobs. Also, due to the burden of unpaid work and the consequent social norms, women are less qualified, particularly in technical and professional fields.

Employers, therefore, tend to employ women mainly as temporary, casual, or contract workers; women who are either young, unmarried girls (without domestic responsibilities) or elderly women who have completed the task of raising a family. In the relatively new garment factories, young, unmarried women are hired as temporary workers. The net result is that the share of women workers in the total 'permanent' workers is very small. This marginalization of women workers in the organized sector is likely to be intensified in the post-quota period, because of the increased demand for skilled labour in the sector. Since the overall literacy and skill levels of women are low in the country, women fail to take advantage of 'permanent' jobs in the organized sector.

## Wage Rates and Gender Wage Gap

The two important features of wages received by workers in the T&G industry are: (a) the increase in labour productivity is not reflected in an increase in the wage rates of men and women workers in the industry and (b) there is a big gap between the wage rates received by men workers as compared to women workers. Gender wage gap is an important indicator of the gender inequalities in the labour market. It reflects occupational segregation of as well as discrimination against women.[8]

Table 11.2 shows that the gender wage gap is the highest in the garment sector (2002–5), followed by silk textiles. The gender wage gap has increased in all the sectors of the T&G industry, except for cotton textiles, which needs a careful investigation. Micro-level studies have shown that women are largely employed in low levels of occupation, that is, in unskilled or semi-skilled production work, in work requiring low-level supervision, etc. (Neetha 2002). The studies also indicate gender discrimination reflected in unequal wages for the same or similar work. Since it is possible for employers to employ women at lower terms by segmenting the labour market, the average wage rate of women tends to become considerably lower than the average wage rate for men.

There are several theoretical presentations that explain gender wage gaps:

1. The *human capital theory*, which is based on supply-side explanations (for occupational segregation) argues that women possess low human capital as compared to men because: (a) they invest less in education and skills due to their domestic responsibilities; (b) they are more likely to work as part-time and intermittent workers due to their domestic responsibilities and, therefore, are likely to acquire low human capital; and (c) they are likely to get crowded in low productivity, low wage occupations and industries.

2. The *taste for discrimination theory* argues that earnings of women who are equally productive are likely to differ because employees and employers have irrational preferences. Employers may prefer men for no apparent rational reason. Becker (1964), however, argues that such an irrational behaviour may not continue in a highly competitive environment, as employers may not be able to afford this luxury when the competition is very high.

---

[8] It is frequently calculated as a gender wage gap using the ratio of average wage rate of women (annual, monthly, weekly, daily, or hourly) to that of man. The measure for occupational segregation is an index of dissimilarity which explains the occupational wage gap between men and women, while unexplained wage gap refers to gender-based discrimination, which is measured through a residual technique called Oaxaca decomposition.

**TABLE 11.2** Trends in Average Daily Earnings by Sex in T&G Industry (1974–9 to 2002–5) (Rs)

| Industry | 1974–9 | | 1985–92 | | 2002–5 | | Gender Wage Gap M/W | | |
|---|---|---|---|---|---|---|---|---|---|
| | Men | Women | Men | Women | Men | Women | 1974–9 | 1985–92 | 2002–5 |
| Cotton Textiles | 14.60 | 11.63 | 42.80 | 29.74 | 78.10 | 73.24 | 1.25 | 1.04 | 1.07 |
| Woollen Textiles | 13.80 | 8.22 | 35.80 | 35.96 | 69.30 | 59.24 | 1.67 | 1.00 | 1.17 |
| Silk Textiles | 10.40 | 7.10 | 30.60 | 25.15 | 64.00 | 39.56 | 1.47 | 1.22 | 1.62 |
| Synthetic Textiles | 0.00 | 0.00 | 40.60 | 42.28 | 62.40 | 40.86 | 0.00 | 0.96 | 1.53 |
| Jute Textiles | 14.70 | 15.59 | 42.20 | 42.00 | 89.70 | 85.99 | 0.94 | 1.01 | 1.04 |
| Textile Garments | 11.30 | 7.12 | 34.00 | 18.61 | 60.60 | 37.83 | 1.58 | 1.83 | 1.90 |
| Coefficient of Variation | 0.17 | 0.37 | 0.16 | 0.25 | 0.17 | 0.37 | 0.46 | 0.64 | 0.46 |

*Source:* Occupational Wage Survey, Labour Bureau, Government of India.

3.  The *statistical discrimination theory,* which is a demand-side explana-
    tion of the gender gap, argues that the gender wage gap exists
    because of market failure. Since market information is not perfect,
    group stereotypes exist. Using these stereotypes, employers dis-
    criminate against women workers. According to the neo-classical
    theory, gender wage gaps should decline with time, as competition
    in the market removes the information gap, irrational tastes and
    preferences, and rising demand for skills (under globalization) will
    raise the skill levels of all workers.

However, this may not happen if it is possible to segment the labour
market based on some of the characteristics of workers. For example,
the high flexibility of women workers and nature of their supply
behaviour (they are docile and have a low interest in unionization)
makes it possible for the employers to segment the labour market and
to treat them differently by providing them temporary, part-time, or
casual employment at low wages. That is, it is possible to employ more
women than men to reduce costs to export in a competitive market.
This raises the wage gap.

The root cause of the wage gap, however, lies in inequalities within
the household that gets reflected in the inequalities in the labour market. Though this factor cannot be isolated as only a labour market
issue, there are feedback effects between macroeconomic and global
economic developments and discrimination in the labour market. In
short, explanation for the gender wage gap has to lie in alternative
theoretical framework that recognizes unequal distribution of unpaid
domestic work within households.

GENDER WAGE GAP IN DIFFERENT SEGMENTS OF WORKERS

Workers in the unorganized sector include casual and temporary
workers, sub-contracted workers, home workers, part-time workers,
concealed workers (such as illegal child labourers), while organized
sector workers are permanent, regular, temporary, or casual workers.
Our study shows that within regular and casual workers as well as
within home-based and non-home-based workers, there are significant gender-based wage differentials. An interesting finding of the
study is that the highest wages are earned by regular, non-home-based

**TABLE 11.3**    T&G Wage Rates by Gender and by Organized/Unorganized Sectors (2004–5)

| Industry | Organized | | | Unorganized | | |
|---|---|---|---|---|---|---|
| | Men | Women | Ratio (M/W) | Men | Women | Ratio (M/W) |
| Textiles | 120.49 | 39.38 | 3.05 | 59.21 | 29.45 | 2.01 |
| Garments | 96.15 | 54.00 | 1.78 | 65.60 | 36.61 | 1.79 |
| T&G (Total) | 117.56 | 46.14 | 2.54 | 60.63 | 31.33 | 1.94 |

*Source*: NSSO Rounds.

working men, while the lowest wages are earned by casual women home workers. The wages of regular workers are higher than that of causal workers, and the wages of non-home workers are higher than that of home workers (Hirway 2009).

The average daily wage rates in the organized sector are higher than those in the unorganized sector (Table 11.3). However, the gender wage gap is also higher in the organized sector: 3.05 and 1.78 for textiles and for garments, respectively, and 2.54 for T&G total as against 2.01, 1.79, and 1.94, respectively, in the unorganized sector. This is perhaps due to the high level of occupation segregation in the organized sector, with women overcrowding in low level of occupations.

In contrast, the occupation-wise differences in wages are lower in the unorganized sector due to the small size of the units, less qualified/underpaid management personnel and predominance of relatively less skilled production workers. Once again, wages are higher in the textile sector than in the garment sector, largely emanating from the higher capital intensity in the textile sector. It is indeed worth noting that the gender wage inequalities are the highest in the top end of the labour market, which is formal, organized, and supposed to be more professionally managed, while the lowest gender wage gap is in the case of casual workers.

## Working Conditions in the Unorganized Sector

In the case of unorganized workers, the working and living conditions are much worse. Employers prefer to hire workers outside their premises in sub-contracted units and as home-based workers because it reduces the overheads of employing. It also gives employers the free-dom of choosing whether and when to use workers; scattered workers cannot unionize easily and bargain for better terms and it saves on payment of social security benefits to workers.

Several studies are worth noting in this context: Neetha's study (2002) of knitwear workers of Tiruppur, a major garment centre that exports more than 80 per cent of the total exports of cotton knitwear from India, shows that most of the processes are contracted out to smaller units and to home-based workers. As a result, these workers, 70–80 per cent of whom are women, work seven days a week in an unhealthy environment, without any social protection. According to the author, this industrial cluster is a classic case of feminization of labour and segmentation of labour market brought out through sub-contracting.

Jeemol Unni's study (Unni and Rani 2002), which has documented the insecurities of informal textile and garment workers in Gujarat, shows that these workers suffer from income insecurity (due to the irregular and uncertain nature of their work as well as low wages), employment insecurity (due to lack of ensured work), and skill inse-curity (arising from their low skills and poor scope for a skill upgrade). They also suffer from food insecurity, insecurity of health and educa-tion, shelter insecurity, etc.

Ritu Dewan's study (2003) has shown that workers, and particu-larly women workers, in export promotion zones are forced to work long hours, earn low wages, and suffer from repressive conditions in general. It is observed that employers are supported by officials, even from the department of labour, in reducing the costs of production by reducing wages and other labour costs. Clearly, unorganized workers under different situations have promoted increasing globalization of the industry, but have been bypassed by its benefits.

## TIME USE OF HOME–BASED WORKERS: INFERENCES AND IMPLICATIONS

The earlier discussion has shown that the home-based sector in the garment industry has expanded rapidly during the period 1995–2010. It has also shown that women are predominant as home-based workers in this industry, and they receive the lowest wages/incomes among all the categories of garment workers. Using time-use data, this section discusses how the workers in this bottom rung of production spend their time and why they need macroeconomic policy support to access benefits of growth occurring in the economy.

This study of home-based garment workers is a part of another study (Phase 2) conducted in 2010–11, sponsored by the International Labour Organization (ILO).[9] The sample of home-based workers has been drawn systematically, based on the typology of home-based garment workers: (a) their work, that is, stitching, finishing, sticking accessories, etc.; (b) the production organization, that is, home-based work taken from traders/contractors, self-employed work, and/or mixed work; (c) socio-religious characteristics of workers; and (d) location of work, that is, the types of location in Ahmedabad city, one of the biggest garment centres, which is also in the business of export of garments.

Three major locations selected for the study were: Ghee Kanta, which is broadly engaged in finished work; Gomtipur, which is broadly engaged in stitching and finishing work usually outsourced by large units; and Shahpur, a Muslim-dominated garment centre, which is involved in stitching as well as finishing. At the first stage of data collection, discussions were organized with the chairpersons and office-bearers of the garment manufacturing associations of Gujarat and particularly of Ahmedabad, followed by discussions with leading units in the three centres. Discussions were also held with a large number of garment manufactures, traders, including exporters in these centres, as well as with home-based garment workers and their leaders.

After identifying the typology of home-based garment workers, 20 units were selected for an in-depth study, including a study of the time use of these workers and their household members (above six years). Two questionnaires were designed: one for home-based workers and their households to understand their socio-economic conditions as well as their production and incomes, and the other was for collecting time-use data of the workers and their household members (above six years of age). It is to be noted that this home-based work is indirectly connected with exports to the EU, US, and/or the Middle-East.

---

[9] The study covers large-, medium-, and small-scale units, in addition to the home-based sector.

## Profile of Workers

All the workers in the sample started working in their homes less than 11 years ago, except in the Shahpur area, where they started working about 18–20 years ago. In Gomtipur, they started only 6–7 years ago. The work was outsourced to them by large and small producers and traders. As mentioned earlier, the three garment centres have grown around increasing exports of garments outside Gujarat and also out of India.

About 60 per cent of the workers are Hindu, all belonging to other backward classes (OBC), while the rest are Muslims (at the city level also, their proportions in home-based garment workers are more or less the same). Ninety-five per cent of these are women workers and 5 per cent are male workers—engaged in higher-level production activities, such as cutting and managing a home-based unit with a few hired workers. Fifteen per cent of home-based workers are illiterates, while 30 per cent have studied up to the fourth standard and 55 per cent have studied up to the secondary level. None of them has studied beyond this level. The educational achievements of household members, however, are much higher, as only 5 per cent members belonging to the older generation are illiterates. Of the remaining, 65.6 per cent have studied up to secondary school, and 12.5 per cent have studied beyond this, with a few attending the college.

Majority of home-based workers are in the age group of 26–40 years, who are married and have young or school-going children. Around one-fourth of the workers are between the ages of 41–55 years and above, while 10 per cent are below 25 years. The average size of the household is 6.2 members with 85 per cent of households living in nuclear families. Interestingly, 60 per cent of the household members are women.

### WAGES, INCOMES, AND ASSETS

Home-based workers earn piece rate wages. Wages are paid, usually on a weekly basis. The piece rate wages depend on the products: for example, in the Ghee Kanta area, the prevailing rate is Rs 6 for finishing (removing threads, ironing, etc.) one dozen shirts or pants, Rs 2–3 for fixing buttons on a dozen shirts, Rs 11–19 for stitching a shirt, and so on. The average wage per day (8 hours) comes to about

Rs 50.16 to Rs 82.46. None of the workers is able to bargain for higher wages, as 'there are many women willing to work at the rate'.

The average annual income of these households is Rs 51,090 and their per capita monthly income is Rs 828, which is slightly above the poverty line (that is, Rs 760 based on the Tendulkar Committee report 2009). However, 8–10 per cent households do live below the poverty line. If we consider only the incomes of the main work-ers, who work for 8–10 hours and some times more than 10 hours, 45 per cent of the households would be below the poverty line. The households are able to avoid poverty due to the large-scale participa-tion of household members.

As one would expect, there are not many consumer durables with the households of home-based workers. Except for the households with less than an annual income of Rs 3,000, all households have some or other furniture, such as chairs and tables, beds, and cabinets. The average value of these assets comes to Rs 6,823. They also have electronic items such as fan, a television, mixer, the average value of this being Rs 5,697. About 40 per cent households have two wheel-ers: a bicycle or a motorcycle, the average value of the vehicle being Rs 33,400. On an average, the value of domestic assets per household comes to Rs 16,600 without counting the value of the home they own, and to Rs 181,780 after counting the value of home.

### OCCUPATIONS OF HOUSEHOLD MEMBERS

About 70 per cent households have stitching as their main occupa-tion and source of income. Ten per cent of households are engaged in a slightly higher-level job within the garment industry—cutting fabrics, distributing work, and earning commission (and also stitching), or running a small home-based unit in garments, as a sub-contracted unit, with a few hired workers. The rest of the households (20 per cent) have other informal work, such as running a tea stall, driving an auto rickshaw, electrical work, as their main source of income.

Around 55 per cent of the household members are engaged in some or other economic activity, including helping in stitching work, as the earnings of one person are not adequate. On an average, 2–3 persons per household have to work to make ends meet. That is, in addition the home-based main workers, children—boys and girls—as well as other adult members of the households have to participate in work to earn incomes. Since the garment work is carried out within the household, several other members extend their help in their spare time in stitching, running errands to get material, etc., or in other related work. It is observed that girls are withdrawn from school by the seventh standard and roped in for stitching, for household work, or in taking care of younger siblings. Even when they go to school (up to the seventh standard), they start helping as soon as they come back home. Boys also help, but they are not withdrawn from school to help the family.

The other subsidiary occupations of these households are factory labour, rickshaw driving, and other petty service or jobs in the informal sector. About 14 per cent household members are engaged in these non-garment activities. On the whole, only 10 per cent households have one earning member in the family. Twenty per cent have two earners each, 55 per cent have three earners each, and 15 per cent have four earners in the family.

## Organization of Production

About 30 per cent of home-based workers do not have a separate room for carrying out their work, while 70 per cent workers have a separate room for it. The former workers live in a one-room home, and, therefore, cannot have a separate space for working, while the latter can spare a room, at least for a few hours for stitching and related work.

About 70 per cent workers own their home and the rest live in a rented homes. About 75 per cent households own at least the main production asset, the sewing machine. Most of them reported that they bought a second-hand machine, the present value of which is Rs 2,000–3,000. Most households also have their own equipment, such as needles, scissors, and other small supplements. (The employer saves all these costs, along with the cost of space.) The average value of the equipment is between Rs 5,000–7,000 per household. In most cases, the employer/trader/sub-contractor provides raw material, cloth, threads, buttons, zips, and accessories, while, in many cases, the workers have to buy thread, buttons, and other raw material.

It is noteworthy that none of the workers has undergone formal training for skills for garment stitching or garment-related work. The workers informed that they had learnt stitching from a friend, relative, or a neighbour, and the skill is acquired on the job. A few workers reported that initially they were doing petty work in a small garment unit and gradually the tailors taught them how to stitch. However, the workers follow the instructions given by the trader or a sub-contractor about specific orders.

## PRODUCTION PROCESS

The usual practice is that the employer provides cut fabrics and instructions, mostly with the required raw material and accessories to these workers and collects readymade clothes. In the case of the finishing work, the employer provides half-finished products and the workers remove threads, put buttons, or iron them and give finished products to the trader/employer. In all the cases, however, it is the responsibility of the worker to collect the cloth and the material from the shop or the production unit of the employer and return the finished products to the shop/factory. This involves hard work of carrying up to 25–30 kg of cloth in most cases. Again, the employer saves on this transport cost. The employer also saves on the electricity used to operate the machines, energy used for running a fan and light, as well as on the cost of providing drinking water and toilet facilities.

It seems that 80 per cent of home-based workers get work through traders, many of whom (60 per cent) are also involved in exporting their products directly or indirectly. Twenty per cent of workers get work from local producers, who are also traders selling their products in India or aboard. Ten per cent of workers also reported that part of their production is sold in the market, as they function as self-employed workers to an extent. Getting work from a trader or a shop is not easy, as they need a known link, such as a relative, a neighbour, or a friend. Frequently, a person who gets work from a trader distributes it to others as job work to neighbouring or known workers and collects a commission, say of a rupee per piece. After the receiver establishes a direct link, he/she does not have to pay this commission. The products cover a wide range of western clothes (frocks for girls, shirts, pants, Bermuda pants, finishing of jeans, etc.) as well as Indian clothes like dupattas and *chania-choli*s.

## EMPLOYMENT AND STABILITY OF WORK

On an average, these workers get work for about 20 days a month. Work is also not available throughout the year, as Table 11.4 shows. The lean months are December–February and July–August, while the peak months are festival seasons (October–November) and the marriage seasons.[10] Eighty-five per cent of households reported that their incomes fluctuate and managing the level of living in the lean season is a challenge. About 66 per cent households reported that they have to reduce their consumption during the lean season.

The global crisis affected 75 per cent of the households, as the crisis resulted in reduction in the garment markets abroad. These households reported that they got much less work for 6–8 months and earned lower incomes during the year 2008–9.

## WORKING CONDITIONS

There are no complaints about the working conditions from workers. As some of them put it, it is convenient to work from home, as they can take care of their homes and can work any time they want, although 20 per cent of workers did complain that they do not have enough space for work. All the workers—without exception—however, complained that they suffer from: (a) back pain; (b) leg pain by running the machine; and (c) eye pain or weak eyes. About half the workers also complained of 'too much noise'. None of the home-based units kept a first aid box.

**TABLE 11.4**  Number of Days of Work Available (2009–10)

| Region | No. of Days of Work in a Year |
|---|---|
| Ghee Kanta | 249 |
| Shahpur | 300 |
| Gomtipur | 236 |
| Total | 255 |

*Source:* The primary survey by the author.

[10] This survey was conducted during a normal period that was neither a peak period nor a lean season.

None of the workers had heard about 'decent work',[11] and when explained, were not very clear whether they want it. May be they thought that by wanting it they may lose their current work. Though some workers in Shahpur (members of Self Employed Women's Association [SEWA]) had heard about insurance, they were not able to access it.

## Analysis of Time Use

In order to understand the impact of home-based work on the time use of workers and their household members, a TUS was conducted. This survey collected data on how the workers and the member of their households (above six years) allocate their time between SNA, non-SNA, and personal (non-delegable) work. The exploratory survey was organized on a small but representative of 10 home-based workers.[12] The sample was selected systematically to cover major typologies of home-based work, and the survey was conducted by trained investigators who used instruction manual designed for the Indian TUS of 1998–9 and the Indian classification (modified) used in 1998–9 TUS for the purpose of analysis of data.

One working day was selected for each worker and her/his household, spread systematically to cover over the weekdays. Based on this selection, weekly estimates on time use were calculated. The analysis of the data is going on at present (for a much larger sample) and in this sense this is a 'work in progress'. The major findings of this study are presented in the following paragraphs.

### TIME SPENT ON GARMENT WORK

There is no uniform pattern of working time, as the starting time, the closing time, and the number of 'working periods' on garment

---

[11] Decent work sums up the aspirations of people in their working lives. It involves opportunities for work that is productive and delivers a fair income, security in the workplace and social protection for families, better prospects for personal development and social integration, freedom for people to express their concerns, organize and participate in the decisions that affect their lives, and equality of opportunity and treatment for all women and men.

[12] The larger TUS has covered about 60 households selected from garment workers in large, medium, and small units.

stitching is different for different workers, depending on the demand from their domestic responsibilities. Thirty per cent of workers start their work at 8.30 in the morning, while the rest start at 10 a.m., 11 a.m. or even 1 p.m. The closing timings also are different, varying from 3 p.m. to midnight, depending on the demand from work and other responsibilities. Except one, all spread their work over 2–5 working periods. That is, the work is done in a scattered manner, depending on the needs of the family as well as of work. Ten per cent of workers distributed their work in five periods, 40 per cent in four working periods and the rest in 2–3 periods.

The working hours, according to the surveyed workers, fluctuate based on the season. In the busy season, some of them work till midnight and put in more than 12 hours of work, while in the lean season they work only for 4–6 hours. As mentioned earlier, the period during which the survey was conducted was 'normal'—neither a peak period nor a lean period.

The average minutes put in by the garment workers for a day was 494.3 minutes (that is, 8 hours and 14 minutes approx.). This varied between 747 minutes (more than 12 hours) to 120 minutes (2 hours). On an average, there are about two household members helping the main worker. The number of helpers varies from zero in one case to 2–3 in most cases. The average time put in by family members in garment work comes to about 378.5 minutes (6 hours 18 minutes), which is not small. This comes to 47 per cent of the total garment working time. In other words, the time spent by family members on garment work, in addition to the time spent by the main worker, comes to 88 per cent of the time spent by the main worker and is a little less than half of the total time spent on garment work by all the family members.

TIME SPENT ON NON-SNA WORK

Home-based workers spend significant time on non-SNA work, that is, household upkeep (washing, cleaning, sweeping, cooking, shopping for the household, etc.) and care work (care of children, the elders, and other needy members of the household). On an average, these workers spend 262 minutes (4 hours 22 minutes) on this work. The time varies from 60 minutes to 293 minutes (4 hours 53 minutes), depending on the presence of young children in the household, structure of the household (presence of elders to take care of children), household income, etc.

The total time spent by home-based workers on SNA and non-SNA work together comes to 757 minutes (12 hours 37 minutes). If the time spent on travelling for these two types of work is included, the total time spent on work by an average home-based worker comes to 817 minutes (13 hours 27 minutes).

## TIME SPENT BY OTHER HOUSEHOLD MEMBERS ON GARMENT WORK

As seen above, on an average, there are 1.9 household members who provide help to the main workers in garment work. Majority of them are women helpers (80 per cent). Three men members (who are all adults) spend 535 minutes (8 hours 55 minutes) on an average to help women workers almost full-time. In the case of women members of the household, who help with the garment work, spend, on an average, 311 minutes (5 hours 11 minutes). On an average, they put in 328 minutes of work per worker. This comes to 76 per cent of the average time spent by the main home-based workers. In short, other household members together spend more minutes on garment work than the main workers put together. This is indeed family wage work.

It is also to be noted that in the case of men, only adults participate, while in the case of women as many women as possible contribute to this family work in different ways.

## CONTRIBUTION BY BOYS AND GIRLS (6–14 YEARS) TO HOUSEHOLD SNA AND NON–SNA WORK

Boys and girls below the age of 14 years help in the 'economic' (SNA) activities (this includes garment and other SNA work) as well as in non-SNA activities. As far as boys are concerned, only two boys out of the total of six participated in SNA activities, bringing their LFPR to 33.33. They spent 15 minutes each on this work. In the case of girls, nine girls out of the total twelve participated in SNA work bringing their WPR to 75.00. They spend, on an average, 20.12 minutes on this work. In addition, the girls also spend 83 minutes (1 hour 23 minutes) average time on non-SNA work that includes household upkeep (that is, cooking, cleaning, washing, sweeping, etc.) and on taking care of their siblings. Boys spend 10 minutes on an average on non-SNA work. Thus, boys spend 25 minutes on work (SNA + non-SNA), while girls work for 105 minutes (1 hour 45 minutes) on work.

It is observed that half of these girls spend more than 2 hours on the total work. This leaves less time for girls to spend on playing, studying, sleeping, and relaxing. The data shows that girls spend 387 minutes on education, implying all their time spent is in school, while boys spend 470 minutes, which implies that they get sometime for study at home. Our discussions also showed that girls are roped into SNA or non-SNA work even before they are 14 years old. They start working as soon as they come back from school.

## Time Spent by Men and Women on SNA, non-SNA, and Personal Time

There are large differences between the pattern of time use of home-based workers—male and female members of the households (6+ years). On an average, home-based workers spend 34.33 per cent of their time on SNA work as against 18.62 by all women and 27.59 per cent by men (see Table 11.5). However, women also spend 31.75 per cent

**TABLE 11.5**   Time Allocation on SNA, non-SNA, and Personal Activities by Men and Women

| Activity Type | Home-based Workers | | Total Men | | Total Women | |
|---|---|---|---|---|---|---|
| | Minutes | % Share | Minutes | % Share | Minutes | % Share |
| SNA Work | 494.30 | 34.33 | 397.33 | 27.59 | 268.09 | 18.62 |
| Non-SNA Work | 262.80 | 18.25 | 34.33 | 2.38 | 457.21 | 31.75 |
| Total work time | 757.10 | 52.58 | 431.66 | 29.98 | 725.30 | 50.37 |
| Personal Activities | 682.90 | 47.42 | 908.34 | 63.07 | 714.70 | 49.03 |
| Total | 1,440.00 | 100.00 | 1,440.00 | 100.00 | 1,440.00 | 100.00 |

*Source*: TUS conducted by the author.

of their time on non-SNA work against 2.38 per cent by men. In all, therefore, women spend 50.37 per cent of their time on work, while men spend 29.98 per cent time on work. Home-based workers spend 52.58 per cent of their time on total work. Consequently, men get more time (63.07 per cent) for personal activities, that includes watching the TV, listening to radio, socialization, relaxation, reading newspapers, as well as sleep as compared to women, who spend 49.03 per cent of the time on these activities.

## Inferences and Implications

This study has shown that the practice of home-based work, which has expanded rapidly under trade liberalization, has given an opportunity to many (mainly women and some men) to get engaged in the production of goods (in this case, garments) within their home. This has allowed them to work with flexible timings, along with taking care of their domestic works, that is, upkeep of the household and care work. As the data shows, this has given a big push to women's WPR in general and in the garment industry in particular.

This supply behaviour of women fits very well in the new environment where producers want flexible production and lowest possible cost of production. Producers who give the lowest kind of production work to home-based garment workers—finishing work (removing threads, stitching buttons, ironing, etc.), stitching cut fabrics, putting accessories on garments, etc.—enjoy two main advantages: (a) they can increase and reduce the production as per the orders received and (b) they can reject their product if it is not of good quality.

In addition, this production system is economical to the producers in several ways: (a) it saves on the space for production, as work is performed by workers in their homes; (b) it saves on overheads like electricity for fans, light, and for running the machines; (c) it saves their expenditure on providing facilities like drinking water, toilets, etc.; (d) it saves expenditure on maintaining safe and clean surroundings for work; and (e) frequently, it saves their expenditure on raw materials. In addition, employers save on social security, including maternity benefits. Not only are home-based workers not compensated for the costs incurred by them, they are also paid lower wages for the work.

As it is possible for employers to segment the labour market for home-based workers, employers are able to pay lower wages. There are many (women) workers wanting this work, creating the supply side pressure on the wage rate.

Globalization policies thus have intensified the practice of home-based work, which has, on the one hand, raised the rate of growth of the economy and foreign exchange reserves, while on the other, it has raised profits for all producers, including exporters who sell their products at a high rate in the global markets. At the same time, it has promoted a highly exploitative system where in spite of generous contribution from family members and subsidies for employers in the form of free space, no overheads, low risk, and no payments for social protection, workers only get pittance as returns. This scenario is likely to have severe negative implications on the economy even though these implications are neither visible nor incorporated in policy designing or policy monitoring.

To start with, the home-based system of work traps the workers in low-skill, low-productivity activities, providing them little scope for improving productivity through skill formation: there is not much scope for providing them new skills or higher level skills due to their production organization and due to their low or semi-literate background. These on-the-job trained school drop-outs have limited capacity to acquire higher level skills and therefore have a limited scope to access upward mobility in productivity, earnings, and jobs. This is a major loss to the economy.

The enormous burden of work, both SNA and non-SNA, on these workers tends to result in human capital depletion. The low wages and low incomes add to this depletion thereby leading to low nutritional status. As a result, their productivity reduces, which, in turn, reduces their capacity to earn. The unequal sharing of total work within the household between men and women puts women in the worst position under this system. The overuse of labour and the consequent depletion of human capital once again implies less than optimum use of labour, which has implications for macroeconomic growth.

The system of home-based work has extremely low wages and flex-ibility of work time, which push women to spread their work, both SNA and non-SNA, from morning to midnight. This leaves less time for relaxation and rest, which affects their overall well-being adversely. They also get less time for acquisition of skills and higher productivity.

Home-based work makes it possible to employ children in the work, with the result that children's contribution, in terms of hours put it, is significant. The condition of girls is particularly difficult, as they frequently perform three kinds of work: garment work, household work, and taking care of younger siblings. There is, therefore, a tendency to withdraw girls after the seventh standard, or even earlier. Even when girls go to school, their time use indicates that they do not get enough free time to play or to study. It is not enough they go to school, it is also essential that they get free time to play and study. Otherwise, it is reflected in their poor quality of education. As girls spend more than two hours on garment work or other market-related work, they are involved in 'child labour' even as they are enrolled in a school.

The time use of children under the system of home-based work can have severe implications on the future of these children. The rapid increase in the home-based work should also be seen from the point of view of children.

### Recommendations for Macroeconomic Policies

The foregoing discussion has important ramifications for assessing and monitoring macroeconomic policies, such as the policy of trade liberalization. If the impact of a policy is assessed on the basis of its impact on exports and GDP, or even on overall employment, it is far from adequate. The impact needs to be assessed in terms of quality of employment, that is, in terms of the characteristics and returns on labour, as well as in terms of changing the production organization, and the pattern of use of labour. It should also be studied in terms of changes in unpaid work of affected workers. Such an assessment provides a realistic picture of the impact and helps in designing and monitoring macroeconomic policies effectively. Time-use statistics will help in making such a comprehensive assessment.

The first major recommendation, therefore, is to make unpaid work of affected households visible. This requires data on the time use of SNA and non-SNA workers as well as on personal activities of affected people. This data can be collected by undertaking an area-based or issue-based TUS. That is, one does not need a large scale or national TUS for this purpose. A focused and small TUS is neither too expensive nor too time-consuming. The other recommendations are discussed in the following paragraphs.

## ADDRESSING HOME–BASED WORK

The study has shown that the production system underlying home-based work needs modifications in order to bring the workers within the purview of mainstream policymaking. This requires multiple efforts.

In this context, the two major challenges emerging from the huge spread of home-based work are: (a) modifying the system of home-based work so as to bring it in the purview of mainstream macroeconomic policymaking in order to open up opportunities for home-based workers in the mainstream economy and (b) including unpaid work within the purview of macroeconomic policy, so that it becomes not only visible (or valued) but is addressed effectively by macroeconomic policies.

To begin with, it is necessary to raise the wage rate of these workers, firstly, by covering all these workers into the purview of the minimum wages act, and secondly, by enforcing this act effectively. The blatant neglect of labour in general and this labour law in particular under the present policy environment is a major weakness of policymaking. It is important to see that benefits of growth achieved under globalization reach these workers for their well-being as well as for the sustenance of the present growth. Increased wages will reduce the dependence of these workers on family members, particularly on girls.

The literature recommends ensuring decent work to all workers including home-based workers, by enforcing effective enforcement of acts like the Minimum Wages Act and a minimum package of social security. However, policy designs have regularly exclude such provisions. As an entry point in this area, one can suggest that no firm should be allowed to export unless it safeguards decent work to all its direct and indirect workers. This should not be very difficult to achieve as most exporters make good profits in the global markets. Such an intervention has the capacity to pave the way for moving to more universal acceptance of decent work.

Another recommendation is to encourage the formation of a producers' company of these wage earners. It is to be kept in mind that these wage earners may not be willing or equipped to run independent enterprises. There is no point, therefore, to train them in entrepreneurship for setting up tiny enterprises. One will have to look for social entrepreneurs to set up such companies.

In order to promote improved productivity and upward mobility of these workers, there is a need to make it mandatory for employers to organize tailor-made skill formation programmes for home-based workers. Relevant training institutes can be roped into this task.

To encourage professionalism and high productivity among workers, it is necessary to bring them out of their homes, which are frequently too small to carry out production work, to work centres or work sheds. Employers and traders should be encouraged to do so. It is to be underlined that though women's supply fits in well with the flexible production structure, there is a need to see that they have an access to upward mobility in their job.

Finally, there is also a need to cover these workers under social protection provisions, including maternity benefits. Access to health insurance, old age pension, maternity leave and allowances, loans for education of children, housing loans, etc., will go a long way not only in improving the well-being of these workers but also raising their labour productivity.

### ADDRESSING UNPAID WORK

Apart from 'recognition' of unpaid work, 'reduction' in unpaid work will also be an important point of consideration here. This requires focused efforts on reducing the drudgery of unpaid work by improving its technology and productivity and by providing basic services/infrastructure to households for taking these activities outside the boundary of the home. For example, ensuring free access to basic health and elementary education, ensuring universal childcare (day care) facilities along with free meals to school-going children can help in reducing the burden of unpaid work on women.

In short, there is also a need to integrate gender concerns into mainstream policy making, that is, in the trade policy, industrial policy, labour policy, etc. Instead of compartmental policymaking by different ministries at present, a coordination committee of all concerned ministries should be set up to plan and monitor macroeconomic policies for the well-being of people and for sustained growth of the economy.

# REFERENCES

Antonopoulos, Rania. 2009. 'The Unpaid Care Work–Paid Work Connection', Working Paper No. 86, Policy Integration and Statistics Department, International Labour Office, Geneva.

———. 2011. 'The Current Economic and Financial Crisis: A Gender Perspective—Macroeconomics & Gender', paper presented at an event, co-sponsored by the Heinrich Böll Foundation North America, the Center of Concern, and the Institute for Women's Policy Research (IWPR) on 22 April 2009.

Antonopoulos, Rania and Indira Hirway. 2010. 'Unpaid Work and the Economy: Gender, Time Use and Poverty', in Rania Antonopoulos and Indira Hirway (eds), *Unpaid Work and the Economy: Gender, Time Use and Poverty in the Global South*, London: Palgrave Macmillan.

Becker, Gary S. 1964. 'A Theory of the Allocation of Time', *The Economic Journal*, 75(299): 493–517.

Blackden, C.M. and Q. Wodon. 2006. 'Gender, Time-Use, and Poverty in Sub-Saharan Africa', Working Paper No. 73, World Bank, Washington, DC.

Charmes, Jacques. 2008. 'Statistics on Informal Employment in the Arab Region', Chapter 3 of *Gender Equality and Workers' Rights in the Informal Economies of Arab States*. Tunis: ILO.

Dewan, Ritu. 2003. 'Ethics of Employment and Exports: Societal Dialogue and Fish Processing Export Units in India'. 31 October to 2 November 2001, SAAT, New Delhi.

Economic Commission for Latin America and the Caribbean (ECLAC). 2007. *Social Panorama of Latin America 2007*. Santiago, Chile: ECLAC.

Esquivel, Valeria. 2008. 'A "Macro" View on Equal Sharing of Responsibilities between Women and Men' (EGM/ESOR/2008/EP.8), Expert Group Meeting on 'The Equal Sharing of Responsibilities between Women and Men, including Caregiving in the Context of HIV/AIDS', 53rd Meeting of the Commission for the Status of Women (CSW), United Nations Division for the Advancement of Women (DAW), New York.

Goldschmidt-Clermont, Luisella. 1987. *Economic Evaluations of Unpaid Household Work: Africa, Asia, Latin America and Oceania*. Geneva, International Labour Office.

———. 1989. *Unpaid Work in the Household: A Review of Economic Evaluation Methods*. Geneva: International Labour Office.

Harvey, Andrew and M.E. Taylor. 2000. 'Designing Household Survey Questionnaires for Developing Countries: Lessons from Fifteen years of Living Standard Measurement Studies', The World Bank, Washington, DC.

Hirway, Indira. 2005. 'Integrating Unpaid Work into Development Policy', paper presented at the 'Conference on Unpaid Work and Economy:

Gender, Poverty and Millennium Development Goals', Levy Economics Institute, New York.

———. 2008. 'Equal Sharing of Responsibilities between Men and Women: Some Issues with Reference to Labour and Employment', paper prepared and presented at 'Expert Group Meeting on Equal Sharing of Responsibilities between Men and Women, including care-giving in the context of HIV/AIDS', United Nations Division for the Advancement of Women, Geneva, 6–9 October.

———. 2009. 'Global Economic Crisis: Impact on the Poor in India: A Synthesis of Sector Studies', UNDP, New Delhi.

———. 2010. 'Understanding Poverty: Insights Emerging from the Time Use of the Poor', in Rania Antonopoulos and Indira Hirway, *Unpaid Work and the Economy: Gender, Time Use and Poverty in the Global South*, UK: Palgrave.

———. 2012, 'Restructuring of Production and Labour under Globalization: A study of the textile and garment industry in India', ILO Decent Work Team for South Asia, ILO, New Delhi.

International Monetary Fund (IMF). 2013. 'Women, Work, and the Economy: Macroeconomic Gains from Gender Equity', IMF Staff Discussion Note, September, Washington DC.

International Textile, Garment and Leather Workers Federation (ITGLWF). 2005. Press Release 2005. Belgium: ITGLWF.

Inter-secretariat Working Group on National Accounts (ISWGNA). 2008. System of National Accounts, UN, New York.

Labour Bureau. 2010. Occupational Wage Survey, Labour Bureau, Government of India, Shimla.

Neetha, N. 2002. 'Flexible Production, Feminization and Disorganization: Evidence from Tirupur Industry', *Economic and Political Weekly*, 37(21): 2045–52.

Textile Committee. 2004. 'Market for Textile Clothing', Textile Committee, Mumbai

United Nations. 2013. 'Report of the Special Rapporteur on Extreme Poverty and Human Rights', United Nations General Assembly, 68th Session, New York.

Unni, Jeemol and Uma Rani. 2002. 'Impact of Recent Policies on Home-based Work in India', Discussion Paper Series-10, UNDP, India.

# Glossary

### African Gender Development Index (AGDI)

The AGDI is a composite index of gender equality introduced by the United Nations Economic Commission for Women and African Economic Development. The index was officially launched at the Fourth African Development Forum (ADF IV) in Addis Ababa on 12 October 2004. Rather than being a collection of individual statistics, the index is composed of two parts, the Gender Status Index (GSI) and the African Women's Progress Scoreboard (AWPS). The AGDI is a specifically African index with an emphasis on the major African charters and documents that have a bearing on gender relations and women's empowerment.

### Anthropological Surveys

Anthropological studies or surveys deal with field data research for human and cultural aspects, working primarily in the fields of physical anthropology and cultural anthropology. While maintaining a strong focus on indigenous populations, they also attempt to document the cultures of other communities and religious groups.

### Centre for Time Use Research (CTUR)

The CTUR is an eminent research centre for time-use research located in the University of Oxford, UK.

### Economic and Social Commission for Asia and the Pacific (ESCAP)

The ESCAP located in Bangkok, Thailand, is one of the five regional commissions of the United Nations.

**Economic Commission for Latin America and the Caribbean (ECLAC)**

The ECLAC, or CEPAL in Spanish, is a UN regional commission to encourage economic cooperation.

**General Production Boundary**

The general production boundary includes production of all goods and services produced by an institutional unit, which could also be a household in which labour and capital are used to transform inputs of goods and services into outputs of other goods and services. The only condition is that the services produced should be delegable, that is, one can produce this for others.

**International Food Policy Research Institute (IFPRI)**

The IFPRI is an international agricultural research centre founded in the early 1970s to improve the understanding of national agricultural and food policies and promote the adoption of innovations in agricultural technology. Additionally, IFPRI was meant to shed more light on the role of agricultural and rural development in the broader development pathway of a country. The mission of IFPRI is to seek sustainable solutions for ending hunger and poverty through research.

**Labour Force Surveys (LFS)**

Labour force surveys are household-based surveys that collect work-related statistics, which are designed by national governments to collect statistics on labour force of an economy. These surveys provide estimates of the employed and unemployed in the economy by carefully collecting statistics from sample households that are representative of the population.

**Living Standards Measurement Study (LSMS)**

The LSMS is a household survey programme focused on generating high-quality data, improving survey methods, and building capacity. The goal of the LSMS is to facilitate the use of household survey data for evidence-based policymaking. These surveys were introduced by the World Bank, particularly for countries where statistics are not very well-developed.

**National Income Accounts**

National income accounts are accounts of the national economy (total output, total consumption, or total incomes) in a way that describes the economic activities of a nation.

## National Modular Time-Use Surveys

When a national time-use survey is conducted as a module of another national survey (such as labour force survey, income and expenditure survey, or a living standard measurement survey), it is called a national modular time-use survey.

## National Statistical Organization or Office (NSO)

Each country is expected to have an apex body that is in charge of all statistics produced in the country. The NSO is responsible for deciding which statistics should be produced, at what frequency, with what coverage, and with what kind of concepts and methods. The NSO is also expected to ensure the quality of the statistics produced.

## Non-Profit Institutions Serving Households (NPISH)

The NPISH are private organizations with tax-exempt status that primarily provide services to households in one of the following categories: religious and welfare (including social services, grant-making foundations, political organizations, museums and libraries, and some civic and fraternal organizations), medical care, education and research, recreation (including cultural, athletic, and some civic and fraternal organizations), and personal business (including labour unions, legal aid, and professional associations). They do not include non-profit institutions that primarily serve business.

## Non-SNA Activities

Non-SNA activities include the production of services not included in the production boundary but included in the general production boundary. These activities/services are not included in the national accounting system. Basically, they include unpaid services of households, production for own consumption, and voluntary services.

## Organisation for Economic Co-Operation and Development (OECD) Countries

The OECD is an international economic organization of 34 countries, founded in 1961, to stimulate economic progress and world trade. It is a forum of countries describing themselves as committed to democracy and the market economy, providing a platform to compare policy experiences, seeking answers to common problems, identifying good practices, and coordinating domestic and international policies of its members.

### Participatory Rapid Appraisal Methods

Participatory rapid appraisal methods are geared towards planning and conducting the research process with those people whose lifeworld and meaningful actions are under study. Consequently, this means that the aim of the inquiry and the research questions develop out of the convergence of two perspectives—that of science and of practice. In the best scenario, both sides benefit from the research process. Everyday practices, which have since long established themselves as a subject of inquiry, introduce their own perspective, namely the way people deal with the existential challenges of everyday life. The participatory research process enables co-researchers to step back cognitively from familiar routines, forms of interaction, and power relationships in order to fundamentally question and rethink established interpretations of situations and strategies.

### Production Boundary

Production boundary defines the purview of national income accounts. It covers the goods and services to be included in national income accounts. The production boundary includes the production of all individual or collective goods or services that are supplied (or intended to be supplied) to units other than their producers, and the own-account production of all goods that are retained by their producers for their own final consumption or gross fixed capital formation. Own-account production for gross fixed capital formation includes the production of fixed assets such as construction; research and development activities; the development of software and mineral exploration for own gross fixed capital formation as well as own-account construction of dwellings; the production and storage of agricultural products; the processing of agricultural products, such as the production of flour by milling; the preservation of fruit by drying and bottling; the production of dairy products like butter and cheese and the production of beer, wine, and spirits; the production of other primary products, such as salt mining, cutting peat, and carrying water; and other kinds of processing, like weaving cloth, the production of pottery, and furniture making.

### Satellite Accounts

Satellite accounts are supplemental accounts that expand the analytical capacity of the main system of accounts by focusing on a particular aspect of economic activity. Satellite accounts are linked to the main accounts, but have greater flexibility in providing more detailed information or in using alternative definitions, concepts, and accounting conventions.

## SNA Activities

These are activities (as well as production of goods and services), which are included in the production boundary.

## Subsistence Production

Production of goods and services for own consumption of a household is defined as subsistence production. Such goods are not meant to be sold in the market.

## System of National Accounts (SNA)

The SNA is the internationally agreed standard set of recommendations on how to compile measures of economic activities in accordance with strict accounting conventions which are based on economic principles. The recommendations are expressed in terms of a set of concepts, definitions, classifications, and accounting rules that comprise internationally agreed standards for measuring such items as GDP.

## United Nations Economic Commission for Africa (UNECA)

The UNECA was established by the United Nations Economic and Social Council to encourage economic cooperation among its member states, that is, the nations of the African continent.

## United Nations Statistics Division (UNSD)

The UNSD, formerly the United Nations Statistical Office, serves under the United Nations Department of Economic and Social Affairs (UNDESA) as the central mechanism within the Secretariat of the United Nations to supply the statistical needs and coordinating activities of the global statistical system. The division is overseen by the United Nations Statistical Commission (UNSC), established in 1947, as the apex entity of the global statistical system and highest decision-making body for coordinating international statistical activities. It brings together the chief statisticians from member states from around the world. It compiles and disseminates global statistical information, develops standards and norms for statistical activities, and supports countries' efforts to strengthen their national statistical systems.

# Index

# About the Editor and Contributors

## EDITOR

**Indira Hirway** is director and professor of economics at Centre for Development Alternatives (CFDA), Ahmedabad, India, and national fellow of the Indian Council of Social Science Research (ICSSR), New Delhi, India. Her areas of interest are development alternatives; employment and labour market structures, poverty and human development, environment and development, and time-use studies and unpaid work. Her recent works include designing curriculum on and coordinating the project on time-use studies for the International Training Centre of the International Labour Organization (ITC-ILO), Turin; implementing the ground-breaking Resolution on Statistics on Work by the ILO using time-use statistics and other data; 'Unpaid Work and the Economy: Linkages and Their Implications' (presidential address to the Indian Society of Labour Economics); *Restructuring of Production and Labour under Globalization: A Study of the Textile and Garment Industry in India* (2011); and *Unpaid Work and the Economy: Gender, Time Use and Poverty in Developing Countries* (2010, as co-editor).

## CONTRIBUTORS

**Omar Ismael Abdourahman** currently works with the United Nations Economic Commission for Africa (UNECA). Some of his work areas include research on time-use data, employment, social protection, migration, and youth. He is also actively involved in international academic and research networks, such as the International Association on Time Use Research (IATUR), Partnership for Economic Policy, and the Gender and Macro International Working Group. He assists member states in Africa in translating international economic and social development frameworks and agreements into national strategies and policies; monitoring progress in addressing economic and social development issues; and building consensus on economic and social development priorities at the sub-regional and regional levels and in building capacity at national and regional levels.

**Rania Antonopoulos** is a senior scholar and director of the gender equality and the economy programme at the Levy Economics Institute of Bard College, New York, USA. She specializes in macro–micro linkages of gender and economics, international competition, and globalization; job guarantee policies and their macroeconomic and employment impacts; social protection and poverty reduction; and the implications of paid and unpaid work on poverty indicators. Antonopoulos has served as the macroeconomic policy adviser for UN Women, expert adviser and consultant for the United Nations Development Programme (UNDP), and, since 2002, as a co-director of the Levy Institute International Working Group on Gender, Macroeconomics, and International Economics (GEM-IWG) Knowledge Networking Program on Engendering Macroeconomics and International Economics. Her work has been widely published.

**Lekha Chakraborty** is associate professor at the National Institute of Public Finance and Policy (NIPFP), New Delhi, India and is also a research associate with the Levy Economics Institute of Bard College, New York, USA. Previously, she worked for the World Bank, UNDP, UN Women, and the Commonwealth Secretariat on short stints. She was the recipient of an award from Department of Foreign Affairs and Trade (DFAIT), Government of Canada twice. She also served as a member of an expert group on 'Classification of Budgetary Transactions', which led to the institutionalization of gender budgeting in India. She has been visiting instructor to GEM-IWG at University of Utah for the Gender and Macroeconomics course.

**Jacques Charmes**, an economist and statistician, is currently emeritus research director at the French Scientific Research Institute for Development (IRD) at the Centre for Population and Development, University of Paris. Earlier, he was director of the Department of Social and Health Sciences at this institute. He has written several articles, reports, and manuals on the measurement of informal sector in the labour force and national accounts, with special emphasis on women, and participated in programmes of international agencies on measurement of size, contribution, and characteristics of informal sector and informal employment across developing regions. Recently he compiled time-use surveys held in 70 countries for the *Human Development Report 2015*.

**Valeria Esquivel** is a researcher at the International Labour Organization (ILO) for care policies in the Gender, Equality and Diversity Branch. Previously, she was Senior Advisor, Social Policy & Gender at the Food and Agriculture Organization of the United Nations (FAO), and research coordinator on gender and development at United Nations Research Institute for Social Development (UNRISD). Esquivel has had a long academic career as feminist economist. She has published extensively on labour, macroeconomic, social and care policies, and on time-use methodologies. She designed and coordinated the Buenos Aires Time Use Survey (2005) and the Rosario Time Use Survey (2010), both in Argentina, and has been advisor in the compilation of the Colombian Care Economy Satellite Account (2013).

**Maria Sagrario Floro** is professor of economics at American University in Washington, DC, USA and the co-director of the graduate programme on gender analysis in economics (PGAE). She also serves as technical adviser to the *Economic and Social Costs of Violence against Women Project*. Her publications include co-authored books, as well as articles on vulnerability, informal employment, urban food security, time use and well-being, financial crises, urban poverty, households' savings, credit, and asset ownership. She has collaborated with researchers, women's groups, and community organizations in Thailand, Philippines, Ecuador, and Bolivia in conducting fieldwork in urban poor communities.

**Kijong Kim** is a research scholar in gender equality and the economy programme at theLevy Economics Institute of Bard College, New York, USA. His research interests include distributional impact analyses of public employment guarantee programmes and other fiscal policies; social care investment; gender-oriented macro modelling; and the application of time-use data to economic analysis. The recent research includes time-income poverty measures and employment policy simulations for South Korea; input–output analysis and micro-simulation of the early childhood care and education in Turkey, of employment impacts of an expanded public works programme in South Africa, and the American Recovery and Reinvestment Act in the US; analyses of household responses to recession using time-use and consumption surveys; and the distributional impact assessment of US climate change policy.

**Hitomi Komatsu** is an independent consultant who works with the International Food Policy Research Institute (IFPRI), the World Bank, and the Inter-American Development Bank. Her research areas include gender, labour, time use, and taxation. Previously, she managed public sector reform projects in Africa and Asia at the UNDP and United Nations Capital Development Fund (UNCDF).

**Sonia Montaño** is a well-known feminist from Bolivia. Previously, she served as the chief of gender affairs division in Economic Commission for Latin America and the Caribbean (ECLAC). She founded the Centro de Iinformación y desarrollo de la Mujer (CIDEM) (Information and Women's Development Centre), a feminist research centre advocating for gender equality. She led the creation of the first national machinery for the advancement of women in Bolivia and was responsible for promoting legislation, mechanisms, and resources to implement international commitments and favour the public participation of women's and feminist organizations. She has published on women's movements, feminism, gender policies in Latin America, and care economy and has coordinated various regional reports on the advancement of women.

**Ajit Zacharias** is a senior scholar and director of the Distribution of Income and Wealth Program at the Levy Economics Institute of

Bard College, New York, USA. His research interests are economic measurement, political economy, and gender disparities. Along with other Levy scholars, Zacharias has developed alternative measures of economic welfare and deprivation:the Levy Institute Measure of Economic Well-Being (LIMEW) and the Levy Institute Measure of Time and Income Poverty. Zacharias serves on the editorial boards of *Journal of Economic Inequality* and *Investigación Económica*. He is also on the advisory board of *Dialectical Anthropology*.